Fallujah' Secrets
&
Nuremberg' Barrier

Who is the Terrorist?

Muhamad Al-Darraji

Copyright © 2016

Published in the United States of America

COPYRIGHT DISCLAIMER

Alpha Academic Press

Fallujah' Secrets & Nuremberg' Barrier
Who is the Terrorist?

First Edition, Paperback

Published May 2016

ISBN: 978-0-9967715-9-7

TABLE OF CONTENTS

CHAPTER 5
Brutal Torture & Abuse of Iraqi Detainees

CHAPTER 6
The First massacre in Fallujah 4 April 2004
Vigilant Resolve Operations

CHAPTER 7
Political Crime Prevented Peace & Caused A Second War Crime In Fallujah

Chapter 12
The Role of International Law Towards Invasion' Crimes

CHAPTER 13

The United Nations and human rights violations:
Paradoxes of human rights and humanity

The war contains within it the accumulated evil of each...

Resolution of the Nuremberg Tribunal

AUTHOR

Dr. Muhamad Tareq Abidalla Al-Darraji

- Birth Date: 30 March 1972
- Birth Place: Fallujah
- Status: Married
- Nationality: Iraq
- Profession: Cryobiologist
- Education: PhD. BioTech

An activist of Human Rights since 2003, he is President and founder of some of the NGOs in Iraqi fighting for human rights and environment protection.

He was the main source collecting evidence inside Fallujah about the invasion force use of chemical weapons in November 2004. These actions forced the U.S. military to confess to their use one year after the crime. He presented this information to the European Parliament and the UN.

Since 2004, he has specialized in the case of Fallujah and other serious violations of human rights, environmental pollution and health risks. He also has followed-up on militia crimes and death squads, which was founded after the U.S. occupation - British Activities

He seeks the true and transitional justice for stopping this violence, prosecution for the crimes and protection for the victims.

He was a member in Fallujah city council (Jaunary – June 2004), a member in Advisory committee of The BRussells Tribunal Committee, a member in Non-violence network of Iraqi NGOs.- Ebril, and a member in International Peace Bureau – Zurich.

ADDITIONAL INFORMATION

Dr. Al-Darraji has supervised the writing
of the following study reports:

- The report on the situation in Fallujah city after final military operations presented to the 60st session of the United Nation Commission on Human Rights (2004).

- First periodical report of Monitoring net of human rights in Iraq, 2005.

- Second periodical report of Monitoring net of human rights in Iraq, 2005.

- Third periodical report of Monitoring net of human rights in Iraq, 2005.

- Open letter and report about torture in Iraq to Special Rapporteure of UN against Torture, 19 October 2006.

- Death squads in Iraq. 2006

- Prohibited weapon crisis in Fallujah, Report presented to Human Rights council of UN. 2008.

- "Testimonies on crimes against the humanity in Fallujah" presented to the United Nation council of Human Rights March 2010.

- Two reports of "Government War Crimes in Anbar Province, Fallujah as Example, 2014".

INTRODUCTION

I am honored to submit this book as a team effort with loved friends in order to be in front of the reader with all the facts witnessed by myself since the beginning of the foreign occupation crimes that occurred in Fallujah.

This book includes parts of the hidden witness war and the fact of major war crimes of the occupation assigned to evidence and proofs. It was not easy writing these facts and events. The pressure of terror and horror that we lived under during the occupation was insurmountable, especially with the accompanying violations, daily crimes and assassinations of human rights. There were the defenders and journalists who exposed or documented those violations. Our mission, at first, as human rights defenders, was limited to writing documented reports, with evidence of such violations, and sending it to international organizations such as the UN, as well as the world press.

The accountability of the perpetrators may have been a fantasy at that time, but at least the documentation will preserve the rights of the people because there is no statute of limitations for these crimes. For this, I thought to publish all the facts, to expose the cover-up and to inform the international community while lacking transparency and confidence in the higher institutions of the UN. This book contains a lot of evidence supported through three different sources, the United Nations, non-governmental organizations and government documents issued by those governments. It makes use of audio-visual media, as well as formal confessions. All of this documented evidence, from my personal testimony, is of events that took place during that period.

I like to recall the wise words of the bold Italian journalist Sigfrido Ranucci (maker of the documentary Italian film: Fallujah: the Hidden Massacre). When asked by Al-Jazeera whether he intended his film to charge American's use of prohibited weapons in spite of Italy being an American ally, he responded,

"The intent is not to accuse the Americans, but if we are talking about democracy, we must seek the truth and honesty in a scientific manner".

This book seeks to accomplish a number of goals:

1. Provide evidence and argument that the concept of terrorism, in contemporary states, was present and directed against Iraq and Iraqis during the occupation period. Provide examples of the war crimes and genocide that took place in the Iraqi city of Fallujah. Hundreds of thousands of Iraqis died due to hunger and disease during this period of the criminal embargo 1991-2003. This was considered a major international crime, which prompted many senior United Nations officials to resign.

2. A large number of the U.S. military and political studies have shown that a majority of their point of views were filled with false motives, while their tongues debunked many of their crimes with misleading facts. On the other side is a very rare number of studies and research that shows the point of view of victims and their suffering. This is a simple and legitimate right for the victims to express their voices and demand justice.

3. Clarify the role of some local and international players in those events, with evidence that supports the need for an independent international investigation and seeking to support the victims and to achieve a lost transitional justice. This transitional justice is considered the real founder that built upon stable peace and security. That would be in front of the responsible international bodies at the United Nations to initiate an investigation, including what came in the book from war crimes and flagrant violations of human rights. Otherwise, they will confirm that administrative corruption and concealment of these crimes which have reached the top of the pyramid of making a decision in the international organization, which would be a disaster in international relations.

4. I hope that any thoughts generated from the events in this book will be a catalyst in pushing for further research and studies, not only about violations in the aforementioned areas but encouragement for other provinces of Iraq to provide greater support. Support, especially in the selection criteria used to determine the factors of international terrorism and the challenges that dominated this approach and are supported by the States in accordance with the rules of international law. These laws are not

of their own political agenda but serve the interest of some political parties, rather than the interests of their people. Events have shown that the so-called sectarian infighting is a creature of a dirty political game, which was intended to divide Iraq according to sectarian divide and rule base. In addition to the economic crisis that hit the Western people have now proved that they were the victim and entered in intervention wars for the interest of global companies supporting the war.

5. To illustrate the similarities between the Nazi mentality that dominated the world and caused the catastrophe of World War II, with the similarity of the terrorism in the contemporary state led by the Bush and Blair governments. There needs to be accountability before and after waging an aggressive war on Iraq. This requires an urgent international criminal court to review the crimes and serious violations committed against the Iraqi people. This requires finding new international conventions that bridge the gaps in the international judicial system in order to prevent future wars and tragedies.

In Chapter 1, we discuss the similarities of the occupation of Iraq with the Nazi mentality that led to the disasters of World War II. It presents strong scientific evidence that refutes false claims about Iraq's relationship with al-Qaeda or terrorism and the possession of weapons of mass destruction. It reviews the manner in which the UN Security Council released resolutions confirming the state of occupation while violating the foundations of international law. This chapter also addresses the lack of real and legal basis for occupation under the pretext of humanitarianism. For this, I address some of crimes and disasters of the embargo against Iraq and its devastating effects on Iraqi life.

In Chapter 2, we discuss the history of Fallujah, in the present as well as the past, especially its history of foreign occupation after World War II. We then discuss the new occupation after the arrival of U.S. and U.K. invasion forces. We also discuss the nature of international solidarity that has arisen with the issue of Fallujah as a global presence and an example of popular resistance against any foreign occupation.

In Chapter 3, we review crimes and human right abuses committed by U.S. forces in Fallujah, which sparked the popular resistance against them and what were the mistakes by them, which led to committing such crimes.

In Chapter 4, we discuss the history of mercenaries represented by private security and military service companies in Iraq. We review the main advantages of using these companies and how they obtained their rapid enrichment from the mercenary industry. The chapter deals also with the official demographic statistics of these companies in Iraq. In addition to talking about the most prominent crimes committed in Iraq, as well as Fallujah, we give a summary about their international danger by reviewing the most prominent previous committed crimes globally.

In Chapter 5, we explain the torture and brutal forms of dealing with prisoners in a detention facility of the occupation forces and their impact on the movement of those methods later in the Iraqi prisons formed afterward under the sectarian governments. This chapter details the brutal torture, arrests and there effects on the victims, as well as to the local and the international community. It also addresses one of the scandals at the Jadiriyah prison, formed as the first Iraqi sectarian government after the transfer of mock sovereignty. We look at the impact of violence, which has been used in prisons to spread this culture of violence to prisons outside of the law of the jungle. We also refer to the U.S. rendition program, which is in fact, kidnapping people from their countries for the purposes of obtaining information through torture, as seen in the Guantanamo prison and other U.S. prisons abroad.

In Chapter 6, we review the first battle in Fallujah, and the most prominent incidents before the battle. We look at the role of the Balakootr agents and the events before the battle. This created a distress call to warn of the mass punishment crimes initiated against the city and its civilians. We report on the most prominent crimes and violations during the battle and how to force the U.S. into a Cease-fire. On one side, they call Fallujah to negotiate with two delegations to find a way to stop the fighting. The main results of these talks mention to the killers, errors in those negotiations preventing stable peace in Iraq. We also focus on the use of chemical weapons, evidenced by white phosphorus found during battles. We finally conclude with the U.S. analysis of the reasons for their defeat in the battle, and the role of the British and Polish troops. In addition to the main lessons learned from this battle.

In Chapter 7, we discuss the Fallujah situation after the first battle and the truth of the Fallujah Protection Brigade activity for the period between these two battles. In addition, the strategies conducted against the city that was too exhausted to fight a second battle. The chapter is also reviews the international mediation of the UN Secretary General, Kofi Annan, and his attempt to prevent the second battle, giving an opportunity for peaceful dialogue in order to avoid more disasters against civilians.

In **Chapter 8**, we discuss the second battle in Fallujah and the U.S. military preparations, especially the massive air attacks, the reasons for choosing the timing of the battle and the battle plans. The re-use of chemical weapons such as white phosphorus, reveals that these were targeted witnesses' crimes accompanied by the making of fake movies, which helped destroy moral in the city. This chapter shows the losses to both parties and the battle reflex, both locally and internationally.

In **Chapter 9**, we discuss the quality and quantity of the weapons used during the first and second battles in Fallujah. In addition to other evidence about the use of chemical weapons and the possibility of using nuclear weapons, which was later confirmed by laboratory results in the scientific research presented in Chapter 10 .

In **Chapter 10**, we discuss the health and environmental status of Fallujah, highlighted by reports, as well as scientific research from such the international agencies as the United Nations. This is concurred by other independent, international and local organizations with examples of other regions of Iraqi with similar environmental and health concerns. We conclude in discussion about this international cover-up relating to these environmental and health pollution crimes.

In **Chapter 11**, we explain that the impasse of military occupation in transforming the reputation of the national armed resistance to terrorism. Also, the creation of death squads against Sunnis in particular regions, Iran's role in the making of terrorism and the completion of the planned cross militias led by Iran's Revolutionary Guards with the prominent role of Qassem Soleimani, the commander of the Quds Force of the Revolutionary Guards. We discuss the onset of the sectarian violence after the shrine bombing in Samarra and most of the evidence of who was involved formally within the local and international authorities. This chapter illustrates the U.S. and British roles, as well as the most prominent players at the beginning of the U.S.-Iranian cooperative in support of the Iranian militia's loyalty in Iraq and the role of militia Hezbollah in Lebanon as well. There is evidence of government involvement of the leaders of the main militias within the government and how they supported terrorism by the governments, specifically al-Maliki.

In Chapter 12, we touch on several legal issues, such as, aggressive war crimes and occupation, the legal description of the various human rights violations by the occupation in Fallujah and in accordance with the international conventions, especially the use of banned weapons and other war crimes. We give examples of similar international issues. The chapter deals with the opinion of international organizations and conventions on the use of mercenaries too in Iraq. Chapter spoke too about the issue of compensation according to Iraqi and international laws and what are some possible ways to take advantage of them.

In Chapter 13, we review the most prominent effects of the occupation and the destruction of Iraq with a statement of the position of the Security Council and their failures, which opposed its role in the protection of international peace and security. The United Nations and the international community were to help the Iraqi people return to a secure and stable environment. I give examples of their failures and reasons from the Office of High Commissioner for Human Rights and the International Red Cross and the World Health Organization and United Nations of Environment Program. This Chapter concludes with the importance of strengthening the role of local and international civil society organizations in the next phase in light of some success that accompanied the support campaigns of Fallujah internationally and the need to strengthen it by the United Nations.

Finally, I am reminded of what was said by German scientist Hans Albrecht Bethe, (Nobel Prize in Physics and the main assistant in the invention of the hydrogen bomb) when he says,

> *"If we are fighting a war and win it with the use of hydrogen bombs, history will not mention the values that we have fought, but the ways in which we used to accomplish"* [2].

That is why the world will remember the brutality of the occupation and the aggressive war waged on Iraq. The occupiers used criminal methods. In addition to the exposure of the falsity of all allegations and vanities that have been used for this act of aggression.

CHAPTER 1

International Law & Invasion of Iraq

1.1. Similarity of Nazi Mentality & Invasion Way of US-UK

T he invasion of Iraq by the neo-conservatives, led by George W. Bush will cast a shadow for many decades. It was the longest war, longer than the American Civil War, and World Wars I and II, and even the Korean War and the Vietnam War. Not surprisingly, the first to launch the label stupid war "dumb war" is U.S. President Obama in 2002 when he was a Senator for the State of Illinois and objected to the war, saying, "I do not oppose all wars, but I am opposed to dumb wars [521].

In order to prove the fact of the similarity of the roots of criminal thinking of some politicians who caused the wars and disasters, and see the effect of authoritarian thinking who came after them. We start with the famous words of Henry Kissinger, U.S. Secretary of State and former engineer of foreign policy for a long time, when it admitted the mentality of their Nazism-like policies when he said,

> *"By controlling the oil we will control the nations, and who controlled the food will control the people'* [362].

Whatever tried the mentality of neo-conservatives to find modern names for a new kind of military tasks that justify their own agendas, such as humanitarian missions to intervene in Somalia, and the stabilization to intervene in Sierra Leone and East Timor. However, these human masks fell with the Western occupation in Iraq, which has not only hit the principles of international law, but also encouraged the spread of the jungle law and the occurrence of other occupation wars later. Therefore, we see that Russian started their occupation of Georgia on August 2008, and the aggressive war of Israeli on Lebanon in 2006, and the Ethiopian invasion into Somalia in 2006.

Thus began the confessions. U.S. General Wesley Clark (The ex-commander of NATO forces, the former presidential candidate) to confirm the new Nazi and colonial mentality. He confessed to the "Conference of Democracy Now," of the Democratic Party, about the intentions of the Bush administration and his

Defense Secretary Rumsfeld for occupation of the five countries in the Middle East. It was during the seven years, including Iraq after it was only for Iraq, even though they did not have any evidence against Iraq, whether in a relationship with al-Qaeda or participation in any way in hitting the World Trade Towers in New York [518].

This was a big shock to global and European opinion including the French in particular. When French journalist Jean-Claude Maurice announced amazing facts that were exposed by former French President Jacques Chirac. The journalist announced this in his book, if it were repeated; I would not believe my ears. Si Vous le répétez, je démentirai, 2008. The author says, "The world has long months repeating broken record on weapons of mass destruction that do not exist only in Iraq, to the point that the war was for international events like the collection holds. According to statements made by Chirac, Maurice published a phone conversation that took place between Presidents Bush and Chirac. A phone call in which the French president indicates that George W. Bush wants Jacques Chirac to change his mind and participate with him in the invasion of Iraq. Chirac said, "I got a strange and unusual phone call from Bush in early 2003, the U.S. President asked me to approve the annexation of the French army allied forces against Iraq, justified by destroying the last dens of Gog and Magog"!

Chirac said in his conversation with the writer that, the U.S. President had assured him that it was "Gog and Magog", hidden in the Middle East, near the ancient city of Babylon, Iraq. Bush responded, "Exactly". "It is a campaign of faith, a blessing to be done, and the duty of the divine and sacred, emphasized by the prophecies of the Hebrew Bible (The Torah) and the Bible "! Chirac confirms, according to the journalist, that he was dumbfounded when he heard this, and that the call was not a joke, that Bush was serious. The writer places the responsibility for this destruction on the U.S. president, who was not joined by French President Jacques Chirac, so the U.S. had to team up with the British. Tony Blair, who shares the "Bush" faith in these religious and priesthood myths, was joined by other Western countries such as Australia and Poland ... etc. One journalist asked and wondered how can the European people accommodate the scandal of Christianity for achieving democracy in the Middle East? That the new president of the largest country in the world is conducting a genocide war against the people on another continent in search of "Gog and Magog", and that the damage to individuals and institutions in Iraq was for this reason! [383].

The occupation authorities created policies and enacted the political process along sectarian lines in Iraq, giving great influence to the parties that supported the occupation, even though it is accused of shedding Iraqi blood were not spontaneous. However, it is the application of the Nazi principle used by Hitler when he said, "If you want to control people then tell them they are at risk, then warn them that their security is under threat, and they will die ... then accuse your opponents of treason and have queried their loyalty and patriotism, finally arrest and kill them.

Among other policies, not the least is to confirm the similarity of the U.S. - British mentality with the Nazi in the use of a large army of mercenaries, whether military or security. Americans do not hide their admiration for the private army, which was founded by a wealthy German Count Albrecht von Wallenstein, which turned out in the end to be the largest of the British army at that time [70]. Neo-Nazi mentality in the U.S. and in British administrative planning increased at a greater pace in the use of mercenaries, especially during their occupation of Iraq. It soon came to be the second largest army beyond the U.S. military in Iraq, and unfortunately became as one of the manifestations of the new World Trade under the global name free of restrictions called the "global military service industry".

One of the historical paradoxes about the war and the invasion, I remember the similarity between the mentality of the Blair - Bush governments and the Nazi mentality. British King GEORGE VI announced, on 3 September 1939, in his speech to join Britain and the Allied forces in World War II against the Axis powers led by Hitler. GEORGE VI explained the reasons for the declaration of war in spite of all the disasters. The paradox was for very similar reasons to those for the announcement of the Iraqi people's resistance against the occupation of the descendants of the king. In his speech, he identifies where the striking similarity in the description of the Nazi mentality, which the British King fought and the same mentality followed by the government of Tony Blair later. He says:

"...... For the second time in the lives of most of us, we are at war. Repeatedly, we have tried to find a peaceful way out of the differences between ourselves and those who are now our enemies, but it has been in vain. We have been forced into a conflict, for we are called, with our allies, to meet the challenge of a principle which, if it were to prevail, would be fatal to any civilized order in the world. It is a principle, which permits a state, in the selfish pursuit of power, to disregard its treaties and its solemn pledges, which sanctions the use of force or

threat of force against the sovereignty and independence of other states. Such a principle, stripped of all disguise, is surely the mere primitive doctrine that might is right, and if this principle were established through the world, the freedom of our own country and of the whole British Commonwealth of nations would be in danger. However, far more than this, the peoples of the world would be kept in bondage of fear, and all hopes of settled peace and of the security, of justice and liberty, among nations, would be ended. This is the ultimate issue, which confronts us. For the sake of all that, we ourselves hold dear, and of the world order and peace, it is unthinkable that we should refuse to meet the challenge. It is to this high purpose that I now call my people at home and my peoples across the seas, which will make our cause their own. I ask them to stand calm, firm, and united in this time of trial. The task will be hard. There may be dark days ahead, and war can no longer be confined to the battlefield, but we can only do the right as we see the right, and reverently commit our cause to God..."

1.2. Allegations of the war on Iraq

There is a lot of evidence that will enable the reader to reject the allegations and the reasons for the occupation of Iraq. Whether it was the existence and continuation of the weapons of mass destruction programs in Iraq, or the Iraqi government liaison relations with al-Qaeda. This was conducted in order to find a relationship between Iraq and destroying the World Trade Center Towers in New York 2001. The U.S. administration and media support her to stress that the evidence of this was strong justification, so she likened the strength of this evidence as bulletproof, but later it turned out to be such fragility of those who worked on promoting this idea [496].

1.2.1. The first claim: The existence of weapons of mass destruction

1. Mr. Hans Blix was the head of the inspection team for mass destruction weapons in Iraq under the United Nations (UNMOVIC). He bowed to recognize that the war on Iraq in 2003 was a horrible mistake and a violation of the UN Charter. He added that it was clear that his office in New York was using wiretapping, which led to support the occupation of Iraq. When Mr. Blix tried to tell the American National Security Advisor Condoleezza Rice that they searched all the sites provided to them by intelligence reports from the U.S. military, but they did not find anything. Ms. Rice responded that Iraq is under trial and not the CIA [405]. It is noteworthy that Mr. Blix had said, before the start of the occupation directly, that his team did not find stockpiles of weapons of mass destruction. That the work was making rapid progress

towards resolving the outstanding disarmament issues, and it was his report to the Security Council on February 14 2003, which reversed the fact that all lies to those who promoted the war in the U.S. and British administrations, which would make it the subject of criticism by them.

2. Mr. Scott Ritter, chief weapons inspector in a unit of the United Nations Special Commission to disarm Iraq of concealment (UNSCOM) from 1991 until 1998, stated that Iraq does not have the capacity for weapons of mass destruction now and the start of a senior political opposition signals war and the invasion of Iraq. He resigned from his job on the inspection team of the United Nations on 26 August 1998 because of the contradictions between the Security Council resolution by the United Nations in 1154 and how to implement it. This was considered an important obstacle to the implementation of his work [542].

3. The U.S. administration was seeking to obliterate evidence and kill Iraqi scientists after they made sure that Iraq was now free of the forbidden weapons programs, and the story of what happened to the CIA agent, Valerie Plame, and her husband, former U.S. ambassador, was the best proof. Despite her work and reports as an expert and a secret spy in nuclear research with the U.S. intelligence apparatus may have helped the U.S. administration to claim the possibility of the use of aluminum tubes Iraq had bought earlier in centrifuges to enrich uranium. Nevertheless, the Bush administration leaked information to the U.S. press about her real character, and this is what led her to think that because of her husband's opinion, Joseph C. Wilson, former U.S. Ambassador, because of his criticism of the Bush administration on lying about the occupation of Iraq [12A]. The U.S. administration sent him to investigate the information that Iraq had tried to buy enriched uranium oxide, also known as yellowcake from Niger. This allegation had not been proved and Joseph considered it as a weak allegation, which angered the Bush administration. It is noteworthy that the diary of Valery in 2007 was transformed in 2010 into an American film titled *Fair Game* [490]. While her husband revealed more assurances about the lies that brought about the war in Iraq in his book, *The Politics of Truth: Inside the Lies that Led to War and Betrayed My Wife's CIA Identity: A Diplomat's Memoir* [491].

4. American professor James P. Pfiffner pointed out in an important article with many facts that refute allegations of President Bush about the danger of weapons of mass destruction in Iraq. At a time when President Bush declared to reporters in opposition to the inspectors mission reports of the United

Nations, experts to disarm Iraq of weapons of mass destruction, as well as the U.S. government departments reports, particularly ones of the CIA [496].

5. The allegations of a fabricated story that Iraq sought to buy uranium from Niger was false, according to information provided by the British government and Italian intelligence sources, which Bush, mentioned in his speech on January 28, 2003. The Italian intelligence source was an Italian journalist named Elisabetta Barba. On October 11, 2002, she gave copies of the Nigerian letters to the U.S. ambassador in Rome. When she was asked later about the reason for the lack of dissemination of these messages, she answered that she was suspicious of the credibility of the messages and believed they were fake! After an investigative visit to Niger by the former U.S. ambassador, Joseph Wilson, he said after his meeting with the U.S. ambassador there that the story is a rumor, which he tells to the CIA. Then the U.S. General Carlton W. Fulford, Jr, with the U.S. ambassador, visited with the Nigerian President to ensure the safety and security of storing uranium cakes. The Nigerian president confirmed to them that the French company was controlling the security and increased the checks on the safety of the storage. In spite of all these facts, the United States handed over a copy of the documents to the Director of the UN Atomic Energy Agency, Mohamed ElBaradei, who revealed the falsification of documents at a press conference on 7 March 2003 [496].

6. When Colin Powell went to the United Nations and gambled away his credibility, the head of the CIA, George Tenet, seated behind him, giving incorrect information based on the lies of an Iraqi person named Rafid Ahmed Alwan al-Janabi. This was a "Curveball" since he provided key testimony to the CIA. He returned in 2011 to reveal that he lied in his testimony and gave deliberately misleading information about Iraq's biological weapons. Al-Janabi said to the British Guardian newspaper, "They gave me this opportunity," "I had the chance to fabricate something to topple the regime" [521].

7. After all these years of occupation come the confession of Colin Powell, former U.S. Secretary of State before and after the occupation period when he said 'I am ashamed of this, which we have done in Iraq, it's stained blood" [438,521]. He said previously in the famous UN Security Council meeting on February 5, 2003, demanding that he authorized the use of force under the pretext of Iraq's material breach of the resolutions of the Security Council when he said "what gives him now are facts and conclusions based on solid intelligence" [433]. The whole world discovered, after the invasion, that Iraq has destroyed all banned weapons since 1991. This indicated that it was more than

12 years from the date of occurrence to the occupation [434]. Kofi Annan said, "Colin L. Powell was more skeptical about the evidence he used to justify the American-led invasion", and he added, "I could only be impressed by the resilience of this man, who had endured so much to argue for a war he clearly did not believe in." Mr. Powell's role, which some historians say irreparably harmed his credibility and derailed his political career [684]. While, after ten years of the occupation, the head of the inspection team of mass destruction weapons in Iraq, Dr. Hans Blix declared that "the war was aimed to eliminate weapons of mass destruction, but there weren't any" [405].

1.2.2. Iraq's relationship with terrorism

Extortion through fabrication of charges and co-opt others were prominent agenda items of U.S. President George W. Bush, which expanded to include intimidate others or the consequences of not participating in the war on terror! Where his mantra has become the basis of U.S. foreign policy, "our nation is at war against terrorism, and will keep on the doctrine of either you're with US or against US" [524]. The U.S. allegation claims about Iraq's relationship with al-Qaeda were based on the theory that the Iraqi government constitutes a threat to the security and safety of the United States of America, as a relationship with al-Qaeda and helping international terrorism, while later proved to the invalidity of the claim and the lack of any evidence to prove it. I found many important facts that reject these claims like the following:

1. The Select Committee on Intelligence of the U.S. Senate conducted a thorough investigation and published information later to prove that these allegations were not responsible and do not have a strong basis in fact [496,441,497].

2. The confessions of U.S. senior intelligence officers in CIA, including Susan Lindauer, came to show the truth about the relationship and the position of Iraq with the September 11th attacks that struck the Twin Towers of the World Trade in New York. The facts announced by Susan pushed the Bush administration to commit the scandalous arrest of Susan for 5 years without trial. However, after coming to the government of President Obama, she was released, and the reason exposed to the relationship of Bush administration with attacks and most of those who were accused of carrying out the attacks were in a relationship with the U.S. Central Intelligence Agency and undercover agents such as Mohammed Atta. This U.S. intelligence officer was responsible for contacts with Iraq and the Libya embassies and confirmed that they were collaborators in the action against the perpetrators of the attacks, and I hope

all of the American people listen to the numerous facts on the internet, especially on YouTube and some satellite channels such as channel of Russia Today [488].

3. The United Nations Committee on Terrorism did not find any link between al-Qaeda and Saddam Hussein's government. The chief investigator Michael Chandler said: "Nothing has come to our attention that would indicate links between Iraq and al-Qaeda, but even if there was some evidence that members of al-Qaeda in Iraq was at one time, it would not constitute evidence that Iraq was linked to the terrorist attacks on 9/11 [544].

4. The testimony of Mr. Salem Jumaili, Director of the American Division of the Iraqi intelligence Service before the occupation, confirmed evidence of the absence of a working relationship for the Iraqi government on the day al-Qaeda evaded the CIA. In addition, of formal cooperation in the delivery of one wanted in the New York bombings, rejected the signing of the document of the meeting for the formal handover of the accused. The U.S. feared confirming Iraq's cooperation in the fight against terrorism and the Bush administration would lose the lie that Iraq was not cooperating with the accusation of terrorism against him [A17]. While the head of the inspection team of mass destruction weapons in Iraq, Dr. Hans Blix declared that the war was aimed to eliminate al-Qaeda in Iraq, but the terrorist group didn't exist in the country until after the invasion [405].

5. On the contrary, the stated facts proved thus far, the strong relationship between the CIA and al-Qaeda through the support they received before, during and after the Soviet invasion of Afghanistan (see Chapter 11). Not to mention all the other facts announced by the official and non-official U.S. destinations proving the involvement of management, which caused former U.S. President George W. Bush a serious breach of security and a threat to the U.S. National Security [488]. For these reasons, it was not surprising then to recognize that the former U.S. Secretary of State, Hillary Clinton, when in front of one of the committees of Congress, declared that "We, AMERICA", have created militants and terrorists to strike the Soviet Union, and are now plagued by them [486]. This makes it clear; allegations of failure confirm the existence of any real threat from Iraq to its neighbors and miss out of any legal or moral justification for committing the crime of aggressive war.

1.3. U.S. - British invasion of Iraq and how to violate international law

According to the rules of international law, the most appropriate word from the legal point in the description of the war on Iraq is that it is a war of aggression. Not only from the side of the UN Security Council's failure to vote in favor of this military action being justified, but because it was threatening international peace and security, through the introduction of the Middle East in a new conflict which will be exacerbated negatively and have an impact on the whole world. This aggressive war initiated officially and virtually since 1992, ended with direct military occupation in 2003. It means that it violated customary international law and the Charter of the United Nations, in Article 2, paragraph 4, which confirmed over-and-over again, the importance of the prohibition of the use of force by a State against another State [284]. While the Rome Convention for the International Criminal Court described, that the war of aggression is a major crime as one of the four crimes that specialize in accordance with the terms of the Memorandum of Association [415].

The standards of the Nuremberg Tribunal, for court cases of Nazi war criminals, which was formed after World War II, described aggressive war as the supreme international crime, also known as aggressive war crimes at the Nuremberg Charter Palate. It is a crime against peace ... and it is the planning and preparation to start waging aggressive war, war in violation of international treaties and the first of the UN Charter. It is an odd coincidence that the U.S. and British states of the occupation were among the judges of the Nuremberg Tribunal. They participated in a wonderful formulation as the decision of being the referee against the Nazis, across every legal section in the extravaganza when they announced that, "the war is basically a wicked thing, not only provoked the Warring States alone, but that affect the whole world. The start of the war of aggression is not only an international crime, but the greatest of international crimes that do not differ from other war crimes, because they contain within it the accumulated evil of each". I liked this speech when reading it for the first time, it stayed in my mind, immortal phrase described, which contains the accumulated evil of each. This accumulated evil, by many countries, was shown in one of the documents of the Pentagon, published by the news site WikiLeaks. This document, dated July 2, 2003, described the number of conspiracy countries that supported this war of aggression. According to the document, there are currently 18 countries with ground forces present in Iraq. In addition, it was the United Kingdom and Australia, jointly supporting America in all the American wars during the past 20 years along with Poland. While there are 14 countries that gave firm commitments to provide forces, now only 11 other countries offer potential support!

In accordance with the provisions of the laws of the Nuremberg Tribunal, which became the foundation, is now international penal law. The administrations of former U.S. President George W. Bush and former British Prime Minister Tony Blair are all participants and guilty of supreme international crimes in Iraq. They all bear the legal and moral responsibility for these acts of violence, killing, and destruction that took place during this war of aggression and throughout with the presence of their troops on the ground in Iraq. It shall not be taken into account that this would have been allowed by the local or national laws of their countries, to declare a war. This is not related to international law, which handles international standards and international conventions of the United Nations. Nazi war was legal according to the laws of the German Government, but considered war crimes under international law. For this, we see the second principle of international law recognized in the Charter of the Nuremberg Tribunal. It is in the judgment of which the imposition of capital law within the national laws of the act that constitutes a crime under international law. This does not relieve the person who committed the act from responsibility under international law. While stressing the third principle on the fact that the person who committed the act, which constitutes a crime under international law and the responsibility of heads of state or prime ministers, it does not relieve them from the responsibility under international law. It is here we see the presence of the international responsibility to those higher international crimes under international law, which has become clear. For this reason, Robert Jackson, the U.S. prosecutor, puts in the Nuremberg Tribunal the following definition "that waging aggressive war, is not only an international crime, it is the supreme international crime differing only from other war crimes in that it contains within it the evil accumulated of the whole".

It is bizarre that international organizations like Amnesty International and the Human Rights Watch Organizations have directed appeals to both sides of the war. They need to respect and observe the laws of war only, without mentioning a single word to legal liability in the illegality of this war or the Supreme criminal responsibility under international law for the leaders of nations committing these crimes! The Organization Human Rights Watch, in one of its reports [421], has documented these crimes of occupation, when entering Iraq.

[10]

International law is very explicit on the issue of banning the use of military force by a State against another State, with the exception of two conditions: the first, according to the valid authorization by the Security Council of the United Nations, and the second in the "strictly defined right of self-defense". See the first requirement of the Charter of the United Nations in 1946, which is binding on all members of the upper and the document of international law treaty. This sought leaders occupying powers (without much success) that there be a third addition, under the excuse of "humanitarian intervention. " Americans sought to justify the war against Iraq by referring to all three criteria. Although the United Nations Charter is a document of anti-war and is described as "a scourge", he says in the Charter, "We the people of the United Nations, determined to save the coming generations from the scourge of war, which brought and twice in our grief indescribable human description".

As the failure of the UN mandate and the international community not to believe the arguments of American and British administrations about the threat of weapons of mass destruction in Iraq for international peace and security, and the failure of alternative arguments for going to war. The international refusal campaign for war continued with the various reports confirming that Iraq is free of weapons of mass destruction. UN inspectors themselves determined a lack of relationship between Iraq and al-Qaeda [56,281]. However, U.S.-U.K. governments tried to deceive their people by the fake mandate according to international resolutions 678, 687 and 1441. The use of force against Iraq was a violation of international law, which has been recognized by many international players of human rights, such as the Dutch Government Panel, The Center for Constitutional Rights, and the International Commission of Jurists, Greenpeace, The Lawyers' Committee on Nuclear Policy, and finally the UN Secretary-General Kofi Annan. While the Commission of Inquiry of the Dutch government confirmed that there was no justification for the use of force and relied on the Security Council Resolution 1441 "does not make sense to be construed as authorizing individual member states to use military force to compel Iraq with Security Council resolutions" [547,284].

The announce by UN Secretary General Mr. Annan received a normal reaction in his speech to the BBC to confirm the fact that the illegality of the occupation, saying, "the US-led occupation of Iraq in the work is illegal and contrary to the UN Charter, and that the decision upon Iraq must be through the Security Council, not unilaterally" [48]. In article II of the UN Charter, it calls for the peaceful resolution of disputes. According to the provisions of article 41 of Chapter VII, only the UN Security Council can determine whether the circumstances justify the use of force. Despite these clear rules and the lack of approval of the Security Council, the occupation governments have embarked on the occupation of Iraq. For more illustration, British lawyer Michael Mansfield confirmed that the terms of United Nations Charter were very clear, saying:

1. The first article explains that the main purpose of the United Nations is "to maintain international peace and security and to their purpose shall take effective collective measures for the prevention and removal of threats to the peace, and work according to the principles of justice and international law.

2. Article 2 [4] discloses this concept in no uncertain terms: "All members of the UN shall refrain in their international relations from the threat or use of force, or be used against land integrity or political independence of any state."

3. Security Council Resolution 1441, dated November 2002 called for the disarmament of Iraq of weapons of mass destruction, and to cooperate with international inspectors. The council explained the continuity of being responsible but did not authorize the use of force against Iraq [404].

Therefore, the UN Security Council resolution, after the beginning of the occupation, was frank and clear, with a description of the two countries as occupation states, they have international obligations in respect of the four Geneva Conventions, which regulate the human rights situation during the war. With the expiration of the first months of the occupation, the fact of the occupation scheme unfolded in the looting, destruction and the lack of any real plan for the reconstruction of Iraq. However, it came to creating the land of Iraq to be an open battlefield with the enemies of the United States through which left Iraq's borders open with the temptations to spread violence as well as to let weapons on the streets. This prompted the commander of U.S. ground forces, Gen. David McKiernan to admit that Iraq will be a combat zone for some time. W. Bush's adviser on Counter-terrorism, Richard A. Clarke stated in his memoirs *Against All Enemies* in 2004 that the ease of the bombing of Iraq after being attacked in the United States by al-Qaeda, "we will have as easily invaded Mexico after the Japanese attack on them in Pearl Harbor " [521].

President Bush's administration had known the difficulty of using its excuses to wage war on Iraq, for this, they initiated, in the use of new phrases in the brainwashing of the American people, such as pre-emptive war phrases (anticipatory), which was quickly corrected by the famous U.S. linguist Noam Chomsky, calling it a preventive war. President Bush said on June 1, 2002, "Our security will require everyone to look forward firmly and ready for preventive action when necessary to defend our liberty and to defend our lives." [185].

Under these excuses, U.S. President George W. Bush asked his Congress to allow him to wage war on Iraq, according to the powers set forth in the domestic U.S. law, known simply as (HJRes. 114 (PL 107-243)). This law authorizes the President to use the armed forces of the United States in the defense of the U.S. national security against alleged threats from Iraq [155]. This authorization was for an unspecified period of time [156]. The actual implementation process of the occupation of Iraq started in 1998 through the adoption of the U.S. Congress for the Iraq Liberation Act. This act authorizes the President to send 100 million U.S. dollars in the form of technical and military assistance to Iraqi opposition groups abroad in order to change the government in Iraq [176]. Despite that, this law is contrary to the whole Charter of the United Nations, in the fourth paragraph, which forbids the threat against sovereign states. The disaster of occupation increased with the international silence on crime disguised as an occupation. This international silence is the one who helped the American Nazi mentality expressed by Secretary of Defense Rumsfeld's rejection of all UN inspection team reports about the lack of any evidence of weapons of mass destruction in Iraq, and by misleading the people saying, "The absence of evidence does not mean evidence of absence!" [405].The strange thing is the continuation of this international silence despite confessions and announcements by many international parties about the criminality of the sanctions program against Iraq before this invasion. There was a report, released in 1995 by two scientists who worked at the United Nations Food and Agriculture Organization (FAO). They may have been killed because of the economic sanctions on Iraq, with at least 576,000 children, there was a sharp rise in malnutrition among young people, which suggests that more children will be at risk in the coming years [389].

The Iraqi government confirmed that the number of children, who died because of the economic sanctions against Iraq between 1991, and January 1999, had reached 400,000 children victimized because of disease and malnutrition [430]. A representative for the U.S. State Department, James Rubin pointed out later about these sanctions as "the toughest and most comprehensive sanctions in history" [548]. Similarly, a select committee of the British House of Commons said that the penal system against Iraq was "unprecedented in terms of longevity and comprehensive nature" [549]. The Security Council of the UN itself set up a research team "humanitarian panel" to investigate the effects of the sanctions. This team released a report in March

30, 1999, where it found that, "In marked contrast to the situation prevailing before the events of 1990 to 1991, the infant mortality rates in Iraq today are among the highest in the world. Low birth weight affects 23% of all infant births, and chronic malnutrition affects one in four children under the age of five. Only 41% of the population has access to regular clean water, and 83% of all schools need substantial repairs. The International Committee of the Red Cross (ICRC) indicated that the Iraqi health care system today is in a dilapidated condition. The United Nations Development Program announced that it would require the sum of $ 7,000,000,000 for the rehabilitation of the electric power sector in all parts of the country to return to its capacity in 1990" [550]. The sanctions imposed on Iraq during the years of inhumane embargo were a crime of genocide, which caused the killing of more than half a million Iraqi children. This was confirmed by the World Childhood UNICEF reports. For 1996, the cause of death of at least 4,500 children under the age of five was due to a lack of water clean, malnutrition and contamination of medical equipment. This increased in 1999 due to economic embargoes. The mortality rate of children under age of five was 131 per 1,000 live births, which were 56 deaths per 1,000 before the imposition of economic sanctions. The infant mortality rate rose for under one-year-olds to 108 per 1,000 compared with 47 per 1,000 live births before the siege [551]. The genocide crime of those children who were killed without mercy is only a common crime of responsibility between the governments of Blair and Clinton, who insisting on the continuation of these sanctions, despite all these international reports at that time.

In spite of these irrefutable facts about the falsity of those allegations and arguments of the war, occupation governments have been using a new argument of the liberation of Iraq and the freedom of their people against the crimes of mass graves is the new mantra of the occupation. Since the only justification remaining now is humanitarian intervention in others words. Here was a new crime in mixing facts and unfortunately, the UN's position despite the variation in its humanity institutions that reject the continuation of the siege inside. Nevertheless, they start to be as conniver or may become joint secondary offense results of these sanctions, which are described according to the numbers of victims, that it was a war of genocide. The United Nations recognizes that the criminal embargo on Iraq was a reason to prevent a lot of the necessary equipment in the health and environmental arenas access to Iraq under the pretext of dual-use [363]. For these reasons, international humanitarian law rejects interference from one side to prevent their use for political purposes and not for humanitarian motives, as happened in Iraq.

[14]

The United Nations Charter did not authorize to change the political system of a country by foreign force and does not the pre-emptive action under the pretext of the potential threat (perceived threat) [404]. Some of the memos showed that there was discussion in early 2001 between U.S. President Bush and British Prime Minister Blair about attacking Iraq without reference to weapons of mass destruction [435]. Both sides spoke at White House about the attack on Iraq on 20 September 2001[436]. While the head of British intelligence, Sir Richard Dearlove spoke during his meeting with Mr. Blair in June 2002, about the falsity of the Iraqi threat allegations to them, saying, "There wangle was going on in the intelligence and facts used in the policy by the leaders in Washington" [437]. Despite this, London government initiated a parallel work of exaggeration and false claims, including two "files or reports" notoriously issued by the British government [439]. In spite of that, occupying powers tried to claim that they acted in accordance with self-defense against an external threat authorized by paragraph 51 of the UN Charter. However, the inability to prove the facts that Iraq was a threat failed to be clear. This is why Mr. Carne Ross, a senior expert in Iraqi affairs within the United Kingdom Mission to the United Nations, to admit and testify as he saw the British and U.S. intelligence move on Iraq each working day for a period of four and a half years. There has not been one report to suggest that Saddam had weapons of mass destruction capability or that he was a threat to Britain or any other country [440].

In spite of all these facts, the series of lies in the form of statements from U.S. officials did not stop. Richard Perle, senior adviser to President George W. Bush at the beginning of the Iraq War in 2003 said. "That the greatest victory of the war on Iraq is to destroy the evil that threatens international law". Although he said, it was illegal but still justified! [545,546]. Because of the failure of them marketing fabricated lies, the U.S. and U.K. stuck with their pseudo-humanitarian arguments. One of these arguments was the liberation of the Iraqi people from dictatorship with frightening violations of human rights. The war would bring freedom and democracy to Iraq! [442]. Here the question arises where humanitarian intervention and human rights among those governments during the inhumane embargo, which described by former U.S. Attorney General Ramsey Clark in 1996, "there is no greater violation of human rights anywhere in the world in the last decade of this millennium than of the sanctions imposed against Iraq".

It has become clear to everyone now that the goal of the governments of the occupying powers after the Kuwait War in 1991 was not regime change in Iraq, but the destruction of Iraq as a people and as a state. In addition, with simple examples from the suffering of the Iraqi people during daily life, we see the continuing problem of power outages during the period of the criminal embargo on the Iraqi people along with the lack of health services and the high cost of living. This prompted one of the U.S. Air Force planners to say then that if the Iraqi people get rid of Saddam Hussein's government, we would be more than happy to assist in the reconstruction and will fix the electricity [429]. However, there was no real reform in restoring electricity in Iraq even after the official departure of their troops from Iraq by the end of 2011 and the passage of more than 11 years after the end of the invasion.

During the first eight months of 1999, the British and U.S. aircraft conducted more than 10,000 air raids on Iraq, in order to target more than 400 Iraqi targets and hit with more than 1,000 rockets or bombs. Although these raids killed and injured hundreds of innocent civilians, the U.S. Brig. General William Looney, commander of these operations, said brazenly, "if they open their Radar, we will strike them with cruise missiles, they know we have the country and the atmosphere of their own. We dictate the way in which they live and the words which declare it, and this is a great thing in America right now, it's a good thing, especially since there was a lot of oil in this region we need" [63 of 28].

Before the start of the invasion and aggression campaign, Washington announced the formation of a "coalition of the willing" to give greater legitimacy to the military action and give it the appearance of a multilateral international effort with support from abroad. Washington announced this "alliance" to attract 49 countries [443]. Many countries in this alliance did not participate in any military contingents, while others participated in units of symbolism, for example, the Kazakhstan military unit was made up of 29 units and Moldavia 24 units, while Iceland has sent only two units [444]. A military force that invaded Iraq was almost entirely composed of combat units from the United States and Britain. The total force was little more than 300,000 ground troops, as well as pieces of a large naval and air task force [445].

The brutal air campaigns began with intensive bombing, and a process called "shock and awe", which preceded the ground campaign. The United States made use of prohibited weapons such as napalm and depleted uranium munitions and cluster bombs, an early sign that the coalition will exercise little moral or legal restraint [425]. As a result, with a huge difference in military power, and after three weeks of fierce fighting, the forces entered Baghdad on 8 April 2003. The occupation became a fait accompli with the control of their forces in the major cities in Iraq after the fall of Baghdad in the hands of the occupation on 9 April 2003. This was followed shortly after, on the May 2nd, with an announcement by U.S. President Bush on board the aircraft carrier U.S. Abraham Lincoln that the task of the occupation "was accomplished"!

In March of 2003, the governments of occupation initiated, after the end of military operations of the invasion, the establishment of management and civil occupation affairs and called it the Office for Reconstruction and Humanitarian Assistance for Iraq. These interim administrations were led by retired U.S. general Jay Montgomery Garner, chairman of the Virginia-based SY Coleman Company, which specialized in providing technical assistance to the U.S. missile systems used during the invasion of Iraq [663]. He had three assistants, including British General Tim Cross. They disagreed on how to rule Iraq. Garner said, "I do not think [the Iraqis] need to go through with the plan of the United States, and I think that what we need to do is set up an Iraqi government that represents the will of the freely elected government by the people. It is their country and their oil [664]. Without clear reason, they replaced this General and administration later with the new administration called the CPA (Coalition Provisional Authority). British and U.S. governments prepared within this authority a letter addressed to the UN Security Council to inform them on the intention to establish a coalition Provisional Authority. This was the first step towards the return of the alleged Iraqis to their land for national sovereignty. This form of the power and responsibility relates clearly to the occupation forces, despite lacking reference to the invasion, to the occupation, to the occupiers and the occupying power [12, 47, 450].

The new management of this authority task force assigned U.S. former diplomat and an expert on international terrorism, Lewis Paul "Jerry" Bremer III. This was a decision issued by the White House and announced by Secretary of Defense Rumsfeld, on 9 May 2003. Bremer actually filled this position for the period between 11 May and June 28, 2003 [665]. It is known that Bremer, after retiring from his U.S. diplomatic work in 1989, he became director of a private company (Kissinger and Associates) as adviser in crisis management. Then in 1999, he was chosen by the House Speaker Dennis Hastert to be president of the National Commission on Terrorism. He issued a report entitled "Countering the changing threat of international terrorism" which was published in June 2006 [666]. He also served on the Committee on Science of the National Academy of Science and Technology in the fight against terrorism, which issued a report in 2002 entitled "Making the Nation Safer: The Role of Science and Technology in Countering Terrorism" [667]. It is known that he does not speak

Arabic and did not previously work in the Middle East before the invasion of Iraq [668]!

Bremer's experience in making and management crisis, in addition to technologies management of terrorism, has become clear in his decisions at the beginning of his work in Iraq. He issued the Coalition Provisional authority's decision No. 2 on the dismantling of the Iraqi army [669], and the demobilization of all employees of the police force. This made Iraqi cities open to looting and arson, while the occupation forces idly stood over the fire in the seventeen ministries of the government, including the ministries of education, culture, health and trade, with the exception of providing protection for the oil ministry only [446]. Paul Bremer admitted upon arrival in Baghdad, saying, "Although it is not desirable, but the word actually found an occupation". Former U.S. Secretary of Defense, Rumsfeld tried in April 11 to justify allowing the looting and theft while minimizing the news that deliberated about the looting of the Iraqi National Museum, which contains historic priceless treasures, saying things happen and freedom untidy [447]. Two days before the end of his mission, Bremer signed "Order No. 17", which gave all foreign contractors with the Coalition Provisional Authority and the U.S. government immunity from Iraqi law. This order was later included in the new Iraqi constitution as well [670]. This helped the violence caused by the U.S. security companies in Iraq, such as Blackwater, which was of great resentment among Iraqi citizens, who view them as private armies acting without law or deterrent effect of punitive damages [671], (see Chapters 11 and 14). Bremer also established the Governing Council, as advisor positions, of the political forces that supported and helped the occupation, and then gave the power to amend and implement the constitution to his authority in the CPA. He proposed a first draft of a ban on political parties that were opposed to the U.S. occupation, to participate in the next elections, and the privatization of numerous Iraqi industries and natural resources. And to allow the unelected Iraqi Governing Council to signing of a binding agreement to regulate cases of forces between Iraq and the United States! This highlights the scandal, that after their departure from Iraq, was the disappearance and without the presence of bills to more than 9 billion dollars, which was allocated for Iraq's reconstruction [672].

In paragraph 5 of the UN Security Council Resolution 1483 references the countries that will be included in the Coalition Provisional Authority now or in the future. They will be part of these authorities, as well as the UN Security Council resolutions including and explicitly recognizing that occupation forces run the Coalition Provisional Authority. In the end, it becomes the Coalition

Provisional Authority as the authority to manage the development of the occupation. This applies to those who enter within it. On 16 October 2003, the Security Council established the multinational forces under resolution 1511. Here, Britain tried to claim that the United Nations is now responsible for all activities and operations of British troops in Iraq, according to UN Security Council Resolution 1511. However, according to Legal Professor Sarooshi, this decision is not related to the nature of the United Nations, it was towards the occupying powers to pressure the formation of a team to serve the policy of those countries and not the mission of UN [211]. The UN Security Council for violating the UN Charter and the threat to international peace and security must punish the invasion countries that launched the war of aggression internationally. The UN must not allow the legitimization of aggressive crimes on an independent state and a founding member of the United Nations.

Some Iraqi politicians, who helped the occupation and supported the opposition abroad, later admitted that the occupation governments deceived them. Perhaps this is highlighted in the confessions of what Ahmad Chalabi previously stated [5, 11 A].

According to international law, the land or territory to be occupied when they are in fact under a hostile army authority [368] must provide the conditions to achieve this definition; 1) the occupier must be in a position to exercise effective control over the land that it does not possess. 2) Intervention is not in accordance with the terms of the legitimate sovereignty, even if this intervention was not part of an armed conflict, which includes hostile acts. These rules apply even if there were no armed resistance [369]. These rules are contained primarily in the three treaties: the Hague Regulations of 1907, the Fourth Geneva Convention of 1949 and Additional Protocol I of 1977 [370].

The description of occupation forces in the rules of international law as described will be considered acts of aggression. The war and the invasion of countries and blockaded ports and regions are all acts of aggression. This alerted America to this matter and imposed itself on the Security Council once again at working out a new resolution 1546 to legitimize the occupation and turning the occupation forces name to multinational forces. This was done in order to insure that there was no responsibility on these forces if any crimes take place [8 A].

The Security Council welcomed the intention of the occupying authorities to establish a democratic government in Iraq, without that, these efforts will be under the direct and complete supervision of the international community as it is supposed to be with the United Nations. This however would only help the UN advisory mission in Iraq without any authority, control or real participation in the decision-making process. Mission work is limited to the review of the events and developments every six months without a real assessment that reflects the reality of what is going on with details in the coming quarters. The violations of international humanitarian law by the occupying forces in Iraq did not prevent the continuation of the UN Security Council to renew the mandate of the multinational forces set up twice by the occupation [448]. Unfortunately, the Security Council did not exercise any meaningful control over the work of the multinational force, as it did not have a full and frank discussion of the Iraq issue. This situation prompted some ambassadors to discuss it at the United Nations, as Mr. Juan Gabriel Valdes of the State of Chile, and Mr. Adolfo Aguilar Zinser of Mexico. However, Washington forced their governments to bring them back to recall them, which makes it very clear that the U.S. will not tolerate any opposition [449]. Since then, several ambassadors have told us, that Washington would not accept questions when viewing periodic reports on behalf of the MNF forces on the UN Security Council [425].

The resolutions of UN Security Council cannot be repealed or amended for paragraphs of international humanitarian law or be a substitute for it. Therefore, not all decisions concerning the occupation of Iraq gave immunity to the occupation forces or international coalition formed by the occupation of the jurisdiction of Iraqi law. The protection given to the occupation soldiers, security and military personnel contractors and civilians has been based on the decisions of the occupying temporary power (CPA) which called decision 17. These decisions remained even after the transfer of alleged sovereignty to the government of Iyad Allawi, the interim authority on 30 June 2004, which did not seek to cancel it upon return to the prestige and authority of the Iraqi judiciary. Paul Bremer has issued Resolution No. 100, which gives the next Iraqi government responsibilities to implement its own resolutions [156]. These decisions were served and protected by the occupation forces in Iraq, because of paragraph 27 of the Transitional Administrative Law of Iraq, TAL, issued by Bremer, confirmed that the laws, regulations and orders issued by the authority of the temporary occupation force until their repealed or amended legislation issued duly and have the force of law. To confirm the occupation management and supervision on the overall political process and the new permanent constitution of Iraq's, Article 130 of it has kept the power of existing laws, including those assumed by the Coalition Provisional Authority, which has not been canceled by the interim government of Iyad Allawi, including the decision notorious No. 17, which remained valid thus far [156]. In case we assume that the Security Council has given authorization mandate of the occupation and joined forces after the invasion for the formation of a multinational force, Resolution 1511, this internationalist authorization needed these forces to provide the highest standards of international law, which is not being during the first and second battle of Fallujah. Violation of customary international law prohibits indiscriminate attacks and causing unwarranted injuries in overcrowded civilian residential areas, which were committed by these forces (see Chapter 12).

Since 19 March to the beginning of May 2003, the date of establishment of the interim Iraqi government, there have been intensive and systematic military operations carried out by the armies of the United States of American and British, with small forces of Australian and Polish. These operations were a flagrant violation of international law and without approval of the UN Security Council [177]. Many forces that entered Iraq after the occupation were not convinced that they were working in accordance with the rules of international law and the responsibilities of international forces and some countries were forced to withdraw. Withdrawing States that adopted its resolution on the military rules of engagement have been precluded from doing tasks, combat or offensive action, while combat missions remained to carried out by only the United States and British forces [230]. This point explains and adds another proof that these forces were not working as authorized international forces.

UN duties towards the occupation of Iraq war fail with many proofs, remember only contradiction in how the Security Council dealt with the entry of the Iraqi army into Kuwait and the issuance of an international resolution by the Security Council to consider it as an occupation. The United States pushed the Security Council to override the principles and purposes of the provisions of the Charter of the United Nations when they jumped straight to Chapter VII in a few hours after the entry of Iraqi forces into Kuwait on 8 February 1990. Resolution 660 was issued which condemned Iraq and asked for immediate withdraw [281]. While the Security Council continues to address the issues of the Israeli occupation in Palestine and the territory of the other Arab countries after more than 65 years later, in the framework of Chapter VI of private settlement of disputes by peaceful means. We all remember before the start of the U.S. project as part of the global war against Iraq campaign, has made most of the Security Council resolutions to punish Iraq. They issued 69 resolutions during the period from August 1990 until the end of 2007, which means more than 20% the total number of decisions that were used during this 17-year period.

The Hague Regulations (1907), the Fourth Geneva Convention (1949) and the first additional Protocol of 1977 governs the status of occupation powers. These laws and conventions dropped the mask on the fact of occupation, and prompting the U.S. and British authorities to talk about the situation of occupation instead of an editing mode of liberation or freedom used in speeches and newspapers before the occupation. The occupation as defined by Article 42 of the Hague Regulations (1907) stipulates that the occupied territories are to be under the authority of the hostile army, and the strength of his power lies in his hand occupier (Article 43). The clarification of occupation duties in the second paragraph of Article II of the Fourth Geneva Convention of 1949, as stated in this paragraph, "all cases of partial or total occupation of the territory of a High Contracting Party, even if the occupation meets with no armed resistance". Here are three clear facts to prove the existence of the military occupation, "the exercise of authority over the land or part of the territory of another country, the presence of a hostile army and the presence or absence of resistance". According to international humanitarian law, the armies of the United States and Britain were hostile armies [11]. While the U.S. Congress report claimed in 2008 that the UN Security Council Resolution 1511 on October 16, 2003 that the authority has handed over temporary occupation (CPA) all obligations and the interim authorities in the administration of occupied Iraq, which will stop with the elected Iraqi government representing the Iraqi people [156]. This violates the occupier powers as described in the Hague Conventions. It is more bizarre that the interpretation of this illegal decision had been based on the Interim Government of Iraq, which will have responsibilities, was formed by an agreement between the occupying powers with the Iraqi Council of rule. This was established by the occupation itself, and not with the Iraqi Council, which was elected by the Iraqi people. The violations of the rules of international law were very clear, "not permissible to recognize the legitimacy of the regional situation, which is achieved by using force and rape". Iraq's national security adviser, appointed by the occupation, Mowafak al-Rubai. He admitted that the Governing Council, which was founded by Paul Bremer, did not have any powers and Bremer managed in a derogatory manner. While Paul Bremer, described the Iraqi Governing Council in his book, *My Year in Iraq: The Strategy to Build a Future of Hope*, that they cannot organize the parade, not to mention the leadership of the country [230].

UN Security Council Resolution 1546 had replaced its initial Resolution 1511 on 8 June, and welcomed the transfer of sovereignty from the civilian occupation authority (CPA), which ends its work on the 28th of same month of June 2004 to the Iraqi Interim Government (IAGO), which was formed under the auspices of the occupation and the false supervision by the United Nations, to result in incomplete sovereign government headed by Iyad Allawi [230].

The former U.S. Defense Secretary Rumsfeld did not hesitate to mention in his memoirs that he had agreed to the transfer of sovereignty in order to give help for reassurance to the Iraqis that the occupation will end soon. This is without mention to end the liberation operation or other phrases echoed by some of the supporters of the occupation. Rumsfeld also admitted at the U.S. leadership meeting on 29 October 2003 in which it identified 30 June 2004 as the date for the transfer of power and sovereign to the Iraqis. This was the first time he gave a specific date in this regard, due to the escalation of the Iraqi resistance [13]. The administration of occupied Iraq was being led by the U.S. administration only as stated in the diary of Rumsfeld when he explained how the decision to schedule the transfer of sovereignty and authority by the scope of President George W. Bush's administration and the U.S. National Security Council [13]. Once the adoption of this resolution, the U.S. President ordered national security adviser Condoleezza Rice to manage the Iraqi file and prepare the post-withdrawal plan. This confirms that the occupation authority (Coalition Provisional) was just a false body to the authority of the occupation's countries, and the international community did not have any real role in making this decision.

It is funny and surprising at the same time that the occupying powers called this period of maintaining the occupying forces in Iraq under the name Operation Iraqi Freedom, including periods of Fallujah first and second battles while the fact that the international resolutions and the confessions of American commanders were confirming a situation of occupation! Since 2003, Iraq has become the deadliest country in the world for aid workers. The International Organization of UNICEF recognizes that 30% of Iraqi children suffer from malnutrition while acute malnutrition rates reached 9%, and with 1.5 million Iraqis displaced internally, Iraq is ranked sixth in the world. While Mental Health become a source of critical concern such as stress and constant anxiety that generate psychological weakness, as a recent study (2006) found that 92% of Iraqi children with learning difficulties, and with that it's very difficult to reach these vulnerable people [219].

However, the most unusual is the issuance of a U.S. military report seen by public readers with lies that falsify history. For example, a report of the U.S. military Faculty of a US Army War College, Carlisle Barracks, and Pennsylvania was issued in 2006, talking about the incident that took place in the month of June 2003. It states, "The U.S. military and the Iraqi army noticed groups of the insurgency in Baghdad along the western edges in Fallujah, Tikrit"! Which Iraqi army was present at the time and working with the occupation forces? We all know they were not present at this time! However, in the same report they describe the coalition forces, which were established as occupation forces by the UN coalition! [60]. The occupation of Iraq is the result of cooperative efforts at the highest levels between the U.S. administration and the British government, especially the intelligence side, which has witnessed the open integration and cooperation relationship without limits in order to strengthen the weaknesses in any issues concerning the interests for both sides in international policy [37].

The Nazi mentality is clarified deeper across the processes of throwing dust in the eyes and the brain washing of the soldiers. Former U.S. Assistant Secretary of Defense Paul Wolfowitz visited the U.S. base near Fallujah, and told the Marines, "What you're doing is fighting another kind of evil. It's not fascism and not communism, but every bit as evil, and I think each piece is a threat to our country!" [240]. As a result, war hysteria has led U.S. soldiers into Iraq to fight in a retaliatory manner until it came out that one of their leaders Capt. John D. Prien III, who gave the leadership of his battalion near Fallujah to a new commander and told his soldiers, "this camp is hallowed ground, where it spilled the blood of the Navy construction battalion soldiers *Seabee* for the cause of freedom and the ongoing war against terrorism" [241]. I am not aware of any of the terror that he talks a about and they know that terrorism groups entered with their occupation of Iraq. Even the media war that portrayed the occupation as acceptable by the U.S. and Western people was a thoughtful terrorist scheme through books and publications, as I read in the most dangerous American book by Robert Spencer. This book, released in 2003 was a hateful book on Islam titled *Escalating Muslim soldiers, how still Jihad threatens America and the West* [286].

Impunity considered an attribute characteristic of the system Bush used to declare the law of the jungle in Iraq. U.S. forces and their spies no longer conceal attacks on civilian targets or eliminate anyone - doctors, clerics, and journalists - they who dares to count the bodies. The administration of George W. Bush has approved official impunity policy with the appointment of Alberto Gonzales in the position of the Attorney General. This man, who advised the President personally "that the memorandum of torture" under the Geneva Conventions may be "outdated". In addition, another thing that helped Bush Jr.

on his re-election is a cover-up Democrats, especially presidential candidate John Kerry on Bush's crimes and lack of legal accountability for serious violations of international law by Bush. This Democratic candidate showed racist style after the scientific journal Lancet published a precise statistical to prove the death of 100,000 Iraqi during that period, John Kerry replied with a lie, "Americans are 90 percent of the casualties in Iraq!" [475]. This situation confirms the spread of Nazism mentality between two ruling parties in America. U.S. politicians were willing even to sacrifice top employees in order to implement their own agenda, after the exposure of the lies of the Bush administration by a committee of the Senate investigation, which spent a whole year, tried this administration to make the Central Intelligence Agency, rather than the White House responsible for the chaos and the decision of the aggressive war [479]. While the British judicial authorities did not dare to investigate allegations of lying by Tony Blair's government to launch an aggression war, they were content with the formation of a parliamentary committee of inquiry on the study of the causes of access to this error in order to prevent future recurrence without legal accountability, which they recognized destroyed Iraq [485].

Colonial mentality of the U.S. administration increases with its use to the presence of crises and wars, as they did after attacking Iraq in 1991. Expanded control of military bases included all of the Arab Gulf states, Saudi Arabia, Kuwait, Bahrain, Qatar, and the United Arab Emirates. After the Yugoslavia war in 1999, they expanded their military bases to include Kosovo, Albania, Macedonia, Bulgaria and Hungary, Bosnia, and Croatia. After their Afghanistan War, they expanded their bases to include in addition to Afghanistan, Pakistan, Kazakhstan, Uzbekistan, Tajikistan, Kyrgyzstan, Georgia, Yemen, and Djibouti. As well as to the huge military bases that still exist since the end of World War II in both Germany and Japan [426]. The U.S. administration recognize that the issue of fighting terrorism is just propaganda for war interests, as senior Pentagon officials indicated to *The New York Times* in 2003. "The idea is to build a counter-terrorism environment globally, so that the issue of terrorism within 20 to 30 years later, like the slave trade, discredited completely" [432]. Crimes and violations of the occupation in Fallujah was the evidence for the Nazi face of the occupation in Iraq [484], which has insulted all the Geneva Conventions and international humanitarian and customary laws.

One of the Chinese Generals, Senior Colonel Qiao Liang, explained to the official Chinese Communist Party newspaper *Zhongguo Qingnian Bao* about his book, *Unrestricted War,* saying, "The first rule of unrestricted warfare is that there no rules, with nothing forbidden" and then added "that powerful states do not use restrictions in the war against weak states because powerful nations are made rules and create a new one when it does not suit the former with its purpose. But he has to show it rules or that the whole world will not trust" [498].

Ten years after the invasion of Iraq, YouGov organization conducted a survey among Americans citizens in 2013, and confirms that 52% of Americans believe the war, occupation of Iraq, was a mistake, while 31% still believe that it was the right decision [521]. The Charter of the United Nations and the Universal Declaration of Human Rights was the embodiment of the rule of law at the international level. No one wants a repeat of blatant aggression wars like that, so it was a charter to replace the gunboat diplomacy and war machine with peaceful measures supervised by the UN Security Council [404]. Kofi Annan said, that the invasion of Iraq was "an event that divided the international community hopelessly — the way Syria is about to do" [684].

The simple look to the following schedule, we will see the reality of mass murder and criminality, which was succeeded by the U.S. – U.K. occupation in Iraq.

Iraq Body Count, March 19, 2003 - August 22, 2008	86,661 - 94,558
Iraq Coalition Casualty Count, April 28, 2005 - August 22, 2008	43,099
Brookings Iraq Index, May 2003 - August 14, 2008	113,616
The Associated Press, April 2005 - February 13, 2008	34,832 dead, 40,174 wounded
The Iraq Family Health Study (the "WHO study") March 2003 - June 2006	151,000
The Lancet, "Mortality after the 2003 Invasion of Iraq" March 19, 2003 - July 31, 2006	426,369 - 793,663

Figure 1.1 - Schedule international assessments of Iraqi civilian casualties [331]

CHAPTER 2

Fallujah' History with Shock and Awe Policy of Foreign Invasions

2.1. Fallujah

Fallujah is located geographically in the Anbar province, about 50 kilometers northwest of the capital of Baghdad. This location places her closer to the sources of the government in Baghdad. There are clans and members of the Arab tribes that live in it and are committed to tribal norms. They adhere to the orders of the Islamic religion; therefore, it has an Islamic awakening. Fallujah comprises an area of up to 30 km² and is rectangular in shape. One of its borders is the Euphrates River from the west. Surrounding Fallujah are three small cities Saqlawiyah, Ameriyah, and Karma. Fallujah is one of the major cities in the Anbar province, one of the largest Iraqi provinces. The Anbar province occupies 30% of the area of Iraq and its capital is the city of Ramadi, 110 km from Baghdad. The Anbar province borders three neighboring Arab countries, Saudi Arabia, Jordan, and Syria. Anbar gained importance more and more because of its location and cultural contacts with these countries.

Fallujah translated from the Arabic language means *arable land*, with its rich soil able to sustain farming when rain falls from the sky. The city's population increased gradually until the number reached, according to the census in 2003, about 650 000 people. The current estimated population of the within the city limits is 700,000 people. Most of Fallujah's population is from large tribes in Iraq descended from Al-Dulaimi clans from all its branches (AlbuEssa, Jumilla, Mahamdh, AlbuAlwan, Fallahat, Zoba, Hallabsa, Albonmr, Alibofahd and Kubissat, in addition to other small clans. The city is also known as the city of mosques (Masjid) totaling approximately 550 mosques and masjid.

There are indications that the area surrounding Fallujah has been known since ancient times and has been inhabited since the time of the Babylonians. There are several theories about the origin of the naming of the city. One of these theories is due to the label assets Akkadian word (Blukato) or (Floqat). Historical studies did not indicate precisely and specifically about the history of

[27]

the emergence of Fallujah or her human settlement. Fallujah is believed to be founded on the ruins of the historic city of Anbar, which liberated by the Arabian leader Khalid ibn al-Walid [6A]. The historic city of Anbar, was established at the time of Caliph Abu Abbas Mohammed bin Abdullah Abbasi (134-145 AH) to be the capital of the Abbasid Empire and center succession before Abbasid Caliph al-Mansur builds the peace city of Baghdad, which became then the capital of the world and the center of culture and sciences.

Fallujah represents an example of the mosaic diversity of Iraqi. There is a variety of minority groups in Iraqi, the broad spectrum of the Kurds, some Sabians and the Christians, who lived here for long periods. Hundreds of Kurds lived in Fallujah after displacement from the Kurdistan region in the north of Iraq during the Iraq - Iran War in 1981. Fallujah was the capital of the province Ramadi, most of the regions of Iraq welcome the kurds and do not feel any discrimination or racial discrimination like the Iraqis over time. For that formed the social roots and strong relationships between the people of Anbar and the Kurds, even after most of them returned to northern Iraq when they became an independent region from the central government of Baghdad at the beginning of the nineties.

Fallujah residents faced a lot of forced displacement outside the city because of the five different wars and military operations. The first was with the Rashid Ali revolt against the British occupation and it is trying to overtake the Regent Prince Abdul Ilah in 1941. The second time was when Fallujah was exposed to the raid by Iranian aircraft in 1981. This was during the war with Iran, and civilian's families stayed for a few days outside the city for fear of the returning planes targeting civilians. They were displacement twice during the battles of Fallujah, the first in April and the second in November of the same year 2004. While the last time, they were displaced when they were exposed to a genocide campaign by the sectarianism regime of PMs Nouri al-Maliki against Anbar and the Sunni provinces, at the end of 2013 and the beginning of 2014.

2.2. History of Fallujah with foreign occupation

2.2.1. English occupation of Iraq

The city's history is defined by foreign occupation, and the animosity and distrust of the Fallujah people towards the new U.S.-U.K. occupation (2003-2011) was not without reasons and historical roots as well. On 12 August 1920, a popular revolution was launched against the British occupation named the Twentieth Revolution, triggered by tribes in southern Iraq after the arrest of

Sheikh Shaalan Abu John by British occupation forces. This started a revolt that spread in the center and north of Iraq with solidarity of the remaining tribes and cities of Iraq. During the Revolution, the famous British commander Colonel Gerard Evelyn Leachman was killed by the son of Sheikh Dhari elder clan Zoba, one of the major clans, known in Falluja, during a meeting between them in the Khan Dhari area near Fallujah. Col. Leachman was buried in the British war cemetery near Fallujah. After this incident, most of the tribes in the west of Iraq joined the rebel clans in the south to emphasize the cohesion of the Iraqis against foreign occupation. Fallujah played a known role in the rejection and resistance to the British occupation not only in the Twentieth Revolution, but also during the Free Officers' Revolution in 1941, known also as the revolution of four colonels or the revolution of Rashid Ali Gailani, who was the Iraqi Prime Minister at the time. During the 1941 Revolution, they tried to sequester the Regent Prince Abdul Ilah and the last King, child at that time of King Faisal II. They then pledged homage to Sharif Razi to be king of Iraq.

The military intervention of the British forces, in the suppression of the revolution to the return back of the Regent to the Protector prince Abdul Ilah thwarted the revolution. There were large numbers of British troops stationed in the Habbaniyah vicinity of Fallujah. They fought a pitched battle with the rebel forces, Iraqi military and the people of Fallujah, at the entrance of the old and iconic iron bridge in Fallujah, named by the British as the long iron bridge. British Captain Alistair Graham led the attack of the British forces coming from Habbaniyah in the late afternoon of 19 May, 1941 and under the supervision of Colonel Ouvry Roberts, they did battle on the iron bridge in Fallujah, Old Bridge, and this was the final result in resolving the battle in advance for the benefit of British.

Iraqi forces supported by the people of Fallujah while British troops supported by some Iraqi puppet groups who were trained at the Habbaniyah base. However, the difference in armament and air superiority was leaked to the rebels, they killed many of the people of Fallujah and the Iraqi army in the massacre. They now reside in the cemetery on the outskirts of the city in Jbeil district, behind the El Alamein flourmill, as known as the flour laboratory of Haji Sami. The English military plan was similar to the plan for the Marines during the first battle in April 2004 in Fallujah. It was based on the closure of all entrances to the city to prevent the arrival of any help and start heavily and barbaric shelling. This was to inflict a psychological and physical effect on civilians and combatants before storming the city. History repeats itself and the policy of shock and awe used by U.S.-U.K. forces by the same military minds in spite of the difference between the generations.

The Fallujah battle against British forces in 1941 immortalized the great Iraq poet Marouf Rusafi with a wonderful poem; perpetuate the occupation crimes and praising starring people to resist the occupation, he sang and saying:

British, we will not forget, your assault in housing 'Fallujah'
That punk will not God cure but, themes wounded and encourage.
It is a disaster, which our loyalty refused, to solve it only by sword
Its disaster which cried Iraqis, and the Levant and corner Mahjojh
infrastructure.
Solve your army wants revenge, a seductive who live as boar
Day wreaked wolves [Athor] where, wreak carries horror.
Disparaged Muslims Stultify, and have taken from Jews as excuse
And you have dropped on unarmed innocent a glass, from blood of treachery
was a fusion.
And you lawful its funds and hewn, between people of homes any glue
Be this urbanization and Sophistication, your people claiming its roots.
Or you drunk to overcome the war, were not emitted in ready
May have vaccine for prematurity, therefore, ended in bad result.
Did you forget your panic army, witnessed cheese coast of the Aegean
Your defeat in fall fort 'Ogarit', and has become an eyesore on the 'eye Vejeh'.
Will carry the shame and mortify, from country want all leave it
No arrogance with false nets, became woven for catching us.
Today, you are only in the tract, like camel chest under it the roller
I lived in the homeland is happy, as free refuses to live forever crooked.
I hope the happiness, but I do not have produced came
God's give fertile land, but I'm not, even care for his fields and garden.
Every day pride sing, making his glory as Dirge
What human life with humiliation, only as bitter when drink as repugnant
Praise and Thank [for two rivers land, and peaceful greeting to Fallujah.

2.2.2. First Gulf War in 1991

On February 13 of 1991 of first Gulf War and after the withdrawal of the Iraqi army from Kuwait, British Tornado aircraft fired a single laser-guided bomb to destroy the old bridge in Fallujah but failed. Despite the success of the second bomb, this hit the modern bridge near to the old bridge. A prominent of its repair was still clear. The bomb fails to target the old bridge, fell on the densely populated area in the old market, which was 100 meters from the Old Bridge. As a result of this accident, it killed more than 130 and wounded more than 80 civilians from Fallujah, many of whom were children, according to statements of the hospital staff. Another source said that at least 100 civilians were killed in this crime [193]. It was a horrific massacre, which I will always remember. A British officer named Capt. David Henderson confirmed the crime and expressed regret to reporters, without further details of the crime. This crime did not take the media dimension it deserved because at the same time, bombs hit a large civilian shelter in the city of Amiriyah in Baghdad. The Amiriyah bombings led to the largest number of victims and fatalities than those of Fallujah. The number of victims was more than 1,500 victims, mostly women and children [428].

At the time of the bombings, I was near the market that afternoon, and just 500 meters away. I arrived at the entrance to the market, and found that a bomb fell at the entrance of the Commercial building beside the Rafidain Bank. The attacking planes were still flying overhead. There were the bodies of the children that sell fresh chicken in front of the bank just a few meters from the bomb. These were the bodies of two girls, not more than twelve years old and a boy who could not have been more than three years old. We found an older man still alive under a large wooden pole that fell from the roof of his shop. The local people contracted to have one of the giant drilling machines to remove the rubble and debris. They tried to save what they could under the shattered shops.

The bodies of martyred civilians, killed by the explosion fire, were carried by civilian cars in addition to the ambulances for a large number of wounded. One of the witnesses', journalist Mr. Bilal Hussein Jurisy said: *""I was very close to the place of bomb, and saw one child running out of the scene and his body covered in dirt and blood because of injury by fragment in the right cheek and pulled out a large part of it. The teeth appear because of lack the right' cheek and is running scared due to the shock and horror of what had happened. Then we take him to the hospital while the parts of his skin scattered in the ground. In addition, there was one civilian car smashed over the ruins of shops and stand someone near it with crying and asking help and saying, my brothers and my father in this shop. We removed the car from the piled debris and we found the bodies of his brothers and his father who may have died. Another witness from Fallujah called Um Yassin said: "many of the bodies were found a week after the crime, all above away buildings, in addition to the head and body separated from the blast". This also was confirmed by the journalist Jurisy saying, "we found a human head on one of the buildings, nine days after the explosion and show that he belong to the victim martyr Hashem Wardi""*.

After all these years, after the massacre, I gather some facts and remember the details of that day. I am sure that the British pilot in 1991 did not miss bombing the iron bridge but that it was a deliberate strike to massacre civilians for several reasons. Firstly, the historical status of the Iron Bridge was in the previous battles due to the resistance against British occupation in 1941. Secondly, the plan was to inflict the greatest number of deaths and injuries causing shock and awe amongst civilians in order to achieve largest psychological and physical impact inside the most prominate logistical city in western Iraq, such as Fallujah. In addition to the difficulty of ratification to commit such an error by the laser-guided bombs being off target by 120 meters, and falling in the middle of the street of the old market while not damaging the tops of the buildings as it was supposed to strike. We consider this massacre as complimentary to the massacre of the British occupation in 1941.

2.2.3. Western occupation of Iraq in 2003

After the U.S. troops occupied many parts of the Anbar province in April 2003, the Army Armored Cavalry Regiment was the first U.S. force that arrived to control the surrounding Fallujah regions [50.64]. Then followed shortly after, arrived the 82nd Airborne forces lead by Lt. Col. Eric Nantz [64]. In the month of September 2003, the 82 Airborne Division led by Maj. Gen. Charles Swannack sent the paratrooper brigade, led by Lt. Col. Brian Drinkwine to Fallujah. Colonel Brian characterized with a calm and political dialogue over the military as I saw during the meetings of the local governing council in Fallujah, which pose as one of the political solutions after the outbreak of the Iraqi resistance. At first, he was a good communicator, but soon we discovered that he was pursuing a policy of deception, especially with the issue of reconstruction of facilities and services that were destroyed in the city. The lies and deceptions of this U.S. commander revealed by his false statements to a local U.S. newspaper when he stated that, "this city has over 45 thousand supporters from the previous leaders and must fight them!" In one of the meetings, he said we would fund $500,000 dollars for the projects and then return in the next meeting, to ask the U.S. how to spend $50,000 dollars for these projects? We tried to correct the number because of all of the members of Fallujah council wrote down the same figures. This situation led some scholars to leave the membership of the council and they invite people to Jihad for the liberation of Iraq from these false leaders of the occupation forces. One of the most prominent religious scholars was Sheikh Abdullah al-Janabi.

2.3. International Solidarity with Fallujah

In Fallujah, its history is the rejection of foreign occupation and resistance because of the suffering of the people. In addition to what its people have traditions of the Iraqi people to preserve the Islamic and Arabic values. These reasons were sufficient to resist the U.S.-U.K. occupation. With the passage of time, the world revealed the lies of the occupation in Iraq to justify their crimes. The occupation did not have a good history, which explains the resistance to injustice in the Iraqis blood since ancient times. That is why the leaders of the occupation were surprised after most parts of Iraq supported the uprising of Fallujah in the first battle. This solidarity threatened the occupation administration and pushes their leaders to recognize this in some of their notes. It was normal in this situation to find an international sympathy by the free world and those who reject the use of force.

In 2005, I visited Spain for a second time in a tour to talk about the crimes of the occupation in Fallujah, both as a victim and a witness. There were a lot of those I met that confirmed to me what happened in Fallujah resembles what happened in a Spanish city. I found during a visit to the Basque region, an internationally famous incident similar to what happened to Fallujah occurred and in the same month for the first battle with U.S. forces. It was a crime for the Nazi's to bomb and destroy the Spanish city of Guernica on 26 April 1937. This was during the Spanish civil war in an operation called Rügen. This bombardment prompted many painters and global anti-war supporters, such as Pablo Picasso, to immortalization in a famous painting bearing the name of this city. In parallel, René Iché immortalized it in one of his most beautiful sculptures, and the poet Paul Eluard immortalized it in a poem, *Victory of Guernica*. This rebellious city, under the former Spanish dictator General Francisco Franco, had lost many civilians during the destruction of their city by aerial bombardment. The Government of the Basque estimated the casualties at 1,654 people were killed, in one of the first air strikes in the modern military aviation history and targeting civilians.

The world commemorates the heroes and is going to spend eternity noting Fallujah as the first city in the modern era, which became popular by uprising against the U.S.-U.K. occupation. It was not surprising that the responses of free world came to remember the next generation's massacres and occupation there. One of the greatest global theater and film productions of Fallujah was by an Italian, who came with the same name, "the confused angels ... Fallujah and open the gates of hell". Angeli Distratti... Falluja: Aprendo le porte dell 'inferno), which directed by Italian Gianluca Arcopinto, and with the help and supervision of Italian Bridge To organization (Un Ponte Per ....). This play was passed in 2006 and inspired by the Italian story titled, "*A song for Falluja about occupation crimes in Fallujah*" [167]. I saw during the show that in this theatre there were some tears from the Italians, declaring its humanitarian solidarity with the Iraqi people, as did the Italians to drop the right-wing government for withdrawing Italian troops from Iraq in November 2006 [168]. The Italians were deceived into entering Iraq in July 2003, inside a coalition of international forces that are not under UN supervision. This situation was the same for the Spanish forces, which pulled out earlier in April 2004 after the rejection of the overwhelming popular opinion in Spain. They were like many of the countries that participated in this coalition and quickly pulled out [169]. Liberals of the British people did the same in the perpetuation of Fallujah with a British theatrical incarnation massacre of Fallujah. The British story was based on interviews with residents of Fallujah and U.S. soldiers who fought there, to prove to everyone that more than 70 violations of the Geneva Conventions took placed. The Play *Fallujah,* was directed by Jonathan Holmes, who showed a picture of revenge at the hands of the occupying forces of the impatient stubbornness of the Iraqis [91]. In one scene of the play, to make it more realistic and quoting an American soldier, a U.S. sniper that fought in Fallujah admits to the barbaric mentality. This was led by saying, "in my country when I go hunting, its sport, but here when I go hunting, it is a personal issue"! The public reaction of the British was full of human emotion for the crimes of the occupation forces, while the U.S. military has not been able to respond to the text of the play, which was sent to them by the director before showing it in public. Finally, Arab and Iraqi Poets, especially poets of Fallujah city, the Fallujah Forum of Poets [90], may immortalize the exploits and the history of the city in several books of poetry published in Arabic.

CHAPTER 3
Beginning Of Invasion' Crimes in Fallujah

3.1. The beginning of occupation crimes in Fallujah:

C rimes of the occupation initiated with the advanced intention after their entry into the capital of Baghdad and the willingness of mass punishment of any opposition to their occupation, which was announced by U.S. Major General Charles H. Swannack Jr., a commander of Special Forces in Baghdad from the 82nd Airborne Division, as he said:

When we identify positively an enemy target, we're going to go ahead and take it out with every means we have available. I like to remember what Viscount Slim said during the Burma campaign. He said, "Use a sledgehammer to crush a walnut." And that's exactly what we will do. We will use force, overwhelming combat power when it's necessary. "[556]

3.1.1. First Crime Suppression and Killing of Protesters (April 2003)

Repression policy was initiated after U.S. troops broke their agreement with the leaders of Fallujah to enter with their tanks and armored vehicles in the center of the city. They initiated the development of checkpoints with a series of violations on the privacy and dignity of the people. On April 25, 2004, they occupied a school building, which is a large two-story building of the primary and secondary school students, which was to be converted to the headquarters of the occupation forces. This confirms that the approval of the previous agreement with a delegation of Fallujah was just to gain time and confidence. So we understood that the cat and mouse game is a game that will prevail and that the false promises will be repeated daily [232]

US forces raised the temper and feelings of anger in the residents when the soldiers committed to acts contrary to the ethics of Islamic traditions in the Iraqi civilian houses near the school, Qaeid, in Fallujah. These abuses compromised the honor and dignity of the people and they should pay for it. They also prevented the schools from educating, depriving the students in the process. This injustice prompted the residents near the school of Qaeid, in the

Nazzal neighborhood, to organize the first peaceful demonstration. This spontaneous event occurred on Wednesday April 28, 2003, just 5 days after the U.S. troops moved into Fallujah city.

The Falluja's rais in this demonstration held signs calling for the U.S. troops to leave the school and respect the traditions and feeling of the city. Demonstrators gathered in front of the Mayor's building, were there was a meeting between the commander of U.S. forces in Fallujah and the new mayor of Fallujah, Mr. Taha Bedaiwi. Then crowds of civilian demonstrators went to a school Qaeid and passed in the streets of Fallujah. The Americans deployed snipers on the roofs of school Qaeid. The powerful logic of the occupying forces, added with their anal thinking, created a bloodbath that open the gates of hell against the occupation forces later. U.S. troops opened fire on the demonstration, killing 17 protesters and wounding 75 civilians. Among the dead were six children. This was the first terrible crime that took place in the city by the U.S. forces. The hysteria of U.S. forces led them to shoot at ambulances, trying to rescue the wounded, according to the testimony of Dr. Ahmed Ghanem al-Ali, director of the Fallujah hospital. The Human Right Watch covered the incident with a report released on 17 June 2003 condemning the incident and demanding an investigation into the circumstances of [172,451].

The U.S. commander in the Fallujah area, Lt. Col. Eric Nantz, has admitted that the soldiers had warned the demonstrators through loudspeakers "the demonstration can be considered a hostile act and will face deadly force"! This commander also claimed that his forces were in the school in front of hostile crowds and were under attack by protestors that threw stones and fired guns aimed at the soldiers. While I was close to the event, I did not hear gunfire from the demonstrators, only that from the U.S. side. The fear of the wrath of the people and the shock of the emergence of an opposition demonstration against the invasion so soon after the fall of Baghdad, with the euphoria of victory of the occupation in Iraq, is one of the main factors that prompted the Americans soldiers to open fire on the demonstrators.

A reporter for the Independent newspaper of London, Phil Reeves, confirmed the fact that there was a lack of gunfire from the protesters. He noted the absence of any trace of bullets or shell casings on the school walls and grounds. The nearby homes in front of the school however, looked like a sieve because of the large number of bullet holes in the concrete walls of the civilian's homes. U.S. commander Nantz responded to a question from a journalist, "where are the traces of the bullets, which you claim were fired toward your soldiers?" Nantz claimed that they passed over the heads of the soldiers and not into the walls! Another American journalist, P. Mitchell Prothero, a correspondent for the American newspaper, United Press International (UPI), was in Fallujah at the time and indicated that among those civilians killed or wounded; only 5.56 mm bullets were found. These are the same type used by U.S. forces. There was no evidence of 7.62 mm bullets from AK-47s, which is usually used by the Iraqis [27].

The events of this horrible crime did not end at this point, but the same forces returned to open fire after two days on April 30, 2004 against a demonstration of mourners from the victims of the first demonstration. They killed two civilians and wounded 14 others, including some children. Journalist Chris Huges was present during this demonstration and documented the second murder crime that he published with images on the Internet [230].

The crime of suppressing these demonstrations spread to other Iraqi cities such as Mosul. The occupation forces began to enter homes and inspected, smashing through doors, destroying furniture, used stun guns to provoke terror in the raids, screamed in the face of people and arrested hundreds of them. This policy by the occupation forces captured dozens of detainees and incarcerated thousands of Iraqis without charges and absence the right of self-defense. During this period of the detention operations, they initiated programs of torture with the knowledge of the occupation authorities .

Fallujah areas remained to protect itself through their sons, despite the prevalence of theft and vandalism in the capital Baghdad and some other cities. These thefts were encouraged by occupation soldiers and some political parties, which came with it and supported this invasion. There was no action by the occupation forces in order to return the rule of law and system in the Iraqi streets as the international law assumes the responsibility of the occupying forces according to the Geneva Conventions. Guarding Fallujah and keeping peace remained in the hands of the cities' sons. They continued for the first six months of the occupation. The civilians felt safer with their own children protecting their areas. This was because everyone knew that the invading forces would not protect them, as they were more concerned with protecting themselves.

The murder of peaceful protesters in Fallujah and the local feeling was that of a lack of justice. The spread of the forest law occurred because of the lack of the rule of Iraqi law, which set off some armed operations against U.S. forces. This forced U.S. President Bush to warn militants attacking U.S. forces in Iraq [233]. These crimes not only inflamed the armed resistance in Fallujah but also other cities of the Anbar province. This drove the spirit of resistance in Iraq as the recognition of the occupation officers themselves [234].

3.1.2. Second Crime, Killing Fallujah' Protection Force and Police (11 Sep., 2003)

Mr. Hamid Bedaiwi was the first mayor of Fallujah, after the occupation that established a Fallujah Protection Force (FPF). This was an idea put forward by one of my relatives' officers with a group of former military colleagues in the military, mostly with high military experience. The aim of the new forces was that they guarded the city government facilities and buildings, and adjust the

[39]

security and traffic control after the occupation decision in reorganizing the army and police. The Fallujah Protection Force weapons, in the beginning, were limited to only sticks and batons. With the success of this simple force to impose the rule of law, the mayor was able to get them on the approval of the U.S. occupation forces using only small weapons like AK-47, pistols, and some cars. This force worked side-by-side with the new police force. The new young members lacked the required experience a veteran officer achieves in time.

At this time came the other crime that I personally witnessed. The Fallujah people played the dubious role of mercenaries while the private security companies worked side-by-side with the U.S. forces. This practice caused the deaths of eight members of the Fallujah Protection Force and wounded seven others, as well as members of the police of Fallujah. A BMW drove by and opened fired on a building of the local government in Fallujah on the night of September 11, 2003. The Fallujah Protection Force was close to the incident assisted the police force chasing the car. This car sped away toward the U.S. military base 22 km southwest of Fallujah on the old road to Baghdad. After this suspicious car entered the U.S. base, both Fallujah security forces decided to return to Fallujah. Just 3 km from the main entry gate to Fallujah, a disastrous situation occurred. The U.S. force located on the side of the road opened fire, focused on the cars of the Fallujah protection force, as told to me by one of the survivors. Those U.S. soldiers went toward the injured to kill them, despite them shouting that they were the police. More criminal than this massacre was that they prevented medical help from reaching them until sunrise. They waited to insure that they would all have died due to severe bleeding, despite the presence of many people and the police just 300 meters from the incident. The American soldiers continued to transfer the wounded and dead to the U.S. base and then returned them to the Fallujah police.

The victims of this crime were the death of eight from the Fallujah Protection Force, Lt. Omar Ismail Mazer, Riaz Malik Waleed Jassim Mohammed, Adnan Amar, Ahmed Mohammed Jassim, Ziad Nazem, Sabah Ali Ibrahim and Ahmed Rehman. Seven others were injured, most of them Fallujah police and the rest of the force protection of Fallujah, LT Essam Ahmed Hussein, M. Mohamed Abdel Mjbas, M. Asim Mohammed Ahmed St., LLC Staff Adnan Ahmed, Abdul Jalil Abdul Mohammed, Alaa Hashim Ahmed and Sam Mohammed Ftikhan [228]. A Majestic funeral occurred for these martyrs, organized by all of the official institutions, religious, social and civic bodies in Fallujah. They were buried in the new cemetery on the northern edge of the city. While the commander of the U.S. paratroopers Lt. Col. Brian Drinkwine, with military responsibility for Fallujah, sent a message of condolence to the families of the martyrs with a small amount of money of up to a thousand dollars each. This was the compensation for the lives of each and every one of them according to the regulations stipulated by the U.S. military. Compensation for Iraqi victims as claimed at the time!

This was a horrible crime towards the security men that were killed, Iraqis began raising doubts about the reality and the nature of the mercenary tasks in accompanying the security companies of the occupation forces in Iraq. This was one of the two sparks that led to the start of the armed resistance against the occupation. In addition to the crime of open fire on civilians during peaceful demonstrations, both departed counter-violence in order to avenge for the martyrs and the dignity of their rights. The violence makes a counter violence in the absence of a national fair judicial system; therefore, law of the jungle will prevail. To evade his troops responsibilities, the former U.S. Defense Secretary Rumsfeld, justifies his troops crimes by trying to describe local fighters as rebels and sometimes as dead-enders, or foreign terrorists or criminal gangs [233].

In the month of November 2003, the Iraqi resistance brought down a U.S. CH-47 helicopter in the north of Fallujah belonging to the 82nd Airborne Division. They used a shoulder-launched rocket. This is forcing the military units to withdrawal out of the city, considering this later as a strategic mistake to allow the resistance freedom of movement within the area where they will receive help from the People's residents [64].

I hear from some political experts question repeatedly, why the Bush administration chose a civil leader, after Gen. Garner, to be Paul Bremer? In particular, who is an expert in terrorism, despite the lack of evidence on the relationship between the Saddam Hussein government and al-Qaeda? With his ominous arrival on 12 May 2003 to Baghdad, the facts revealed more about the spread of the mercenary army crimes that he brought it under the leadership of the Erik Prince. He left with the most prominent scandal after the discovery of the disappearance of nine billion U.S. dollars from the funds for the reconstruction of Iraq, according to auditing by the U.S. special inspector general for Iraq.

I liked what American author Jeremy Scahill wrote in the wonderful book about the history of the international mercenary company Blackwater and its roots *Blackwater, Rise of the world's most powerful mercenary army* -- revised and updated. This book, which won several international awards, and I agreed with the writer in most things, not only because of the large amount of evidence presented by the book, but from the experience of reality that I have seen myself. The warlords side with fellow Paul Bremer, who made terrorism and justified their crimes and their thefts under the pretext of fighting terrorism. It was true that they were similar to computer company pirates who paralyze websites and then marketed himself as a specialized security informational network. The entire world knows, and U.S. officials themselves admitted the role of the United States in the emergence and development of al-Qaeda, for they are no stranger to terrorism. Industry experts from the formation of new groups penetrate al Qaeda or work with them to implement their desired goals (See Chapter 11).

Bremer expressed upon his arrival in Iraq the fact that his job came forth when he said, "the occupation is an ugly word, but this is the truth", to stop the lies of those who claim that it was the liberation process and the start of the era of false democracy and freedom. Bremer's decisions were not stupid when he began his mission, as there were preparations for a new strategy intended to make Iraq a battlefield with terrorist groups who were prepared internally and externally. His decisions, such as leaving open the border for a long time and leaving the weapons stores accessible to everyone, as well as to dissolve all of the army and police systems. In addition, they expelled the Baathists from their jobs without any pension, all this was part of the preparation for Iraq creative chaos that would allowed them to liquidate those who want to break down the barriers that prevent their strategy of rewriting Iraq as weak and scrawny.

The supporting evidence revealed by another author, Jeremy Scahill, confirmed that Blackwater started, beginning in 2004 and acquired the first contracts to protect the occupation officials in all its offices throughout Iraq. The Time's

London magazine described the real commercial situation then, "most trade sought-after war is not oil, but security" [2 of 6 (371)] "and from this we can know why the security situation has not stabilized to some extent now, despite the fall of thousands of innocent Iraqi civilians a year among the dead and wounded. The most dangerous role of the, *security*, mercenary companies was the open door for every professional in the murder or violence to come to Iraq and make fast money. This allowed them to exercise a dangerous and exciting hobby, under the facade of a Holy War, fighting terrorism like a Hollywood film with Heroes and criminals as actors.

After the U.S. occupation forces committed these crimes, then came the legitimacy of armed resistance that took a stronger self-defense. This occurred after they lost a Chinook helicopter near Fallujah, killing 17 U.S. soldiers and wounding others. The escalation of the Iraqi armed resistance against the occupation occurred during the months of October and November. Escalation of their numbers from 12 attacks per today to 36 daily attacks, according to the former U.S. Vice President Cheney's in his memoirs (page 446). During the period of November 2003 to January 2004, there were three attacks on three helicopters of U.S. occupation forces near Fallujah, killing another 25 soldiers [101].

This events prompted the U.S. occupation forces to arrest and target journalists, preventing the widespread news of the resistance. They were detained near Fallujah on January 2, 2004. The staff of the Reuters news agency, cameraman Salem Ureibi and photographer Ahmed Mohammad Hussein al-Badrani, and car-driver Sattar Jabar al-Badrani, along with a photographer satellite channel NBC Ali Muhammed Hussein al-Badrani. They were trying to document the U.S. helicopter that was shot-down near Fallujah that day. After three days of detention and torture at the U.S. 82nd Airborne Division base at Forward Operating Base 'Volturno' they were released from the operations base St. Mere [130].

The occupation leaders tried to outwit the world and give a different description to get away with a plan for the national resistance against the occupation operations. The commander of the U.S. forces in Iraq, John Abizaid used the term guerrilla warfare [52 from 13 (371)]. The idea was not favorable to the U.S. leadership. The fact that America has previously supported guerrilla warfare in the past, in Latin America, as brave fighters attempted to change the authoritarian regimes in their countries. While U.S. former defense Secretary Donald Rumsfeld used with caution, the term insurgency, but he soon discovered that the insurgency means a movement organization for an armed group to overthrow the local government. One secret training military document confirmed that their specifications to define the insurgency do not fit the situation of National Armed resistance, which was launched against an aggressive occupier or foreign occupation by the people of an independent sovereign state [187].

This improper description prompted Rumsfeld to assign his experts in the Ministry of Defense to offer their advice on the most appropriate term, especially with the fear of using the term *War on Terror* again because of the fear that he would regret this choice [13]. Therefore, he requested, in November 2003, to gather all the available information about the historic rebellion that was faced by the British in Malaysia. According to Rumsfeld, Paul Bremer was not concerned with the large number of reports received from the U.S. President, Vice President and Secretary of State. Bremer said on September 7, 2003 that the Iraqis are on their way to sovereignty in an attempt to alleviate the resistance. This initiated an increase in the resistance that was larger than Rumsfeld's push to prescribe insurgency. Documents surfaced from Gen. Ricardo S. Sanchez, of the U.S. Army in Iraq. They were dated 14 September 2003, and had exposed the use of the name of resistance in the official correspondence with his guidance in applying violations of the International Convention Against Torture standards within what he called, his orders then Counter-Resistance Policy and he did not mention the rebellion [137].

Rumsfeld's confession came in a frank memoir of the state of occupation with the escalation of Iraqi resistance that rejects invasion. The decision to transfer the alleged sovereignty was not in the U.S. leaderships mind until they saw the intensified resistance. This prompted Paul Bremer to announce the intention to transfer sovereignty to the Iraqis without informing the Minister of Defense, Rumsfeld, in advance. This meant that the decision ocurred in haste and in a narrow level within the U.S. command only [13].

The following documents confirm the massacre:

1. Letter from the US military commander in Fallujah to one of the victim's familes.

2. Report from the Fallujah police center to the office of the interior ministry about the accident.

3. Diagram of accident sent by Fallujah' police center to interior ministry in Baghdad.

4. A statement from a civil NGOs and government offices in Fallujah condemns the incident.

Department Of The Army

Headquarters, 1-505th Parachute Infantry Regiment
82nd Airborne Division
Fort Bragg, North Carolina 28307-5100

مم : مكتب القائد

Office of the Commander

17 September 2003

الى : عائلة الــــيد رحمن أحمد خلف

The family of Rhman Ahmed Kalaf
al-Fallujah, Iraq

السلام عليكم و بعد التحية والتقدير

Permit me to extend my condolences for the recent loss of your loved one, who was a casualty in the line of duty.

اسمحوا لي ان اقدم التعازي في فقيدكم المحبوب الذي اســتشهد أثناء تأدية القيام بالواجب

Our mutual goal in the city of al-Fallujah is to establish and maintain a safe and secure environment for the city and its residents. Included in this goal is the security of all who live here. I hope that your loss does not deter you from continued cooperation with Coalition Forces. It is the combined efforts of the government of al-Fallujah, its people, and the Coalition that will build a city where all are safe.

ان هدفنا المشترك هو ان تقيم مدينة الفلوجة بالامن والاستقرار وابناؤها يعيش سكانها بالامان. ان احد اهدافنا تتضمن هذه المدينة عند الجميع الذين يعيشون بها. ان امن الامن والاستقرار مدينة الفلوجة بالامان. انه بالتعاون لبناء مدينة باسمه جميع جيران الفلوجة وسكانها والتعاون سوف نجعل بناء مدينة يأمن بها نزل الجميع

Again, my condolences for your loss. As an expression of my sympathy, and the sympathy of the Coalition, I ask that you please accept this gift as a small measure of solace. Of course, this gift is not meant to make up for your loss. Instead, we offer it as a way to honor the memory of your loved one. My wish is that we will emerge from this time stronger, and with the bond of a common goal: the security of this great city and all its inhabitants.

مرة اخرى، اريد الوزراء تعازي وتعبير عن تعاطفي وتعاطف الحلفاء سلم جزءا من العزاء نابتي ارجو ان تقبل من هذه الهدية الرمزية الرمزية لقد سكن الامر التعازي تعبير عن ان هذه الهدية لم نعوضكم وذكرى المحبوب لعنى ان نبزغ جميعا من هذا الموقف اقوى مذا جنبه مال المدينة الاوقر

Sincerely,

دمتم،

المقدم براين درنكواين

قائد قوات التحالف

لمنطقة الفلوجة

Brian M. Drinkwine
Lieutenant Colonel, US Army
Commanding

SICLY   SALERNO   NORMANDY   HOLLAND

DOMINICAN REPUBLIC   VIET NAM   GRENADA

[47]

بسم الله الرحمن الرحيم

مديرية شرطة الفلوجة
العدد / ١٧٨١
التاريخ / ٢٠٠٣/٩/١٢

الى /وزارة الداخلية ــ مكتب السيد الوزير

في الساعة 2430 من ليلة 2003/9/11 قامت سيارة نوع B M W زرقاء اللون برمي عبارات نارية باتجاه قائم مقادمة الفلوجة وعلى الفور قامت قوة حماية الفلوجة بمطاردة السيارة المذكورة وباسناد سيارتين من دوريات شرطة الفلوجة ونجاه وبذلك على الطريق القديم ولدى وصول مفارزنا بالقرب من المستشفى الأردني قامت قوات التحالف باطلاق نار وبشكل كثيف باتجاه دوريتنا مما ادى الى استشهاد ثمانية منتسبين من قوة حماية الفلوجة ولاصابة سبعة من منتسبي شرطة الفلوجة وقوة حماية الفلوجة وقد تم نقل المصابين الى مستشفى الفلوجة ورفع ارسال الشهداء في الطبابة العدلية في الانبار وان الحادث ادى الى عطل ثلاث سيارات بسبب اصابتها بالعديد من الاطلاقات وندرج لكم اسماء الشهداء والمصابين . وسنوافيكم بما يستجد لاجتاه " للاطلاع والتكرم مع التقدير .

المدير
رياض عباس أحمد اللطيف
مدير شرطة الفلوجة
٩/١٢

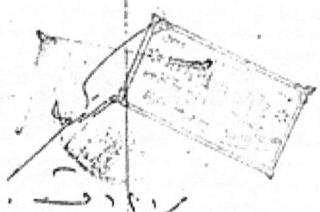

قائمة الشهداء
1. الملازم انور اسماعيل ميزر
2. رياض خلف
3. وليد جاسم حاكم
4. غزلان صبار
5. احمد سعيد حاكم
6. زيد نظام
7. صباح علي فرحان
8. رحمن احمد مطلك

قائمة المصابين
1. الملازم عصام احمد حسين
2. ش / محمد عبد عباس
3. = عاصم محمد احمد
4. = اركان عدنان احمد
5. عبد الجليل عبد محمد
6. علاء هاتم احمد
7. وسام محمد اكيطان

Falluja Police Center
11/10/2003

Diagram of Accident

On basis of the news coming to us about death of the victim RAHMAN AHMED KHALEF one of the Falluja Force members by coalition forces, we present the following:

1. The location of accident is far about 4 km from the police center.
2. The accident is death of RAHMAN AHMED KHALEF.
3. The victim was charged with patrol duty of Falluja Protection Force near of Jordanian Hospital.
4. I haven't seen the victim in location of accident as he had been moved to the hospital then died there.
5. I haven't seen anything else useful in the investigation.

The Diagram

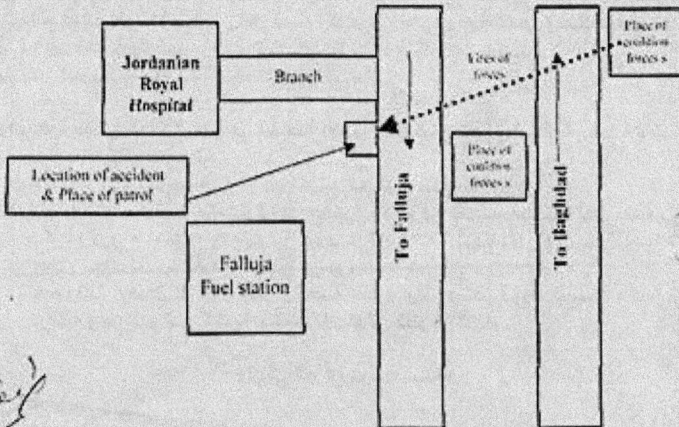

Lieutenant
Ali Hameed Jasim
Investigation officer

بسم الله الرحمن الرحيم

((ومن المؤمنين رجال صدقوا ما عاهدوا الله عليه فمنهم من قضى نحبه ومنهم من ينتظر وما بدلوا تبديلا)) صدق

يا أبناء الفلوجة البواسل .
أيها الشعب العراقي الأبي.

ارتكبت القوات الأمريكية المحتلة مجزرة بشعة أخرى فجر يوم الجمعة
(٢٠٠٣/٩/١٢) بحق أناس نذروا أنفسهم لحماية مدينتهم الفلوجة الباسلة وهم قوة حماية
المدينة والشرطة الوطنية أثناء قيامهم بتعقب مجموعة من اللصوص والسارقين دون مبرر
لهذه المجزرة .
يا أبناء الفلوجة :
ان هذه الكوكبة من الشهداء كانوا يؤدون واجبهم الوطني الشريف دفاعا عن أرض مدينتهم
وحماية أهلها الطيبين فلتقف مدينة الفلوجة إجلالا وإكبارا لهؤلاء الشهداء الأبرار ولكن هذا
الحدث دافعا للتعاون والتوحد بين جميع أبناء المدينة من المواطنين الشرفاء والأحزاب
والقوات السياسية والهيئات والجمعيات بجميع أنواعها وليستمر العمل الوطني الداعم لقوات
الحماية الوطنية بمختلف فصائلهم ولنغرس كل الأسنة التي تتطاول على هؤلاء الشرفاء
وليسمع قادة وجنود الاحتلال ان أهل المدينة قادرون على حماية أمنهم وسلامتهم وليكفوا
أيديهم عن المدينة وترك مسؤولية الأمن .
يا أبناء الفلوجة الباسلة : أننا بإسمكم ندعو شي مبني :

١- دعوة مجلس الحكم المحلي في محافظة الانبار وللاجتماع الفوري لمناقشة الحالة واتخاذ
ما يلزم بما يتناسب مع الحدث الجلل.
٢- مشاركة أبناء الفلوجة الغيارى في التشييع الجنائزي للشهداء الأبرار .
٣- قيام كافة أبناء الفلوجة بالمشاركة في الإضراب العام في المدينة احتجاجا على المجزرة
وتكريما لأرواح الشهداء واعتبار يوم ٢٠٠٣/٩/١٤ أضرابا عاما لمدينة الفلوجة .
٤- إعلان الحداد لمدة ثلاثة أيام اعتبارا من يوم الاحد الموافق ٢٠٠٣/٩/١٤ .
٥- تحية وأكبار وإجلال للشهداء الأبرار تحية احترام وتقدير لكن قوات الحماية والشرطة
الوطنية وعوائلهم الخيرة تحية خالصة لكل اهالي الفلوجة الكرام .

وليبقى العراق موحدا مستقلا.

الإدارة المدنية لمدينة الفلوجة
رابطة اهالي الفلوجة
النيئات والجمعيات الثقافية في الفلوجة

عجلس شيوخ عشائر الفلوجة
علماء الدين في الفلوجة
شيوخ عشائر الفلوجة
القوى السياسية في الفلوجة
اتحاد المعلمين في الفلوجة

CHAPTER 4

Use of Mercenaries of Private Companies & Their Role in Iraq

4.1. History of the use of mercenaries

Private military contractors are also known as privatized military firms [71]. This is a condition, adopted universally since the start of the Romanian and Greek civilizations, using mercenaries or special combat units for a financial goal. These phenomena used by the occupation forces, is a concept that has perpetuated throughout the ages [216]. In the United States, the civilians begin military service ever since the emergence of the republican system. However, the first official statement on the hiring of civilians did not appear until 1954 at the beginning of World War II and known as (OMB Circular A-76, which is still in effect today. Most of these services are in the field of logistics, arms procurement and basic food rations for soldiers. This also includes many aspects of uniforms, supplies, transportation, etc. In addition, the American arms industry began to expand, making the U.S. government turn to suppliers of small arms and bayonets from the private sector [217]. The Civil African Wars and the Iraqi War proved the importance of the potential applications of private military companies, as well as the risks they are exposed to working alongside the United States Government. Those working under contract with the U.S. Department of Defense and these companies can help fill the gaps that are most needed in the U.S. military force structures, especially in the field of logistics and security services [216].

The U.S. reliance on mercenaries during war times started expanding with the beginning of the Vietnam War, they relied on them to help with sophisticated and complex weapons management, in addition to communication platforms for espionage and intelligence [70]. In addition, the crimes of torture and brutality at Abu Ghraib prison revealed that these mercenaries were also involved in interrogations and torture at U.S. detention centers in Iraq [71]. The mercenaries were estimated at approximately twenty thousand contractors in 2004, according to the Human Rights Watch, which also considers it a serious violation of the rights of prisoners. The inflicted abuse, although per the Geneva Conventions of 1949, considered to be torture and inhuman treatment of prisoners, is a war crime. This is also a violation under customary laws of war. If you look at the percentage of participation of the civil elements for conflicts that fought by the United States since their independence from the British Crown, it is substantial. We see that the U.S. government was more dependence on civilian service contractors within the armed forces in their own struggles, while reducing their dependence on them in wars International waged within an international coalition to its dependence on the regular army elements are larger (see Tables 1 and 2) [217].

Table 1. Estimated Civilian Participation in U.S. Conflicts			
War/Conflict	Civilians	Military	Ratio
Revolution	1,500	9,000	1:6
Mexican/American	6,000	33,000	1:6
Civil War	200,000	1,000,000	1:5
World War II	85,000	2,000,000	1:20
World War I	734,000	5,400,000	1:7
Korean Conflict	156,000	393,000	1:2.5
Vietnam Conflict	70,000	359,000	1:5

Table 2. Estimated Numbers of Contractors deployed to Theaters during Conflict			
Conflict	Contractors	Military	Ratio
Gulf War I	9,200	541,000	1:58
Bosnia	1,400	20,000	1.15
Iraq	21,000	140,000	1:6

4.2. How mercenary companies are entered into Iraq

The beginning of work' story of the mercenary security companies in Iraq started before the coming of the civil governor and the occupation authority named CPA. Writer David Isenberg stated in his book, *Shadow Force, Private Security Contractors in Iraq*, that the beginning of hiring private security contractors initiated with the advent of the reconstruction efforts of the alleged official by the United States in Iraq, which was headed by retired U.S. Gen. Jay Garner. The U.S. military commanders told Garner there was no likelihood that they would have a soldier protect him. This forced the Garner to ask for the help of private security companies. Among those recruited were two South Africans known as Lion and Lucky, two veterans of the South African Special Air Service [371]. However, after Paul Bremer replaced Garner in May 2003, there was a new chief of the police, former commissioner of the New York Police Bernard Kerik. The Africans bodyguards found themselves unemployed, but Kirk needed bodyguards and assistants in the training of police operations, therefore Garner, helping them train the police within the Iraqi Interior Ministry, under a new solution, the so-called Meteoric Tactical Solution. In June 2003, they were granted a contract with the U.S. government for U.S. $ 600,000 as the first of two contracts. These contracts have a total value of more than one million U.S. dollars, which they received by two guards from South Africa during the summer.

Garner, Kirk, et al, did not care for the illegal employment of such guards. The laws of the State of South Africa prevent hiring former members of the armed forces with foreign governments without prior permission. One of these guards, Lorenz Horn, nicknamed Lucky, arrested in March 2004 in Zimbabwe on charges of involvement in a plot to overthrow the government in Equatorial Guinea with the assistance of a private security company, in which British soldiers and South Africans were working. In the end, Zimbabwe released Lorenz Horn, but the South African authorities arrested him and found him guilty of the cause of action as mercenaries and breaking anti-mercenary laws. This prompted the South African government to reopen the investigation at the end of 2004, concerning hundreds of its nationals working illegally in Iraq [125]. In May 2003, Tom Davis (R-Va.), a representative of one of these private security companies, indicated that there are 8,700 contractor employees that have been deployed to the Middle East to help the process, (the occupation of Iraq, called falsely *Operation Iraqi Freedom*.

4.3. Advantages of the use of mercenaries

The process of using mercenaries or military and security company contractors has some advantages and disadvantages from the point of view of the Americans. Especially, since it became the second largest army after the U.S. military forces participating in the operations in Iraq and larger than the British Army. The Director of the International and Global Studies Institute at George Washington University, Deborah D. Avant, and author of *The Market for Force* [217] shows the most important quality advantages for its part, which is very dangerous also because of the international laws as follows:

1) Provide additional forces without the need to pass the political and bureaucratic approvals of the state.

2) Provides twice the salary or wages that can be obtained from the ordinary citizen in his country.

3) The possibility of contracting for short-term periods not exceeding six months and thus the possibility of dismissal and transfer of forces more easily.

4) Provide people with specialized skills who have experience in special operations.

5) The lower incurred costs compared with the costs of the use of military personnel of the regular army to complete the same task.

The main disadvantages fall into two categories. In the short-term, there are the practical problems of high cost, reliability, mission integration and legal uncertainty. While in the long-term, there are political risks including the importance of military professions and democratic restraint.

The international definition of mercenary is, "a person who serves in order to get financial remuneration". The legal definition of mercenaries have been explained in the first additional protocol 1977 [79], as well as it was specified in two international treaties which criminalize mercenarism [83,84].

According to a report of U.S. General Accounting Office on 5 June 2003, the mercenaries' work extends from the responsibility of maintaining sophisticated weapons and the establishment and operation of telecommunications networks. It also includes to provide security at the gates and perimeter of the camps, as well as the translation of foreign languages, preparing meals and washing clothes of the military forces. The report also recognizes that the policies and directives of the Ministry of Defense, in overseeing the distribution of the contractors' staff, were inconsistent. Then the same report admits that there are no contract clauses for where they are [115]. This means that tasks are identified upon arrival at military bases, through coordination with the military leaders, according to their needs. These were the most dangerous missions in Iraq. It was the responsibility of the military or security contractors who perform armed roles in the battle space, as well as guarding facilities and escorting convoys. Contractors, such as Blackwater, use arms and military training to carry out their tasks as an integral part of the success of the operation in the battlefield against combatants. In 2006, the director of the private security company association in Iraq stated that 181 of these companies were operating in Iraq, with a little more than 48,000 employees [171]. These companies create and promote the culture of lawlessness among its mercenary employees and encouraged them to work within the financial interests of the company, lacking interest for the life of innocent Iraqi people. They were encouraged to use unnecessary excessive and lethal force [288].

It was mentioned that the mercenaries of the military contractors, who during the invasion, assisted in the operation of military combat systems of the Army, such as Patriot missile batteries, and the Aegis defense system on U.S. Navy ships [148]. This confirms a combat role for them in addition to the role of private companies in prolonging the continuity of occupation. In February 2005, the founder of Blackwater, Eric Prince, suggested creating the contractor brigade in order to supplement the U.S. military forces. He indicated, "there is panic in the U.S. Department of Defense (DoD) about increasing the permanent size of the Army, if they want to add 30,000 people at a cost of 3.6 to 4 billion U.S. dollars, which means $ 135,000 per soldier, but we can offer these services cheaper" [79 from 125 (371)].

I liked the facts mentioned by Jeremy Scahill the author of the wonderful book, *Blackwater, and the emergence of the biggest strength of the mercenary army in the world,* when he describes the character closest to their duties under government protection, America's frightening Praetorian Guard [371]. This company offers mercenary services, being one of the companies of the American businessman Erik Prince, which belongs to a group called The Prince Group and EP Investments LLC [288]. The United States has relied on a very large scale on Private Security Contractors (PSCs) in providing security in the hostile atmosphere in Iraq more than they did in Afghanistan [85]. Private Military Contractors played an important and harmful role within the United States efforts to quell the growing Iraqi national resistance that reject the occupation under his efforts of counterinsurgency in either the strategic or planning level [171].

4.4. Rapid enrichment of the mercenary industry trade

The Civilian occupation authority (CPA) contributed in the theft of Iraq's money through a lot of contracts for civilian contractors without the slightest controls to prevent this administrative corruption [49]. It is amongst the highest type of rapid enrichment by the security companies of the mercenaries, especially after the killing of four Blackwater mercenaries in Fallujah. But after some of the new laws, legislation such as the **Transparency and Accountability in Military and Security Contracting Act** (S.674), the U.S. administration was forced to admit not to acquire any census about the number of contractors in Iraq during the first three years of the invasion of Iraq. The U.S. Military's Central Command announced in 2006 the presence of 100,000 contractors working in Iraq, not including sub-contractors. The Associated Press, in 2007 stated that there are more than 120,000 contractors working in Iraq [125]. While the internal Defense Department census acknowledged the existence of over 180,000 contractors working in more than 30 countries. Those serving in Iraq alone numbered 165,000 [171]. The great administrative corruption facilitated by the occupation authorities, especially during the first three years of the occupation of Iraq was clear. The Washington Post has debunked part of this corruption, as published in August 2007. This information showed that the U.S. military had been paid 548 million U.S. dollars over the past three years to two British security companies, *Aegis Defense Services* and *Erinys Iraq* in order to protect the U.S. Army Corp's of Engineers. These personnel, working on the Iraqi reconstruction projects, were pay $200 million more when compared to the original budget [95 reference of chapter 125 (371)]. It's known that *Erinys Iraq* had hired more than 14,000 Iraqi security personnel to protect the oil fields during 2003-2004 and was in agreement with the Coalition Provisional Authority (CPA) [125]. It was clear during this period that there was a lack of documentation for oil exported from Iraq. This is additional proof on the systematic theft by the occupation policy.

British security contractor companies, in March 2004, numbered more than the 8,700 British troops in Iraq in that time. Occupation forces hired many security contractors from other countries after America and Britain [71]. Many of these 400+ large and small security companies, employed thousands of former soldiers and police officers from Britain, United States, Australia, New Zealand,

South Africa, Fijians, Gurkhas, Israel, Ukraine and Bosnia. There are those who had their doubts about using mercenaries from Chile, trained by the United States during the rule of Dictator General Pinochet's [81,158]. The Pentagon admitted that 30% of the civilian security contractors in Iraq are from third world countries, aka, third-country nationals (TCNs) [159]. The press in 2005 estimated that there were 5,000 to 10,000 people from South Africa working with private security companies [160]. It was believed that the security companies also hire veterans of the anti-insurgency in Colombia, former Russian soldiers from the Chechnya war conflicts [161]. The press reports confirm the employment of large numbers of mercenaries from Latin American countries such as Guatemala, El Salvador, Chile, Nicaragua, and Colombia, which pervaded the thousands of former military and police with experience in counter-insurgency [162]. Jeffrey Shippy confirmed this in 2005, while working on the ads in the site of business jobs of the company DynCorp in Iraq. Jeffrey confirmed that the United States trained more than 1,000 Colombians with good combat experience and high rigidity in fighting the rebels, and they were willing to work for in $2,500 -5,000 in wages monthly, compared with $ 10,000 paid to the U.S. [163].

There are different salary levels for mercenary's dependent upon their nationality. A former member in the U.S. Special Forces will get $1,000 USD per day, especially in areas such as Fallujah [509], while mercenaries like a former member of the armed forces of South Africa gets a salary of $4,000-6,000 per month. Mercenary fighters from Ghurka get a salary of more than $ 2,000 a month [148]. In 2006, the Honduran government fined the local branch of the American private security company, Your Solutions, $ 25,000 USD, because they trained 300 illegal Honduran's alongside foreign fighters from Chile, Nicaragua, and send them to work in Iraq in 2005 [125]. While other reports indicate that the salary of a retired member of the U.S. Special Forces, working with the military and security companies in Iraq, ranges between $100,000-200,000 USD annually. One of the contracted mercenarys' received $175,000 per year, an amount four times what he got after 27 years of service in the military. International contractors, non-U.S. or British citizens, are paid less than the salaried contractors are. Those compensated the least were the Iraqi contractor's, who were paid $150 a month in 2004, while the third-country national mercenaries received 10-20 times more, while the international mercenaries received 100 times that value in salaries [217]. According to the report of U.S. Congressional Budget Office, the United States has spent over $85 billion on contracts to private contractors. Contracts for military operations related to Iraq for the period from 2003 to 2007. This was part of the $446 billion USD that the United States spent on their activities in Iraq during that period. There was $63 billion USD that the U.S. spent in Iraq, and $14 billion USD through bases in Kuwait and the rest through military bases in neighboring Iraq and other countries. This report admitted also that $76 billion USD was for private contractors through the U.S. Department of Defense (DoD). This amounted to between $6.1 billion USD for security tasks carried out by private contractors, who ranged in number from 25-30 thousand people, mostly militants. The same report confirmed spending between $17-21 billion USD annually since 2004 on the work of private contractors [287].

One of the British companies estimated the level of profiteering by these companies. David Claridge, director of security firm Janusian, stated that profits of British companies a year after the invasion of Iraq reached 800 million pounds. Another example was the civilian contractors from Charlotte's Zapata Engineering, while working for the United States in Iraq, received millions from the U.S. military in order to get rid of the seized ammunition. This was an average of 10 times the actual cost charged by the ordinary soldier or the U.S. National Guard, conducting the same this business [152].

As described by one author, the criticism of the mercenaries remains to push and encourage war-makers and not encourage peace. This is like pretending that weapons designed to kill cannot be life-saving [149]. The best evidence is from the larger companies that won contracts after the invasion of Iraq. The Halliburton Company, owned by U.S. vice president Dick Cheney, was one of the decision makers of the war and the invasion of Iraq [148].

4.5. Mercenaries army numbers and their role in Iraq

The Los Angeles Times report in 2007 was the most accurate and based on the statistics of the U.S. Central Command. This was obtained under the American Freedom of Information Act and revealed the following [129]:

1. The presence of the military and security contractors exceeded the number of the U.S. military in Iraq. The number of contractors reached 180,000 while the number of U.S. military personnel was 160,000 at the time in Iraq.

2. There are 43,000 contractors from foreign nationals and neither American nor Iraqi.

3. From the total number of mercenaries, there were 130,000 contractors working with 632 contractor companies in cooperation with the U.S.

Department of Defense only in Iraq, while the remainder was working with other federal agencies and ministries of US.

In addition, you can note that there are tens of thousands of people who served in the U.S. military who were not American, at least not before the year 2009. The number increased from 28,000 to 39,000 from 2000 until 2005 only [14 from 125 (371)]. U.S. laws and procedures allowed immigrants to obtain U.S. citizenship after four years of service in the U.S. military [17 from 125 (371)], and these immigrant fighters, many of whom were killed were not citizens of the countries they defended. As of March 2008, U.S. citizenship was granted to more than 100 foreign-born immigrant fighters due to their deaths in Iraq [18 from 125 (371)].

Confession by the American military researchers indicate that Private Security Providers are a contributing factor of instability in the security missions of the United States, as well as in the U.S. military missions. This indicates that they would be more harmful factors of instability for peoples who were under their occupation [70]. In a search titled, the privatization of war and violence, security, military and private companies, factual and legal approach to human rights abuses by those companies in Iraq, 2011, which was published by a Spanish organization, Nova-Institute for Active Non-violence, in collaboration with several Iraqi and international organizations [177]. This research has found 105 private security and military companies operating in Iraq and registered in the following states:

1. United States (45 companies),
2. Britain (18 companies),
3. Israel (2 companies),
4. United Arab Emirates (6 companies),
5. South Africa (4 companies),
6. Kuwait (1 company),
7. Canada (2 companies),
8. Australia (1 company),
9. Germany (2 companies),
10. Barbados (1 company),
11. Czech Republic (1 company),
12. Spain (1 company),
13. France (4 companies),
14. Iraq (16 companies).

The tasks' nature of military contractors in Iraq can be estimated through their casualties, which in September 2004, reached losses of up to 150 killed with 700 injured. These figures exceed the victims of any force within the coalition of international forces that joined the occupation forces at the time, which is statistically higher than obtained in any division or corps in the U.S. Army in Iraq [148]. The number of dead personnel of security and military contractors in Iraq was estimated at 1,000, with 13,000 injured. This was in 2007, when the outcome of the private contractor forces reached 50% of the U.S. armed presence in Iraq [171]. Their role before the invasion of Iraq, and help them in the configuration of it, was limited to only some of the bases in Gulf, such as Camp Doha in Kuwait, considered to be the largest base for launching the invasion. It was built, managed and protected by the private contractor mercenaries [148]. The bodies of the mercenaries killed from these companies were not published in the statistics of daily losses issued by the occupation authorities. This downplayed the daily losses of wounded and dead [81,509]. There were 780 killed in Iraq from mercenary contractor companies including Blackwater, excluding the crimes they committed, and thus are not held accountable [315].

It is strange that the U.S. congressional investigations about killing four Blackwater contractors in Fallujah concentrated on the main reasons for the lack of adequate protection for them without trying to show many things that it is right for U.S. citizens to know, such as the fact of their duties and their violations, which created hatred towards them. This confirms that the U.S. House of Representatives covers up the facts of the mercenaries tasks. This policy is a clear violation of the Geneva Conventions of 1949 by using a means of violating the rights of the people to self-determination under the occupation recognized internationally. Professor of Strategic and International Relations at the Australian National University, Dr. Michael McKinley, description of the private security companies as very attractive for the governments because they are working in the world where there is no law and became a kind of evil as being necessary for the circumstances of Iraq [315].

From August 2004 to the beginning of June 2007, there were 138 private security contractors killed in Iraq, while 451 were wounded [40 from 125 (371)]. In May 2007, the *New York Times* published an article that the total number of contractors killed in Iraq was 917 with 12,000 injured, whether on the battlefield or at work [41 from 125 (371)].

These private security or military companies were operating from the declared official perspective in Iraq as to provide protection for individuals, transport convoys, operating bases, buildings, and the economic infrastructure, in addition to the training of police recruits and members of the Iraqi army [85]. Soon, the facts were released about the hostile and combative activities of U.S. security and military company personnel, making them internationally and legally like fighters on a mercenary mission. This makes the United States guilty of committing international crimes, with evidence that confirm this as follows:

1) The participation in intelligence and combat operations is confirmed by events before the killing of four contractors in Fallujah, as well as work on the collection of intelligence information from prisoners [86]. The role of the CACI company members in scandalous torture at the Abu Ghraib prison, and their combat role in the second battle in Fallujah is a clear example [372].

2) Their participation in missions to storm houses, killing of civilians and torture of civilian detainees occurred in the Abu Ghraib prison scandal [79, 86]. There are several others cases, such as the assassination of the young Sinan Abdul Ilah al-Mashhadani incident and the arrest of his child brother Amin, who was tortured by private contractors in civilian uniform. On 17 May 2004, the federal grand jury accused the contractor working for the CIA, David Passaro, of committing acts of torture in Afghanistan when he assaulted Afghan detainees in Asadabad base with a dangerous weapon [71].

3) The private military and security contractors used bribery, during their work as Blackwater employees, done to cover up the violations. Blackwater setting aside changed its name, but the mercenary approach remained in their work. The U.S. Justice Department in February 2011 admitted doing investigations into the Blackwater's work about using bribes to Iraqi officers as one million U.S. dollars in order to allow them to continue to work in Iraq after the killing of 17 civilians in the Eagles Square in Baghdad [291,292,315].

4) The violations of selling Illegal and hidden weapons, which exposed the issue of charging five executives of the Blackwater company with conduct violations related to sell weapons without government authorization and lying to federal authorities. This is merely one of the true aspects of the work preformed by these companies.

[61]

US military commanders have not only recognized the role of the military contractor in combat missions, but their modern studies recommend more coordination between the Joint Task Force and field commanders. These recommendations, in order to take into account the role of mercenaries (contractors) in the next tasks, through coordination and pre-planning in Joint Operational Planning Process (JOPP), are to prevent any conflict in work between whom the U.S. government hired and the combat missions for the U.S. military [77].

4.6. Crimes and violations of mercenaries in Iraq

On 3 April 2012, the American magazine *Harper* published some articles that emphasize many of the crimes and violations of the mercenaries of Blackwater over the killing of Iraqi civilians and the wounding of others. It also shows the engagement of their Helicopters in combat operations against ground targets. This indicated by former Blackwater employees in Iraq, to the American Journal reporter Charles Glass [157].

The American media [124,125] revealed scandals, torture and the famous Abu Ghraib abuses. Two military special companies were implicated, CACI International, Inc. based in Arlington, Virginia was responsible for 50% of the interrogations, alongside the Titan Company based in San Diego, California. Investigators from both companies assisted in the secret U.S. Army investigation by Maj. Antonio Taguba. The names of four men were revealed as follows:

1. Steven Stephanowicz, U.S. contractor as an investigator in CACI Inc., worked with the brigade's military intelligence 205. He was giving false information to the investigation team on places and activities that did not exist, in addition to encouraging others to intimidate prisoners while clearly knowing that the instructions were equivalent to physical abuse.

2. John Israel, American translation contractor of CACI Inc., worked with the brigade's military intelligence 205. He misleads the investigators. Despite his testimony that he did not witness any misconduct, but the report admits that he did not have security clearance authorized to enter the place of the investigation, and it is not known how he could gain access to this place, only if he was an extremely intelligent man!

3. Torin Nelson, the report does not disclose the truth about what happened with him during the investigation.

4. Adel Nakhla, fielded tough questions about the charges of rape of some prisoners, and he admitted that the two sergeants had leprosy which is why the prisoners were naked and in strange positions on top of each other.

All four of them were appointed to work with the Military Intelligence Brigade 205, a unit stationed in Germany and Italy for supporting the U.S. Fifth Corps.

Many crimes committing by Blackwater mercenaries spread after the release of several films, but the crimes of killing Iraqi civilians, covered by the media, were two crimes and the media focused on the second one only. The first crime was on 9 September 2007 when the Blackwater heavily armed gunmen opened fire indiscriminately and without justification on a group of Iraqi civilians in the Al Wathba Square. This incident resulted in the death of five civilians and wounding others with various injuries. One of the martyrs is the citizen Ali Hussam Eddin Ibrahim al-Bazzaz, killed in front of his shop near the Wathba Square, and his family has asked for compensation in U.S. courts by the lawyers of the U.S. Center for Constitutional Rights [288]. The second was on 16 September 2007 when the crime was random shootings in the Tayaran Square in Baghdad, killing 17 civilians under the pretext of being under fire during convoy traffic in that area. These crime sequences revealed the combat and criminal role of security companies with the occupation forces. The occupation forces, followed by the Iraqi government, granted immunity to the mercenaries, private security and military companies from legal accountability in front of the Iraqi judiciary. The Iraqi government was unable to take any legal action except to not renew their work in Iraq and demand that the U.S. government replace them with other security companies. The Iraqi government, without the ability to intervene, oversees the rules of work of the mercenaries to protect the Iraqi civilians in the street, as well as to allow for the use of the mercenaries operating in Iraq, which is internationally prohibited. The lawsuit raised against these mercenary companies in the U.S. courts, although the incidence of crime on Iraqi ground was recognition of Iraqi government about the false sovereignty! The legal responsibility of the Iraqi government was to participate in these crimes despite the Maliki government admitting that this type of crime is deliberate murder. Because of this, they gave immunity that prevented and halted the Iraqi judiciary authority even after the transfer of sovereignty from the occupation.

The decision of the American judge in Virginia about the case against refusal to confirm, or not to accept accountability, to accuse those mercenaries for their crimes and not to accept compensation for Iraqi victims, was despite the U.S. courts recognition of the presence of these criminal elements. This decision confirms the need for new local and international laws for the return of the rule of judiciary to prevent impunity, and provide suitable compensation for victims of mercenary company violations. In addition, it is to illustration the human rights obligations by these companies in the international conventions and legal system [2]. Surprisingly, a spokesman for the U.S. State Department, Sean McCormack, has said, "that his ministry did not give protection from legal liability, but limited protection and can be set up to legally charge them"!

One expert in U.S. law at the University of Baltimore [3] believed that the immunity given to the mercenaries of the U.S. security companies came from the understanding of the 'Fifth Amendment Privilege against Compelled Self-Incrimination'. This gives the right not to answer questions posed by the U.S. government and any answer may lead the U.S. citizen to incriminate himself in the future! From this is given alternative immunity to the U.S. government, which in turn yields to the members of these companies, as government contractors, without being identified in a clear framework, to protect the human rights or the victims in accordance to international law. The U.S. government has decided if the protected person is compelled to submit testimony to the court or reject it, in accordance with the protection afforded under the Fifth Amendment. The last amendment by the U.S. Department of Defense called, Bill, S. 552, gives the U.S. military contractors trial conditions within the military court in circumstances during the war.

Despite the targeting of journalists and prevention of a lot of news of crimes and violations of the mercenaries against the Iraqi people, the simple look to some incidents opened fire on Iraqi citizens by mercenaries of security contractors according to the agency Associated Press [73] gives realistic and tangible evidence of their criminal behavior:

- September 2007, contractors from North Carolina working in the security of the U.S. Blackwater had opened fire, killing eight civilians, and wounding 13 others in an exchange of fire after an explosion near the U.S. State Department motorcade in Baghdad. The Iraqi government said after the incident that it cancelled this company's work license because of this crime.

[64]

- In May 2007, the employees of Blackwater shot an Iraqi citizen and said he was driving very close to the U.S. convoy. She claimed to a representative for the company that the incident reports with accounts of other witnesses were identical; the employee had acted lawfully and appropriately, not knowing whether they were Iraqis or Americans!

- Inside the Green Zone in December 2006, an employee of Blackwater was drunk during New Year's celebrations and opened fire, killing the bodyguard of Iraqi Vice President Adel Abdul-Mahdi. This was according to a statement by Iraqi and U.S. officials. The procedure, ordered brought him brought back to the United States by the company, while the investigations were ongoing, according to the authorities [171].

- In 2006-2007, two employees at the company's headquarters in Virginia, Triple Canopy, Virginia-based Triple Canopy, accused their supervisor of shooting at Iraqi civilians for fun and filed a lawsuit against him in a U.S. court. The supervisor told them, I am going to kill someone today. The company expelled three employees for not immediately informing them about the shootings. Two guards also claimed that the supervisor fired his M4 rifle towards the windscreen of an Iraqi driver taxi. A spokeswoman for the security company Jayanti Menches claimed that the internal investigation did not find any aggrieved person from this fire [164].

- In 2006-2005, former employees of the Custer Battles Company, based in Rhode Island US, accused their colleagues at work of firing indiscriminately at civilians and crushing a car full of Iraqi children and adults while they were trying to make their way in the traffic jam, but the company denies these accusations.

- In 2005, the staff of the Aegis Defense Services Company, based in London, put video on the internet showing company guards firing at Iraqi civilians from a moving car. The AEGIS company said, "that shooting was part of the protocol allowed for contractos, guards, to shoot at vehicles that were too close or that were speeding. The U.S. military has agreed with what was said by the company.

- On 28 May 2005, the U.S. Marines in Fallujah imprisoned 16 U.S. security guard staff from the Zapata Engineering Company, based in North Carolina, who were released of the alleged fire on U.S. troops and Iraqi civilians together, and them. They later returned with those guards to the United States without being charged. Eight of them were former soldiers in the Marines and they are not enrolled in the Iraqi Interior Ministry. Thus, they were working illegally [221,223].

Brigadier General Karl Horst, deputy commander of the U.S. 3rd Infantry Division, responsible for security in the Baghdad area at that time, admitted that 12 incidents of shootings by mercenaries, private contractors, in his sector during two months of 2005, led to the deaths of at least six Iraqi civilians and the wounding of three others. His exact description of the mercenaries' work was that, "Those guys are a work unavailing and working stupid things, and there is no authority over them, so you cannot ease their effects when stepping up their strength, they shoot people, and someone must deal with their successors" [77,171]. American journalist, Robert Pelton, describes this period living with the contractors of Blackwater for a month in Baghdad, indicating, "They were using machine guns, against people in cars". As the working groups in the private security guards of the Unity Resources Group, which is an Australian company Headquartered in Dubai, they killed two women in a civilian car in a town near Baghdad [171].

4.6.1. Mercenary Crime in Fallujah

The US Special Forces, accompanied by Americans civilian's, people with earrings in their ears and their faces covered by beards for the murder' mission of an Iraqi child. They arrest and tortured his brother. The incident occurred in the police district of Fallujah city. Armored forces backed by helicopter aerial droppings at sunset of Sunday 18 June 2006, broke into the house of Mr. Abdul Ilah Najim al-Mashhadani. They intimidate them with their neighbors who have suffered from beatings and humiliation during the incursion. Attacking forces entered the house of al-Mashhadani in the usual way of battering the doors and using sound bombs to terrorize civilians, along with sniffer dogs. They asked the family of al-Mashhadani about the young Sinan Abdul Ilah, and Sinan, and requested that they prove their identity. They detained his mother and sister in one room and arrested his younger brother Amin, 13 years of age, and then they executed Sinan in another room via the launch of a barrage of bullets and threw over his body the bed to hide him until they left the house. His younger brother, Amin Abdul Ilah, strongly exposed to the beatings on his small body with the presence of dogs, biting his hands and taking him to the U.S. camp near Fallujah. After three days under arrest, Amin was released. He spoke about his brutal treatment by those people with beards, wearing earrings and in civilian clothing. They used dogs for torture Amin and caused a distortion of his left hand during the investigation. This incident revealed for the U.S. in Fallujah, additional evidence of the involvement of mercenary security companies in the crimes of the occupation forces [4].

The young martyr Sinan Najim Abdul Ilah al-Mashhadani (22 years) after his assassination by U.S. special force supported by mercenary's security companies.

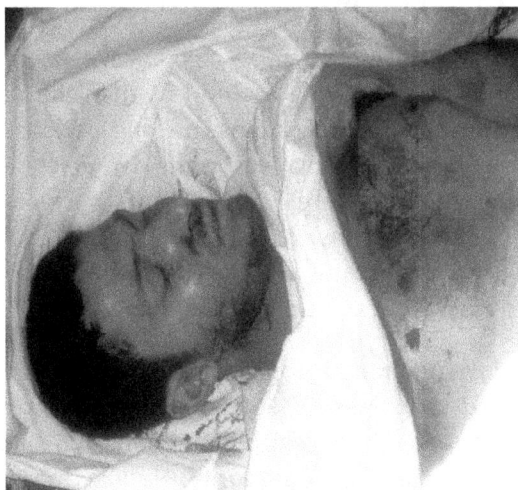

Sinan was a student in the third level of his studies at the University of Mustansiriya, where he was the sole breadwinner for his family, after the death of his father in the U.S. bombing of the city of Fallujah during the military operations of Vigilant Resolve in April 2004. His family, headed up by his mother, sister and younger brother Amin 1-year old.

Blackwater arrived in Fallujah to continue their work from a private British security company, Control Risks Group, which criticized the action of Blackwater after the killing of their four agents in Fallujah because they do not benefit from the British company's experience in the prevention of accidents in this dangerous region [239]. Blackwater changed its name later to Xe Services after the Iraqi government withdrew its permission to work in Iraq, and the U.S. Department of Defense stopped working with them. Nevertheless, they returned to work under a new company name. This new company soon repeated crimes of the past. While in Afghanistan, two of their mercenaries killed an unarmed Afghan civilian and wounded other victims in the car [290]. Despite the issuance by a U.S. judge in June of 2011, who sent them to jail for two and one-half years, however what caught my attention about this case was

[67]

that the mercenaries were discharged from the military base without permission! This incident is similar to the killing of four Blackwater mercenaries in Fallujah and how they violated advice not to enter the city on that day which raises many questions. These Incidents violate security controls and indicates one of two things, either their recklessness in their work, or the existence of secret missions.

4.7. History of mercenaries and death squads globally

The history for using the mercenaries has always been associated with massacres, wars, and mass genocide are no less than the risk of weapons of mass destruction. These have implications for long periods. One example of their role in the civil war in Colombia was in the early eighties with disastrous results for the country. There were 30,000 deaths per year and 75 political executions a week and dozens of kidnappings per day. These crimes demonstrate how the United States and the CIA interfere in the sovereignty of that country under the pretext of helping Colombia [26].

The CIA is organized governmental groups of death squads in Guatemala (1953-1990), which claimed casualties of 200,000 victims [9]. The United States supported the military in Chile, which helped in the success of General Pinochet's coup against the civilian authority. He was the head of the leftist Salvador Allende that ruled the country through criminal dictatorship. This led the country to the execution of 3,000 with the disappearance of thousands of civilians and torture of tens of thousands of others [24]. These crimes persuaded the international courts to arrest this dictator because of his crimes against humanity. In addition, the U.S. Treasury spent 6 billion U.S. dollars to assist with the Civil War in El Salvador. They used small groups of military trainers and consultants with CIA agents and the result of this Civil War (1980-1992) were at least 75,000 civilian casualties with the emergence of a handful of very wealthy warlords left to rule a large portion of the poor country's economy [28].

In Nicaragua, the CIA helped the Contras militias, one of the remnants of the private guards of Nicaraguan dictator Anastasio Somoza Debayle. He was ousted in a popular revolt in the July of 1979. These militias fought forces of the FSLN Sandinista National Liberation Front of the Nicaraguan government. The Militias Contras preformed serious violations of human rights. They paid the Nicaraguan government to file a complaint to the International Court of Justice in The Hague (ICJ) against the United States government for violating international law. This was for the U.S. support to the Contras in their rebellion against the Nicaraguan government. Actually, the International Court of Justice ruled in favor of the Nicaraguan government and concluded that the U.S. government committed international crimes after this Court found that the United States government and CIA encouraged acts contrary to the general principles of humanitarian law, such as:

1. The edition of a manual titled, *Psychological Operations in Guerrilla Warfare*, and published this guide for the Contras militia fighters.

2. Provided advice on how to rationalize the operations of killings of civilians

3. The recommendation of hiring hitmen to carry out specific tasks [224].

During this conflict, more than 50,000 civilian men, women, and children were killed. This was the result of the Contra militia and their CIA support. The United States offered protection of a senior death squad leader in El Salvador. He was a former commander of the Salvadoran armed forces, Gen. Jose Guillermo Garcia, accused of killing thousands of people with his death squads that were linked to his troops. He now lives in the state of Florida in the U.S. using his illegally obtained income since 1990. The U.S. Department of Immigration of judicial conduct seeks the possibility of his deportation from the United States for illegal entry into the country!

It came as no surprise to the United Nations work group that the use of mercenaries in Iraq in 2011 was the largest scale operation of private security and military companies. The major incidents that occurred were related to these companies. One such incident, the shooting in the courtyard of the Eagles in 2007, focused attention on the negative status of their activities against human rights. Such incidents confirm that the security companies and individuals are responsible for human rights violations [177].

It is important to note this paradox. The U.S. forces estimated the number of Arab fighters within the fighting armed forces number between 5-10% of the total fighters [343]. While all of the information and figures previously presented show the reality of the Second Army mercenaries in competition with the number of occupied U.S. military Forces in Iraq!

CHAPTER 5

Brutal Torture & Abuse of Iraqi Detainees

5.1. Torture & US International Politics

There is published evidence of the ill-treatment of detainees by global organizations. This has become useful in tracking down the perpetrators of torture crimes internationally. Two pieces of key evidence have emerged for questioning, by the CIA in 1997, after the American newspaper received a copy of it, the Baltimore Sun, through the Freedom of Information Act (FOIA). The images from Iraq and Guantanamo indicate that the tips in these notebooks are still being applied: [533].

The first report dates back to writings of 1983, written for use in Honduras. Titled the "Human Resource Exploitation Training Manual" [534], which states: "The purpose of all coercive techniques is to induce psychological regression in the subject by bringing a superior outside force to bear on his will in slope resistance," says Sgt Frederick, at the Abu Ghraib prison. He remained detained, in isolation, for up to three days in a room without windows. According to the CIA guide, "A person's sense of identity depends on continuity in his surroundings, habits, appearance, relations with others ... detention planning should enhance feelings of detainee disconnection for known and reassuring stuff". According to the CIA guide, threats of electrocution may be better than the real thing. "The threat of coercion usually weakens or destroys resistance more effectively than coercion itself" [533].

The second report dated back to 1963, called the "Counterintelligence Interrogation," or KUBARK, which depends on the torture the receiving prisoner. Some were techniques used in sexual humiliation, by inflicting anxiety to disrupt the emotional and psychological aspects of familiarity. This is done drastically to bring about a psychological shock or paralysis to affect dramatically the mental state of the prisoner [534].

The torture' scandal at the Abu Ghraib prison was one of the contributing factors in the continuation of the resistance. This prevented numerous Iraqi insurgents from delivering their weapons out of fear of being subjected to the same torture as the prisoners at the Abu Ghraib prison [230].

5.2. Start torture policy and arbitrary detention

In his speech to the United Nations at World Day on June 26, 2014, reflecting on helping the victims of torture, former U.S. President George W. Bush said; "The United States remains committed to firmly supporting the Geneva Conventions", which has been the cornerstone of protection in situations of armed conflict for more than 50 years. These agreements provide important protection that aim to reduce human suffering in armed force conflicts. We expect that other countries will treat our military members and civilians according to the Geneva Convention. Our armed forces are committed to complying with and holding accountable, members of our military who do not abide. [141]. This is typical of the higher authority of the U.S. politicians, in their deception of the torture of Iraqi detainees, especially in the full areas of resistance to the occupation. These methods expose the brutal and sadistic practices that forced the leaders of the occupation to try to stop the resistance [137]. After the Abu Ghraib prison scandal, Director of Human Rights at the United Nations Mission in Iraq (UNAMI) said to the Reuters news agency, "Those who have found in the Abu Ghraib prison were among an estimated 14,000 people and were imprisoned in violation of UN Security Council resolution of 1546 ".

The 2004 International Committee of the Red Cross reported that the treatment by the occupation forces of the war prisoners and other persons protected under the Geneva Conventions in Iraq during their arrest, detention, and interrogation showed serious violations of the Geneva Convention. This use of these techniques violates agreements and includes the following: "stress positions" questioning for 20 hours and stripping, which played on the phobias of the detainees. This induced stress, by using dogs. Their deceptions were to make the detainee believe the investigator is from a country with a great reputation for torture. They utilized false documents and reports; and inflicted isolation for up to 30 days, creating sensory deprivation [134].

The U.S. government's investigation, aka Fay-Jones investigation [136] confirmed the presence of misconduct and abuse by the U.S. Military Intelligence Brigade [205]. This brigade was responsible for the Abu Ghraib prison in Baghdad. The investigation found that the same techniques and methods investigators used and developed at Guantanamo were being used in Iraq and Afghanistan. General Karpinski recognized this. A team of investigators working at

Guantanamo visited the Abu Ghraib prison and transfer their technologies and expertise to these investigators (533). These investigative methods include:

1. Sleep adjustment, which is the opposite of sleep timing from night to the day.

2. Forced nudity and placing them in an upside down position. This was a tactic to force the detainees to cooperate.

3. Mistreatment of detainees using dogs.

4. Isolation.

5. Sensory deprivation and holding the detainee in hot or cold temperatures. Solitary confinement with limited light and ventilation (136).

6. Using insects during their torture techniques [653].

According to official government reports in 2001[135], U.S. Defense Secretary Donald Rumsfeld and other senior military leaders abandoned absolute prohibition against torture. On April 16, 2003 Secretary, Rumsfeld personally approved the use of 24 techniques or methods recommended by the investigation committee. This committee, formed on January 15, 2003, was selected to choose investigative techniques [144]. On September 14, 2003, Gen. Ricardo Sanchez gave permission to use these techniques in the course of the investigations [137]. Some leaks occurred from the investigative files of Abu Ghraib, which state that Major General Antonio Taguba conducted abuses. It also states that the military intelligence staff of the Central Intelligence Agency, and private contractors "interrogated the guards at the prison and other witnesses sitting in on these psychological and physical treatments. In this interrogation method, they forced detainees to respond to questions asked by the investigators [533]. A report conducted by the Deputy Inspector General of the intelligence Ddepartment of the U.S. Department of Defense reinvestigated this on August 25, 2006, showing the following results:

The report, submitted to military leaders, claims not to document cases of torture and abuse against the detainees. This prevented senior leadership in the U.S. military from being aware of such violations. It called for the issuance of publications outlining the responsibilities used during intelligence investigations.

The report also claims that the investigations in Iraq lacked effort in the unity of command. Many of the formations in the Pentagon had planned and carried out various interrogation operations without a clear and shared objective relationship and common understanding to direct questioning. This confirms Sanchez's memoirs [36]. The intensification of the resistance led him to create large detention centers in those areas to minimize the resistance. This rejects the presence of occupation.

It is recognized that counter resistant interrogation techniques were transferred to Iraq for many reasons. This includes the personnel of investigation operations who believe that traditional interrogation techniques are no longer effective with all detainees. The supervision policy of the interrogation is effective. As a result, there have been exceeded border assessments for the interrogation techniques set forth in the army manual for interrogation intelligence [52-34] dated September 28, 1992. The report is demanding of the joint leaders' implementation of the policies to prevent, escape resistance, introducing survival, and evasion techniques.

The increased operations of armed resistance against the occupation in 2003 pushed them to arrest and target journalists preventing the spread of news of the growing popular resistance against the occupation. Occupation forces were detaining camera operators near Fallujah on January 2, 2004. The staff of the Reuters news agency Salem Uribe; photographer Ahmed Mohammad Hussein; al-Bahrain, taxi cab driver; Sattar Jabar al-Badrani, a photographer; and satellite channel NBC Ali Muhammed Hussein al-Badrani. They were trying to record a U.S. helicopter shot down near Fallujah that day. After three days of detention and torture by the U.S. 82nd Airborne Division at Forward Operating Base 'Volturno', they were released from the operations base 'St. Mere'. [130]

One famous incident of torture, done by British troops against Iraq detained civilians, is that of Iraq's eight young that were arrested in Basra, abused and tortured by British soldiers. This led to the death of Baha Mousa while detained and in the custody of British soldiers.This event occurred according to the military and medical records reviewed by *The Independent*. Amnesty International protested and made personal demands to Prime Minister Tony Blair about the death of Baha Mousa. It was demanded that an impartial and independent investigation into the torture of prisoners in Basra take place. The Speaker in the field hospital [33], outside the southern Iraqi city, said that one of the survivors suffered from "acute renal failure" after he faced beatings. He had severe bruising on the upper part of the abdomen, the right side of the chest, and right arm [515].

The issue of the death Iraq detainees faced in U.S. occupation prisons was revealed in a documentary of the U.S. military. General Ltc.C Patrick W. Williams issued instructions to all departments within the occupation prisons, dated February 19, 2007. It stated that documentation is required for the death of detainees and needs to include whether misconduct of the detainee was the cause of death. This documentation indicates that his colleagues in detention until handed over to his family prevent them from washing the corpse. There is no reference to neither the abuses, the ill situations of the detention centers or the loss of the most basic human rights standards! [188].

According to the Ministry of Human Rights, the total number of detainees for the entire country was 30,842 on December 1, 2006, of which 14,534 are in MN I detention facilities [687].

5.3. Effects of the torture crime on the victims and community

The most brutal crime in the scope of torture and arbitrary detention was set up in secret prisons and unannounced jails. Legally, secret detention centers are irreconcilably in violation of international human rights laws, including detaining during emergency and armed conflicts. It is a violation of international humanitarian law during any form of armed conflict.

Secret detention violates many human rights such as:

1. The right to personal liberty and the prohibition of arbitrary arrest or detention.

2. It has no jurisdiction and allows individuals to be deprived of their personal liberties, in secret, for periods that are likely to be indefinite.

3. It is established outside the scope of the law, without recourse to legal proceedings, including habeas corpus. Usually, detainees were deprived of their right to a fair and speedy trial, state authorities did not intend to charge detainees with a crime or have a fair trial.

4. Criminal excuse, secrecy, and insecurity caused by the deprivation of contact with the outside world, and the fact that family members have no knowledge of their whereabouts, violated the presumption of

innocence and lead to confessions extracted under torture or other forms of ill-treatment.

5. If the cases of enforced disappearances almost systematic or permanent, or systematic and on a large scale, the secret detention has reached the threshold of crimes against humanity.

6. The suffering of family members of a secretly detained person (i.e., disappeared) may also be tortured or any other form of ill-treatment, and at the same time there is a violation of the rights to the protection of family life [516].

Seymour Hersh, a journalist who published the story of Abu Ghraib, is one of the few American reporters known for neutrality. Hersh said in a lecture, "some of the worst things that happened that you do not know about the video, which show that there are women in Abu Ghraib. Some heard that they were passing messages, or making connections with their men ... and women were stating in their letters, "please come and kill me because of what happened". Those women were arrested with young male boys. Videos acknowledge that the boys were sodomized. In the background is of the sound of shrieking children". It is known that these films were viewed during a secret session to members of the U.S. Congress and not shared with the general public for opinion [505].

Occupation forces ran secret operations with the use of thousands of Special Forces such as Army Rangers, Navy Seals, and the Delta Force. In addition to the British Special Air Service Services, [452] there were units from the U.S. Central Intelligence Agency (CIA) and (MI6), as well as private collections of military intelligence and the :"Black-Op forces". Under the pretext of searching for Saddam Hussein and prosecuting terrorists, many of these secret military operations used brutal tactics in their interrogations of these suspects in these secret camps [453]. With the availability of security mercenaries or contractors, they relied on them as investigators in the occupation jails [454].

Unfortunately, the elevation of the U.S. military using violence and aggression in the Abu Ghraib prison has been transformed. Americans soldiers, of mere mortal's ordinary to sufferers, according to a scientific study published in the Journal of aggression and violence in 2009. Despite the attempt to establish the facts of the torturous scandal at Abu Ghraib's prison as one of the most corrupt groups, similar reports of war crimes in the collection across Iraq are still being uncovered. This study suggests that the U.S. military has converted ordinary soldiers to brutal harsh prison guards at Abu Ghraib prison. By the basics recruitment strategies and general training, they gave them a license to increase their aggression and violence after the events of 9/11. The specific authorization for interrogation became more aggressive with increasing pressures for protection. In addition, this became the dehumanization of prisoners [220].

Some cases of torture against civilian casualties by U.S. forces were documented in Fallujah, which I handed over as part of a special report to the Special Rapporteur of the United Nations' anti-torture and all inhumane treatment methods Mr. Mark Noah in the UNAMI office in the capital Amman in 2005 [552]. Many Fallujah victims were incarcerated for periods ranging from weeks to several years. All of these cases confirmed the existence of a fixed policy, or systematic plan of the occupation authorities to pursue daily repression, violence and intimidation of civilian detainees.

5.4. Aljaderiah scandal

On November 14, 2005, U.S. troops inspected the Jadiriyah district of Baghdad. They found 168 detainees, aged between 15 - 60 years old. Many of the detainees said that the shelter was under the responsibility of Brigade 9 Badr. Others said people in uniforms, detained them at the same time most of them said they were arrested at checkpoints, and a few of them said they were arrested because they were blackmailed by a third party. Medical examinations revealed that 101 out of 186 prisoners were subjected to ill-treatment and signs of beatings, electric shock, and had stab wounds on their bodies. According to testimony of the detainees and prisoners, 18 died or were killed during their interrogation. Documents submitted by the witnesses confirmed the deaths of 14 prisoners from this group. On the other hand, 95 were arrested in accordance with a court order and all of their information was documented. Seventy-One were arrested and convicted under a court order, but their testimony was not given during a court proceeding. The investigator documented seven certificates but did not submit their papers to the justice.

The Office of Human Rights of UNAMI collected reports indicating that the interior minister and senior officials in the ministry were aware that using this facility as a detention center was illegal. According to other allegations, U.S. forces knew about these facilities and their violations. They visited the shelter before November 13, 2005 to treat some people who were arrested.

Many people believe that the judiciary also knew of the detainees and detention conditions. Some judges belong to the Directorate of Special

Investigations, which oversees the shelter on behalf of the Ministry of Interior. In June 2005, the Special Investigation Department was established under the control of Deputy Prime Minister for the affairs of the General Intelligence Department. The Special Investigation Department hired about 26 officers into Special Investigations. They received detainees from police offices, in addition to the Special Forces, the General Intelligence Department, and the provincial police.

On November 15, 2005, the government announced that it opened an investigation about the Jadiriyah scandal and its report would be ready in a week. On November 18, 2005, a judicial commission was formed to investigate the legality of the detention procedures that were followed in the case of the people found in the Jadiriyah center. This was to make sure whether the detainees were subjected to ill-treatment. The government formed a third committee to look generally at the issue of detention in the country and it was expected that the Commission would issue its report by the end of 2005. After the inspection, which took place on November 14, other government officials backed by U.S. troops identified detention facilities. There were 625 detainees found on December 8, 2005 in another detention facility, run by the Interior Ministry in Baghdad. Reports indicated that many of these detainees were in poor health due to ill-treatment and showed signs of the effect of torture [650]. There were meetings of the representative of the secretary-general in Iraq, Mr. Ashraf Qazi, with Prime Minister Ibrahim al-Jaafari and President Talabani in an attempt to involve the United Nations in these investigations of mistreatment, but all efforts failed. So far, the governments of Jaafari and al-Maliki later refused to announce the results of these investigations into these crimes. Although many of the calls from the United Nations described the clear and dangerous challenges to the international community, as well as the cover up of the death squads that were placed in the context as the security system in Iraq.

5.5. Torture as a catalyst for the continuation of violence and revenge

An Australian officer, who worked with U.S. forces in Iraq, from 2005 – 2008, as an adviser on counter-insurgency, said in his book that in 2007, there was a dramatic rise in the sectarian killings after the bombings of shrines in Samarra. The spread of sectarian killings by Shiite militias penetrated the heart of the government. This situation forced 70% of the participants in this violence to become detainees with no other way to defend themselves against a terrorist and brutal environment, which threaten their community or their region [498].

This brutal torture methods and repression by the occupation forces remained, even after their departure from Iraq. The use of torture during the interrogation of detainees in Iraqi prisons was under the spread of corruption, bribery and death threats [316]. Indiscriminate detention policy based on suspicion becomes a normal policy [317]. Despite the U.S. recognition of the torture, the Jadiriya's shelter of the interior ministry was formed after the first elections under occupation. Occupation complicity of criminals who gave orders to torture, continued to support these criminal groups and sectarian militias inside the Iraqi Interior Ministry. This is clear evidence of their plan to replace these militia criminals, conducted to punish all of those who rejected the existence of the occupation [357].

In 2006, the Committee against Torture "CAT" of the UN studied the file of the United States detention practices of interrogation used against detainees within the so-called war on terror. The Committee noted that the United States practiced methods including sexual humiliation, waterboarding, short shackling, and using dogs to induce fear. This is in violation of the Convention Against Torture [142].

The report of the human rights office in UNAMI for the first two months of 2006, acknowledged the existence of many of the detainees still not charged with a crime. Since 2004, detainees are languishing in occupation jails and the new Iraqi government prisons [649].

In September 2010, Amnesty International, in a report titled the new system and abuses continue; warned that the illegal detention and torture in Iraq resulted in 30,000 prisoners held without rights and subjected to torture or ill-treatment. Malcolm Smart from the Amnesty's Middle East and North Africa branch said, "The Iraqi security forces were responsible for systematic violations of the rights of detainees which were allowed. The U.S. authorities handed over thousands of people detained by U.S. forces to face this governmental violence and systematic assault to evade any responsibility for their human rights [525].

On October 22, 2010, WikiLeaks declared some of the war documents failed to force the U.S. authorities to investigate hundreds of reports of ill-treatment, torture, rape and murder by Iraqi police and soldiers whose behavior was a systematic nature of the punishment. U.S. troops abused prisoners for years after the Abu Ghraib scandal [526]. Corruption in the United States has led to dealing with the establishment of the new police order and prisons in Iraq. The U.S. government has referred the contract to re-establish the police buildings and prisons in Iraq to a company involved in a scandal, which involves trading prostitutes in Bosnia. *'The Observer'* had reported that Washington had contracted with DynCorp to create a police force to maintain security in Iraq and oversee the establishment of the facilities. This company has already donated more than £100,000 GBP to the U.S. Republican Party. The British employment tribunal has already ruled £100,000 GBP was compensation from the company to the UN officers, which had worked with the company in Bosnia. They were dismissed from work because they told the press about the company's violations of sexual and immoral work. Former Minister of Labor Defense, Peter Kilfoyle, criticized for his handling of this company. He stated, "I find it hard to believe that in the time that we seek to impose law and order in Iraq, we need to handle carefully and with great sensitivity, the task entrusted to a private U.S. company such as DynCorp which is unreliable for such work" [520].

Human Rights reports of UNAMI continued to refer to the continuity of torture in the Maliki government prisons and said, "continuing reports of the widespread and routine torture or ill-treatment of detainees, particularly those being held in pre-trial detention facilities, including police stations" [651].

5.6. Rendition Program

Of the things that helped to marginalize the rule of international law and respect for human rights were the secret programs of arrest and torture, which are among the most fundamental violation of the rights of unlawful arrest. Here we highlight the role of American policy in this file through the transfer of suspects from one country to another without any court hearing or delivery, which is the process of abductions. This policy began under the former U.S. President Ronald Reagan. The joint team, between the CIA and the FBI, brought drug dealers and suspected terrorists to the United States. These terrorists have their rights and attorneys are provided for them as they are brought to trial. In the aftermath of a truck bomb attack at the World Trade Center in 1993, they replaced these arrests, known as "renditions", to a wider process called policy of "extraordinary rendition" with the suspects and their transfer to a third country. CIA officers decided that the fight against Islamic terrorism had to hold on to some of the suspects outside the courts of the United States due to the fear of exposing their sources and to protect

[80]

intelligence officials from other countries to be called as witnesses [532]. It is well known that U.S. President George W. Bush gave the order to the CIA to set up secret prisons outside of the United States [147].

Finally, I would like to remember what the American *Time* newspaper said in 2009 for the comparison between Iraq and America after the White House released torture memos previous to the Bush administration as another step toward closure in what President Obama called "a dark and painful chapter in our history,". In Iraq, torture, is not a thing of the past. This is according to the results of a new study about civilian casualties [651].

CHAPTER 6

The First massacre in Fallujah 4 April 2004
Vigilant Resolve Operations

6.1. Pre-Fight Period

F allujah was not the only city that launched the signs of popular rejection of the occupation. Most of the Iraqi people realized the truth ly with the escalation of theft, lack of security and lack of job opportunities, with other lies that promised to assist with occupation operations. Before giving details of that period, we should firstly correct the media mistakes, which were repeating what the occupation had to say about the launch of the rebels on the insurgents especially in Fallujah and generally in Iraq. Iraq was then formally under occupation and recognized internationally that there was no elected Iraqi government with sovereignty. This mistake was recognized by former U.S. Secretary of Defense Donald Rumsfeld [13].

The course of events confirmed that the first American massacre against the people of Fallujah was a U.S. decision with full participation and support of the British within the joint command of the leadership of the international coalition forces. Therefore, this was the framework of the international dispute between joint forces of U.S. - British occupation and Iraq people, who defended themselves in the absence of international protection, under the methodology of violence and the logic of force against those who reject the occupation and its agenda. Some Iraqi political collaborators of the invasion tried to overlook this when talking about the fight. They spoke only about the second battle because of the legal difference between the two battles which condemns the occupation with full responsibility.

On Thursday, 15 January 2004, the downing of a U.S. helicopter near Fallujah was the third attempt to bring down a U.S. military helicopter in less than two weeks, while US troops opened fire in two separate incidents on the same day, killing four civilians [51]. The U.S. Navy Marine Corps initiated access to the

Anbar province in mid-February in 2004 and initiated a formal action in the Anbar province on 4 March 2004 with full responsibility, which it moved from 3rd Armored Cavalry Regiment "Brave Rifles" on 14 March 2004 [50].

On 24 March 2004, Marines arrived, under the command of *Col. Gregg P. Olson,* commander of the 2nd Battalion. They were the first Marines in Fallujah to replace the Parachute Brigade with military responsibility for the city. They wanted to show their strength to force the people to accept the orders of the occupation, confirmed by statements in the U.S. press on 28 March 2004. They came to do what the paratroopers were afraid to do! Two days after their arrival, the first armed clashes between them and local fighters in the Alaskari district occurred. The result was the killing of a U.S. soldier and wounding of seven others. Also killed were 15 Iraqi people, among them a photographer of ABC News American channel, as well as a two-year-old Iraqi child. This, according to the same American newspaper [414] (13 reference of chapter 7 [371]). This incident, in which innocent civilians were killed, prompted residents to boil because of this new strategy of the occupation forces. The Marines clearly utilized force, principle and punishment instead of dialogue and respect. Therefore, things turned to an increase in violence, because violence made violence.

Hatred of the people initiated and increased against the occupation with a new crime in Palestine. When an Israeli helicopter shot and fired against the spiritual leader of Islamic Resistance Movement Hamas, Sheikh Yassin, killing him and others after dawn prayers on 22 March 2004. This incident was born in anger and outrage amongst Muslims in the world, including Fallujah. The timing of this was wrong. The Marines were trying to show power with their new offensive against Israel with this murder. This gave an indication that the people felt both sides were working as one against the Muslims. Unfortunately, this mistaken policy has not understood by the U.S. command. After failing in the first battle of Fallujah, they began to open dialogue with the local civilians.

To confirm the new aggressive policy of Marines towards the people, U.S. forces initiated a campaign of arbitrary arrest, accompanied by the proliferation of tanks and armored vehicles on the roads, digging trenches on the outskirts of the city. Then came the U.S. Naval military activities stating on 27 March 2004, that they are doing offensive operations to promote and secure a stable environment for the people. "Those who chose to fight against them have chosen their destiny and they will engage them and destroy them." (18 reference of chapter 7 [371]). The proliferation of U.S. vehicles in the streets of Fallujah, broadcasting through loudspeakers, that Fallujah would be a battleground if the terrorists did not drop their weapons. This caused some of the people to leave the city. Shops closed in the early hours while American ambushes and checkpoints spread abruptly each time. These actions prompted Brig. General Mark Kimmitt, deputy commander of military operations in Iraq, to say to reporters on 30 March 2004 that they were pleased with the success of the Marines in dealing with Fallujah and their work progress. "The Marines were happy about how to stream into force things in Fallujah, and look at the continuity of progress in establishing a secure and stable environment, rebuilding the province of Iraq" (23 reference of chapter 7 [371]). Kimmit did not realize that the Marines policy and violations in Fallujah were counterproductive leading to disastrous results. This created increased hatred and revenge against them by people who suffered from injustice at the hands of their troops without guilt or fault. This situation in Fallujah created a city of armed resistance, which became an example of the national resistance against foreign occupation. However, Kimmitt returned the day after the killing of four Americans contractors to say, "that what happened is a small massacre" [506].

6.2. The truth of the Blackwater' role in Fallujah

In mid-February 2004, the author was invite with a colleague in the Fallujah Council, Eng. Fawzi Almudan, to a meeting at the U.S. base near Fallujah. They told us that the American side called upon us because we had scientific degrees, and were to meet with an important civilian representative from the U.S. administration. We were supposed to discuss new development plans for the City. Arriving at the meeting, we were surprised that Bremer's representative was a CIA agent, who usually attended meetings on the military side. We understood that the discussion of new projects and the presence of an important politician from the U.S. administration were a mere false pretext for this meeting. We soon understood the reason for the meeting when private security agents from Blackwater attended later, unexpectedly wearing civilian clothes of Iraqi style and Arabic headdress (keffiyeh). We were surprised that they were former members of the CIA because their facial features were Arabic. The spokesman from Blackwater was heavily muscled with tattoos on both arms, with a blonde mustache looking like a cowboy. Behind him sat three of his colleagues, also with mustaches, and one of them with a light beard.

They started to talk to us about their decision to stop the work of 50 members of the Iraqi police for facilities protection under the pretext not needing them as surplus labor. We rejected this decision because it affected 50 families in

Fallujah, and cutting out their salaries meant cutting off their only source of livelihood. After a lengthy discussion, the Blackwater representative suggested that these officers return to work but with a new task, using spies to find out who targets U.S. forces. We rejected this proposal as well, for trying to exploit the difficult economic situation in Fallujah to protect U.S. forces, while the opposite is what should be, because occupying forces are obliged to protect the occupied people. The course of the meeting turned into a verbal argument between us. A Bremer representative tried to frighten us by asking us to inform the people of Fallujah that the paratroopers would leave Fallujah and the Marines replacing them would make a tougher response to any attack on them. Here the author tried to advise them to take advantage of the mistakes of paratroopers, to ensure the non-recurrence of crimes and violations that occurred with the paratroopers, and to try to understand the culture and traditions of Fallujah, especially regarding the issue of justice and the need for revenge in the absence of justice. We tried to give an example for clarification, but they understood my example as a threat to their troops. The author explained that by tribal traditions, it is the right of the people of the slain victim to extract revenge from the killer's family, because judicial justice did not exist to be levied the killer since Bremer had demanded immunity for his troops before the Iraqi judiciary no matter how they many crimes and abuses they had committed. We had desired to illustrate the need to avoid violence, as a way to avoid counter-violence in reaction, as natural self-defense.

Here, Bremer's representative became furious and said no one threatens the Marines! Then he grabbed the neck of his shirt, and said with a smirk, tell the people of Fallujah that the current forces are not the paratroopers but Marines and we will respond to the killing of one U.S. soldier by killing ten civilians of yours. This prompted us to loudly refute this logic and my colleague Fawzi intervened; he said to them, "Do you want a sea of blood? We came here in order to help the Fallujah and we do not accept your verbal threats". The U.S. side ended the meeting under the pretext of another meeting that demanded their attention.

The more important surprise was when we left the meeting tent, we saw modern civilian cars with Iraqi license plates and some of these cars were BMWs known to be used by Blackwater contractors. This confirmed that the terrorist car, that opened fire on a local Fallujah government building on the night of November 9, 2003 and then fled to the US base, was likely from Blackwater. This raises questions about what the role of Blackwater really was, and was their role to fight in Iraq?

6. 3. Killing of Blackwater mercenaries

Four days later, responsibility was transfered in the Anbar province from the paratroopers of the 82nd Airborne Division to the Marines (MEF) [230]. On March 31, 2004, four Blackwater contractors' cars left their headquarters in the military base west of Fallujah heading across Fallujah towards the town of Habbaniyah. Strangely, they took the road that passes through Fallujah, rather than the outer road they were instructed to use by their employer. It is strange that international and U.S. parties did not call for an independent investigation to determine the causes of this incident, particularly since the Fallujah citizens did not resist the U.S. occupation forces after the fall of Baghdad on April 9, 2003, since the mutilation of enemies would be morally abhorrent to them. To understand how this event happened, one must first understand the role and function of this "security company" and how it impacted civilians' minds. Secondly, what was the nature of the Fallujah tradition in particular, and of the Iraqi people in general toward the occupation and their right of self-defense? The American's story, stated by a Marine spokesman, Gen. Mark Kimmitt, alleged that four contractors from Blackwater were carrying out humanitarian tasks by providing food and humanitarian aid in the region. A senior Pentagon officer, John R. Ballard, in his book *Fight for Fallujah*, also made this claim. However, all the facts indicate that these were of the second rank militarily in Iraq in terms of the number and nature of armaments and military tasks (see Chapter IV). It's sufficient to remember that Blackwater delayed in answering the American Committee's inquiry, and that they used obvious evasions such as claims of being stymied by document classification errors regarding Fallujah incidents or waiting for reclassification of these to non-classified status by the U.S. Department of Defense. This manipulation to avoid accountability, confirmed the doubts about their legal privileges and the classification of non-humanitarian operations [239]. This was in addition to our meeting with them and discovering their intelligence role in Fallujah.

According to a U.S. Marine officer at his base near Fallujah, Blackwater mercenaries refused to inform their leaders or anyone at the base about the nature of their mission [371]. U.S. congressional sources revealed much about this incident in 2007.

Many of the warnings had told them not to enter the City due to the seriousness of the situation and the likely response of the inhabitants. Blackwater they confirmed that they would not enter the city. Unfortunately, they entered and this action, was interpreted by others as negligence [371].

There are security contractors who had warned them before the night of the incident, not to travel inside Fallujah because they lacked many essential supplies such as maps adequate for the region and the city, and adequate weapons or armoured vehicles to protect the trucks. Four contractors arrived the night before the incident at the wrong military base near Fallujah, and were forced to sleep there for security reasons before they set off the next day in a hurry and without adequate preparations [239].

The four Blackwater contractors had begun their mission before the start of formal contracts between the U.S. government and their company. In spite of all alarms, they travelled with several people in each car that should have contained two people sitting in the back to provide protection. Two of their colleagues remained at the company's headquarters to perform administrative duties and complete the mission. Just four people went, raising difficult questions regarding their decision [221]. It's worth noting that a British security company, Control Risks Group, that had been doing security work near Fallujah before the advent of Blackwater, refused to do this work, twice arguing that they refused to bear unacceptable risks. Nevertheless, Blackwater accepted the job without worrying about the warnings from the British company [239].

It is important to consider information cited by Jeremy Scahill from Blackwater for its importance in the sequence of events [371]. A Bremer spokesman, Dan Senor, confirmed that they had full confidence in the Blackwater men protecting Mr. Bremer and providing security in all of Iraq! [371]. This meant that the main task for them concerned security and not humanitarian tasks as they claimed after the incident. There had even been explicit calls by political pundits in the U.S. media to make Fallujah a bloodbath! Bill O'Reilly said on Fox News, "I don't care about the people of Fallujah. You're not going to win their hearts and minds. They're going to kill you to the every end. They've proven that. So let's knock this place down". (17 from 8 [371]). While former Democratic Presidential candidate General Wesley Clark said to MSNBC: "The resistance is not declining in Fallujah, so far as I can determine. It's building and mounting. And we can't have that challenge to our authority" (20 from 8 [371]). Some statements confused being a target in your own home with being an occupier who may kill anyone without any criticism. Host Tucker Carlson opinioned in the CNN program Crossfire that, "I think we ought to kill every person who's responsible for the deaths of those Americans. This is a sign of weakness. This is how we got 9/11. It's because we allowed things like that to go unresponded to. This is a big deal." (8 from 24 [371]).

[88]

Despite the condemnation of the mutilation of the four contractors by all official, religious and social spokespeople in Fallujah, the situation continued to deteriorate [235]. The first meeting after the incident was between the Governing Council in Fallujah and the U.S. side at the military base near Fallujah. The first speech was by Bremer's civilian representative in the Anbar province. He spoke roughly with the fire of revenge lighting his eyes, red from crying. He stood next to the new commander of Marines who was in his first meeting with us. The next speech was made by the Vice President of the Fallujah Council, Sheikh Mohammed Hamid Shihan. He spoke about the killing of the four security contractors. The Council denounced mutilation as contrary to Islamic Sharia Law and Iraqi traditions. Then the new Marine commander in Fallujah followed saying, "The Prophet David also decried the mutilation of corpses", a reference to his Jewish religion. Then Bremer's representative in Fallujah added that they were my friends and colleagues and he would avenge the murders. Interestingly and strikingly he was wearing a bullet-proof vest during that meeting with us, despite our meeting at a U.S. base near Fallujah. He had never worn a bullet-proof vest before, even during the meetings prior to the incident, even including those held in the youth center hall in Fallujah!

6.4. Configuration to storm Fallujah and crime of mass punishment

This incident presented a good opportunity for American politicians, especially for President Bush, who had started his Presidential campaign saying that those terrorists will not intimidate the United States and will not undermine her will. That's what made them use the incident as an excuse to dramatize their will to fight terrorism and to prevent its arrival in America. This prestaged the continuation of the deception that the occupation of Iraq was to fight terrorism.

General Sanchez noted that the political push for revenge is what forced the Marines to decide on a quick and comprehensive response, despite having hoped for more time to prepare their mission. Paul Bremer vowed in his first comments on the deaths of four contractors during the graduation of the first batch of trainees at the police academy in Baghdad, "that the killing of the Blackwater men would not go unpunished" [202]. There were five Marines killed on the same day, March 31st near Habbaniyah, only 20 miles away from Fallujah. But the media did not focus on *them* and the leaders of the occupation did not threaten to avenge *them* [193]. There was no media focus as well on the same day when a car bomb was used to attack a convoy of new Iraqi police, claiming 15 victims [506].

After the U.S. president made the decision to invade Fallujah, and before embarking on military action, the U.S. sent Jim Steele into Fallujah with an American - Iraqis team. Steele assisted Paul Bremer. Jim Steele is a prominent player in the history of the U.S. dirty wars in some Latin American countries. He was the key to starting up a formal rebellion in the U.S.'s bloody war in El Salvador, through his supervision of the training of Salvadoran death squads. A Congressional investigation exposed his role in supplying arms to the death squads in Nicaragua too. He worked on training the Panamanian police after the United States ousted the Panamanian President [57, 56 and 55 from 8 (371)]. That is convincing evidence that he was the instigator of the "Salvadoran" death squads in Iraq [61 from 8 (371)]. Mr. Steele knew how to organize an armed rebellion led by local forces [62 from 8 (371)]. After he returned from his mission in Fallujah, Steele claimed, "his mission was to retrieve the bodies of the four Blackwater men and to assess the enemy situation internally" [63 from 8 (371)]. While the truth was that the Fallujah police cars had already carried the corpses to the U.S. base. The actual purpose of his mission was to get intelligence to assess the internal situation before the U.S. started the attack. Steele asserted that, "In Fallujah, a heavy hand makes sense," he said. "That's the only thing some of those guys will understand. Down south, too, where the United States faced a mounting Shiite rebellion. We can't be seen as weak. Otherwise, this kind of thing can happen everywhere" [64 from 8 (371)].

The military role of the corporate mercenaries escalated with the participation of the Marines. Soldiers were protecting the occupation authority's headquarters in Najaf called Camp Golf, and began armed clashes in the city of Najaf against the followers of Moqtada al-Sadr on the very day of the attack on Fallujah on April 4, 2004. On March 28, 2004, Paul Bremer ordered the al-Hawza newspaper of Muqtada closed, and the arrest of a senior cleric, Yacoubi. This fueled a massive demonstration against the occupation that urged Bremer to leave. The men of Blackwater gave the order to shoot at the Marines, and led the clash that took place on April 4, 2004 in Najaf. This event confirms a combat role for Blackwater, in addition to their security role. (See Chapter IX for published allegations about the presence of Arab fighters in Fallujah.) Here we review some of the facts that refute Bremer. The top U.S. commander in Iraq, Gen. Ricardo Sanchez, admitted that in July 2003, there were three different wars taking place in Iraq. The first aggregated unstructured groups from the former regime whose main task was decentralized fighting, and carrying the insurgency against coalition forces. The second engaged Sunnis extremists who unpredictably attacked any foreign presence in their neighborhood. These extremists were concentrated in the western part of Baghdad near Fallujah, (See page 251.) [36]. Sanchez's analysis confirmed this by a National Gound Intelligence Center (NGIC), [1] report issued after the end of the first battle. This document did not mention the existence of any non-Iraqi groups, as would be taken up later.

6.5. The beginning of the siege operation of Fallujah

6.5.1. The last meeting with the Marines

On April 4, 2004, we, as members of the Fallujah Local Council, met with the commander of the U.S. Marines in Fallujah. This was the second meeting for us with them after the killing of the Blackwater security mercenaries. The Council members who lived inside the City made it to the Council building, but other members who lived outside of the City, a majority of the Council, were not allow to enter. The Chairman of the Council, Dr. Mohamed Hassan Albloh, was out of town. The delegation members consisted of his Deputy of Council, Saadallah al-Rawi, Eng. Fawzi Mohammed Alamadan, Shiek of Alroyen tribal Taqi al-Rawi, the religious scholar Imam Ahmed al-Janabi, management director of the Council Hazim Al-Jumaili and the author.

On this morning, coinciding with the anniversary of the killing of Iraq's King Ghazi Faisal in 1939, everyone was surprised because of the U.S. forces shutting down all vehicle and pedestrian traffic leading to and from the City's port, a route that passes across 14 roads or crossings. We went to the military checkpoint on the main road close to the U.S. camp. We informed them that we had a meeting with the military leadership. After one hour of having contacted their military leadership, they let us pass escorted by U.S. patrol vehicles. We found Marine Commander Lt. Gen. James T. Conway waiting for us at the meeting tent. He was holding a message that he handed us, and then asked us to spread it to the people of Fallujah. The U.S. planned a military action against those suspected of killing the four contractors. The U.S. leaflet instructed residents, according to the Geneva Conventions, not to go out of the City. In case of necessity and urgency, people should raise a white flag in front of American soldiers to ask for food or medicine only. They had decided in advance to make Fallujah a big prison, and allow only the food and medicine to enter that was brought by their forces. This was the first violation of the Geneva Convention before the start of the battle. Strangely, an American military study falsely alleged that the U.S. military had encouraged the Fallujah people to get out of the city before the start of the battle, [55], refuting this, international aid organizations confirmed that American marines had prevented civilians in Fallujah to exit or enter the City and snipers targeted a lot of them. [219].

We tried to discuss with the Marine commander the justifications for this operation and asserted that he has no right to punish the entire City, especially since he could capture whoever killed the four contractors. As their statements imply that they know the perpetrators from TV broadcasts, since they held many of the spies' captive in the City, they could capture them at any time and arrest them. Considering that the Marines enter the city each day and night to arrest people whom they want, why this collective punishment? The U.S. Commander replied as he tried to leave, "these orders came from Pentagon" and he had no authority to discuss the orders, he was only required to carry them out. Before we left the tent, he took the initiative to say that we should reassure the people of Fallujah not to panic if they saw our soldiers in different dress, because the U.S. would conduct quality operations against terrorists. This speech took our delegation by surprise, and we interpreted this as psychological warfare, intended to keep us wondering whether they might use selected Special Forces or perhaps mercenary fighters?

6. 5. 2. Relief Call of Fallujah

After our Fallujah delegation returned to the City, we started thinking about the effects of this mass punishment imposed by the military. We came out unanimously thinking that this punishment might rise to the level of genocide or indiscriminate killing. Therefore, we decided to launch an appeal via satellite to save the City from the crime and destruction that lay ahead. Mr. Fawzi Alamadan, jointly with Mr. Saadallah al-Rawi, started to prepare a distress call for the rescue of Fallujah. The Al-Arabiya TV correspondent, Abdulkadir Abanndakja, arrived, followed shortly thereafter by Al-Jazeera reporter, Hussein Daly, to record and to broadcast a distress call immediately. During the broadcast, Mr. Saadallah al-Rawi's voice was filled with pain and fear for the fate of civilians. He called on all Iraqis to help in the rescue of Fallujah after the U.S. decision to impose mass punishment on the people of the City. The appeal spread across the Arab and international satellite channels and launched a campaign of solidarity with us to a level not anticipated. The appeal plan won the media battle in this conflict thanks to the support of the Al-Jazeera and Al-Arabiya channels. People's Solidarity shared by diverse Iraqi groups caused our hearts to rejoice, and we felt that the battle would not be contained just to Fallujah.

The whole world had been listening to only one side in the media, especially with the many showings of videos of the four dead American contractors. That is why the appeal for help was made, and following that, many pictures were published showing dozens of Iraqi civilian casualties due to the U.S. shelling and sniping. This all changed world opinion by allowing people to see who were defending themselves, and who was committing crimes against innocent civilians.

On April 4 and 5, Al-Jazeera's correspondent in Fallujah started to speak in a broadcast about civilian casualties and a humanitarian disaster, which sparked a wave of anger. The Islamic Party warned that it would withdraw from the Governing Council, formed by the Civil Governor Bremer, unless this situation stopped. [230]

In the early days following the U.S. massacre, on April 6 or 7, 2004 a body arrived at the new medical unit near the mosque Hadra. A martyr, killed by a sniper's bullet to the head, appeared to be smiling and smelling of musk. There were five martyrs on the first floor of the medical unit waiting until a place to bury them was found. The new cemetery could not be used because of its location within range of the U.S. snipers and small arms fire. In the meantime, a delegation from the Sadrist movement headed by Sheikh Aqeel arrived at the mosque Hadra as I recall, and with him a convoy of food and aid. They were met by some of the notables, representatives and leaders of Fallujah with some of my colleagues of the local council. They brought the greetings of Moqtada al-Sadr, and the solidarity of the Sadrist movement and Mahdi Army, to the people of Fallujah. At the end of the meeting, the notables of Fallujah gave thanks to the al-Sadr delegation for the solidarity and feelings we experienced because they were the first arrivals to support our rescue. Before leaving the delegation, they asked to see the bodies of our martyrs and we were wondering about it at first glance, but we went with them to the morgue. When they arrived at corpses' room, the smell of musk filled the place, then began the Takbeers voices, **Allah Greater**, while some of them started crying over the bodies of the martyrs. Some decided to stay, saying we are with you on victory or martyrdom! During the unloading of food from a car, I noticed a 5-kilogram bag of flour! I was amazed and asked the driver, a man in his forties, what is this? He answered that the old woman of Naser weal Salam city was trying to catch up to his car in order to contribute this flour because she does not have anything else to give! Such national sentiment spurred convoys of solidarity, humanitarian aid and medical supplies to reach Fallujah. Donations of food, medicine, money, gold jewelry and even blood donations flooded in to support the people of Fallujah. It was then we became certain that the victory of God would come after strengthening and unifying the hearts of Iraqis against the occupation and its crimes. I've had moments where emotions were mixed between scenes of indiscriminate killing and the arrival of the various delegations of Iraq and its sects in support, despite the gravity of the security situation in Fallujah. Therefore it was natural given the coverage by the U.S. newspapers, although some were righteously outraged at the war and the Bush administration, that fraternal cooperation and synergies between the Sadrists and the people of Fallujah and full support was achieved between them for the uprising against the occupation - this was one of the greatest crises faced by the occupation [105]. We did not plan all of this, but we raised our voices honestly and we won the media battle, thereby securing popular solidarity ever since the beginning of the battle.

6.6. The beginning of first battle in Fallujah

The U.S. side claimed that they had asked civilians to raise their hands before speaking with American soldiers, after they completed their siege of Fallujah. [8 from 10 (371)]. Contradictorily, they started to shoot many civilians who naturally just wanted to survive this massacre. The Marines also set up arrest camps before the start of the offensive on the City [1 from 10 (371)]. On May 4, 2004 military operations were launched on the city of Fallujah, [64] 30 attacks in the same month [231]. The U.S. special forces were sent to hit specific targets inside the city. Three battalions of U.S. Marines entered, backed by intimidating tanks. Soon they began asking for additional troop support after the battle with the armed resistance had started in the interior [9 from 10 (371)].

On April 8, 2004, U.S. warplanes started to rain bombs down on Fallujah [64]. One of the strikes done by a U.S. fighter jet, F-16, threw a bomb weighing 500 pounds on a mosque in Fallujah [12 from 10 (371)]. Disregarding that such an action was a flagrant violation of the Geneva Conventions that prohibit targeting centers and places of worship, the U.S. side claimed it was a center of fighters, which transformed it into a military target! [13 from 10 (371)].

U.S. Marines captured the general hospital of the City and prevented the wounded from getting medication [15 from 10 (371)]. US forces bombed a Fallujah power station at the beginning of the offensive with predictable consequences, more suffering for the ordinary people! [16 from 10 (371)]. Marine commander Lt. Col. Brennan Byrne vowed that if anyone resisted he would break their back [19 from 10 (371)].

These U.S. crimes committed in the early days then spread to the world via Al-Jazeera television, energized anti-occupation demonstrations, and spurred massive condemnation. Worldwide humanitarian donations were collected and sent to Fallujah. There also appeared aid convoys and volunteers arriving in the City. Employees in the Fallujah Hospital informed the rest of us that more than 280 civilians had been killed and more than 400 others wounded [25 from 10 (371)]. In spite of the denial by U.S. forces about targeting civilians, tellingly, Maj. Larry Kaifesh admitted the difficulty of distinguishing fighters from civilians during the battles [27 from 10 (371)]. Although the U.S. Defense Secretary Rumsfeld had falsely alleged, at the beginning of processes, that the Marines were moving systematically in the City, seeking out specific targets from photos. Rumsfeld further contended that they know who they want; they know what they want; and they recognize who should be arrested, this person or others [52].

6.7. Other Crimes of Invasion Forces

Because of the continued siege and fighting in urban areas, preventing ambulances from rescuing the injured or transferring the bodies, there was an inevitable accumulation of civilian bodies in the streets. The smell of death clung all over Fallujah. Temporary health clinics were created during the battle, because the U.S. prevented the injured fighters from getting to the General Hospital that was outside the city. Undeniable was the lack of basic humane health conditions. Dahr Jamil, a well known journalist with teammate Rahul Mahajan, witnessed in the City, the tragedy brought home to noncombatant Iraqi women and children by U.S. snipers [32 from 10 (371)]. The author's relationship with Mr. Jamil strengthened after that battle. It precipitated a flood of published articles and news directly from the people of Fallujah, giving a free voice for them within the United States and abroad. Rahul Mahajan confirmed that U.S. aircraft, stealth S – 130s, dropped bombs weighing 500, 1,000 and 2,000 pounds on Fallujah districts. Rahul also had a presence in the medical clinic and watched the arrival of more than 20 civilians wounded by a sniper, some of them were women, as well as children as young as 10 years old. This demonstrated the heavy deployment of American snipers widely throughout Fallujah, showing no mercy for any civilians, whatever their age or sex! The ambulances also were not spared from American snipers [35 from 10 (371)]. This immense suffering and carnage prompted the people's decision to transform the Fallujah football stadium into a new cemetery for burying the new martyrs. Despite the U.S. announcement of a ceasefire, their planes continued to bombard the districts of Fallujah, which was exposed by Al-Jazeera photographs. The journalist, Ahmed Mansour, with his staff on April 3, entered

Fallujah a day before the start of the siege and attendant military operations. The photographic/video record of the massacre in Fallujah and the digitized evidence given by medical and humanitarian staff show the tragic situation without the need of explanation. The Latin legal term for this is "Res Ipsa Loquitor" – the thing speaks for itself. The angry statements by a Marine spokesman (Kimmit) and a spokesman for Paul Bremer, Dan Senor, were not surprising in their defensive criticism and accusation of Al-Jazeera and Al-Arabia. Donald Rumsfeld opinioned that Al Jazeera's coverage of the massacre was evil, inaccurate and not justified) [49 from 10 (371)]. Then came an even more shocking revelation when the British newspaper, the Daily Mirror announced, citing a confidential document from the former British Prime Minister Tony Blair's office that said, "Bush told him that he was willing to hit Al-Jazeera in Qatar and the rest of its offices" [50 from 10 (371)]! This document confirmed and dismayed many that a war criminal President was governing a modern and civilized country like the United States!

Meanwhile, President Bush continued lying to the American people. He proclaimed in a weekly speech on U.S. national television on April 13, 2004 that terrorists from other countries had entered Iraq and began to incite organized attacks. He falsely contended to Americans that the violence that we saw was the seizure of power by cruel extremists, not a popular uprising! [55 from 10 (371)]. If this cohesion among Iraqis were not considered a popular uprising, what would it say about the American mentality? Would the internal displacement of more than 200,000 civilians from Fallujah and imposition of a mass punishment strategy as inhumane as this, be justifiable revenge for the killing of four mercenaries?

This author saw many hurt, injured and wounded civilians, mostly by American snipers, as well as injured by fragments from inhumane cluster bombs. Some of the written testimonies of the victims of this battle were collected immediately afterwards. It is impossible not to recall the images of civilians who were killed or wounded nearby, suffering mortal injuries. The most difficult to forget were the four following cases.

The first was a man about fifty years old with his son of nearly 11 years of age. They were waiting beside the Hadra mosque in front of a car transporting food. Suddenly, a U.S. sniper's bullet killed the father with a head shot. Everyone there tried to hide behind the walls of nearby buildings, while the child remained crying over his father and trying to stand him up with blood gushing from his father' head. Some men hurried to save the child, rushing the body of his murdered father to a nearby clinic.

The second incident involved two families in a civilian car. They tried to get out through one of the dirt roads on the outskirts of Fallujah, but American soldiers opened fire on the car, which ended up looking like a sieve with all of the bullet holes. The car arrived at the clinic of the Hadra mosque filled with blood. Most of the victims were women and children. The car was driven by one of the wounded men.

The third incident occurred on April 13, 2004, with the U.S. intensification of aerial bombardment using cluster bombs. The clinic of Hadra took a call from a family in that police district that experienced cluster bombs dropped near their house. They heard the screams of the wounded but they could not go out to rescue them. The horrorible danger of that night for them was not only because of the sniper fire but also because of the intensity of the cluster bombing. The cluster bombs could be recognized by the two distinct sounds they made when launched. The author, with Haj Mahmoud Zobaie and Haj Qasim Mohammad Jumaili went out to transport the victims for medical care by ambulance. It was a horrible shock to witness the site of destruction. The explosions created a hole two meters deep with shrapnel piercing everything in the vicinity. We found bodies' mutalated by these cluster bombs. The stench of burning bodies and explosives assaulted our nostrils. The first body that Haji Qasim attempted to move was missing it's torso and was lacking a foot.

The fourth was during one of the nights when the author was travelling with the two aforementioned young men to deliver humanitarian aid to one of the homes in the battle zone, which contained the parents, a daughter and two young sons. This was in the Thubat neighbourhood, Officers district. We distributed the food and other supplies. We then we went up to the roof to scout out what was happening. It was a surprise when we found the Marines playing American songs over loudspeakers to lift the morale of the soldiers, some of whom were crying. The collapsed state of their morale is a righteous payback for their inhumane reprisals in targeting ambulances and unarmed civilians.

6.8. Start negotiations stage

On 9 April 2004, Bremer ordered a temporary halt to offensive operations, which was a total failure. Negotiations started at a high level on April 13, with a formal cease-fire on April 22 [64]. The temporary occupation authority (CPA) agreed to the decision of this cease-fire after a meeting of the U.S. and British ambassadors, as well as Bremer and Commander Ricardo Sanchez. The Marine commander in Iraq, Lt. Gen. James Conway, objected to this decision, but his objecting did not stop the implementation of this resolution [230].

Since the start of the military operations, several attempts were made by the Notable Shieks of the clans and Imams of Fallujah in order to persuade the government council, formed by Bremer, to stop the battle. However, the responses were negative due to not a pursuit of most of them with the exception of the Sunni representatives in the Council. The real negotiations began when a delegation headed by Sheikh Mohammed bin Sheikh al-Yawar visited Fallujah. Sheikh al-Yawar was running at the time for the presidency of the Governing Council in Baghdad. Sheikh al-Yawar announced his rejection of the military operations against Fallujah and threatened Bremer that he would withdraw from the political process. The delegation was in constant contact with the parties of conflict and joined him later with members of the Iraqi Islamic Party such as Hajim Hassani and Alaa Makki. We heard that a lot of peaceful demonstrations of support and solidarity with Fallujah were suppressed in some areas controlled by militias loyal to the occupation parties, according to the aid convoys that were arriving from different parts of Iraq in solidarity with Fallujah. We did not know that the situation was much like a massive popular revolution and has reached the point that they cut off supplies to Marines in some parts of Fallujah. This pushed Bremer to declare a ceasefire unilaterally with the call to negotiate. We had hoped the cease-fire would protect civilians, but the main problem was a lack of confidence in the U.S. promises that we have become accustomed to being only for win time.

In the meantime, some international sides intervened to mediate between the parties. They asked Fallujah to send a second delegation representing Fallujah to the Jordanian capital of Amman to meet with UNAMI and international organizations operating in Iraq. Most international organizations transferred their headquarters to Amman after bombings of their headquarters in Baghdad. Fallujah notables had chosen a delegation of four people and I was one of them. Leaving Fallujah on April 17, 2004 were Qasim Muhammad Jumaili, Mohammed Abdul Latif al-Shammari and myself. The fourth person

[98]

was Sheikh Mohammed Al-Mohammadi from Saqlawiya. He waited for us in the city of Ramadi. The only available route for us to leave Fallujah was from the west area crossing of the Euphrates River from the Shuhada neighborhood.

We found one boat with many holes and people trying to escape through it to the other side by pulling a rope between both sides of the river back and forth. We entered the boat with two other civilians. Everyone had their heads down to avoid U.S. sniper rounds that could be heard above us. Some civilians were killed before. We arrived on the other side, but we walked in the land of black, moist and moldy clay. We started to sink in the mud, which reached to the level of our stomachs, and we held our bags on our heads with great difficulty. Then we found a friend waiting for us to take us to his home in the nearby village of Alboalon. The dawn of the second day, we drove to the city of Ramadi to find Sheikh Al-Mohammadi waiting for us and then we set off together towards Jordan. We arrived at its capital at the night of 18 April. We started immediately planning and preparing the schedule of our meetings with the international humanitarian organizations that were led by UNAMI.

The first meeting was with the Human Rights Office of UNAMI. They were shocked by the information we brought about the situation in the city. Our most prominent discussion was about requesting mediation between us and the U.S. side as we gave them the terms of Fallujah for a ceasefire. The conditions include intervention of the United Nations as a mediator and guarantor for the negotiations and to monitor the cease-fire agreement between us. In addition to converting soldiers of the Jordanian military hospital located near Fallujah to the U.N. uniform forces for monitoring the ceasefire and control of the outskirts of Fallujah. The first delegation of negotiations in Baghdad had reached an impasse with the Americans there. A few days later, the U.S. side agreed to our terms and the international mediator told us that a meeting with the U.S. side would take place over the next three days. Prior to the expiration of the three-days deadline, the first delegation of our colleagues reached a peace agreement with the U.S. command in Baghdad without coordinating with us and without international guarantees as we asked in Amman. At this time, we realized the reason for the three-day waiting period to prevent an uprising under the pretext of negotiations. They are seeking the best solutions to avoid defeat scandal and prevent the continuation of the popular revolution.

6.9. Ceasefire Agreement

On 21 April began the use of a protection force of the Fallujah people, the Fallujah Brigade, assumed responsibility for security and protection in Fallujah under the leadership of former Iraqi Gen. Maj. Gen. Jassim Mohammed Saleh Mohammadi. The U.S. side agreed to the proposal and reached the elders of Fallujah, via the first negotiating delegation, to the cease-fire agreement with U.S. forces and no permanent peace agreement. This new force started to spread inside and around Fallujah. The Marines withdraw just over a month of fighting and siege. In addition to the American withdrawal, the process of reconstruction was supposed to begin in the city, with the main facilities and to start compensating victims [19]. This did not get more real because the main objective of the Americans was to calm down all the areas have raised, not just Anbar province.

Colonel Coates was responsible for coordination with the new Fallujah Brigade about a cease-fire and the distribution of security measures tasks, because he had good experience from his previous work in El Salvador. On 30 April, the Americans were informed about the arrival of the first battalion of 300 men from the brigade of Fallujah for their tasks around the city, as well as to enroll hundreds of volunteers over the next few days [19]. Our second delegation returned to Fallujah at the end of April 2004, but in spite of many victory celebrations, the defeat of the Marines and the establishment of a military brigade from Fallujah people, I was apprehensive of permanence or usefulness of this form of agreement for many reasons, perhaps the most notable:

1. Previous American promises with the local council of the city before the battle was a lack of respect. Especially the presence of Iraqi sectarian parties in Governing Council paid occupation always for a crisis with the Sunni areas to prevent stability and extend their plans.

2. The absence of an international guarantor and mediator in the negotiations which gave Americans the freedom to the bombing and re-military operations under any pretext. International mediator and U.N. forces will monitor any military violation and check the causes. Therefore, citizens are under international protection with control of the Geneva Conventions governing the status of civilians and prisoners of war under occupation.

3. The strength of Fallujah people' negotiations relied on the support, solidarity and uprisings of other areas in Iraq. This was a mistake from

the first negotiating delegation to limit negotiations to Fallujah only, which the uprising loses real power and isolates people of Fallujah alone. Failure to protect areas of Fallujah that were damaged and destroyed was the beginning of a turning point for the occupation.

6.10. The Role of Media Coverage

We communicate via mobile devices when there is good coverage of the communications network, with the addition of e-mail in times where there is electricity supplied by small generators. These allow us the possibility to make contact with international relief organizations and the international press. Although there is a large staff from the Al-Jazeera channel present, we have also been able to communicate with international journalists and American by sending preliminary reports on the violations to one of international organizations to be published in the meetings of the Commission on Human Rights of the United Nations (called now Human Rights Council of UN) in Geneva.

What happened during the battle was terrifying not only to civilians but even amongst Western journalists who are with the Marines. One British relief and activist volunteer, Jo Wilding, was present near Fallujah at the time and he wrote his observations in an article to the New York Times on 21 April 2004. He exposed what he saw of the mass punishment and joint targeting of both combatants and civilians together. He stated in his letter dated 11 April 2004, saying, "Americans snipers were shooting at ambulances, old women and even aid workers that were carrying medical aid and walking on foot [555,554].

American journalist, Pamela Constable, who was working with the Washington Post, witnessed crimes of the Marines. Pamela said in her article dated 15 April 2004 that, "U.S. convoys were ambushed between several buildings and faced heavy fire that lasted for three hours, injuring some of the Marines. Marine casualties were heavy trying to free the military convoy. This intervention was a collective punishment of the area by the troops. Pamela described it by writing, "before the advent of sunset, U.S. aircraft a so-called stealth launched destroyer raid punitive six surrounding blocks of the place where the convoy came under fire, with the release of dozens of artillery shells that shook the city and lit up the sky. Marines officers confirmed that they destroyed most of the region and there is no activity observed for the fighters". They did not make reference to the extent of the damage and casualties among civilians in those areas [25].

This particular incident was referenced by a group of American researchers, Richard Jackson, Eamon Murphy and Scott Poynting, in the introduction of their book, *The contemporary state terrorism, Contemporary State Terrorism, 2010.* The authors announced Fallujah' example and what happened in this particular incident as evidence of terrorism of this civilized army from a developed country like the United States of America [143]. Although the issue of Fallujah was not part of the case studies detailed in their important book, but they admitted and considered this crime as a collective punishment and a form of terrorism led by the state in order to warn civilians in Fallujah from helping the fighters.

6.11. Health aspect

During the first five days, more than 300 people in Fallujah were killed. This came from the barbaric bombardment use of heavy bombs 300-500 kg. The use of cluster bombs led to the destruction of hundreds of homes and killed more than 600 people, according to hospital director Dr. Rafe Hiad Issawi [302]. Most of the victims were civilians; women, children and the elderly. The injured totaled at least 2,000 people, tallied from those treated in Fallujah medical centers alone. While no one counted the number of Fallujah' victims, the dead and wounded were taken to Baghdad and Ramadi hospitals or other nearby cities.

U.S. forces did not report the number of dead or wounded in Fallujah. The authorities in Fallujah did not formally announce the casualty figures for fear from the American public and government reaction. The health authorities in the city indicated statistics that more than 731 civilians were killed and 2,847 others wounded. 25% of the victims were women and children, with the failure to extend this figure to the victims who were taken to hospitals out Fallujah [17].

From the U.S. side, Lt Col Brennan Byrne tried to underestimated the enormity of civilian casualties in Fallujah, saying, "what I think you will find 95% of those in the military age males to participate in the fighting" [302]. The U.S. authorities estimated the deaths of 600 people from Fallujah on 13 April 2004 with 39 soldiers or Marines killed [22]. British sources pointed to the deaths of more than 1,000 civilians from the people of Fallujah because of the use of repressive tactics of the Americans, *Heavy Handed*, as described by the British minister [238]. The Office of the U.N. for the Coordination of Humanitarian Affairs estimated the number of unarmed civilian deaths reached 500 victims until the day of 15 April 2004, without mention to how many of the wounded who were being treated in hospitals Baghdad and some of them died as a result of their injuries and were not counted [483].

The process of preventing people from passing on the two bridges over the Euphrates River prevented them reaching the hospital and targeting of health centers inside the city in order to prevent any civilian from getting the medical assistance. These actions can be considered as war crimes according to the Geneva Conventions. It also resulted in the destruction of thousands of homes forcing thousands of civilians to live in school buildings and incomplete structures. They became internal refugees. The most shocking concern was preventing access to the cemetery outside the city in order to bury the dead in Fallujah which prompting residents to convert the stadium of football in the center city to a new cemetery and to remain a witness for this massacre

British journalist Naomi Klein pointed out that the information of the loss of hundreds of victims and dead civilians came from three different sources as [474]:

1. Medical doctors, *USA TODAY* newspaper noted in its issue on 11 April of the same year, the statistics and the names of the civilian victims who were killed in the first battle had been collected from four health centers in addition to the general hospital in Fallujah.

2. Reporters of Arab channels. Doctors released the death statistics for both Al-Jazeera and Al-Arabiya have put a human face on these statistics, with the presence of many photographers in Fallujah. Both TVs networks worked on broadcast footage of women, maimed children and wounded to all parts of Iraq and the Arab-speaking world to spread to the international media.

3. Clergy. Reports from journalists and doctors about killing hundreds of civilians arrived at the prominent clerics in Iraq. Many of clerics gave fiery speeches condemning the attack and turned worshipers against U.S. forces, which sparked the uprising that forced U.S. troops to withdraw.

American authorities denied the killing of hundreds of civilians during the siege and battles in April 2004 and drew criticism of the sources of these reports. One of the U.S. officers told the *New York Times* in November 2004, where he described the Fallujah General Hospital "center of propaganda". But the strongest words against the Arab television networks was by Donald Rumsfeld when he asked about the Al-Jazeera reports on the Arab channel about the hundreds of civilians killed in Fallujah, he replied that "what the Al-Jazeera is the work of a vicious, inaccurate and inexcusable". The media in the world picked up the scenes from video of one of those massacres when the U.S. F-16 aircraft bombed civilian families. Between 25-30 people from different ages were waving a white flag and trying to get out of the city. Because of this video, the U.S. Pentagon announced opening an investigation but never announced the results [510]. U.S. bombers, such as the giant C-130 were used extensively in the bombing of Fallujah, in addition to the F-15 - and helicopters.

6.12. Crime of using white phosphorus weapons

The use of white phosphorus, as one of the weapons in this battle, was a crime not formally acknowledged by the Marines in the second massacre; however the evidence of its use is irrefutable. Twice evidence appeared of its use, which did not allow for any doubt about the crime of using white phosphorus as a weapon against the people in the first battle of Fallujah, as follow:

• The first evidence was exposed by the U.S. war correspondent, Darrin Mortenson, an U.S. war photographer Hayne Palmour while covering what happened during the battle in their article dated 11 April 2004 [16]. Those journalists publish a statement from Corporal Nicholas Bogert, aged 22 and living in New York, a weapons mortar team leader. He had ordered his soldiers to fire mortar shells containing a mixture of white phosphorus against the city on Friday and Saturday in what is known as the *Shake and Bake* process. This means they are using these types of shells in parallel to be like the principle of bread-making. The white phosphorus shells are working on a bottleneck of fighters to push them out of their bunkers and then come the role of intense missile blasts to kill them. This Corporal admitted he did not know the goal that hit, what type or the size of the losses caused by this strategy, according to what was said by journalists in their article [16]. The journalist added, "shelling continued repeatedly and sent a combination of caustic white phosphorus and highly explosive materials toward a group of buildings that barricaded the rebels throughout the week".

In response to a question by an e-mail message of the British newspaper *The Independent*, American military correspondent confirmed the nature of the fighting that took place in his article above, saying, "that white phosphorus shells were used as firepower against a palm grove and concrete buildings were used as cover for Iraqi snipers who fired heavy machine guns at American helicopters" [306,303].

• The second evidence was pictures of civilian casualties, their bodies terribly burned. The images were shown by doctors from the Fallujah' hospital in the documentary film by Japanese journalist Toshikuni Doi, *Fallujah, April 2004* [17].

In contrast to this fact, the U.S. General Richard B. Myers told more mockingly when he said, "that this was no more so than humanitarian operations ... and this applies to operations in Fallujah" (Radio BBC April 15, 2004).

At the end of the first battle of Fallujah, 30 April, a U.S. Navy convoy of soldiers faced an ambush from an IED blast in the Anbar province, killing two Navy soldiers, Jason B. Dwelley and Christopher M. Dickerson [240]. On 2 May, five more soldiers were killed, Michael Anderson, Trace Dossett, Ronald Ginther, Robert Jenkins and Scott McHugh, and all of them were from the 1st Marine Expeditionary Force [24].

Marines (1st Marine Division) that committed the first Fallujah massacre (which was named Operation Vigilant Resolve) in the month of April 2004 were led by Maj. Gen. James N. Mattis. He is the same that played a role in the cease-fire negotiations during the first battle. Then he helps the preparation for military operations in the second massacre (November 2004) which it called by the US military later as Phantom Fury Operation. This General admitted later in a television interview with CNN network about his mentality that he was led during his service in Afghanistan and Iraq when he said (in fact, was very enjoyable fight them, as you know. It's been hell, "he added," but it's fun to launch fire on some people. I love the fight !!!) [24].

The US military studies admitted that pushing of Marines inside Fallujah have a lack (violation) of the US commitment guidelines that must be followed in fighting guide in urban warfare manual which so-called military name (MCWP 3-35.3) [23]. These principles calling to isolate any cities surrounding the city are storming to prevent any assistance or support from other regions. Ignore these instructions may be due to vanity and excessive confidence in victory inevitable for Marines which equipped and supported with the modern weapons under the need for a rapid response in order to punish the city for the killing four mercenaries of Blackwater. Despite this evidence points to the need to use a military band for every area containing one hundred thousand people (and the band usually consists of three battalions of infantry units with attribution) [30]. Since the Fallujah contain three hundred thousand people, it means the need to use 3 military bands in the attack, while the force that used in the first battle was only two battalions of the army and force fighting was not enough, according to their opinion !!. These documents we see that the occupation

[105]

forces were considered all the people of Fallujah as an enemy. This is not surprising, but interesting of pride that the military is known that the 1000-1500 fighters can defend the city containing 100,000 inhabitants [119], but Fallujah fighters did not exceed 600 fighters at the latest end in a city of 300,000 people .

6. 13. U.S. Analysis of the Defeat' Reasons

The US military intelligence report appeared with the documents revealed by WikiLeaks site and had been issued by the National Ground Intelligence Center NGIC (1) and report number (SECRET // NOFORN // 20310306). It's admitted and contains a lot of facts that tried to hide by the occupation. Document has revealed the characters of the people, who fought the Marines in the first battle of Fallujah, saying:

1. The groups that fights them were dispersed and uncorrelated with each other and rely on hit-and-run in the attacks.

2. The groups of fighters were bound together by a kind of social and tribal relations and other natural ties between the people of any region or city in Iraq, and this confirmed by explained the strong social structure and knit between tribes and regions all of Fallujah.

3. The report acknowledged that these groups fought were not linked by a unified command before the battle but only small groups.

4. The report pointed to the escape of a large proportion of the Iraqi National Guard, trained by the Americans because they refused to fight against their countrymen. This was confirmed also by other American Military Studies [181].

The report attempted to justify striking mosques, schools, and the rest of the services building under the pretext used by the fighters. But everyone knows the place of worship in uniting the people in front of the occupation. If we assume that the Iraqis are occupying America for Americans gathered in churches to urge the American people to fight the Iraqis. Hollywood movies always show US civilians to resort to the churches in the event of a hurricane or an emergency hits the towns, so how about if it was an occupation?? From another side, if these places were used as hospitals for the wounded people, because the US Marines occupied the only hospital of the city and indeed outside the city to prevent any civilian from accessing it as a form of collective punishment of civilians. But the most unusual is intelligence Marines statement that they found evidence indicating the nature of the fighters who have been fighting in Fallujah through finding the gripping of the former military during their inspection of the houses of some civilians on the outskirts of the city, or the possibility of finding images of the former Iraqi president's hanging in one of the houses, making them believe these families that is Baathists or military who are fighting them now!!! [300].

The report also recognized that the battle was a political and media battle with going of Marines as to the battle as egotistical pre-victory. Marines forgot that they are occupiers and the people of the city are the people of the land and fiercely defend their land and their lives and their freedom. The lyrics report were explicit signs of how the loss of political and media battle because of the media coverage (for example, the announcement by Al-Jazeera television in the deaths of 600 civilians by US troops, reinforced its news pictures of the victims of the martyrs and the wounded spread rapidly around the world). Like this news helped in losing media war at the beginning of this battle [63].

That is why the experts recognize that after 2006, the Battle of VIGILANT RESOLVE in Fallujah was the biggest example of the loss of the media during the war [723]. Thomas P. Odom a military analyst recognized in 2006 that the press operations are an important part within the IT operations for the US military. Press relations is an important fighting wars tool to help decision-operational, and he adds that they are in the year 2006 saw the press is part of the battlefield because the war in the twenty-first century is the fight in four dimensions, and this is what must be understood and train during the fighting by both senior leaders and field commanders and soldiers. CPT David Connolly from Command and General Staff College, Center for Army Tactics said that the press in the battlefield is one of the non-lethal fire or nonkinetic targeting that affect the completion of the task [184].

As stated in previous report [1], about the IT operations of the enemy (they mean here the statements and facts that were issued from residents, doctors and representatives of the city through the press and TV channels, which showed the facts that it was not expected by Americans to appearance so quickly, both results of murder and destruction or insistence of residents to defend their city). The report said that the fragility of the political situation, which ordered a halt to military operations by imposing (and here may not entirely agree with this point). When launched military operations and announced three members of the Governing Council withdrew from the board and threatened to withdraw also of other five of Council [87], but the US did not care much. The political process was set up under their approval and cares which still in its infancy, and it is easy to change the faces outs. But the main problem in my opinion were two things, the first being the start of the popular uprising in different parts of Iraq, and popular support and international political and media who put Fallujah as a symbol of resistance in newspapers and magazines titles. That is why Americans became the in the aggressor and occupied' position if they continue in the battle against those who defend themselves and US' confessed that the fighters were defending against comprehensive punishment' crime of Fallujah. Therefore was not surprising that recognize that May of 2004 was the worst on their forces and their security situation [87]. US forces have been committed a war crime through considering all the inhabitants of Fallujah as fighters and all them must be punished and to prevent male in the age of fighting from leaving the city [196]. A lot of children and women stayed in the city, as much as the British Observer reporter estimated the number of remaining citizens in the city between 30000-50000 civilians, mostly women and children [197].

They've confessed in the same report [1], as Rumsfeld acknowledged in his memoirs too [13] that Mehdi Army led by Muqtada al-Sadr and groups (they called them Sunni) in different parts of Baghdad and in Anbar initiated to fighting them after the outbreak of the first battle of Fallujah. And most honest what was Rumsfeld' recognition that Paul Bremer feared that the continuation of military operations in Fallujah would lead to uprisings will be deployed in Iraq [13].

Followers of Sadr's movement were driving another uprising in Najaf, Karbala and Kut cities in addition to Sadr City after the occupation forces in several steps, including on 28 March, closing the newspaper Hawza which follow to Sadrists by Paul Bremer direct orders, under the pretext of encouraging violence. Besides the arrest to military official of the Sadrist movement Mustafa Yacoubi Mustafa al-Yacoubi for the murder of Ayatollah Abdul Majid al-Khoei in May 2003 in Najaf, with the issuance of an arrest warrant against Mr. Muqtada al-Sadr under the same charge [230]. Members of the Governing Council during a meeting with Bremer referred to exit comprehensive demonstrations in parts of Iraq against this military operation. All these reasons are why the Ambassador Paul Bremer instructs the US commander in Iraq, Gen. John Abizaid to stop the fire by US forces on 9 April 2004 with the continuation of the siege on the city for three weeks of fighting then stopped officially on 30 April after reaching understandings that resulted in the formation of the Fallujah Brigade [19]. While Rumsfeld that refers to President Bush on 10 April has not issued a decision to stop operations or its continuation but left it under appreciated brass officers on the battlefield, but he returned to admit that it was a defeat, prompting even the British allies that asking to halt military operations because of the terrible pictures which was carried by satellite from the shelling of hospitals and mosques, and the emergence of the painful scenes of civilians dead and wounded them to the bodies [13].

NGIC report [1] estimated of Fallujah's population as 285,000 people, then they point in the same report they allowed more than sixty thousand to go out the city without reference to the fate of 225,000 a number of the rest of the civilian population!! Also, it's claimed the destruction of 75 building including two mosques during 150 sorties in spite of their recognition of the same report that the air strikes were 1,000 times!!! For your information, it has not been an official estimate of the damage assessment in order to compensate victims. It is known that US forces did not allow the departure of children, women and elderly men as claimed the report. Evidenced by the arrival of many of them to health centers are dead or wounded or shocked by the horror of gunshot or explosions of missiles falling on them while trying to get out of the city.

The report also referred that the decision of the massacre, destruction and punishment had been issued by the Minister of Defense Rumsfeld and former Gen. Abu Zeid and the US Civil Governor Paul Bremer. While the US commander Ricardo Sanchez diary refers to a direct order from US President George W. Bush after meeting with his assists such as Colin Powell and Rumsfeld to decide mass punishment policy. This is making all those people internationally wanted for war crimes. While another US military source said that the decision to strike Fallujah on 4 April was issued by Lt. Gen. James T. Conway [52]. The former British Prime Minister Tony Blair added to his series of lies a new one when he defended the massacre saying (that US forces were acting on behalf of the majority of ordinary Iraqis!!!) [107]. Thomas Ricks reporter *Washington Post* summed up the battle by saying (rebels surprised US soldiers by coordinate their attacks, they use of indirect fire, and the enemy effectively maneuvered, and stop, then fighting) [30 and 29 from 10 (371)].

6. 14. Who are the foreign forces participated with Marines in the First Battle?

6. 14. 1. British Role:

During the first battle in Fallujah, US LT Gen. Ricardo S. Sanchez (general commander of the occupation forces (Coalition Joint) from the period June

2003 to June 2004) admitted in the diary book (WISER IN BATTLE, A Soldier's Story) about the role and participation of British officers and other leaders of the coalition forces in the first massacre in Fallujah by subscription in planning after the first days of the battle, saying in chapter twenty on page 389 (in addition to Bremer, members of the coalition countries have been put tremendous pressure on us to stop fighting. In the early days of the attack Fallujah, it became very clear that the US government may do not allow participating in the decision to launch the attack with political leaders of the coalition countries. That is why the anger of the leaders of these countries on this subject. Vice-British General (deputy commander of coalition forces) start taking part in all internal planning, and all the leaders of the coalition forces were full partners in the implementation of the offensive plan. British general three-starlets and his member in the staff of CJTF-7 has been involved in all stages of planning and send our intentions to London on a daily basis. The constantly, his government has expressed concern about the planned attack by us, and I'm sure that the current discussions have taken place between the White House and 10 Downing Street. London thought that we are very far from achieving our goals because of us using heavy-handed tactics. But President Bush still gives it an attack [36]. Here Ricardo Sanchez confirms in his memoirs that the international pressure by America's allies in coalition to halt the military operation against Fallujah has revealed that the US government's decision was individually and without any consultation with these countries. And that it is the start engages assistant British general in all internal planning pertaining to the operation in Fallujah, which led to stop the attack because of the difference opinion between them [36].

6.14.2. Polish Role

According to US military sources, it has subscribed of a new US special force (Marine Corps Special Operations Command Detachment One) in assigning Marines in Fallujah operation [21]. This force after being frozen previously, it has been activated again on 19 June 2003 after it was suspended operations in 2006. This force was led by Col. Robert J. Coates as he was served as commander of First Force Reconnaissance Company [20]. It was to strengthen the work of this American force by providing with Polish special force called Operational Mobile Response Group which known in Polish "Grupa Reagowania Operacyjno Mobilnego" in order to chase resistance groups initiated arise against the occupation in Anbar province and the start of the siege and attack the Marines on Fallujah [19]. This is joint forces turned its work after 28 May 2004 only in order to protect the important politicians in the

Interim Governing Council. This American evidence on the involvement of Polish troops in military operations in Fallujah and its outskirts. It will put Poland among those involved in war crimes that took place in the first Fallujah battle and requires from the European judicial investigation for violating the European Convention on Human Rights.

6. 15. The lessons learned from the first battle

Despite the US decision to punish the city as a collective and comprehensive punishment came from one party at the beginning of the conflict, and this led to problems occurred between the Iraqi Governing Council (IGC) and the occupation authority (CPA). The council felt that he did not report the decisions belong to Fallujah. Particularly with regard to the attempts failed to use the new Iraqi forces to control of Fallujah. Except commandos battalion 36 that stayed fighting, while the two military battalions 505 and 506 of Iraqi Civil Defense Corps (ICDC) refused to fight in Fallujah because link family relations or friendship with the families of Fallujah. In addition, the second battalion of the First Brigade was ambushed during the month of March in while traveling from Taji area of Baghdad to Fallujah. Sadrist militias in the Ameel zone fired them to prevent them from going to Fallujah, the battalion refused to continue after the ambush, while some of the soldiers who had joined the side of Fallujah fighters [230].

The Facts of Fallujah' victory can be seen from US official's statements. Deputy of US forces commander in Iraq and Deputy of Sanchez, Brigadier General Mark Kimmitt had promised a crushing response to the killing of Blackwater security contractors saying (we will pacify this city), while he returned after failing to enter the city and their request to negotiate, saying (to stop hostilities and to allow the political process and discussion can go ahead). While US President George W. Bush admitted on Sunday, 11 April that the week's events were the tough, and it is difficult to know whether the worst clashes had ended [302]. Rumsfeld admitted in his memoirs that his interest after the killing of the Blackwater mercenaries in Fallujah not only capture whom wanted, but to send a message across the country that any person who participates in acts of resistance will face the might of the US military [13]. US leadership planned the massacre as punishment for the purpose of comprehensive frighten the other cities, but Rumsfeld returned to admit that the first battle and its name were not assertive and no solution as been named. The siege of Fallujah and hit random decision became the beginning of the first Iraqi popular uprising against the occupation and become an example of resistance in the Middle

East against the evil represented by the occupation itself [105]. Therefore, the secretary-general of the Arab League Amr Moussa saying (the recent fighting in Fallujah, it is unacceptable and very dangerous) [302].

US General Assessment Office in its report to the US Congress (GAO, 2006) admitted that a series of attacks against the occupation forces (Alliance) has initiated spread since April 2004 in the western, central and southern areas of Iraq. Local Sunni fighters attacked occupation forces in Fallujah, Baghdad, Ramadi, Samarra, and Tikrit, while they were attacked by the Sadrist fighters starting from Baghdad and Basra in the south too. The report also adds that the Iraqi forces (trained by the US have been battling with the US) often were helping Iraqi militants [118]. In conjunction with the siege of Fallujah and military action against it, there were fierce battles also taking place at Abu Ghraib, and there was dropping US helicopter (AH-64 Apache) and killing two pilots. Iraqi battalion also refused to go to Fallujah because its members did not sign up to fight Iraqis, which means refusing to fight against their countrymen [302]. For your information, this new Iraqi forces were under the full control of the US side in terms of preparation, training and appointment of leaders or change them or directing them even after the second battle of Fallujah [230], which means not following any official Iraqi side.

Uprisings starting in Sunni and Shi'ite areas were a defeat for new politicians who tried to gain popularity bases on a sectarian basis. The first battle of Fallujah revealed the fact that all Iraqi political and military actors are merely advisory bodies and take orders from the temporary occupation authority (CPA) [230].

This popular cohesion between the various sects of the Iraqi people in support of Fallujah was not welcome even to some international sides that they want to increase sedition among Iraqis to push far the occupation scenario from their country. For this many international actors sought to recruit gangs publishing mesmerized sectarian and hit national unity and under the knowledge of the occupation. On the other hand, attempts for media politicization of reports occupation was initiated after the first battle by naming recipe of a 'insurgency' or 'unrest' on the resistance movements in the Sunni areas especially in Fallujah, while referring to the status of the 'uprisings' on the resistance movement led by the Sadrists [87,13]. Which confirms the beginning of the occupation in sectarian segregation option across begins teams clog theory and then practices the Salvadoran example of death squads in Iraq. Sectarian strife is still the most dangerous threat against Iraqis, and this explains why the continuation of daily bombings and assassinations (see Chapter XI).

Although the most people considered the result was victory on the occupation by the efforts of all rose up against the crime of mass punishment, but the fact it was a massacre and a crime against humanity as first class which led to loss the lives of more than 700 killed and more than 2,500 wounded, most of whom were civilians [17]. While British minister admitted that it left more than 1,000 victims among civilians. Paul Bremer said the day after the men Blackwater four killed (The events of yesterday in Fallujah is a shining example of the conflict between human dignity and barbarism), but after this battle of Fallujah, the whole world has known far is the one who defends the dignity and who came with barbarism agenda.

CHAPTER 7

Political Crime Prevented Peace & Caused A Second War Crime In Fallujah

7. 1. Fallujah Responds after the First Battle

During the cease-fire agreement following the first battle between the Fallujah defenders and US forces, the Mujahideen Shura Council was formed in the city. This advisory council, including groups that fought the Marines during the first battle, gathered as the people of Fallujah, to respond to the collective punishment on the city imposed by the furious Marines. This was confirmed by U.S. military intelligence after the battle. [1] According to the Center for American Studies, Fallujah during the summer and Autumn of 2004 became a symbol of resistance and embarrassment for the new Iraqi interim government (IIG), which was formed in June when its forces seemed powerless to subdue the city. [62]

After the withdrawal of US troops to outside Fallujah, the personnel of the Fallujah Brigade forces were located both on the outskirts as well as inside the City. The relentless U.S. aerial bombardment of Fallujah continued without a stop. Gen. Richard B. Myers, Commander of the Joint Chiefs of Staff, announced that AC-130 aircraft and fixed wing aircraft would continue to attack specific targets in the city. He claimed that these attacks killed many fighters [52]. The US air raids on the city killed many civilians [193].

The commander of the Marines that attacked Fallujah in November 2004 again justified what happened under the pretext that the cease-fire agreement, after the first battle in Fallujah broke down with the delivery of heavy weapons to the Fallujah fighters. The US also continued to investigate the killing of four Americans contractors on 31 March 2004 [232]. Two questions stand out here, would the occupier respect his agreements to stop the attacks? The facts militated against this. The U.S. would not allow the United Nations into Fallujah as an observer in any agreement. It also demanded an investigation into the killing of the Blackwater contractors without taking up the many civilian victims killed in the battle of Fallujah in an orgy of mass punishment!

In May 2004, President George W. Bush ordered a Presidential National Security Directive stating that after the transfer of sovereignty to the Iraqi government, the U.S. Department of Defense (DoD) would be responsible for U.S. activity in Iraq. This applied to security and activities related to military operations; it established the Central Command (CENTCOM), as manager of all U.S. government activities to organize, equip and train Iraqi security forces. By the Summer of 2004, plans and strategies for the work of the multinational forces in cooperation with the U.S. embassy in Baghdad had been developed. A new plan was issued to transition joint security responsibility to the U.S. and Iraqi security forces. [118] On May 10, the first joint patrol of U.S. troops, Iraqi Civil Defense Corp soldiers and the Fallujah police entered Fallujah, arriving at the City Center peacefully without any interference. Master Sgt. Arthur Trader Jr told the Marine's reporter: "Everyone has the impression that we will have a battle because they did not purge the city." He added, "We did not have a surprise engagement with the enemy because the Iraqi army was the only one in the city a short time ago." It should be noted that only ten vehicles from U.S. forces had entered the city as part of the joint patrol while the other elements of the U.S. battalion remained outside of the gates where one entered Fallujah. According to the statement of Maj. Andrew J. Petrucci, Executive Officer of the third battalion, writing for the same newspaper to inform that, "Our goal is to show interoperability between the coalition and Fallujah Brigade Forces" and "to show in front of the citizens of Fallujah, that the banner can provide a safe environment for both citizens and coalition forces" [299]. The first joint patrol parade ended with their expulsion by civilians with hiking civilian boots in the face of the troops leaving the city to express the disapproval of residents to the crimes committed by the occupation forces during the first battle. The Commander of the 1st Marine Division, General Maj. Gen. James N. Mattis, met with the Iraqi commander of the Fallujah Brigade, Gen. Mohammed Latif. Mathis commented that the meeting was a first step to developing relations for peace and redevelopment of areas affected by the battle, in all parts of the city. Mathis added that, "we have synthesized a good history because it did not turn into a battle - we did not come here to fight, we need to continue to build the capacity of a single day of peace, and re-build a house here or repair damage there and shake hands with the Iraqis" [299].

7. 2. Preparations for the Second Battle of Fallujah

There were some major changes in the organization of troops under U.S. control. In July 2004, General George Casey was appointed General Commander of the so-called Multi-National Forces (MNF-I). Many would have guessed that Lieutenant General Ricardo Sanchez, commander of the force Combined Joint Task Force 7 (CJTF-7) during and after the initial phase of the military operations of the occupation in Iraq would have been chosen instead. Lieutenant General Thomas Metz became an assistant to Gen. Casey. Both had worked under the command of Gen. Abizaid when he was the commander of the U.S. Central Command (CENTCOM) in Tampa, Florida. At this moment, allied forces in the coalition became known as the Multinational Forces in Iraq.

This formalization of the coalition was in preparation for an anticipated national uprising or armed resistance. The alleged semi-international nature of these forces was to provide cover and protection from accountability for ignoring the new UN Security Council resolutions.

The U.S. command re-arranged units that had been scattered because of the first popular revolution against the occupation. They sought excuses to bomb Fallujah from time to time under the pretext of violation of the ceasefire agreement. Instead of strengthening the capacity of the people to administer their city, Marines had admitted that they exploited the Fallujah Brigade as a port to collect intelligence information to support tactics for future operations in Fallujah. It became clear that the U.S. planned to attack the City again. They tried to distort the image of the Fallujah Brigade, falsely asserting that it was part of the former Iraqi army. U.S. commander Colonel Robert J. Coates acknowledged a plan to exploit division among the fighters in the City and to help a new Iraqi unit to fight them [19]. During this period, the Americans deployed some members of the Iraqi intelligence sources to gather information on the Fallujah fighters. These members were under the command of Colonel Ron Makuta [193]. A ground control officer who planned air attacks during battles, Lt. Col. Greg Harbin admitted that the most important lesson of Fallujah was the necessity of pre-planning to reduce his troops casualties. He explained that we must know alleys and streets better than they do [52].

The leaders of the occupation forces accompanied the preparation with justifications for another attack. Gen. John P. Abizaid declared that there are things we will not tolerate, such as the presence of foreign fighters in Fallujah [52]. This was even contradicted in their own reports that admitted that they fought in the first battle with people from Fallujah [1,36]. The obvious contradiction was the focus on potential Arab fighters in Fallujah as the problem, while they considered the presence of foreign occupation forces, including Iranian militia and intelligence, as very reasonable and acceptable. They made such hollow excuses while preparing for a criminal act far more extensive than the range of Fallujah and Najaf (see the Salvadoran option chapter).

The former Iraqi intelligence service director during this period, Gen. Mohammed Abdullah al-Shawani, said that the coalition forces "occupation" and the Iraqi government had not given an adequate opportunity to the Fallujah Brigade troops to prove themselves. He added that the Fallujah Brigade succeeded in securing the city for five months without firing a shot, there was not a single killing in Fallujah, and not a single bullet fired against the occupying American forces. This situation reflected the agenda of the Iraqi government, as the Iranians were helping the continuing conflict in Anbar [230].

Mowafak al-Rubai was appointed by Bremer as an advisor for national security. He had admitted that the withdrawal of Marines from Fallujah after the first battle and the formation of the Fallujah Brigade, which took over responsibility for security in the city, had been a major turning point in the war for many reasons:

1. It manifested the ability of local fighters to repel attacks of the occupation forces.

2. It gave more credibility to the Fallujah Brigade, comprising former members of the Iraq Army, in maintaining security in the City.

3. It caused Fallujah to become a symbol of resistance in much of the Arab world [230].

The widening circle of armed resistance and popular rejection of the presence of invaders pushed the occupation to form an unelected and transitional Iraqi interim government, headed by Iyad Allawi. The security and military files stayed in the occupying forces' hands. This government did not have the support of parties opposed to the presence of the occupiers. The Shiaa side, like the Sadrist movement and its leader Muqtada al-Sadr, announced their opposition to the government and called upon his followers on August 2004 to join a popular revolution. The arrival of the Marines mechanized quick reaction force in Najaf city which spurred clashes on August 2. Although Sadr had called for a cease-fire, as was the case after the first battle of Fallujah, the governor of Najaf, Adnan Alzyreva, rejected the al-Sadr appeal. Ultimately, force of hand drove Sadr's Mahdi Army from Najaf city and its huge cemetery. Then a round of peace negotiations initiated between the Deputy Commanding General, Marine Corps Brigadier Dennis J. Hejlik, and representatives of the Iraqi interim government on the one hand, with the Mahdi Army officials, on the other hand. Despite this, the fighting continued, and they attacked the house of Sadir to get many documents and information about his involvement in criminal activities, according to Colonel John R. Ballard. Then hostilities ceased temporarily by Marines commander General Metz on August 13. However, battles began to break out strongly on August 26 with the announcement of the Commander in Chief of the Marines to stop operations to give another chance for peaceful dialogue between Iraqi politicians and officials of the Mahdi Army. This dialogue ended with the delivery of management of shrine Imam Ali Ibn Abi Talib to the Sistani's office by Muqtada himself to end the battle of Najaf with 1,500 killed from Mehdi Army fighters [193].

The battle of Najaf was noticeably similar to the hit-and-run between the two sides both militarily and politically. Periods of intermittent fighting were accompanied by leaving the door open for Iraqi peace negotiations to stop the fight. Shiite parties rivalling the Sadrist movement, helped occupation forces reduce popular support for the Sadrist uprising as they fought against it. The fundamental question here is, why the government of Iyad Allawi, which claims to reject secularism and sectarianism, did not take the same policy with the City of Fallujah, rather than storming aggressively and destructively, burning everything and everybody, thereby preventing any chance of peace? The government of Iyad Allawi and the role played by Mowaffak Rubaie exposed sectarian duplicity in their dealings. They reached an agreement with the Mahdi Army militia to disarm and to leave Najaf city, and not to return to the city as an armed militia. *While turning the issue of the order of the arrest of Muqtada al-Sadr for the murder of Ayatollah Khoei in the Iraqi courts and giving him enough time there, freezing the case.* Afterwards, Iyad Allawi met with the Sadrist clerics in Sadr City and they agreed to sell their weapons, even the old ones, to the government for $12 million USD [230]. One delegation of the Sadrist movement, headed by Sheikh Fadel, visited Fallujah after the first battle and before the battle of Najaf. They asked for help by giving more medical equipment. Fallujah's local officials agreed to provide them with what they needed. When one man asked Sheikh Fadel about why they sold their weapons with Iraq still being occupied, Sheikh Fadel replied, the money paid for its old weapons had been used to buy new weapons from Iran!

In the meantime, U.S. B-52 flights increased over time in the night-time bombardments of Fallujah. This was under the pretext of chasing the fighters. The use of cluster weapon bombardment returned in some areas, along with 500 kilograms bombs, which turned three neighbouring houses, in the engineers area, into a large crater. All three families were killed. In this time of increasing raids, British newspapers justified the massive air strikes in the middle of October (2004) as revenge for the killing of British hostage Ken Bigley, while they conveniently ignored the presence of a lot of innocent civilian victims under this bombardment, and failed to mention the number of deaths it caused [108].

Air strikes were targeted to weaken the defences of the City that challenged the occupation led by United States at every turn. "Fallujah is very important", according to retired Greg Newbold of the Marines [778]. On September 8, 2004, an armed group kidnapped four people from an Italian-Iraqi group working for a humanitarian organization and a group opposing the war on Iraq. A Bridge To Un Ponte Per. Three women and one man, Simona Torretta, Simona Pari, Mahnouz Bassam, and Raad Ali Abdul Azziz were kidnapped in the center of the City. The details incriminate those attacking Fallujah. The organization's headquarters, surrounded by concrete blocks, was attack by about twenty armed men according to a Newsweek newspaper report. Fifteen minutes after the kidnapping, a U.S. convoy of Humvees passed near Headquarters. The Iraqi Ministry of the Interior acknowledged that the kidnappers wore military uniforms and body armor! Especially relevant is that this humanitarian organization had a significant support role during the first battle in Fallujah. After the Najaf siege that preceded the second battle in Fallujah, one day before the abduction, *Torretta and Barry* told Iraqi colleagues that they intended to do a great humanitarian mission despite the dangerous situation in Fallujah, including the danger to witnesses of the coalition military activities. [476]

7.3. The Failure of Negotiations with the Allawi' Government

The military actions in Fallujah created a sense of threat that prompted negotiation. The negotiations initiated between the Allawi interim government represented by the Defense Minister Mr. Hazem Shaalan, while the Fallujah delegation included Sheikh Khaled Hamoud Jumaili (Chairman) and representatives of Fallujah like Dr. Rafie Hiaad al-Issawi and the Fallujah Brigade Commander. Negotiations continued nearly two months and ended with a peace agreement. Its most prominent points were to withdraw heavy weapons from the city, the people of Fallujah vowed to withdraw dozens of Arab fighters who were stationed on the outskirts of the city after the first battle. Mr. Shaalan asked for 3 days before signing the agreement for submission to the Council of Ministers. But he invited the head of Fallujah delegation to meet after two days just before the requested deadline. Mr. Shaalan reported that Sheikh Khalid al-Jumaili was unable to sign the agreement because of the refusal on the part of the US, and that the people of Fallujah should put pressure on the Americans to stop the next military action. These facts contradict Iyad Allawi's contention reported in a US military bulletin alleging that he tried to take all means to negotiate until the very last minute. [230]

Prime Minister of the Transitional Government Iyad Allawi disclosed during a press conference that he had asked the people of Fallujah to hand over or surrender Zarqawi, and this condition was not presented during the negotiations which led to making it fail. This contention made despite that Allawi knew the Americans had failed to apprehend him. Nevertheless, he requested it from the people of Fallujah! One wonders why this condition was not raise during the negotiations, but later used to account for the failure of negotiations. At the same time, the head of the Fallujah negotiating team arrested for a few days in a bid to stop his activities and those of the movements that were trying to find a peaceful outlet to spare the city and civilians against any military action. At this moment, the Fallujah Brigade was maintaining security inside Fallujah with the help of the police, and had not failed in its mission as falsely alleged by the US and British authorities. [231] In short, it made clear that the coalition intended to hit the City again.

An interview with a Fallujah negotiator familiar with the facts suggests two contradictory stories had been float. The first alleged that the Allawi government wanted to reach a peaceful agreement to avoid the destruction of the city and the resultant suffering of the people as happened in the first fight. While the second story, according to Ricardo Sanchez' Memoir, [36] was that the US command saw negotiations as merely a ploy to gain time to prepare another attack on the City with no genuine intention to reach an agreement. Sadly, the American mentality was only to avoid the many consequences that led to the failure of the first military operation in April 2004.

7. 4. Request for UN Mediation

After the release of the head of the Fallujah negotiating delegation, Sheikh Khaled al-Jumaili, who had been arrest by the Marines, I went with two journalists in order to meet him and find out what the facts were. Sheikh Jumaili himself confirmed for us what we described above, about what happened during the negotiations. In response to this intractable situation, we came up with the idea of seeking United Nations political intervention to head off the next impending tragedy. I contacted the Human Rights Office of the UN mission in Iraq (UNAMI) to ask for help in holding a meeting between a Fallujah spokesman and the representative of the Secretary-General of the United Nations in Iraq, Mr. Ashraf Qazi. The meeting was arrang and I took the Fallujah negotiating delegation headed by Sheikh Khaled Jumili, also including Rafie al-Issawi, the Fallujah brigade commander and some other notables. The Chief of Staff of the Human Rights Office in UNAMI Mr. Elio Tmburi also participated. The Fallujah delegation initiated by describing developments in the negotiations with the Iraqi government, and how they had reached a peace agreement that had been reject by the Americans. On this basis, the Fallujah representation appealed to the Secretary General of the United Nations Kofi Annan to intervene, and seek to stop the upcoming military operation, and to allow for a more peaceful dialogue under the auspices of the United Nations.

Mr. Qazi responded that he would do all he could to prevent more bloodshed as a Muslim as well as acting in his role as a representative of UN. He promised to send an urgent letter on the same day to the Secretary-General of the United Nations, Kofi Annan. True to his word, he sent an open letter published at the time throughout the media. A letter also addressed to both President Bush and British PM Tony Blair as well as to the Iraqi Prime Minister Iyad Allawi asking them to forestall the next military action and to protect civilians from more bloodshed and suffering, and to provide an opportunity for peaceful dialogue under the auspices of the United Nations. As we left the meeting, one of the delegation members who was a minister in the Maliki government turned to me, saying now that we have met with your friend, let us see if he can do something. I answered that whatever the result, this is the proper approach and we should persist in using all the ways and means of international support to give the peace dialogue a chance to succeed. Now it is evident that the Fallujah delegation's efforts did not go to waste because it provided evidence of our intention for a peaceful solution that prevented by the occupying powers, intent to massively punish the City and its inhabitants for their righteous resistance to occupation.

[122]

The three leaders of the occupiers rejected the peaceful solutions offered to pursue military action using all means available. The British Prime Minister lied to the British House of Lords, falsely claiming that the people of Fallujah rejected disarmament, had refused the peace agreement and should be defeat by force. Blairs' lying precipitated the transfer of 5,000 British troops from Basra City to the outskirts of Baghdad and the highways around Fallujah. The plan was to get them involved and to participate in the second massacre that Fallujah faced in November 2004. Blair had warned before the start of the second battle that British troops could face serious reaction if the United States' ended their attempt to seize the insurgent stronghold in Fallujah.[297,238] Thus, commission of a lying crime by a government employee led to an international war crime. (See the paragraph pertaining to British courts in Chapter XII).

Iyad Allawi described the message from Annan as "confused," adding sarcastically that if Mr Annan thought he could prevent Fallujah's insurgents from harm that he was welcome to try.) [101]

7. 5. Exposure of the Intention of Aggression

Before embarking to the storm of Fallujah, the occupation forces attacked the Najaf city that had become the second stronghold of popular resistance to the occupation after Fallujah. According to the divide and conquer policy, the occupation tried to deceive the world that Fallujah is the only city having rebels, while recognizing at the same time they fought fierce battles in Najaf before the attack on Fallujah. [64] What happened was the realization of what we feared. During the period between two battles, American forces under the pretext of pursuing gunmen, inflicted constant bombardment on residential and industrial areas. They dropped huge bombs weighing 500 kg, and sometimes cluster weapons, that I witnessed. The pre-planning of the attack included forcing residents out of Fallujah under the pretext of reducing civilian casualties during the attack. Actually, it meant to prevent the international and local pressure to stop another attack. Americans had learned their lesson and knew the extent of the power of international pressure and resulting responses to negative images of wounded civilians during warfare in cities in the modern era. [193]

Per their strategy for American forces in urban warfare to suppress the popular rejection of their presence, they intended to impose mass punishment on the City and its citizens before the first battle in Fallujah. They realized after failing to win the battle that military success in populated urban areas depends on many factors. The most important is the extent of popular support and willingness to sacrifice their troops.[119] It was evident that the US forces during the period between the two battles carried out US military strategy. [120,119]

US strategy included:

1. Scouts, Special Forces, snipers, and Human Intelligence (HUMINT) agents, to map the terrain in detail and in three dimensions. This mission for identifying positions, equipment and intentions of the enemy, with consideration of the opinion of the people in those areas and the start of psychological operations at this stage to force civilians to flee.

2. Urban areas to be attack must be completely surrounded and isolat to be attacked quickly and strongly.

3. Combined Arms attack along the axis of penetration, to gain a foothold in the city to establish a beachhead for the deployment of troops.

4. Finally, the common units of weapons to enter the city and the systematic removal of the sources of resistance encountered.

This new military strategy is complementary to the strategy followed in Fallujah, based on the developed strategy for the US Marines in the second half of 1990. They elaborated the battlefield view in urban warfare that based on the concept of Three Block War. This includes training based on the attack scenario, and the ability to switch between high and low intensity operations with a joint media, integrated with the concept of the Network Centric Warfare. [235]

The timing of second military operation against Fallujah with all the war crimes that punctuated it was not arbitrary, although the initial plan prepared by General Casey and government of Iyad Allawi had been scheduled later for December 2004. [314] However, US politics pushed the attack to an earlier date. The presidential election in the US in early November 2004 was more important than the timing of the first Iraqi elections under occupation that took place later in January 2005. US President W. Bush sought a victory to renew his presidential term. The price for ensuring his personal victory was the blood of Iraqis. Available evidence confirms that US forces were planning to re-storm Fallujah following the end of the VIGILANT RESOLVE operation and the team responsible for the planning processes was the Regimental Combat Team-1 (RCT-1). [230]

The US insistence on destroying largest city in Anbar province and in imposing the re-tragedy of war in such a large and comprehensive way satisfied two agendas. The first was to rehabilitate the reputation of the US military that had failed to enter Fallujah in the first battle. But was also at work was an Iraqi sectarian politician's desire to undo the national cohesion beginning to spread between the Iraq communities of Sunnis and Shiites. This cohesion threatened the sectarian political divide promoted by Paul Bremer. Therefore, any revelations of the real forces that pushed for the war and prevented a peaceful solution should also reveal who is behind the sectarian killings that begin in 2005, causing the killing and wounding of tens of thousands of Iraqis annually over the years 2005, 2006 and 2007 (UN figures).

The important note that I have found in this period between two battles of Fallujah, is that the policy of occupation in attempting to inspire the national armed resistance worked against the Iraqi people. It intended by the US as cover to justify before their own populace, the legality of the horrendous crimes committed against Iraqis. This policy started by separating Shiite areas, then politicizing it through bargaining, considering previous activities as uprisings, and finally ending its participation in the political process overseen by the occupation. In contrast, Sunni areas were to be as terrorist enclaves, and insurgency branded as the continuation of the Sunni Triangle resistance. This meant to provide a big role to Iran and Syria in this direction by supporting al-Qaeda groups in these areas.

CHAPTER 8

2nd Massacre in Fallujah

7 November 2004

Operation Phantom Fury

8. 1. US Initialization before the battle

Rumsfeld admitted that he was confident after the cease-fire of the first battle in Fallujah that they will come back sooner or later, and they were facing two resistances (insurgent) in spring 2004. The first was in Fallujah, west of Iraq and the other in the south with the Sadrist movement of Muqtada [13]. Rumsfeld returned to confirm at a news conference at the Pentagon with Gen. Richard B. Myers chairman of the Joint Chiefs of Staff (We can't allow that Fallujah remains as center of resistance in Iraq) [106]. So before the attack on Fallujah, they carried out the attack on Najaf because it was easier to have and to give moral impetus to move their troops before the battle to Fallujah. But the work was different because fighting and political solutions were operating at the same time in Najaf. And in order to create strife among Iraqis have called "the uprising" began on clashes with Sadr's movement while prescription rebellion against Resisters Fallujah and regions [105].

The United States brought its finest expertise and equipment for urban warfare to this battle. Jeffrey White, a researcher at the Washington Institute for Near East Policy who worked for the Pentagon's Defense Intelligence Agency for more than 30 years, said "we must win the battle in a few days because if it lasts for two weeks and is broadcast on television worldwide with civilian deaths, the United States will lose the support of the Iraqi interim government and its friends and others allies. Speed is of the essence" White adds. "If we entered into a long-term battle, the government will lose its political will, and the rebels record another victory" He adds, "You can win in the city, but if the global picture is the deaths of women, children, and innocent civilians ... you have a problem in your hands" [778].

[127]

The Fallujah Brigade was firm in its aim to prevent any problems or friction with the Marines, and to avoid the painful memories left by the Marines in Fallujah. The American officer Col. Larry K. Brown from the force of MEF G-3 noted the high discipline to this brigade. He said, "They were doing what they promised. This is the first time that I see Iraqis do anything they promised on time without delay."

The Commander of the Marines in Iraq, Lt. Gen. Ricardo Sanchez, was asked by US President W. Bush about the Fallujah Brigade. He replied, "It seems not good so far, but it's the best option available for this moment" [36]. The advance planning of the Fallujah strike was to end the engagement of the Fallujah Brigade on 12 September 2004, after it emerged that the delay in the storming of the city was to fight with the lowest losses. [19] Iyad Allawi admitted he did some work on the Fallujah Brigade before the start of the second attack to enhance intelligence and participation of Iraqi forces. He appointed an Iraqi commander from Fallujah to lead joint Iraqi forces in the attack. Accompanied by a media campaign, he held meetings with people linked closely with Fallujah fighters [230].

US military operations against Fallujah did not stop as agreed in the ceasefire. US sources admitted that since July 2004 they had collected images captured by aircraft and satellites in order to identify targets before the storming of the city. They even collected the data for all buildings and streets of Fallujah, estimated at 800 buildings. The data was sent to ground and air crews, in addition to planners of air strikes. US military personnel on the ground could then easily request planes to bomb the buildings in the way of their progress in Fallujah [52,67]. Marines completed the planning for the measurements of air control over Fallujah. They defined squares covering Fallujah. These made up the military high-density combat zone in the region (HIDACZ.) It included a diameter area 30 nautical miles (55.56 km) to a height of 30,000 feet. Another five nautical miles around Fallujah was defined to provide rapid reaction in support of aircraft in the area of operations against Fallujah resistance fighters [68].

Aircraft involved in the bombing were from the carrier JOHN F. KENNEDY (CVW-17), based in the Arabian Gulf. They hit the main targets at a rate of 38 missions per day, in conjunction with the US Air Force and aircraft of US Marine Corps. Carrier commander Capt. Dennis Fitzpatrick proudly announced that success in Fallujah was due to the efficiency of the professional bombardment group!! [191]. But he shamelessly forgot that this huge number of aircraft crews, enough to face a regular army of the State, faced instead only the small city of Fallujah!! At the same time there was a military operation against the city of Samarra (125 km away from the capital, Baghdad), which lasted from 1 to 4 October 2004, called Baton Rouge by the Americans. [230].

Fallujah was divided into several longitudinal segments. US troops started the break-in on the northern and southern parts. The process was similar to the storming of Berlin by the Soviet army, when the Marshal Zhukov and Marshall Konev raced to be first to arrive at the Spree river. One of them took the north of Berlin while taking the other took its south. Occupation forces sought to use the same strategy of Soviets, in the massive destruction of the city in order to reduce their losses through a scorched-earth strategy [119].

8.2. Mad attacks of US air forces

US strikes continued for months before the second battle in spite of the weakness of targeting intelligence about targets inside the city [193]. The bombing displaced most of civilian population, who fled for their lives only to become internal refugees. This fact is contrary to the American claim that the Whisper Campaign of leaflets dropped over the city caused residents to get out of town [230]. The leaflets commanded the 300,000 residents of Fallujah to leave the city if they want to avoid war.

Lt. Col. Michael Ramos, first battalion commander of the Marine Corps in Band III said, "This is the Hue City of our generation," referring to an urban battle of 1968. The U.S regained control on the city after four weeks of block-by-block fighting led to the deaths of more than 142 Marines [478].

A scorched-earth strategy was followed before the ground assault on Fallujah. More strikes were made during the months of August and September. On 13 September, the Associated Press reported that at least five air raids had been carried out on Fallujah during the past week under the pretext of killing al-Zarqawi [52]. As usual, he "escaped at the last moment." From the first moments of the attack the occupation and the Allawi government promoted a rumor about the escape of leaders of fighters from Fallujah, led by Abu Musab al-Zarqawi [104]. General George Casey claimed al-Zarqawi escaped from Fallujah on 9 November [303]. He said it to prepare public opinion for the failure to find the leaders of combatants, and justify the occupation's crimes after the massacre.

The important question is, if they knew about the escape of the leaders before and during the offensive, why did they use this enormous destructive power against those who remained in the city, although they were aware of the presence of many civilians? It is known that Special Operations Forces (SOF) has played an important role in intelligence gathering during the months preceding the attack [231].

Ariel bombardment, the scale of destruction, and the civilian casualties reached a peak in October 2004. It drew attention to the use since August and revealed the use of two types of war crimes. The first was use of cluster bombs that are particularly dangerous to children because they explode long after being dropped. The second type is the use of the weaponized AC – 130 aircraft, which has a 155 mm cannon. From the first moments of use of these weapons we were aware that their purpose was not to kill fighters in the city, but a continuation of the policy of shock and awe, which started on the first day of the occupation.

The intense bombardment was designed to terrorize the city's population before and during the attack. More than 200,000 of the population fled [193,100]. A US report recognized there were at least 5,000 civilians stayed in the city during the attack [230]. Another source revealed the escape of 70-90% of the population to seek refuge in neighboring cities [304].

Two days before the start of the attack, the US aircraft destroyed the small Emergency Hospital in the Nazzal neighbourhood. It was turned into rubble with an unknown the number of casualties. As noted by UK BBC Radio, the deliberate destruction of the hospital this clear indicator that the US military wanted to ensure that residents of Fallujah brought to hospitals would be killed or wounded to hospitals in the city. The aim was to hide the number of civilian casualties. The anger of Iraqis in solidarity with Fallujah in first battle was successful in forcing US troops to make a cease-fire decision [101]. Unfortunately, the homicidal mentality was shared among occupation soldiers. It was summed up by 20-year-old Lance Corporal Joseph Bowman on 7 November 2004 in an interview with Associated Press. He said, "I want to go and kill people. Then I can return home. That's all we can do." [100]

On 2 October 2004, the so-called international coalition troops in Iraq of MNC-I (Multinational Corps-Iraq) issued Warning Order 15. It concerned operation "Phantom Fury", assigned to the 31s Marine Expeditionary Unit as a backup strategic force. On 3 October, MNC-I issued "required instructions" about the Preconditions for Operations in Fallujah which set forth the fundamental forces of the attack, and more detailed attack information. On 21 October, the 1st Marine Division released the first order, No. (04-363). It set the time and date of the main attack on 8 November. It was to be preceded by the start of operations twenty-four hours earlier, on 7 November.

A new issuance from MNC-I followed two days later with order No. 891 to confirm and strengthen the role of the interim transitional government in this battle. Before the end of October, a luxury car on a convoy of the 1st Battalion vehicles from 3rd Marines exploded. It had arrived on the outskirts of Fallujah base to join forces preparing to attack. The bombing killed eight marines and wounded many them. It was a sad day for the occupation base near Fallujah [193].

The famous American writer Noam Chomsky described the horror of air attacks on Fallujah. He said the Fallujah attack resembled to a large extent that on Srebrenica (a Serbian city), which was condemned internationally as genocide. The United States did not bring women and children out of the city it bombed. During about a month of bombing, somehow two hundred thousand people were able to flee. The men stayed in. We do not know what happened after that. There are no estimates of casualties which that attack is responsible!! [662]

8. 3. Timing of the battle

The timing of battle with the beginning of the holy month of Ramadan month was a great violation of the Muslim sanctity and religion on the US side. Perhaps they thought the people of Fallujah would perform rituals of fasting and ask the help of God in such difficult circumstances, thus to weaken the physical and combat capabilities against attack of the defenders of Fallujah.

Before the beginning of military operations the US base near Fallujah was visited by the former Democratic Party presidential candidate, Senator John Kerry. He met with a former member of the local council of Fallujah, Engi. Fawzi Alamadan. Kerry asked whether the people of Fallujah were interested in participating in the scheduled 2005 elections. Mr. Fawzi told him yes, but Fallujah, like a lot of cities, rejects the occupation. If you carry out military operations, Fallujah will refrain from participation in the elections. The coming carnage must be prevented to make way for people to participate freely.

The US Senator said he was surprised at this response because the impression given by the Bush administration to the American people was the opposite. Kael Weston, representative of the US State Department in Fallujah, confirmed after the battle that its timing was too soon before the election, and may have prevented thousands from voting. He said that if the battle had taken place after a fatwa from Fallujah's imams on October 15 to participate in the elections, that more than one hundred and eighty thousand (180,000) citizen in Fallujah would have voted in the elections [230].

On 25 September 2004, the Coalition Joint Leadership (MNF-I) announced resolution No. 306, titled "Integrated Operations Prior to Ramadan." It stipulated that their forces would begin counter-insurgency operations in coordination with Iraqi security forces to neutralize foreign terrorist networks. They meant which mean to take decisive action before the end of November. General Sattler immediately went to Baghdad to brief General Metz for the second and third phases of the process. They agreed to call it 'Phantom Fury'. By the end of September, all efforts were focused on preparations for the attack on Fallujah, in spite of the presence of smaller operations in western Iraq as part of Anbar province. Four Marines were killed in western Iraq on 3 September, while on the outskirts of Fallujah seven Marines were killed on September 6. On 8 September Army Private First Class Jason L. Sparks was killed, as were two Marines on 12 September including First Lieutenant Alexander Wetherbee. On 13 September shells of Fallujah fighters penetrated the headquarters in Camp Fallujah, wounding Colonel Larry Nicholson and killing communications officer Lieutenant Colonel Kevin M. Shea. September was the bloodiest month for the Marines, with 17 killed [193]. The military operation was renamed New Dawn by Iyad Allawi [231].

Shelling and attacks by aircraft were approved by the supreme commander of US forces in Iraq General George Casey, after obtaining the approval of the Secretary of Defence Rumsfeld, and recognized by an officer, John R . Ballard [193]. The main role in the aerial bombardment was assigned to giant AC-130 bombers. Most of Fallujah was bombed indiscriminately and brutally. The bombardment used special bombs and missiles in the early days, and then changed to bombs weighing 300-500 kg, and cluster bombs, which are internationally banned. They killed and wounded thousands of civilians and displaced thousands more. It destroyed homes and public property. I saw a lot of these incidents from the train across the city. Americans did not expect that people of Fallujah to fight against the crime of mass punishment. They were surprised by the fierce resistance to the entry their forces. Lt. Joshua Jamison from Marine Corps 2nd was among the first to enter Fallujah. He said, "I did not expect that I would request mortar and air strikes, just to get into the city!!) [52].

8.4. Starting the second massacre in Fallujah

The second battle of Fallujah was initiated at the end of September. There was aerial bombardment and random destruction before the entry of ground forces, which began in November 2004. I was in Baghdad with my family and I could not reach the outskirts of Fallujah to see the humanitarian situation. The number of military checkpoints prevented humanitarian aid agencies and the independent press from getting access to the area of operations. I knew before the battle that the poorest families remained inside the city, because they spent their savings money during the displacement of the first battle. These families were the first civilian victims of the battle. Thousands of families were displaced to villages and towns around Fallujah. They were suffering from a very tragic humanitarian situation because of the lack of food, water and medicine, in addition to the lack of fuel in the winter holy month of Ramadan.

On 7 November 2004, Fallujah was isolated from the southeast side by electronic attack (dynamic cordon) by a unit of 2BCT of the 1st Cav Division. They occupied a general hospital outside the city on the west. That is an explicit humanitarian offense according to the Geneva Conventions. Meanwhile the while 3rd Light Armored Reconnaissance Battalion (3rd LAR) controlled the bridges of Fallujah [230]. Iyad Allawi claimed 38 persons were killed in the attack on the General Hospital. The US military said it was quickly and easily and there were no victims. A military spokesman, 1st. Sgt. Steven Valley later announced 47 people killed in different parts of the city. Doctors declared 10 killed and 11 wounded as a result of one night of bombing and indiscriminate shelling [478].

In 30 October, aircraft and artillery attacked specific targets in Fallujah as a warning. This was followed by a 5 November cut-off of the power supply and drinking water for the city, in spite of the nearly 50,000 civilians remaining, according to an estimate in the UN report [197]. Occupation warplanes dropped warning leaflets over the city asking civilians not to go out of their homes and not to use their cars. On 7 November Allawi's interim government announced a state of emergency in Iraq (excluding the Kurdistan region of Iraq) for a period of 60 days. These measures caused 75-90% of residents to flee the city, according to a US military source [62]. At the same time the US forces in cooperation with Allawi's interim government completely closed the Syrian-Iraqi border to prevent any supplies or assistance to reach the fighters in Fallujah [231].

Military source indicate that military operations of Phantom Fury were launched on 2 November [193], although the official announcement said 7 November 2004 with the participation of 15,000 of American Marines, British soldiers and 2000 of Iraqi soldier [13]. These forces included one battalion of the British army, three battalions of the US-trained Iraqi army, six battalions of US Marines and three battalions of the United States Army [88.353]. It is worth mentioning is get splits in one of the Iraqi battalions which refusing to participate in the attack before beginning, because Iraqi soldiers refused to fight against their countrymen [106].

The planning and supervision of the attack was by Lieutenant General Tom Metz, commander of III Corps Marine. Direct leadership of the attack led by the MEF commander General Sattler and his assisted Brigadier General Hejlik. The director of Operations, department G3 of the General Staff, was First Marine Col. Mike Regner. The chief of staff was Colonel John Coleman, the director of intelligence was Colonel Makuta[193]. Col Craig Tucker was the commander of RCT-7 which was responsible for the attack from the east [230].

The General Command of the 1st Marine Division was held by Major General Richard Natonski, consisting of four battalions of US Marines. Also, two battalions of the US military, two infantry task forces (Task Forces 2-2), and mounted forces (2-7 Cavalry) fought in the streets of Fallujah. The Army's 2d Brigade and the 1st Cavalry Division cordoned off the city during the attack [62].

BBC reporter Paul Wood, who accompanied US forces outside Fallujah, said a convoy of armored vehicles and Humvee vehicles probed the outskirts of Fallujah in order to expose the positions of fighters in Fallujah for aerial and artillery bombardment before the start of the comprehensive attack. Marine commanders meanwhile claimed that they were waiting for the permission of Iraqi Prime Minister Iyad Allawi, to start mass attack!!! [101].

Heavy bombardment and massive use of excessive force led to the violation of the war basis by violating the pro-rata with the attacking forces and the size of the required destruction. As example on 8 November 2004, the US Navy aircraft dropped eight 2000 pound bombs on the berm adjacent to the train station to the west of Fallujah, before ordering their forces to occupy the station [194].

On 9 November 2004, Dexter Filkins of the New York Times wrote that US military officials estimated that 70-90% of the people of Fallujah left the city at the beginning of military operations, in spite of the testimony of many journalists who confirm there were thousands of civilians remaining in Fallujah[165]. The US side claimed that they avoided hitting mosques in their attack[103]. All the facts and figures and images collected by the Rehabilitation Committee of Fallujah (we retain a copy of this document) confirm the massive destruction of mosques and all public and private buildings in Fallujah.

The double-faced policy of Iyad Allawi's order was revealed by US military report. Allawi claimed that he respected the Geneva Conventions, which obliges respect and avoidance of targeting of places of worship and historical monuments. He ordered that only Iraqi soldiers should enter the holy shrines during battles in cities of Najaf and Samarra (2004) (230).

The mosques in Fallujah were left without sanctity and without respect for the Geneva Conventions, however. They became places for station breaks for the soldiers of the occupation after the deadliest crimes reported by the media. US journalist Filkins also indicated intense battles near the residential district of the railway in the north of the city, where F-18 aircraft firing 3,000 rounds per minute and the AC-130 aircraft fired from guns (155 mm) rounds to left enormous damage. The jihad' Takbeers from mosques constitute a nightmare for US soldiers in psychological warfare. They pushed the American commanders to set up loudspeakers near their attacking troops to play American songs like the cavalry charge in order to raise the morale of their troops [103].

On the south side of the city, there was a special task force known as TF2-2IN, short for Task Force 2nd Battalion, 2nd Infantry. This force was among the troops of fifteen thousand that participated in the battle under the supervision of Marine Expeditionary Force I that divided Fallujah into six combat areas or breakers. This force had to admit the presence of civilians in the south of Fallujah while they storm edit. Shuhada neighborhood held tough resistance areas [34]. This neighborhood is a poor area, a population forced to stay because of their inability to pay to the live outside the city. They had to stay under the threat of death. But it is better to have their dignity and self-esteem than to become internally displaced refugees and request help from others.

8.5. Invasion of hospital and prevent the entry of medical and humanitarian aid

Noam Chomsky described the assault on Fallujah Hospital saying, "but what was really dramatic about Fallujah was not a secret. It's what we saw on the front page of The New York Times." There is a picture a person lying on the ground, guarded by soldiers. There is a story that tells of patients and doctors arrested. Patients were taken from their beds, patients and doctors were forced to lie on the ground, their hands tied, under guard, imagine it!!! The President of the United States could be subject to the death penalty under the law the United States for that crime only. The Geneva Conventions that say unequivocally that hospitals, medical staff, and patients must be protected by all combatants in any conflict. There cannot be a more serious violation of the Geneva Conventions [662].

The medical staff of the general hospital was prevented from entering the city according to hospital director Dr. Rafe Chiad. He confirmed that US authorities refused all his requests to enter the city to help the wounded and sick people. The most criminal thing according to all human and divine laws was the bombing of the health clinic in the Nazal neighborhood at 5:30 am at dawn on 9 November. There were 35 wounded patients, including two girls and three children under the age of ten. As well there were 15 medics, four nurses, and five health support staff, including the martyrs Sami Omar, Omar Mahmoud, Ali Amini, Omar Ahmed, and doctors Muhammad Abbas, Hamid Rabia, Saluan al-Kubaissy, and Mustafa Sheriff.

Nonetheless the health center provided food and water to civilians, as testified by Dr. Sami Al-Jumili. Fadel Badranni, a correspondent for Reuters and the BBC, estimated the number of casualties at 40, including dead, and wounded. Fifteen were medical staff and aides. Dr. Eiman al-Anni, from the general hospital of the city, said when she reached the crime place that the entrance to the clinic had completely collapsed. James Ross from Human Rights Watch (HRW) condemned the crime. He said, "it is the responsibility of the US government now to demonstrate that this center is used for military purposes and that this response was proportionate. Even if there were snipers on the roof, that does not justify the absolute destruction of the hospital". Hamid Salaman Hamid of Fallujah's general hospital told an AP correspondent that five patients in an ambulance had been killed by the US bombing. Dr. Sami Jumaili confirmed the death of three children from thirst, due to inability to find drinking water during the battle [166].

A Marine leader, John R. Ballard, called the staff of Fallujah General Hospital assistants of terrorists because they announced the number of casualties directly, regardless of the reasons why they were hit by U.S. fire!! He also revealed that the order that targeted the ambulance came from the Marine commander, General Sattler, under the pretext that it was moving weapons and fighters. He acknowledged the existence of civilian casualties because of the bombing. The most absurd thing was the claim that "smart" laser-guided weapons had high precision in targeting fighters in Fallujah after it was surveyed for days via satellite.

He lost credibility when he admitted there were weaknesses of intelligence information on the civilian presence in the city. He further lost credibility when he admitted the difficulty of hitting targets without civilian [193]? Many doctors and aid workers in international humanitarian organizations witnessed US forces attacking ambulances and hitting medical health centers [482].

This situation motivated aid agencies to send a warning that civilians were left inside the city without food or water [153]. The smell of dead bodies became unbearable. Many died of hunger, wounds, or lack of medical assistance. Many families had to bury the bodies of martyrs in their gardens [154].

Convoys of humanitarian aid from organizations such as International Red Cross and Red Crescent were prevented from entering the city [219]. Staff members of a Muslim relief agency in Fallujah feared that a third of Fallujah's of 300,000 inhabitants who remained there suffered from hunger and lack of medical care, due to the barring of relief from the city. Ahmed Nasser from the Iraqi Red Crescent confirmed they were detained in a hospital without permission to enter the city to serve humanitarian needs.

Dr Salih al Issawi from Fallujah hospital told the South African Press Association that the US Marines prevented ambulances from delivering patients to the emergency room [100]. It is known internationally that a large number of difficulties in coordination of humanitarian aid during combat lead to a doubling of losses. That is why there is an implicit consensus in the international community to avoid battle in cities [119]. Under cover of the lie in the Marine Corps Gazette about the absence of civilians, it was admitted that lethal weapons were used. Marines used explosive blasts to enter houses used as pillboxes [198]. Unfortunately, humanitarian convoys were not allowed to enter. Only one convoy entered after the start of the battle, on 5 December, which was too late for the wounded civilians [219]. Note that the US military estimates confirmed that at least 50,000 civilians remained in the city [778].

Photos and movies showed civilian bodies that had been burned and melted by incendiary or unknown materials, while their clothes remained intact. We collected this evidence from various sources. The most prominent is the photo and movie collection made by the rescue team of Doctor Mohammed Jazzae Jumaili and Haji Mohammad Adnan Hamdani. In addition there are films from a friend who worked with the Iraqi Red Crescent teams, Mohammed Khalaf al-Issawi. His home in the Shortta district became a temporary center of the Iraqi Red Crescent, made up of some dozens of civilians of all ages who remained in the city. US forces did not allow their extrication even after the end of the battles. They were forced to stay in the temporary shelter, which also confirms that many civilians were present.

8. 6. Testimonies for war crimes and genocide

BBC correspondent Fadhil Badrani witnessed bodies of women and children lying in the streets of Fallujah [154]. This was also confirmed to me by one of my relatives who came to the city a month after the battle, during the collection of bodies from streets and houses. He was one of the many locals who witnessed the collection of bodies. He saw the bodies of some of his neighbors, women, children, and old people. He cried during their burial. For several days he could not eat because of the severity of the pain and trauma of what he saw.

I also met many families who lost their sons, and those who do not know their fate. The official estimate is more than 1,400 people missing, according to local sources. One of those known to be missing is an older man named Shaker Abdullah Hamdan Al Fayad Kubaisi. According to the testimony of his son, Sheikh Abdel Moneim Shaker Kubaisi, after a brutal arrest he was put in an American prison in Basra. It is not known if he was killed, or died, or transferred to an another secret place.

The US commander of the second battle, John F Sattler, admits in his assessment that more than 500 civilians remained in the city during the fighting and a few of them were injured [199].

The crimes of killing civilians or imprisoned fighters in Fallujah by occupation forces were many. Former Marine sergeant Jose L. Nazario Jr. led a squad of 13 Marines from Kilo Company, 3rd Battalion, and 1st Marine Regiment. [92] Hewas tried for his involvement in the killing of four captured fighters on the second day of the battle. Nazario killed two captives while a third prisoner was killed by Sergeant Jermaine Nelson. The killer of the fourth captive has not been announced so far [72].

[138]

A reporter from NBC, Kevin Sites, showed a clip of Marines opening fire on an old man in a mosque, executing him in cold blood [109]. CNN showed footage after the battle, which shows a wounded Iraqi on the ground. Marines returned fire and killed him, and then bragged about the crime [102].

Many civilians were killed indoors and in mosques. Hamid Sultan Abdul Razzaq, a native of Fallujah, saw his pregnant wife and four sons killed in front of him by US attackers on 9 November, 2004. Four members of Fawzi Hussein Salman al-Issawi's family were butchered by US forces in front of the eyes of their daughter Huda.

On 11 November US troops of the so-called "RCT-1" and "RCT-7" continued to penetrate from the south of the city. On 13 Nov. came to begin The third phase of the plan, "Phase III-B", began on 13 November. It included search and attack. Allawi's announced of the return of security to the city. The RCT-7 force withdrew from Fallujah in the middle of December to begin the hunt for militants in the vicinity of Nassir Wal Salam, to the east of Fallujah. The BCT forces of the 1st Cavalry Division continued operations on the outskirts of Fallujah until mid-December [230]. Marine officers Lt Col Gareth Brandl admitted to BBC Radio that people from Fallujah were targeted, not all of them people from Syria and Jordan "as Rumsfeld wants us to believe." [477].

The bodies of hundreds of civilians and combatants remained on the streets of Fallujah or inside wrecked homes for more than a month, and feral dogs ate them. In mid-December (2004), the Marines approved the request of residents outside the city to allow teams of volunteers to enter the city for collect the bodies and bury them. A British Channel 4 report took testimony from many of those who had lost family members, or saw civilians, children, women and the elderly killed in the inner city [173]. US troops left snipers in the inner city, who each night targeted anyone they thought was a fighter, or to kill on suspicion only [153].

In order to prevent media exposure plans were prepared specifically to prevent independent press coverage, thus to avoid the mistakes of the first battle [231,1,63,]. Many journalists from independent agencies, especially the staff of Al-Jazeera and Al-Arabia channels, were prevented from entering the city during the fighting. Ninety-one journalists with the US forces, representing 60 news agencies and newspapers, were barred from publishing news of military operations that jeopardized civilians only, according to Sattler [231].

On 26 August 2004, before this battle, the independent Italian journalist Enzo Baldoni was killed because he was gathering information for a book about the Iraqi resistance. He was on his way with a humanitarian aid convoy of the Italian Red Cross to the city of Najaf, which was also gearing up for its own second battle. Enzo Baldoni visited Fallujah before the second battle. He asked us for help to stay inside Fallujah to complete part of his book about the resistance there. We advised him to return immediately to Baghdad out of fear for his safety, due to the hazardous security situation inside the city.

A few local journalists remained inside the city. The most prominent was Fadhil Badrani, who provided his reports to international news agencies such as Reuters and the BBC World Service [154].

On 4 February, Italian journalist Giuliana Sgrena was kidnapped in an area of Baghdad controlled by the militia of a political party. It was after she gathered tragic information from refugees from Fallujah.

Sgrena reported on a meeting in Baghdad with some displaced families from Fallujah. The women interviewed tried to enter their homes in Fallujah. They found dust all over their houses. They tried to clean it up. But soldiers are advised to use detergents because of hazardous substances in the dust [127].

Giuliana Sgrena was released on 5 March 2005. A US tank parked on the road to Baghdad International Airport opened fire on the cars of an Italian intelligence group that helped with her release. The tank fire injured an Italian officer, and killed intelligence officer Major General Nicola Calipari.

US reporter Dexter Filkins recounted his observations in his book, *Forever War*. He entered Fallujah with the Marines. In his book he reported the use of white phosphorus (WP) against the people in the massacre, but not in his news reports to the *New York Times*!!!

White fire fell upon him when he was with the Marines. Someone yelled "phosphorus!!" A Marine threw him to the ground and told him to take off his jacket immediately, with the sleeping bag on his back. Another Marine yelled a warning it could reach his bones. Filkins rushed to throw off his bag. The litter resembled white feathers due to the combustion of WP.

Although he was one of the few journalists who entered the city, he wrote little in his book about areas that had seen earlier battles. He reported viewing the bodies of slain Iraqis in central Fallujah without mentioning the battles that captured these areas. This confirms he came after the main battle, and saw secondary battles after removal of the remains of fighters. An Australian photographer accompanied him, but he did not dare to show a single image of Fallujah other than those of streets cleared of dead bodies and wrecked vehicles!!

The other interesting thing in the novel was his report of seeing four men fighting with the troops, but not from the Marines. They wore flak jackets, tennis shoes, and reflective sunglasses, and moved briskly in the shade. They looked like executioners in a script. Their role was seen by a journalist as local hunters. According to his claim they were hitmen. This was conclusive evidence on the use of mercenary security companies such as Blackwater in take vengeance on the people of Fallujah for the killing of four Blackwater mercenaries before the first battle [372].

Filkins did not tell the full story in his newspaper dispatches. But he did write a documentary film script that described the boost in morale of Marines as they heard a song called "Hells Bells" over loudspeakers. It was accompanied by the roar of US aircraft bombing and destroying the houses before them, with amplified voices heard from fighters chanting in Fallujah mosques!!!

The intent was to give a picture of a battle between two civilizations or religions. It was the same pattern used by President Bush to justify the crime of aggressive war to the American people The same immoral imagery was used in the US media to anesthetize the American people during the Vietnam war, when Americans pilots were shown listening to loud music while they dropped napalm bombs on Vietnamese villages that supported the Vietnamese National Resistance.

The intensity of the second Fallujah massacre was also shown by the major part played by snipers. Col. Michael McCarthy also exposed the full reality when he told the story of another sniper who was missed by Filkins, unfortunately for the success of his Hollywood story. McCarthy exposes the violation of US war rules in the use of proportionality in the use of force. He referred to a sniper holed up in a three-floor building. Marines responded with fire from rifles, machine guns, bombs, and artillery, but the sniper continued shooting. The US aircraft then dropped two bombs weighing 500 and 2000 pounds on the building, but did not succeed in killing him. An M-1 tank finally stopped the sniper fire with 10 rounds of 120 mm shells. But the big shock on the faces of the Marines came as they watched the sniper leave from the back of the building and get away on a bicycle [75].

Every morning started with at least 20 minutes with the carpet-fire by mortars, artillery, bombs, missiles, and rockets. An enormous amount of hell was inflicted on sites believed occupied by fighters [245].

Toby Harnden, a British journalist working for *Telegraph*, revealed the use of white phosphorus in an article written on 9 November and published on 20 November 2004. He wrote that white phosphorus shells lit up the sky, created barriers across roads, and delivered fire on rebel positions. He added that Marines expected big enemy losses, as had occurred in the Golan area. [69]. The BBC confirmed that pitched battles in the Golan which imposed a tight streets alleys lack of importance of the control of US forces on the surfaces of some high building in the area. This situation prompted soldiers to stay inside their tanks. Their armored convoys were dependent on air cover for 24 hours a day. [154] A month after the end of second battle (December, 2004), US state department thumbed its nose at allegations of the use of banned weapons in Fallujah. They said the widespread rumors were myths. They asserted that white phosphorus shells are not prohibited from use. They said they were used sparingly in Fallujah for lighting purposes. They were fired into the air to illuminate fighters' positions in the evening, not at enemy fighters!! [245].

8.7. The use of chemical weapons and incendiary

The official US recognition of use of white phosphorus by the Marines in this battle came after a full year of denial, and being ignored by US and the Western media. The case confirms political control of the media. It ratifies the statement at the Nuremburg Tribunal by U.S. magistrate Robert Jackson that aggressive war is "the supreme crime, containing within itself the accumulated evil of the whole."

But the will of God to expose the crime came in a documentary film by the Italian satellite channel RAI News24, on 8 November 2005 [90] , a day of the arrival of puppet Iraqi President Jalal Talabani to Italy on an official visit [245].

The film raised the prospect of a worldwide scandal like that of the use of chemical weapons in Vietnam. The film showed injuries to the bodies of women and children similar to the effects of napalm or WP. There are painful images of bodies of women and children who were burned alive, comparable to the bodies of victims of the bombings of Hamburg and Dresden in Germany during World War II by US chemical weapons bombs [535]. The *Washington Post* reported on 10 November that some artillery fired white phosphorus shells that inflict fire that cannot be quenched by water. The militants said they were attacked with a substance that caused melting of the skin, a reaction consistent with white phosphorus. A doctor at a local hospital in Fallujah told the newspaper that the bodies of the militants were burnt and some were melted [308].

Many of the civilian population in Fallujah confirmed they witnessed the use of chemical weapons and incendiaries on the city [481]. Doctor Kamal Hadeethi, who works at a health center in Fallujah, said to the *San Francisco Chronicle* that "the bodies of the Mujahideen were burnt and some were melted" [480]. The testimony was repeated by Dr. Mohammad J. Haded, and also by the coordinator of the Iraqi Red Crescent in Fallujah, Mr. Mohammad F. Awad, who said that the bodies of many of the dead in the city were charred. [482].

A spokeswoman for the United Nations expressed concern despite the announcement by the government of Iyad Allawi of an investigation into the use of prohibited weapons. [252]. US officials responded to the film with denial and disbelief. Pentagon spokesman Todd Vician categorically denied the use of any chemical weapons in Iraq. He claimed that people were trying to tarnish his country's reputation by inventing false accusations. The denial was repeated by Lt. Col. Steve Boylan, the Director of the Pentagon's Combined Press Information Center in Baghdad, in an appearance on the American program "Democracy Now" on 8 November 2005. He denied the evidence and confessions in the Italian documentary film "The Hidden Massacre" on the use of white phosphorus against Iraqis [127]. But in a news conference on 18 November, Boylan admitted that WP is a munition that can be used to force people out of hiding by heat and smoke. He said U.S. forces launch it against military targets. He said that in Fallujah, the military targets were "terrorists and insurgents." [259.260].

On 15 November 2005, the US ambassador to London Robert Holmes Tuttle wrote a letter to the British newspaper The Guardian. It stated that US forces participating in Iraqi Freedom Operation use legal weapons against legitimate targets. US forces do not use napalm or phosphorus as a weapon) [204,14]. The US Ambassador's lie held up for only one day.

On 16 November 2005 the truth of the crime was revealed. Brig. Gen. Donald Alston of the US Air Force, deputy chief of staff for strategic communications, and a spokesman for the official multinational forces in Baghdad, told CNN that, "We have not changed our position that we did not use white phosphorus against civilians in Fallujah during Operation Dawn." (al-Fajr) [248]. But on the same day, Lieutenant-Colonel Barry Venable, a Pentagon spokesman for the Pentagon, was interviewed by BBC. He said that they actually used white phosphorus as an incendiary weapon, and perhaps used against enemy combatants. "It is not a chemical weapon," he said!!! [30;789;259]. Ambassador Tuttle tried to apologize for his lie in the *London Times* newspaper, saying "We've done the best we can with the information available to us, and we regret that it was not entirely accurate." [261]. US officials' statements started circulating among Western journalists as examples of ridiculous humor.

White phosphorus is known to generate smoke clouds that kill any living organism within miles, as well as causing burns that melt flesh. Therefore is does not differentiate between combatants or unarmed civilians, or even animals or plants. Bryan Whitman, US Deputy Secretary of Defense for Public Affairs, told reporters he was "not aware of any civilian casualties due to the WP attacks in Fallujah" [262]. At a US Department of Defense press conference attended by Defense Secretary Donald Rumsfeld, Gen. Peter Pace, Chairman of the Joint Chiefs of Staff, said that white phosphorus "is a legitimate tool for the Army" that can be used for lighting, smoke, and incendiary purposes. [263].

Incredibly, US Department of Defense had previously clarified in a press conference that white phosphorus is not used as an incendiary weapon [264]. According to Pace, it is allowed by the laws of war to use white phosphorus for "labeling and sorting." [263]. This was despite all the confessions and testimony by the US military and by Iraqi civilians about the use of white phosphorus as a weapon against civilians and fighters in urban areas [248]. This was the final official statement about white phosphorus, without any discussion of the legality of chemical substances as anti-personnel weapons in the laws of war or the Chemical Weapons Convention.

The US State Department declined to comment on the scandal. It described the confessions as a public relations failure [252]. On 8 December 2004 the US State Department posted a statement on its official website. It denied news reports after the battle that said the United States had used the illegal weapons of napalm and poison gas, and phosphorus (such as Mark-77), in Fallujah. It claimed that international law does not prohibit the use of incendiary weapons such as napalm against enemy forces, which were used during the occupation operations in Iraq in 2003 [254.95]. Overlooked was the prohibition of targeting the enemy in civilian areas, which was the case in the Battle of Fallujah.

The website of the US Department of Defense has already admitted using Mark 77 bombs in Iraq without mentioning the name or nature of the areas where they were used [225.227]. The use of incendiary weapons by powerful countries against fighters in areas populated by thousands of innocent civilians is an atrocity and a war crime.

A statement of the Iraqi Ministry of Health confirmed that it had evidence of civilian casualties due to white phosphorus [252]. But the US leadership repeatedly insisted that it used WP very sparingly in Fallujah for purposes of lighting the positions of combatants, not directly against the fighters. Because of the scandal the American expert Daryl G. Kimball, director of the Arms Control Association, demanded that the US Department of Defense and possibly an independent body should review whether or not the US use of white phosphorus was in line with international arms agreements [252].

According to Paul Wood of Radio BBC, this demand was as a public relations disaster for the United States of America before the world because it came after a full year of repeated denials [89]. The Italian film and the American confessions prompted some countries to withdraw their troops from, or plan withdrawal, when they became aware of war crimes committed without their knowledge or involvement.

The timing of Italian film on the first anniversary of the second battle was a big shock to the US Department of Defense and the White House, because it came despite all the blackouts and concealment of the crime. It revealed conclusive evidence of their lies, without the need to wait 30 years for the lifting of secrecy of US government documents, as happened in the Vietnam War. The film [90] confirms a lot of facts, The most important of them are reinforced by other evidence, which follows.

The use of WP and the Mark 77 bomb, a type of napalm bomb (militarily nicknamed Whiskey Pete), including the night 8 November 2004, was confirmed by a US military document [34]. This document was written by three US artillery officers, and listed munitions used. In addition, its use was mentioned by a Marine, Jeff Englehart, who took part in the battle [245].

[145]

An order was given to the occupation soldiers that anyone over the age of ten considered to be a rebel, of whatever sex, should be targeted and killed in the attack [90]. This was confirmed by Chris Kyle, one of the most infamous US snipers in history. He killed dozens in the second battle, and admitted his crimes in his book *American Sniper* [373].

In an interview with the BBC, a senior US military commander, Gen Peter Pace, defended the use of WP. He said it is a legitimate tool for the Army. WP burns when exposed to oxygen and burns brightly on the battlefield, it produces clouds of white smoke to conceal troop movements. He said it's not a chemical weapon, it is an incendiary weapon [151]. That conflicts with the confession of Marine soldier Jeff Englehart who said bodies were burned, women burned, and children burned because white phosphorus kills indiscriminately. It does irreversible harm if it even touches the skin, burning flesh down to the bone [90].

Occupation forces took about 7 weeks to gain initial control of the city, but sporadic fighting continued in some areas until the end of December [212,353]. Requests for air emergency assistance against resistance fighters continued through the month. According to Lieutenant Rex McIntosh of the third battalion of the Marines fifth division, the Marines lost dozens in fierce battles, especially in the northern part of the city [313].

8. 8. After the Fighting Stopped

The 3rd of December 2004 saw the beginning of the transition phase with the arrival of the Public Order Brigade. Major General Mehdi Sabih Hashem al-Garawi, who led the brigade, described the day he entered the city as most difficult in his life. Many soldiers refused to enter the city. Fourteen officers rebelled. He was forced to work all of the time to keep control of them, even during periods of eating and sleeping. He acknowledged that the people of Fallujah had no confidence in the occupation's Iraqi soldiers.

The Ministry of the Interior delayed establishment of a new police force in the city until September of 2007. At that time the second battalion of the Iraqi army withdrew and turned over responsibility for security to the local police [230]. That meant keeping the city of Fallujah from 23 December 2004, the date when people were allowed to return to their homes, until September 2007 in the condition of a big military prison. Thus Fallujah was ruled by martial law for a period of three years.

At the beginning of January 2005, I entered to the city as an assistant of Iraqi journalist Dr. Ali Fadel, who was working as a reporter for British Channel 4. We collected documentation for more than 25 hours of film reportage, which confirmed many violations [173]. An Iraqi journalist saw beheaded bodies near Rawi mosque. These bodies were much like the Crucifixion of Jesus Christ (peace be upon him). They indicated the possibility of the execution by decapitation, followed by crucifixion. Unfortunately, the channel did not show this evidence. The American writer Filkins also noted a decapitated and crucified body found on Tharthar Street!! I received a copy of the Channel 4 documentary film from Channel 4 a week after it was shown. I showed the film to a special meeting at the World Health Office in Amman, Jordan, which, included

1. The Special Representative of the Secretary-General of the United Nations in Iraq, Mr. Ashraf Jehangir Qazi.

2. Mr. Elio Tamburi of the senior staff of Human Rights Office of UNAMI.

3. Dr. Naima Algasseer (Bahrain), Director of the Iraq Office of the World Health Organization

4. Press spokesman for UNAMI in Iraq, Mr. Ayman Al-Safadi from Jordan, who later worked as a media consultant for Jordanian King Abdullah II.

5. Dr. Ahmed Hardan Mohammadi as Technical Representative of WHO in Baghdad, who gave a detailed explanation of the terrible humanitarian and health situation in the city.

I presented the documentary film to them showing the reality of the city after the battle. Mr. Ashraf gave instructions to expedite two separate written requests to US forces to allow entry of two teams to Fallujah to investigate abuses shown in the film. One team would be from the WHO and the other from the Human Rights Office of UNAMI. The US military refused as usual under the pretext of the bad security situation. Their real motive was to prevent any investigation that would reveal the facts. The interesting thing that struck me in this meeting was the shock of Mr. Ashraf at the content of the film. He asked how to get this, and said the Americans told us not to get like information like this!! There was shock on the faces, and silence among the rest of the representatives. US forces at that time denied destruction of the infrastructure of the city. They stated that imaging facilities of the Marine forces that attacked did not confirm the destruction of the city and its infrastructure [30]. But the reports of Ministry of Industry teams that surveyed the damage were to the contrary. That explains why the US refused entry to UN investigational teams.

8.9. Losses of Parties

There was a media contrast on official reports of losses from fighting. The reports that went out conflicted to confirm the absence of credibility.

The American McClatchy Newspapers reported that 95 US soldiers, 200 fighters, and 6000 civilians had been killed in Fallujah [76]. ABC News Online said 71 US soldiers, 1200 to 1600 fighters, and 2,000 local civilians had died [305]. Another source referred to the wounding of 275 US military [304]. A press report in Marines Magazine admitted that the US toll was 95 dead, and 560 injured, 1350 fighters killed, and 1500 arrested. [353]. BBC Radio estimated that more than 2000 people were killed [536]. Another US source gave 70 U.S. military deaths, and 609 wounded.

Before the battle the US commander, John F Sattler, estimated the number of fighters in Fallujah at about 3,000. The figure was very close to the number of fighters and civilians killed. Refrigerated potato warehouses on the edge of the eastern Fallujah were used to keep the bodies of fighters and civilians, especially those disfigured by unconventional weapons [231].

When official reports came out the numbers of casualties also differed greatly. According to one report, 51 US troops were killed, and 425 wounded, the death toll of Fallujah fighters was estimated at 1200 [32]. A US Congress report estimated Fallujah fighter losses at more than 500 [87]. A US officer said there were 70 US military deaths and 600 wounded 600s [194]. American reporter Richard S. Lowry gave losses of US forces at 95 dead and 1,000 wounded, and Fallujah fighters lost 1400 [213].

Gen. John Sattler confirmed the deaths of only 50 Marines, and 600 wounded [536]. The discrepancies among the various US military sources show they tried to hide the true numbers of casualties in order to avoid outrage.

After nine years of battle, Sheikh Khaled Hamoud Jumaili, chief of Fallujah negotiating team before the second battle, accused the puppet Iraqi army of involvement in disappearances and killings of 480 people from Fallujah after the battle. Sheikh Khalid said in a statement released by the agency Voices of Iraq, that a complete file had been sent to the Maliki government and the Iraqi parliament, but they did not investigate. Instead they covered up the crime and protected those involved [10 A].

[148]

Major General Richard Natonski declared that 1,200 rebels had been killed in battle [99]. It is noticeable that the US forces have largely avoided accurate official statistics on the number of people killed in Fallujah. Any clear and precise announcement of figures could make it necessary to show the required number of bodies. That may expose them to a risk of disclosure of the weapons used, or to probing questions from the international press.

Lt. Gen. Thomas Metz, commander of US ground forces in Iraq, said in Baghdad that, "We've got great losses among the enemy more than we expected, but the military does not maintain a formal outcome for losses among the enemy." [104].

Eleven years later, Metz' statement was shown to be deceptive when the *Washington Post* revealed the existence of a record of bodies kept by the Marines called "the green logbook." They put bodies in potato warehouses, with bodies of fighters and civilians together. The newspaper confirmed the presence of several bodies of civilians as well as fighters. They were recorded in a register, according to whether a civilian identity is unknown, ("civilian unidentified"), or a fighter's identity is unknown, ("insurgent unidentified"), or a body is incomplete ("unassociated portion"). They had a supply of 900 black body bags, more than half of which they used [689].

What is known to few people in Fallujah is that the Marines recorded images of bodies collected after the battle on compact discs. They gave the CD's to the Fallujah General Hospital administration (the old hospital, near the river) to help the families of the victims to identify their son's bodies. But the Marines returned a few days later to take back all the pictures and even the computers for fear of later use as evidence to crimes. But they were too late. The CD's were copied and distributed. We got a full copy of these images (as shown some in the following pictures).

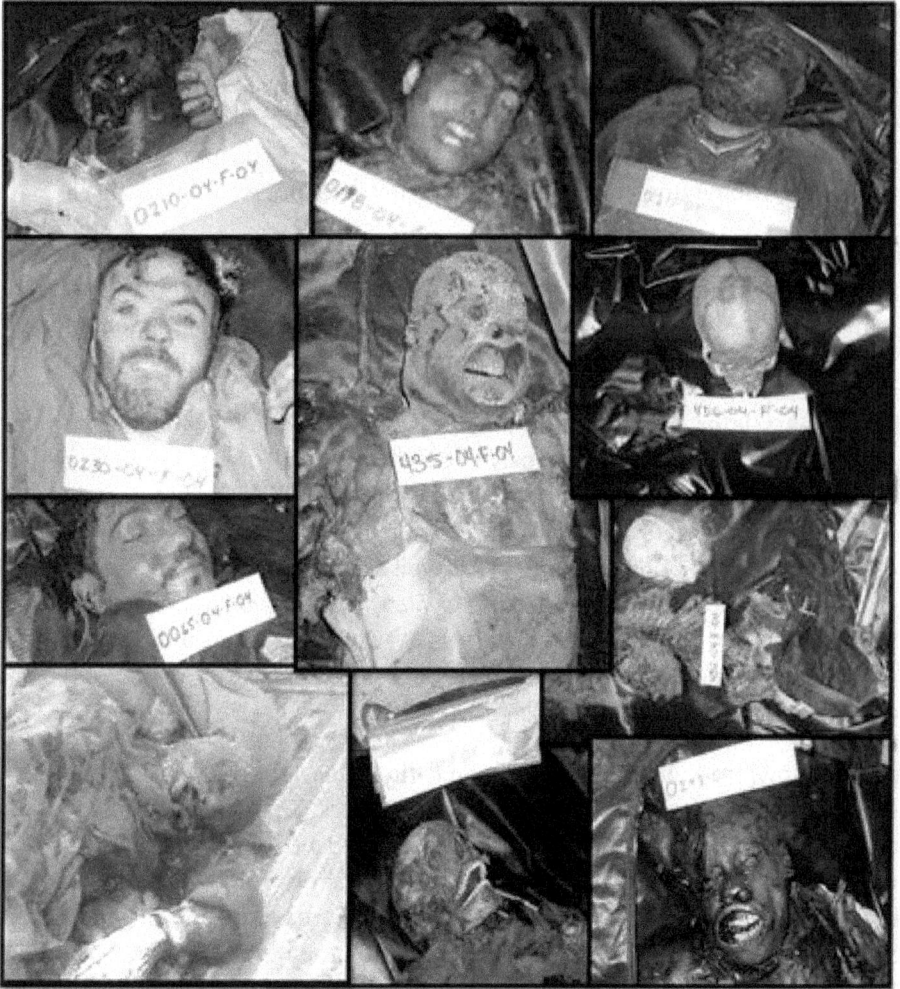

US intelligence officers feared that disclosure of heavy civilian losses would not only lose Sunnis, but Iraqis fighting in areas other than Fallujah. Walter P. Lang, former head of the Middle East Analysis Department in the Defence Intelligence Agency said, "We'll see if this is just a small rebellion that can be removed by weapons only, but if popular support continues it is something bad for us." [106].

American commanders were proud that their losses were very few. They avoided catastrophic losses like those of Russian troops in Grozny in Chechenia, or those incurred by the Israeli occupation forces in Jenin city in Palestine in 2002. Fallujah II was one of the most ferocious urban battles U.S. forces had seen since Hue in Vietnam in 1968 [34]. Despite the informational confusion at the battle's end, their confessions revealed their preference for remote slaughter. They used the entire range of remote sensing techniques combined with weapons of enormous destructive power and high accuracy, rather than risking battle face to face [67]. It was a dirty war of devastating technology from a distance, not one of knights who show their courage face-to-face.

The fighting destroyed or damaged 18,000 buildings of the total of 39,000 in the city [88]. While another source referred to the destruction of 36,000 homes and more than 9,000 stores, as well as 65 mosques and 60 schools. Two power plants, three water treatment plants, the sewer system, and the communications network were destroyed. Hundreds of women and women were killed [182]. In mid - January 2005 civilian families were allowed to return to the city, but few of them returned. More than 220,000 others became internal refugees in the surrounding areas and in the cities of Baghdad and Ramadi [219].

A report of the UN Emergency Working Group, "Fallujah Crisis, 2004," was published in an Australian newspaper. It said 210,600 people (35,000 families) fled Fallujah before the US attack and did not return. Many of them were in dire need of aid, with near-freezing temperatures, and the United Nations declared a new state of emergency. [312].

8.10. Genocide of witnesses to war crimes

The Canadian journalist Naomi Klein revealed hundreds of civilian deaths from the first US attack on the city. That showed the American forces and their partners no longer bother to hide attacks on specific civilian targets. In the second battle, doctors, clergy and journalists who keep count of victims were a particular concern that should be eliminated. Klein's information, published in the Guardian newspaper, came in response to a message to the US ambassador in London. According to Klein, the evidence pointed to the following:

1. *Elimination of doctors*. The first major objective of US Marines and Iraqi soldiers was to seize Fallujah General Hospital, arrest the doctors, and put the facility under military control. The *New York Times* reported that "the choice of a hospital as an early goal because the American military believed it was a source of information about heavy estimates of losses." It noted that "this time, the US military intends to fight its own information war, and silence what was one of the most powerful weapons of resistance." The *Los Angeles Times* reported one of the

doctors as saying that soldiers "stole the mobile phones" at the hospital, to prevent doctors from communicating with the outside world. But that was not the worst of the attacks on health workers. Two days before the health emergency clinic had been bombed and turned to rubble, as well nearby medical supplies. Dr. Sami al-Jumaili, who worked in the clinic, said bombs killed 15 paramedics, four nurses, and 35 patients.

2. The *Los Angeles Times* published a statement of the director of Fallujah General Hospital. He said he had informed an American general of the position of the temporary downtown Medical Center before the bombing. Whether US forces targeted the clinic or destroyed accidentally, the effect was the same, which was to eliminate many of the doctors in the Fallujah war zone. Dr. Jumaili told *The Independent* newspaper on 14 November: "There is not a single surgeon in Fallujah now". When the US and Iraqi forces fought in Mosul, a similar tactic was used during entry into the city, with immediate seizure of control of the Al-Zaharawi Hospital.

3. *Elimination of journalists.* The photos in the global media of second battle came almost exclusively from reporter accompanying the US forces. That was because Arab journalists who covered the siege in April had taken the perspective of the civilians. Al Jazeera did not have any cameras on the ground because it had been banned indefinitely from any reporting in Iraq. Al-Arabiya correspondent Abdul-Qader al-Saadi did not join US forces, although he remained in Fallujah. On 11 November 2004 he was detained by US forces for the duration of the siege. *Reporters Without Borders* and the *International Federation of Journalists* condemned the arrest of Saadi. The latter said "We cannot ignore the possibility of intimidation just because he trying to do his job". This was not the first time journalists in Iraq faced this kind of intimidation. When US forces invaded Baghdad in April 2003, the US Central Command urged all non-journalists accompanying US forces to leave the city. Some of the escorts the U.S. forces insisted on staying, with the result that at least three paid with their lives for their stay. On 8 April 2003, US aircraft bombed Al-Jazeera offices in Baghdad, killing reporter Tareq Ayyoub. Al-Jazeera has documentation proving it gave the coordinates of its location to US forces. On the same day, a US tank fired a shell at the Palestine Hotel, killing José Couso who was working for the Spanish network Telecinco, and Taras Protsiuk from the Reuters

news agency. Three US soldiers face criminal case from Couso's family, which claims that the US forces were well aware that journalists were in the Palestine Hotel and that they committed a war crime.

4. *Elimination of the Clergy.* Just as doctors and journalists were targeted, so were many clerics who spoke out strongly against the killings in the siege. On 11 November, Sheikh Mehdi al-Sumaidaie, Chairman of the Supreme Assembly for Guidance and Advocacy, was arrested. According to the Associated Press, "Sumaidaei called Sunni areas in the country to launch a civil disobedience campaign if the Iraqi government does not halt the attack on Fallujah". On 19 November AP reported that US and Iraqi forces stormed a prominent Sunni mosque, Abu Hanifa in Adhamiya, killing three people and arresting 40 including the chief cleric, who was another opponent of the siege of Fallujah. On the same day, Fox News said that "US forces also raided a Sunni mosque in Qaim, near the Syrian border". The report described the arrests as "retaliation for opposing the attack on Fallujah". Also arrested were two Shiite clerics associated with Moqtada al-Sadr in recent weeks. According to the AP "both raised their voices against the attack on Fallujah". Gen. Tommy Franks of the US Central Command said "We do not do body counts". The question is: What happens to people who insist on counting the bodies? Doctors who should talk about their patients may have been killed, as well to journalists documenting the loss, and the clergy who condemns those crimes. Evidence is increasing that these voices are silenced systematically through a variety of means, from mass arrests, to raids on hospitals, prohibition of the media, and physical assaults that are overt and unexplained.

Naomi Klein concluded, "Mr. Ambassador, I believe that your government and Iraqi followers are waging two wars in Iraq." One war was against the Iraqi people, and an estimated 100,000 people were killed. Another was the war on witnesses [474].

8.11. Recording Hollywood Movie

I met with many parents and friends who entered in the first days of allowed civilian access. They entered only to see their homes and for no purposes that would keep them from leaving before dark. Strangely, I heard from them that the Americans did report the wars at home. This was the reason we heard the blasts and gunshots. One friend of mine said that he visited his house and found broken doors and windows and destruction of furniture. (We thought he was lucky to come back and find the walls standing).

On his third visit he found the house was entirely crushed. He went to one of Marine officers to ask why. The response was that they found bodies of their dead colleagues there, therefore they bombed the house!!! My friend had not found any dead body during two visits to his house before.

Later I found parts of the American documentary program on YouTube. It spoke about tournaments of American soldiers in a Hollywood style. The program was called "Military Channel Podcast: Fight for Fallujah". There is a shocking scene that shows soldiers in Fallujah shoot their weapons supposedly against ghost fighters. Playacting with live weapons during the bombing added more destruction to a city which saw most of its citizens, more than a quarter of a million, displaced. The only thing that I found honest in this film was that soldiers recognized the voices of civilians, distraught from the massive destruction and daily killings they experienced during the attack on their neighbourhoods.

8.12. Reflections on the Fallujah massacres locally and internationally

US commanders admitted they had difficulties during the first battle in Fallujah in April of 2004. They had to temporarily halt military operations, a cease-fire, and withdraw from the city. Most of these problems were overcome during the second battle, most importantly in information operations. In a campaign of lies, they claimed they succeeded in separating groups of combatants and civilians [230.64]. The fact was, information management succeeded in preventing neutral media from entering the city. Western news agencies loyal to their agenda were allowed instead. The media also reduced international attention by giving more coverage to the death of Palestinian President Yasser Arafat, who died four days after the battle started, than to the battle.

The American side claimed that news from an Al Jazeera satellite channel telling of the storming of Fallujah hospital and the arrest of its staff was a surprise to them, and outside the scope of their control. But the management planning of Information operations by US forces had been carried out in cooperation and coordination between Public Affairs Office (PAO) and Psychological Operations (PSYOP) [230]. The Al Jazeera channel was accused of not helping the new Iraqi government.

The serious human rights violations in Fallujah, and the subsequent torture scandals at Abu Ghraib strengthened the popular demand to get occupation troops out of Iraq [33]. The Iraqi Islamic Party withdrew from the puppet government of Iyad Allawi after the battle. It did not want to assume responsibility for the shedding of Iraqi blood without a legitimate excuse, as stated by Mr. Ayad al-Samarrai Iyad al Samurraie [100]. The party remained a participant in the elections that followed the attack on Fallujah, while Muqtada al-Sadr called it an attack on all the Iraqi people and said no Iraqi should help the invasion [105].

Politically the Islamic Party and former Iraqi President Sheikh Ghazi al-Yawar were opponents of the second attack, and asked for further negotiations. Mowaffak Rubaie raised the possibility of postponing the attack until after the Iraqi elections scheduled for January 2005 to give time for further negotiations. That was also supported by the Islamic Party [230]. At the beginning Britain had some reservations about the the participation of its troops alongside US forces. They were summed up by British Foreign Secretary Robin Cook:

1. US forces lacked the policy of restraint that distinguished British forces.

2. The real danger in sending a British battalion into a sector where the United States Army was present was that British troops could become associated in the minds of Iraqis with the methods of the United States. The last time US forces attacked Fallujah they left 1,000 civilians dead. Their heavy-handed tactics raised an uproar.

3. If Britain participated with US forces in the attack may bear equal responsibility in the eyes of Iraqis for what happened to the people of Fallujah [297,238].

In the US, revelations of years of criminal use of chemical weapons and the exposure of lies about it throughout, led to a decline of support for the war. Opposition increased, as shown by some American news programs like "Democracy Now." This international crime was increasingly exposed [652].

After two and a half months of battle the occupation forces allowed the people of Fallujah to return to a city contaminated city with remnants from weapons (see Chapter IX). This additional war crime was confirmed by the US commander in Iraq, Gen. George W. Casey Jr., who said before the end of military operations that the "medical relief and reconstruction assistance will arrive immediately after the attack" [106].

[155]

Iyad Allawi announced on 9 December 2004 that he would enable the return of people to Fallujah on 23 December. He appointed Mr. Hashim al-Hassani (Islamic Party and Minister of Industry Member) as coordinator on Fallujah management and reconstruction [230].

Although diplomats and the American military considered that the Iraqi government should not rush the return of civilians to the city, the return was confirmed by the director of the Civil-Military Operations Centre (CMOC) Fallujah, Lieutenant Colonel Scot Ballard. He said the possibility that the Iraqi government would allow the return of civilians in a matter of days rather than weeks seemed reassuring, "but all plans are still hostage to the security situation . . . 5 days ago we had active battles with 50 insurgents and killed them." (310). Many people said they found the city in a tragic condition. The returning civilians said the fighting was still going on, there was no food and no shelter, and all of their homes had been looted. [311].

Other questions have not been answered so far after the massacre. Who kidnapped and killed foreign hostages?? Allawi's government was authorized in Fallujah and some other cities to restore security and law enforcement. But why was not any evidence provided about the killing of an Irish-English hostage bearing an Iraqi passport as Mrs. Margaret Hassan? Who is the beneficiary of the killing of a person supportive of the Iraqi people?? [504]. The use of double agents to commit massacres and violations and cover up clients is one of the official methods of US and British intelligence. (See Chapter 11th about death squads in Iraq).

The American writer Noam Chomsky said, "The Battle of Fallujah, which is one of the major war crimes, is very similar to the Russian destruction of Grozny 10 years ago, a city with almost the same size, pounded until it became rubble and empty of people) [662]. From another side and after 11th years, some Marines Chaplains describes their testimonies of this battle. "I have not spoken of the battle of Fallujah hardly at all during the past 11 years; it was an absolutely heartbreaking and horrific event that took a toll on myself and my fellow chaplains and RPs," said Col. Willard A. Buhl, commanding officer for Expeditionary Operations Training Group, I Marine Expeditionary Force. He added "and I can tell you now that there was nothing, absolutely nothing that compares to the devastation our forces experienced in the past 11 years during that battle," said Buhl. "We owe them everything.". Lt. Cmdr. Ron Kennedy, the 1st Marine Regiment, 1st Marine Division chaplain recounted his personal experience during the battle and his role as a caregiver and religious guide to wounded Marines:

"I knew what was coming from the reports and stories I heard from that area of Iraq. When we got there it was shocking," said Kennedy. "So many Marines had been disfigured and torn apart that I was hard pressed to push it all aside and focus on guiding them to a place of spiritual peace." [700]

We end this chapter with an acknowledgment in a report of the US Institute for Defence Analysis about the most important results of the Second Battle of Fallujah. They considered that the use of various weapons, and what took place, would be a warning to all cities that if they act like renegades they will face a Fallujah-like fate [230]. It leaves no doubt on the terrorism policy of a superpower state against an occupied people.

CHAPTER 9

Weapons Types Used Against Fallujah & Forbidden One

9.1. The First Battle

Information was not available until near time about the quality and quantity of the weapons used by the Marines during the first battle in spite of the presence largest Western media coverage with the of these forces and the emergence of a small portion of facts by some journalists or peace activists or Westerners relief near the battlefield. But the big part was with the emergence of the documents of National Ground Intelligence Center (NGIC) [1].

This report said that the census of attacking Marines (without the non-support from outside the city) had 2,000 troops armed with modern American weapons of the fighting machine guns and grenade launchers. They supported by 10 tanks of M1A1 type and 24 armored amphibious (AAVP-7) as well to battery howitzers (M198). NGIC' report explains the types of weapons used by the occupation forces during the first battle in April 2004. Air support had includes two types of aircraft: Firstly, the qualitative helicopters like Cobra (AH-1W Cobra) and Huey (UH-1N Huey gunships), which they used rockets like: Hellfire (these missiles had also been used in the battle of Najaf against the Mahdi Army in August 2004), TOW (which seen as modern missiles and unknown composition of the material explosive, which confirmed also be used to a report by the Marines [301]), HE, 2.75 high-explosive and flechette rockets, as well as to shells caliber (20-mm, .50-cal and 7.62-mm). Secondly, Combat aircraft (fixed wing) were the aircrafts (F-15E), (F-16CG), (F-16C +), (AC-130U), (F-18C) and (F-14B). Aircrafts carried out more than one thousand (1000) aerial sorties to shot of 70 shells type (GBU-12's), and two shells of the type (GBU-31's) (These bombs were also used in the battle of Najaf against the Mahdi Army in August 2004), and one shell of type (AGM-65H), with many of shells (20-mm, 105-mm, 40-mm, and 25-mm).

All of these forces and fortified weapons with the latest modern technology was fighting Fallujah fighters who were estimated report between 500 to 1000, while many confirmed to me during the fighting at home they do not exceed

500 fighters and remain from them just to last day of the battle at least 250 fighters only fighting with simple weapons compared arming US soldier. But the most powerful weapon which possessed those fighters had the strength and hardness of their faith that they are defending their land and their honor and dignity as well to their future against the occupation proved the days its came to destroy their country and steal it.

The properties of the weapons used in the first battle only according to this report was realize the cumulative effect of the weapons used and how this led to start a health and environmental pollution from these weapons in Fallujah for both Qualitative (this has been mentioned in the report above without reference to the real contents of the type of heavy metals or even the amount of them shot during the first battle, but the mere mention of the word (many) these words open quantity), and Quantitative for weapons used (this reported as type and quantity in the report above).

- Hellfire missiles: There are different types both fired from the shoulder or the air - land to targeting anti-armor for helicopters. The destructive power back to the unknown material so far, and possible that a laser is routed after being fed by information of ground observers [385].

- TOW missile:

- Missiles of 2.75 high-explosive:

- Cluster bombs (flechette rockets): It is a weapon in the form of container published submunitions (or smaller bombs in size) explosive them (each weighing less than 20 kg), which is designed to explode during deployment or after deployment, depending on the model. A cluster munition contains several dozen to more than 600 small bombs. While the bombs that contains less than smaller units of bombs and can be detected and is equipped with obsolete electronic self-destruction, it is not prohibited, but regulates the use by international humanitarian law [45]. The other international sources have confirmed the use of cluster munitions by the occupation forces [469].

- Shells of GBU-12's:

- Shells of GBU-31's:

- Shells of AGM-65H:

- Shells of 20-mm, .50-cal, and 7.62-mm:

- Shells of 20-mm, 105-mm, 40-mm, and 25-mm:

If we look at the nature of arming to aircraft from and its huge air strikes that have exceeded a thousand, we will know that this report did not mention the full facts.

Despite the existence of this evidence indicating the magnitude and quality of weapons that have been used, but what exciting for laughter is the talk of a US military commander attributed the loss for the first battle in Fallujah because of few air and artillery cover them with a few of their forces compared to census the population of Fallujah [30]. This confirms that they have considered all the residents of Fallujah are enemies, especially with their recognition of supporting people of the resistance to protect their city from mass punishment and destruction crimes [61].

9.2. Second battle

The second battle was different in terms of weapons and strategies through comprehensive targeting and indiscrimination shelling during the battle which continues from 7 - 30 November 2004. Despite boasting American commanders for few losses in this battle [32], but the fact that the use of sophisticated and lethal weapons with huge quantities of their forces in order to prevent real exposure of confrontation during the battle and rely on the destructive power from far of different weapons to kill anyone located in the center of operations before go head. Which means less evidence of possible genocide policy, armed heavy tanks has been used the most lethal ammunition, while aerial and artillery bombardment were freer than the prior authorization before the bombing [30]. As their admission, the second battle was a chance to test and demonstrate the impact of new launchers or sensor technology when integrated with other forces in joint operations because it did not allow them the opportunity tested during the process of occupation of Baghdad [52]. But despite the boast of US senior leaders for using only smart munitions and bombs in the second battle of Fallujah, but the recent US military studies have shown a lack of effectiveness of these weapons in the fight inside urban areas [75].

US Lt. Col. David Steven commander of USAF, Commander 9th Expeditionary Air Support Operations Squadron in its report published on 12 November 2004 pointed out (that at least 20 species of warplanes had been involved in the second battle of Fallujah including 10 kinds of aircraft fixed wing and three types of helicopters in addition to the 7 types of unmanned aircraft. There were ten groups of personnel land checkpoints that move within the city with Marine and US army fighters in order to lead the aircraft to areas that must be bombed. They gave the orders for aircraft and artillery bombed buildings and homes that hinder their progress with the work of this air cover during 24 hours a day [67]. Among the fighter fixed wing aircrafts were AV-8B Harrier, AC-130, F-14, F-15, F-16, F/A-18. One of Marine officers described the power of destruction of AC-130 aircraft, saying (this plane gave direct assistance to battalions during the progress, and formation eight forms all the time waiting for their chance to hit, they were beaten on the basis of the sites targeted by mortars and artillery 155 mm and within four minutes, all weapons systems which work like a fireworks). Another soldier describes the impact of weapons of this plane bombers in conjunction with mortar shells falling together, said happily (Explosions with artillery shells lighting the night sky, this shelling cut southern districts of Fallujah, you can even see those fireballs orange scattered from massive explosions over the surface homes) [67].

US tanks called Bradley were called to participate in this battle alongside tanks (M1) which previously participated in the first battle in Fallujah, and also it is used the AT4 shells with the Javelin missiles [212].

US source pointed out that this military operation (second battle of Fallujah) has included the 540 air strikes, with the launch of 14,000 mortars and artillery, while tanks fired 2500 bomb from artillery [88,87].

Indirect fire also used by artillery fire of cannons 155 mm from less than 5 miles of the east of Fallujah inside occupation camp there (Former Presidential farm), as daily bombing during and after the fierce fighting that took place in this period [64]. Only in the period of 7-10 November US artillery batteries shot with more than 800 shells at the city and its center, while the number of sorties on the first day only 24 sorties, including the four huge bombs dropping 500-pound [31]. In addition to the artillery launching total of 2000 shells and mortar with more than 10 tons of precision Air Force munitions. The close air support (CAS) threw more than 15 guided bombs units GBU-12s, which has 500 pound per bomb and directed by laser (and these bombs were also used in the battle of Najaf against the Mahdi Army in August 2004) As used too four bombs weighing 2,000 pounds labeled (JDAMs), which is GBU-29 Joint Direct Attack Munition and one missile type (Maverick). Besides there were a six hours of combat aviation roaring giant of aircraft stealth (AC-130 Specter gunship support) [34]. But one of the US military reports indicated that the most favored weapons to throw from the air during the second battle was Hellfire missiles and an ammunition of direct vector multiplication via GPS weighting 500-pound as the type JDAM and also known as (GBU-38) [67]. This last one according to a US military source considered as the modernist weapons munition what US Navy arsenal have from ammunition because allowing high accuracy in injury with massive destruction capability. Strangely they point to it usefulness in reducing injuries among innocent civilians while they forget its great destructive power!! [191].

The Maverick missile from model of air-land missiles with precision and multi-warhead with 9 different models used against large and small targets that moving or fixed, as well as to high value targets such as ships and communications centers ... etc. Its weight ranges according to its kind between the 207- 365 kg and carrying explosive materials on two types of quantity (57 and 135 kg). It has been used during the first Gulf War in 1991 and hit 85% of the targets (which means that it has an error ratio of 15%) and can target from a distance of up to 13 sea miles [66] .

The main tactic to push US forces inside the city of Fallujah was included to send Marines in specific buildings while launching laser-guided bombs, artillery and tank shells on the nearby buildings [64]. The US strategy to do collar during a military attack depends on the control of the time factor to minimize the loss between their soldiers and this requires the use of precision firepower and sensor technology to defeat an opponent with fewer sacrifices [65]. This means the absolute use of all kinds of ammunition to ensure extermination of Fallujah fighters and prevent confrontation near to minimize losses [75]. Goals holed up inside buildings and homes of Fallujah have been destroyed through precision targeting rockets and artillery shelling to prevent the need to send the soldiers themselves to make sure the death of people in each room inside the building or house [67]. This explains the mass destruction of the city after the battle in which US military avoid the traditional confrontation as a man to man, despite the large numerical superiority compared with those who were inside!!

On 3 March 2005, a director in the Ministry of Health Dr. Khalid ash Shaykhli held a press conference in Baghdad after 4 months of the end of the second battle of Fallujah to profess publicly US military using banned chemically weapon includes nerve gas during the storming of Fallujah. Quoting Al Jazeera network news, Dr. Khalid said (that research prepared by the medical team, prove that US occupation forces used banned substances internationally, including mustard gas, nerve gas and other incendiary chemicals in their attacks on the city's war-torn). Sheikhli said that during an attack by US forces,

[163]

fleeing' residents described "seeing corpses that had melted, which suggests that US forces used gas bombs, napalm, a poisonous compound of polystyrene of jet fuel which melts bodies". He also said that his researchers found evidence of the use of mustard gas and nerve gas. "We found dozens if not hundreds of stray dogs, cats, and birds that have died as a result of these gasses". He revealed this information in a press conference held at the Ministry of Health building in Baghdad and was attended in addition to Al-Jazeera more than 20 Iraqi and foreign media networks, including Sharqyia, Iraqi TV network, Al-Sabah Iraqi newspaper, US Washington Post and Knight-Ridder service [226].

However, this news was limited deployment in the United States, where the press conference mentioned in the Christian Science Monitor newspaper site, in addition to the annual US State Department report on the record of other countries for human rights on 7 March of the same year. The Christian Science Monitor newspaper based in Boston reported that "quoting Al Jazeera that Dr. Khalid ash Shaykhli, an official at the Iraqi Ministry of Health, said in a press conference in Baghdad that his ministry has made in the conflict in Fallujah and found that US forces had used" internationally prohibited weapons" during the attack last November, including napalm with jet fuel. The United States did not sign the treaty which prohibits the use of napalm against civilians.

In spite of that little aware at the time, there was a military article published by Field Artillery Magazine, American Journal of the monthly issue published in the March / April 2005 and in an article named ''fighting for Fallujah'' [34] a description of the process of using WP as a weapon during the second battle (November 2004) in Fallujah. They describe the use of this weapon as following: (proved WP weapon to be ammunition effective and versatile. We used to use in the lighting operations and later used it in combat as a psychological strong weapon against the rebels in the trenches and holes spider which we can not influence them using high explosives (HE, high explosive). We started operations of shake and bake against the rebels. WP' using were expelled them from their places and using HE has been killed them [16,14,34]. Then the same article said (it is possible to use other types of smoke munitions and keep WP ammunition for deadly tasks!!). From this recognition, which is added to other confessions, it is assert that the chemical weapon white phosphorus was used as a deadly weapon.

The phosphorous bombs which are modified from the napalm bomb and have fluffy pot containing fuel powder ignites immediately upon contact with air and published gelatinous, sticky and incendiary material within a wide area as soon as contact with oxygen. Gel fuel has evolved over the years, was used during World War II (gasoline with material naphthenic and acids, palmitic palmitic acids), while developed in Vietnam and the Korean Wars to include (kerosene, gasoline and polystyrene polystyrene), then arrived evolution during the occupation of Iraq war to produce bombs (MK-77) containing jet fuel (kerosene) with polystyrene, in addition to contain oxidizing agent makes it difficult to put out the fires. These types of bomb have developed from species (M-47 and M-74) and their light aluminum containers are characterized by lack of fins to help them stabilize and making it far from being accurate weapons targeting [54,225]. The MK-77 bomb is one of the main incendiary weapons used by the United States Army and weighs 340 kg (750 lbs.). Its containing 110 gallons of gel fuel, which is one of the modern mixtures of napalm mixture that contains the oxidizing agent in order to prevents extinguish the flames as well as to contains WP (white phosphorus) [94]. The marines also used the weapons equipped by head containing 35% thermobaric novel explosive (NE) beside 65% standard high explosive, and has been used in order to cause the collapse of the roof and killed Fallujah fighters holed inside interior rooms, and were used over and over again for homes purge tremendously [200]. This type of weapon was used by Russian troops in the city of Grozny, Chechen (Grozny battles) as was referred by the US journal *Marine Corps Gazette* in an issue published in August 2000. They spoke about thermal weapons or also known as the fuel-air weapons. US military newspaper showing the nature of these weapons, saying (they form a cloud of volatile gases or fine powder fly, this cloud will ignite and eject rollers wounds in the surrounding area while consuming the oxygen in the region, the lack of oxygen leads to overpressure dramatically leading to killing of all human beings under this cloud, while outside the cloud area blast wave up to a distance of 3,000 meters per second, which makes this type of explosives have an effect of a tactical nuclear weapon without radiation traces. Injuries resulting from normal aerial bombardment may be burns, broken bones and possibly blindness, combined with the effect of excess pressure that will produce air embolism within the blood vessels, with concussions, and multi hemorrhages internal in the liver and spleen with collapse the lungs, accompanied by rupture the eardrum and the removal of the eyes from its place) [201]. For this, it is hard to believe Lieutenant Colonel Barry Venables that admitted on the use of these weapons without killing civilians!!

It is worth mentioning that the British Ministry of Defence has admitted that US Marines using of thirty bombs MK-77 type during the progress of Baghdad' occupation during the period from 22 March until 2 April 2003 [96]. Also that at the time, Col. James Alles leader of the group of 11 Air Force Marines stationed at Miramar admit to shoot down dozens of incendiary bombs near bridges along the Saddam Canal and the Tigris River and added (I've to watch a video through the cockpit, many people who are in these areas before the hit, they were Iraqi soldiers there, it is not suitable method for death). The bombing campaign has helped these weapons to eliminate pockets of resistance from the race track to the US Marine Corps to get to the capital, Baghdad. Maj. Gen. Jim Amos Commander of 3rd Marine Air Wing admit their use of napalm in several times during their progress toward Baghdad, especially near transit the bridge to the city of Numaniyah, about 40 km from Baghdad [95].

Although US side not recognition the amount of shells and prepared, but they also admitted using the following weapons and ordnance species in the Second Battle of Fallujah (severe munitions explosion (155-mm high explosive (HE) M107 (short-range)), shells long-term (M795), folds WP-luminescent (WP, M110 and M825), with fuzes bombing point-detonating (PD), different kinds timings, mortar shells 120 mm which is loaded with munitions WP and ammunition high explosive (HE), and lighting, with different fuzes species and ammunition of 81 mm [34].

One of the military sources also recognized that Marine engineers used 20 pounds of explosive and very dangerous material called C4 in the course of their holes in the concrete walls, which faced to their progress in some areas of Gulan neighborhood [194].

In addition to the use of the drones like Tactical UAVs (TUAVS) and these planes were used many kinds (Predator, Shadow, Hunter and Pioneer) in order that the target is very precise besides its intelligence role of places well fortified in the battle depth. It was known as the most efficient one called Predator which is capable of carrying several different missiles with a camera very accurate with full movement in the forefront of helping to drive by a computer in the base platform. In Fallujah dropped two unmanned UAVs at least of its heavy machine gun battalion called TF2-2 [194]. US military use also the shells weighing 500 pounds of the type of GBU-38 JDAM, which they considered at least in terms of collateral damage associated with bombs laser-guided, in addition to Hellfire shells unknown number, and directly hit ammunition guided by satellites [52]. While they used 2000 pound bombs since the early days [194].

At the end of Second Battle, the military outcome of air and artillery support there were 76 appeal for support by US ground forces inside Fallujah through backing by air and artillery bombardment different armament, resulting in 135 mission of close air support and throw 1898 artillery shells and 218000 pounds of ordnance [68].

9.3.1. The use of chemical weapons (WP)

White phosphorus is a white or yellow color solid with a smell similar to garlic. Ignites on contact with oxygen and cause significant a burn to the body and does not stop these burns or ignition only if stop the presence of oxygen [128]. It is used for the purposes of signaling, or the work smokescreen or incendiary, and has a second name known as Willie Pete and short "WP". It is used against human targets, such as the use of napalm [318].

Jeff Englehart from US Marines admitted the participating in the second battle and WP gases spread in the air but once contact with the skin and the harm can not be stopped in terms of burning flesh to the bones. It is not necessarily to burn clothes, but it will burn the skin under clothes and for this reason that masks does not help against the incendiary weapon that will burn the rubber component of the mask. If someone inhaled it then will cause Blister of throat and lungs until full choke and then burn the body, in addition, its usually reacts with the skin and oxygen and water [90,127].

WP burns easily over 10-15 ° C heat above room temperature and is used in the manufacture of chemicals and smoke ammunition. Because of a hypergolic property when exposed to air, it causes burns and irritation of liver, kidney, heart, lung, or bone damage, and death [128]. Which explains the lack of full combustion Knits with many of the bodies of the martyrs while a full open body was burned to the air.

9. 3. 2. Evidence of use of nuclear weapons

New Medical scientific analysis showed evidence of the use of nuclear weapons in Fallujah [5], in addition to the survey conducted by the inter-ministerial committee (see Chapter 10). United States deny the use of depleted uranium weapons during the Second Battle of Fallujah (Phantom Fury), but at the same time indicated it does not have any records on the use of depleted-uranium munitions before June 2004, which means that if they had used this ammunition during the first battle (Vigilant Resolve), it can not be verified. This answer has been come from US Department of Defense to a question by a British activist group (International Coalition to Ban Uranium Weapons) under The Freedom of Information Act (FOIA) [378]. It is known that the occupying armies had been used by the Fallujah battles also depleted uranium weapons against Iraq [468].

In an article written by journalist Christopher Bolleyn for the American Free Press in December 2004, he reports:

"Having seen what appeared to be a depleted uranium (DU) missile fired at a building in Fallujah on CNN during the first week of the fighting, AFP asked the Pentagon if DU weapons are being used in Fallujah. "Yes" Yoswa said, "DU is a standard round on the M-1 Abrams tank."

Because U.S. marines in Fallujah are very close to the poison gas produced by exploded DU shells, AFP asked Yoswa if anything was being done to protect the troops from DU poisoning. Yoswa seemed unaware of the dangers posed by the use of DU.

Marion Fulk, a retired nuclear scientist from Livermore National Lab told AFP that "The Marines exposed to DU in Fallujah, and elsewhere, face greatly increased risks of cancer, deformed children, and other health problems in the future." [705]

At least, two models of weapons that could fire depleted uranium shells were used in the second battle of Fallujah, Abrams tank, and Bradley AFV tank. In spite of doubts about the feasibility of the use of depleted-uranium munitions (APFSDS mm120) by Abrams tanks in a street fight against irregular forces!!! [379]. Despite all this information that confirms the magnitude of the military operations against the city of Fallujah, as if they are facing a modern army, but the American generals tried to claiming the easily entering to the city after the second battle [480], which was denied by the facts presented here of the magnitude of the arms and joint forces in this battle.

The weapons internationally banned and unknown composition of contained heavy metals and unknown influence but its known the destructive effects brought about both during the battles or after its completion by the horrific results of distorted daily birth and many diseases of cancer (see Chapter X).

Through the above, we see that the total number of weapons that shoot the city was danger to the public health and the environment depending on two important aspects: first, the qualitative side, which includes new destructive weapons, it is not known the nature of the explosive composition. Secondly is the enormous amount of explosives and missiles in all kinds and what caused of pollution from large cumulative results emerged quickly spread of dangerous diseases every day and embryonic malformations.

Chapter 10

Health Disaster & Environmental Pollution

10. 1. The health and environmental pollution by the battles of Fallujah

On 32 December 2004, and after six weeks of fighting between the US army and fighters of Fallujah, dozens of civilians gathered outside the city of Fallujah, in order to return to their homes between the rubble [310]. The return process of the contaminated and disaster city was the beginning of the health catastrophe that kills civilians successively. Fallujah remained as stricken city and under a full closed control of the US in the entry and exit to September 2008, when security powers transferred to the Iraqi government [353].

Official statistics for the Iraqi government show that the period before the outbreak of the first Gulf War in 1991, the incidence of the cancer rate in Iraq was 40 from 100,000 people. However in 1995 solutions, has increased to 800 from 100,000 people, and by 2005, this figure had doubled to at least 1,600 from every 100,000 people. Note that current estimates show the trend continuing to mount [384].

In order to highlight the fact that the health impact of chemical weapons, including white phosphorus specifically, because of the large number of evidence and confessions to use it as one of the lethal weapons types in Fallujah. US report (GAO, 2004) showed for the first Gulf War in 1991 growing conditions unknown among US soldiers returning to their country of this war. According to the US Defense Department's 700,000 patient's disease was not

[169]

diagnosed but attributed to exposure to chemical warfare (CW). This disease because of the elements of the plumes of smoke coming from Iraqi places bombed by US, according to the assumption of the US Department of Defense (117).

10.2. White Phosphorus (WP)

It is one of the forbidden and main weapons in the battles of Fallujah and one of the causes for the deterioration in the health of the city. US Environmental Protection Agency, which it described WP as a very toxic to humans [309]. While the Agency for Toxic Substances and Disease Registry that affiliate of the American Health Ministry issued more detailed information in September 1997 and showed that anyone of the ways to enter WP within the environment in the case was used by the military, it is very toxic and dangerous advantages to human life as following [128]:

1. Possibility of WP deposition in the water and the bottom of the river near the place of use or spread it, and reacts with water in the presence of less oxygen found to produce a highly toxic chemical compound is Phosphine, which is usually evaporates into the air to produce less harmful substances. White phosphorus can remain in the soil for many years without change.

2. There is a minor proportion of it in the fish' body that live in contaminated rivers with WP. For this, the exposure of white phosphorus may be through eating contaminated fish by phosphorus, or even drinking or swimming in contaminated rivers, or contact with contaminated soil.

3. The report admits the lack to provide sufficient information as to whether the exposure to white phosphorus affects the ability to reproduce or births malformations as well to missing studies indicate its impact leading to cancers. In addition, there is no medical test shows the exposure of white phosphorus.

4. US Environmental Protection Agency (EPA) was listed the WP as one of hazardous air pollutants that must be reported in the case of leakage or spread in the environment.

Lyophobic materials were known as flammable automatically when exposed to the air, where oxidized phosphorus pentoxide for forming during this process, then enormous heat is released in the form of bright flame with dense white smoke. This process continues until all the phosphorus will be oxidized or even deprived of oxygen. When burning particles come into contact with the skin can cause serious burns as a second and third tier. It penetrates the skin quickly to cause a deep and painful burn [309,318].

An attempt to extinguish the burning body by water is not useful because it is flammable phosphorus renewed once dry the water and phosphorus contact with oxygen because is penetrated and stationed under the skin. Delaying a little ignition or death, and in both cases will be the destruction of the heart, liver and kidneys, and in case of inhalation only white phosphorus particles in the smoke will cause serious damage to the lungs and throat [128]. Also, the smoke of WP has physiological effects on the human body and its smoke particles composed of phosphorus pentoxide which reacts with moisture in the air or the body for the formation of phosphoric acid. This acid, depending on the concentration and duration of exposure, may produce a variety of injuries or topically irritative injuries to the victim [318].

Exposure to low concentrations of smoke white phosphorus (phosphorus pentoxide 0.188 mg / m^3) for five minutes led to that half the people under test (volunteers) suffer from respiratory distress, coughing, congestion and throat irritation. While the high concentrations (phosphorus pentoxide 0.514 mg / m^3) for 15 minutes resulted in the exposure of all people under test to tightness of chest, cough, nose irritation, and difficulty speaking. Exposure to phosphorus pentoxide for 3.5 minutes and a concentration of 592 mg / m^3, which led to a similar irritation of the respiratory tract the tightness of chest, coughing and difficulty breathing. After this experiment, the volunteers refused to be exposed to the highest concentration in the belief that it would be impossible without more serious effects to perform any work or physical exercise in that focus. While one of the volunteers' faced acute bronchitis during the experiment [319]. From this evidence shows that white phosphorus is a volatile chemical and can cause serious burns with irritation of respiratory tract and mucous membranes, and under these effects of WP is considered as an incendiary or a chemical weapon.

[171]

10. 3. UN agencies

UN Agencies ones in such a health disaster, unfortunately, were not efficient on it international responsibility in accordance with its internal law towards such serious medical condition and previous evidence confirmed beyond any doubt about the use of chemical weapons and material with lethal specifications within the small town of Fallujah area. If you look at the reports and responses of World Health Organization (WHO) during the battles of Fallujah will find its periodic report on its activities in the international crises during the middle of April 2004, just referred to a little small exodus from the city of Fallujah [255]!!! Although the media and official reports confirmed the exodus of most of the city's 300,000 inhabitants during the first battle, and I do not know based on which measure they called this forced displacement as small size!! This confirms the deliberate politicization of hiding the facts. They only reference to medical aid sent to the Iraqi Ministry of Health and the Iraqi Red Crescent. While its periodic report came after the end of the second battle of Fallujah in reference only to deliver the humanitarian aid and health through the Iraqi Red Crescent to the internally displaced people of Fallujah, with their preparing for draft action plan for environmental relief for the displaced people of Fallujah [256]. Two months after the second battle, they pointed out in its January report of 2005 to convening of a meeting of the emergency action in Fallujah, without giving any further details [257].

According to the report of the British Royal Society, the most important methods used to identify chemical and biological agents and pollution prevention in the United Kingdom is the recognizing and diagnosing the effects of abnormal cases [351]. Whenever deepened more on how the preparations and the nature of the common tasks between the government and all official and popular apparatus about any chemical or biological contamination possible, I realized more the size of the crime they involved against Iraqi people and their present and future, and how they tried to conceal pollution facts, despite the appearance of each medical evidence and documented statistics.

10. 4. Scientific Reports

After two years of second massacre and as a result of worsening the bad health and environmental situation, we have done as NGOs in cooperation with the Fallujah hospital and over the years 2006/2007, for collecting official statistics ones in particular serious diseases. It was action to issuance of the first scientific and medical report about the real situation of the health in the city after three years of the end of the battle to attract the attention of global public opinion about this humanitarian disaster and criminal findings against civilians. The report titled Prohibited weapons crisis in Fallujah 2008 of CCERF-MHRI organizations was presented to the seventh session of the Human Rights Council of the United Nations (3-28 March 2008). The report show for first time the data of the medical staff in Fallujah' Hospital collected and confirmed the presence of 5928 seriously ill in 2006, (Meningitis, Thalassemia, Congenital Spinal cord abnormalities, Congenital Renal abnormalities, and undiagnosed cases). There were 70% of these cancers and congenital malformations were affecting the age group of 1 day to 12 years old. While the unknown and dangerous diseases were in the first half of 2007 are 2447 included 50% of it into the group of children.

This report spread for many international bodies, but most of the press we contacted did not refer to it exception of Al Jazeera English-speaking show it on Riz Khan Show [174]. However, with the help of peace activists and opponents of the war in America, it was sent to the secretariat of some American Congressmen. Two of them (we believe that one of them was Dennis Kucinich, a representative of the state of Ohio and who expressed his sympathy with the report), accompanied by the leader of Marines of the western region of Iraq were visited Fallujah on August 2008. The first place they were visiting fastly with exasperating to Fallujah General Hospital in order to ensure the information contained in our report. The way of visiting the hospital with a large military force sown terror among the staff of hospital and patients to end either. Unfortunately, the delegation was not trying to find the solutions of this disaster after it confirms our report, but they just held a meeting with members of the municipal council in Fallujah city with making promises to facilitate the recent grant disbursement of compensation on the damage of the second massacre that belonged to only the industrial zone, which was facing obstacles in the disposal of the former finance minister at the time (Bian Jabr Solag).

Beginning of 2009, international media began to bring the world's attention through the deployment of high credibility talking about high birth defects rates in the city of Fallujah. Researchers suggest a possible link between the remnants of war and health problems like the birth defects rate reached to 15% of the total births, especially among the highest proportion of fetal heart defects and neural tube defects [375,376,377].

Then began to appear successively studies that confirm what was in our report, one epidemiological surveys in mid-2010 and published international as a study research team British researchers - Iraqis by conducting my knowledge questionnaire included 711 houses (4843 people) mentioned about the spread of cancer and birth defects and rate Infant mortality during the period from the beginning of 2005 to the date of this study in Jan / Feb 2010. They proved to increase four times the size of the infant mortality rates, with the disruption of sex ratio between the births of males and females to reduce the birth rate of the male, and the increasing rates of deaths due to cancer, especially cancer of the blood in the aftermath of the Fallujah battles (2004). The results was to compare with those of other countries such as Egypt and Jordan, and found for 62 cases malignant cancer among this group (of which 16 cases of cancer among children aged 0-4 years), 20 case of leukemia (spread between the ages of between 0-34 years), and 8 cases of cancer of the lymph glands (spread between the ages between 0-34 years), and 12 cases of breast cancer in females (aged 0-44 years), and 4 cases of brain cancer among different ages [7,206].

While the infant mortality rate, according to statistics of births among 2006 - 2009 is up to 1/6th adding to Statistics above. There were 34 cases of death for infants between the ages of 0-4 years, and this gives the ratio of 80 cases from 1000, while the rate in Egypt, Jordan, Kuwait are 19.8, 17 and 9.7 of 1000. In addition to signs of destruction stress genetic, this has caused an imbalance in the sex ratio between males and females.

Scientific research of the American - Italian - Iraqi team published in the international journal at the beginning of 2011 showed there is a 15% increase in congenital malformations of the newborn babies, which topped Congenital heart defects first grade followed by neural tube defects. The similarity of the proportion of these cases with the same proportion of cases in contaminated areas during the war, and according to the questionnaire also conducted between the cases studied show high birth defects from after 2003, but the main cause of the increases remained unknown and need study more broadly[6].

Recent reports stir the attention to developments in congenital malformations anomalies and cancer in Fallujah, which it blamed on a genetic defect and genetic stresses caused by contamination with depleted uranium and chemical weapons in the battles witnessed in the city 2004 and the start of the important question is going on between the various researchers about the nature of the weapons increases used in the battles of Fallujah and what were the contents and nature of the destructive levels on short or long-term?

For this reason, British - Iraqis team of researchers in 2011 [5] conduct an analysis study of samples from the hair of 25 pairs of parents whom born deformed children using a device (Inductively Coupled plasma Mass Spectrometry) to determine if the uranium was found with 51 heavy elements. It is a full-length hair analysis can be obtained on the radiation exposure information by the time that affected him. And to analyze the samples of water and soil for determine the existence of uranium' isotopes.

Between the mothers were ratios of elements Ca, Mg, Co, Fe, Mn, V, Zn, Sr, Al, Ba, Bi, Ga, Pb, Hg, Pd, and U high moral natural proportions compared with average levels for women in Sweden for example. The high increase was in ratios Ca, Mg, Sr, Al, Bi, and Hg. The Hg element considered as the only cause of Congenital anomaly. High levels of uranium in the mothers were higher than in the fathers. But the big shock in this research was the type of uranium discovered in the samples is radioactive uranium (which is much more dangerous) and not depleted uranium as expected. Researchers attributed the presence of radioactive uranium as the main reason or connected to the spread of diseases, birth defects, and cancer. These recent results were a shock to many of the proponents of the occupation and they began to launch a campaign to discredit the work of British Professor Christopher Busby.

These results have been confirmed on 10 February 2012 when a team of several Iraqi scientific and official bodies (Iraqi Commission for control of the radiation, and the Ministry of Science and Technology, Ministry of Environment, the Council of Anbar province, the media in Fallujah Hospital) conducted a survey comprehensive on different areas of Fallujah in order to measure the radiation rates. They found a very high percentage of radioactivities in the two areas in the industrial district in Fallujah, near the new hospital. They collect radioactive waste war and sent it to the laboratories of Iraqi Atomic Energy Organization in Baghdad, according to what was issued by a member of the Anbar province council (Dr. Taleb Hammad, official environmental department in the Anbar governorate) and news published on media committee' page of Fallujah hospital confirmed by those pictures below.

The following are photos from the web site of Fallujah General Hospital called (Birth defects in FGH).

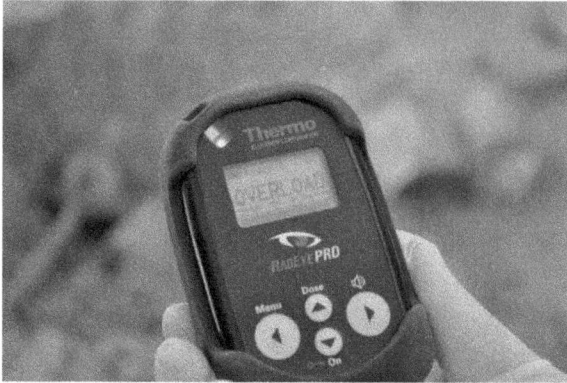

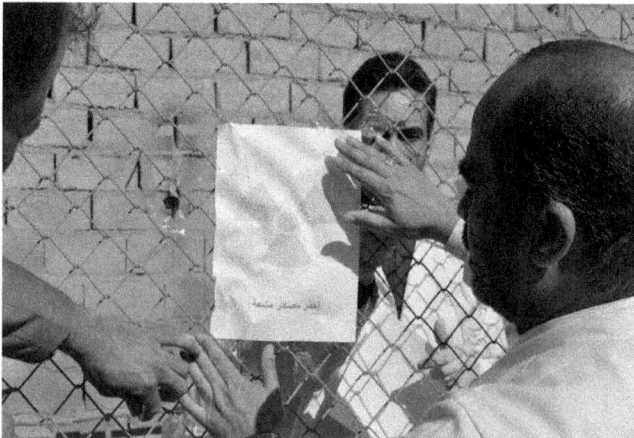

Scientific team from Fallujah General Hospital confirmed the incidence of cancer in Fallujah appears to be higher than the other regions in Iraq and other Middle East countries. The incidence of cancer in Fallujah is 96 per 100,000, while was 34.5 per 100,000 in 2002, before the US invasion in 2003, which mean increase 3 fold than before. Carcinoma of the breast, lung, stomach, and colorectal are leading cancers in Fallujah, according to medical data of Fallujah hospital in 2001 and was published in international journal (Health) on 2012 (699).

But what about the effects of chemical weapons used during the first and second Battles of Fallujah (April and November 2004)?? As everyone knows, the Israeli army had used also WP weapon against the Palestinian Gaza City during military operations in 2008-2009, which resulted in the increase 28% of birth defects, according to a research study of Italians - Palestinians scientists and published in the International Journal of Environmental Research and Public Health. Perhaps this is the only scientific study that proved scientifically a great relationship between exposure parent or one of them to an effect of WP or tailings for making a genetic change in the new children [192].

The effects of cluster weapons that have been used extensively, especially in the first battle of Fallujah, depending on a large proportion of deadly unexploded submunitions remain their effects polluting stricken. Occupation of Iraq in 2003 brought a huge force with huge equipment were distributed to more than 300 military bases inside Iraq. During the ten years of staying in Iraq, they left a lot of wastes and beyond without the accountability of any party, so they left unexploded ordnance, cleaning solvents, oils, and oil waste, and radioactive depleted uranium shells. Unfortunately, there is no formal policy on environment clean after the military operations. There is no list of laws, not of US Code, and in international law, or otherwise, which can be controlled and hazardous waste management in emergency operations such as the war in Iraq. In this war, the environmental consideration is not a high priority for the military. In accordance with the principles of guidelines from the US Central Command, "During combat operations, the environmental considerations are manufactured to accomplish the task and the preservation of human life" [208]. If we look at the security convention which was held between the US and Iraq in 2008, we will find that it contains a short paragraph about the general environmental responsibilities on the United States in which it says (on the parties to implement this agreement in a manner consistent with the natural environment and human health and safety protection). While Iraq's neighbors made after the first Gulf War of 1991 complaints against Iraq, demanding compensation for environmental damage because of this war to the Compensation Committee of the United Nations, valued at more than $ 80 billion. But the United Nations later gave them for environmental damages in the amount of worth more than 5 billion pounds [209]. It is worth mentioning is the US and British forces recognition of dumping more than 350 metric tons of depleted uranium on the combat zones during the first Gulf War in 1991 [354,255]. While the British Ministry of Defense recognized to use 1.9 metric tons of depleted uranium against Iraqi forces during the occupation of Iraq operations in 2003 which is equivalent to twice what they used during the War of 1991 [355,356].

According to the medical staff in Fallujah General Hospital, BBC and Al-Jazeera English-speaking chanels reported that rates for congenital heart defects in Fallujah are 13 times what is happening in Europe. The city is witnessing for 2-3 birth deformation cases per day, and the big rate of which congenital heart defects, compared with one case for every two months in 2003 [385,.325]. According to the BBC the Iraqi Ministry of Health has requested of World Health Organization and its country offices to provide technical support and expertise, although they organizing workshops with international centers working with the World Health Organization, such as ICBDSR and CDC. But the activities focused according to claim of BBC Radio to help Iraqi Ministry of Health to develop a monitoring system in areas likely to be affected in Iraq with training in the field of monitoring of birth defects [349]. These activities have been without the knowledge or participation of any environmental or health centers in Fallujah.

At a time of the proportion of birth defects in Fallujah increased, the Fallujah hospital lacked the necessary facilities to diagnose and treat a lot of cases, as organs sonar for the early detection of congenital malformations and fetal hardware required tests chromosomal DNA in addition to the acute shortage of many medicines and health supplies. It is hoped and awaits the announcement of the report of the World Health Organization in partnership with Iraqi Ministry of Health, who formed a team research on the topic and collect as many samples from posting program areas including Fallujah, and it was hoped to issue a report at the beginning of 2013, which has been issued so far [403].

10. 5. Confessions of Pollution in Similar Areas of Fallujah

The environmental pollution after Fallujah battles disaster did not stop at the borders of Fallujah alone, but overtaken by the cities of Anbar and other as Ramadi and Qaiem which also witnessed fierce battles with US Marines after the second battle of Fallujah. The statistics released from the Iraq western Center for recording and monitoring of congenital malformations in the teaching hospital for children and motherhood in Ramadi [10], showed the presence of 744 cases of congenital malformations in less than two months and for the period from (1/10/2011) until (02/28/2011).

If we look at the environmental and health disaster for the occupation outside the province of Anbar, we will find the province of Najaf, for example, suffer from the effects of pollution of depleted uranium weapons used by US and British forces during the wars of 1991 and 2003. Despite the contaminated area of fighting with weapons of depleted uranium is about 180 miles far from the city Najaf, but the escalation of cancer diseases was a remarkable rate of 28.21 per 100,000 people in 2006. While the natural ratio should be 8.12 cases per 100,000 people [8]. Another scientific team noted to increased rates of birth defects in Fallujah, Basra at high rates [381]. Recent US studies have shown transmission-genetic damage from parents (who were exposed to the effects of depleted uranium weapons) to children or the new birth as happened with the soldiers who were not the target of such munitions during the 1991 Gulf War [393]. Scientific Reports have proven the existence of Chromosome Alterations in lymphocytes among veterans who participated in the Gulf War 1991 and Balkans war in 1994 [396]. While Environment Programme of UN noted in its report for 2007 that US troops were fired during the Gulf War 1991, about 50 metric tonnes during the tanks' battles and 250 metric tonnes in the atmosphere of the ground battles. The same report pointed to the fact that the amount used during the occupation of Iraq war 2003 was ranging between 170-1700 metric tonnes [397].

British official report issued by the British Royal Commission also admitted that the 340 tonnes of depleted uranium weapons have been used in the first Gulf War 1991, and the proportion of 70-80% of the gear and equipment contaminated with uranium weapons have been buried on the battlefield. Despite the recognition that the risks of these weapons is the occurrence of congenital malformations and cancers of new births, but they claimed that the epidemiological studies on reproductive health of soldiers who participated in the first Gulf War 1991, as well as Iraqi civilians, did not appear the effects at time of writing the report 2002, although that the report's recommendation to invite further investigation in the case of the emergence of such effects, according to the report allegation !!!! [352]. The ability of depleted uranium activity is less than 40% from the irradiated uranium [354], but it increases to 80% of the activity rate of radioactive uranium months after its production, but keep the same level of the chemical toxic effects of radioactive analogues [374]. As well as this recognition was confirmed by report of UNEP on 2003 saying that US forces had used the 290 square meters of depleted uranium shells (DU projectiles) compared with the use of 9 tonnes in the Kosovo war, and 3 tonnes in the Bosnian War. Note that this quantity of depleted uranium has been used in Iraq by US military as different proportions. US military tanks and marines (the two types of tanks M60 and M1A1 Abrams) fired about 16%, while the US Air Force planes of type II (LNP) (A-10 Thunderbolt II) or named pig or tank Fool ('warthog' or 'tank buster') fired about 81%, and Marines Harrier aircraft type (AV-8 Harrier) threw about 3% [363]. Another source pointed to the use of the US for more than 440,000 Kg of depleted uranium during the wars of 1991 and 2003, after he had been tried in the joint military exercises in Egypt before the 1991 war [395,388,374]. Another US source pointed to the launch of the armies of the United States for about 900,000 rounds of depleted uranium during the Gulf War 1991 [395]. UNEP had estimated the amount of what has been thrown on the Iraq from nuclear weapons depending on satellite images after the end of military operations in 2003, about 1,000 to 2,000 metric tonnes [390,380].

International scientific report published in the Journal of Bull Environ Contam Toxicol in 2012, pointed to obtain an increase seven-fold increase in the number of birth defects of new birth in the city of Basra, between 1994 and 2003. There were 23 cases of fetal malformation of every 1,000 live births. As the concentration of lead in the deciduous teeth of sick children in Basra, nearly three times to a similar value in areas without a fight. This study concludes that it did not happen before such a high rate of neural tube defects "open back" as it was recorded in children of Basra, and this rate continues to rise. The number of hydrocephalus cases "water on the brain" among newborns is six times in Basra than it is the case in the United States [514].

According to US General Office Accounting, US troops were fired in Iraq and for the period between 2002 to 2005 by about six million bullets (6000000000) [384]. Another example of pollution of Iraq by remnants of the US Army is what announcement by American newspaper The Times, on the associated main roads with Baghdad, Fallujah, and Mosul, where the fighting was at its peak. The spread drums of hazardous waste with oil filters and sprays, drums non-liquid waste known and unknown. While some contractors appointed by the US military for the disposal of hazardous waste mixed with metal scrap to be distributed to Iraqi traders, complained that scrap yard Iraqis workers got a disease such as coughing and rashes and other diseases after dealing with the US scrap contaminated with hazardous waste. The amount of hazardous waste generated by the US forces as estimated according to the same newspaper about 11 million pounds of hazardous waste, while an estimated US responsible for the reconstruction of infrastructure in Iraq, Brigadier General Kendall Cox that more than 30 million pounds of Iraqi soil has been contaminated with oil, and both of these figures do not include unexploded munitions or munitions used previously and containing depleted uranium [210].

According to a US - Iraqis medical team in the maternity hospital in Basra, the proportion of fetal malformations in Iraq between 1994-1995 is 1.37 per 1000 born children and increased the rate in 2003 to up to 23 per 1000 born children to confirm an increase of 17 times. At the same time there is a high proportion of heavy metals such as lead in the hair, nails, and teeth samples for children who live in Basra as nearly three-fold compared with the population of unimpacted areas [350]. While leukemia rates have risen in childhood in Basra more than doubled between 1993 and 2007. In 1993, the annual rate of blood cancer (leukemia) in childhood is 2.6 per 1000, and by 2006 had reached 12.2 per 1000 [389].

It is understood also the psychological effects remain with the population for a long time, as one global studies conducted by Jonathan Dworkin team (2008) on the population of the Halabja city, Iraq, which hit by chemical weapons also in 1998. The study indicates that after 18 years of incident that the war and violations Human rights contribute to the increased prevalence of PTS (post traumatic stress) and low social performance among the population and remain these ratios are high between the different ages and sexes, even after decades of war and the incident of human rights violations [492].

According to the documentary report photographer from Russia Today channel, doctors and researchers confirm the high rate of cancer in the city of Basra at alarming proportions in recent years. Experts consider this phenomenon as a new war on the Iraqi people left by the wars against Iraq, and a foretaste of the terrifying future of the second largest city in Iraq as density population. What make matters worse are the high prices for the treatment from these diseases and the weakness of government support and the lack of specialized centers for the treatment of cancer stand without control it. As well as the existences of new forms of cancers are the result of the use of weapons against Iraq they contain radioactive materials and toxic [12A].

In Iraqi city Hawija, they found Titanium (Ti) and magnesium (Mg) are heavily used in war industries. Exposure to Ti and Mg has been linked to the dust in occupation soldiers' lungs. Hair samples of children in Hawija, Iraq contained significantly higher levels of Ti compared to Iranian children living near the Iraqi border. Magnesium was 1.7 times higher in Hawija children compared to Iranian children. In samples from Hawija, Ti was 1.3 times higher in children with neurodevelopmental disorders, and Mg was 1.9 times higher in children without neurodevelopmental disorders. Lead, arsenic, and cadmium in Hawija children with neurodevelopmental disorders were 2.5, 2.2, and 1.37 times higher compared to non-disabled children. Although this city is witnessing lower proportion than found in the cities of Fallujah and Basra, according to Iraqi - US team' results were published in the Journal of Environmental Monitoring and Assessment, 2015 [698].

10. 6. International Cover-up About The Crime of Pollution

Chris Busby said that the health crisis in Fallujah represents "the highest proportion of genetic damage in any population studied than ever". Busby is the co-author of two studies on this subject and he added: However, it is difficult to determine accurately the cause of defects. It also can cause deformed Spinal chord from a lack of folic acid in early pregnancy as an example. Moreover, very few of the Iraqis doing regular pregnancy tests on the opposite of what usually happen in Europe or the United States. Wolfgang Hoffmann, an epidemiologist at the University of Greifswald in northeastern Germany, has in collaboration with fellow scientists in Basra for years. He says, "birth defects often look very annoying when you see them in the pictures, but in each case their circumstances and not necessarily that the pictures are specific to the causes, and the overall data and questions epidemiological reliable shortages also affect. However, indicators to increase the incidence of cancer in Basra should be taken seriously, because data of Basra is more reliable [513]. International cover-up on this issue was flagrant. In the United States, did not publish yet any of the famous newspapers about genetic disorders in Fallujah, with the exception of Al Jazeera English. British Guardian criticized the silence of the "West" and describing it as a moral failure.

In an evaluation study by the United Nations Development Group (UNDP) about birth defects in the six governorates of Baghdad, Anbar, Basra, Dhi Qar, Sulaimaniya and Diyala. It stating that there is a survey conducted in 2006 had congenital birth defects has shown that 20% of children under 5 years of age have some form of disability, and some of these cases have been attributed to birth defects. This means the need to develop a comprehensive program to better understand the distribution and size of the trends and birth defects in Iraq [382].

Wikileaks' documents also revealed the role of the remnants of the US bases (more than 500 military bases, predominantly located near the main roads of Baghdad-Mosul and Baghdad-Anbar) to add another type of direct pollution of the Iraqi environment by burning US troops dangerous and polluting materials, mostly hazardous chemicals are buried after cremation in Iraqi territory to add another type of pollution [186]. The United Nations Environment Programme select 311 contaminated places needs to several decades for cleared, especially with regard to the uses of depleted uranium and white phosphorus in their war on Iraq in 1991 and 2003. UNEP director program in Iraq Mural Thummarukudy told that there are hundreds, probably thousands of other sites with the need of assessment [553].

The US secret document pointed about the bombing of high explosives and white phosphorus shells by US team performs operations to deal with unexploded ordnance munitions (UXO Operations), including the bombing revealed by one of the documents were conducted outside Baiji base (NAD Bayjis) on 4 March 2008. This operation included five bombings containing 124 shell of Armor Piercing, and the bombing of one of them was Includes 59 shells of High Explosive and High Explosive Anti-Tank. The second bomb place was Includes the ejected from ammunition WP MM 105 (White Phosphorus Projectile). With poor safety procedures, the explosion of unintentional to ejected WP injuring the supervisor of this project (John Carter) across burns caused by WP on both hands and eyes with a ruptured cornea of left eye [189].

In the new study on the reality and the effects of the use of depleted uranium in Iraq, has issued by a Dutch organization (IKV Pax Christi) and funded by the Norwegian Foreign Ministry report titled (In a state of uncertainty) [374], and it revealed the following facts:

1. The lack of transparency in the provision of information from the occupation forces (Alliance) during the wars of 1991 and 2003, especially around the coordinates of launch to this missile and launch' amount and type of ammunition used. The lost important information makes it difficult to make any real effort to cleaning contaminated places by these substances, risk assessment and implementation of the repair work.

2. Use of depleted uranium in populated areas against armed and unarmed targets, usually states defends that use these weapons they used to defend against armored and armed vehicles, but its use in Iraq was widely used in populated areas, causing a very big problem because of the nature indiscriminate of depleted uranium dust.

3. The difficulty to assess and manage contamination with depleted uranium because the effective and influential management of the devastated areas require significant cooperation between several UN experts, such as UNEP, International Atomic Energy Agency and World Health Organisation. More than 300 contaminated sites are still in the evaluation process of cleansing.

4. The impact on the health and civil environmental as pointed out by many reports and published research referred to a dangerous increase in congenital malformations.

Ironically, the first Iraqi government created by the occupation in 2004, in front of the meeting of High Commissioner of human rights in United Nations, had admitted of increase the proportion of projections and birth defects among newborns, but it did not dare to address the issue of pollution as a result of the use of prohibited weapons against the Iraqi people since Gulf War 1991 until the end of military operations of the occupation of Iraq 2003 [7A].

Abdul Hussein Shaaban, Iraqi activist of human rights referred to some important facts [19 A]: US troops left after the withdrawal from Iraq (30 December, 2011) All of the hazardous waste in Iraq instead of returning to the

United States, as required by international laws and conventions, in particular the international Basel convention (Switzerland) 1989 for controlling the movement of hazardous waste across border and disposal. As well as the Acts of US Department of Defense, "Pentagon" have the same prohibition (the United States has not ratified the Basel Convention, but US laws prevent to transfer these toxic substances to another country). *Times* newspaper said " the toxic substances include about 130 thousand tons of waste, in addition to getting rid of 14500 tons of oil and soil contaminated with it that has accumulated during the years of occupation. Narmin Othman Iraqi Environment Minister on 30/6/2010 has revealed that the US military landfill huge amounts of waste and toxic waste in 30 locations. Gen. Kinneral Cox has admitted before a year of US troops leave Iraq (2010), saying: We have accumulated (during our stay) millions of pounds of hazardous waste, but he tried to evade responsibility by the US Constitution and the responsibility of the US governments who decided the war in Iraq or hide its crimes now.

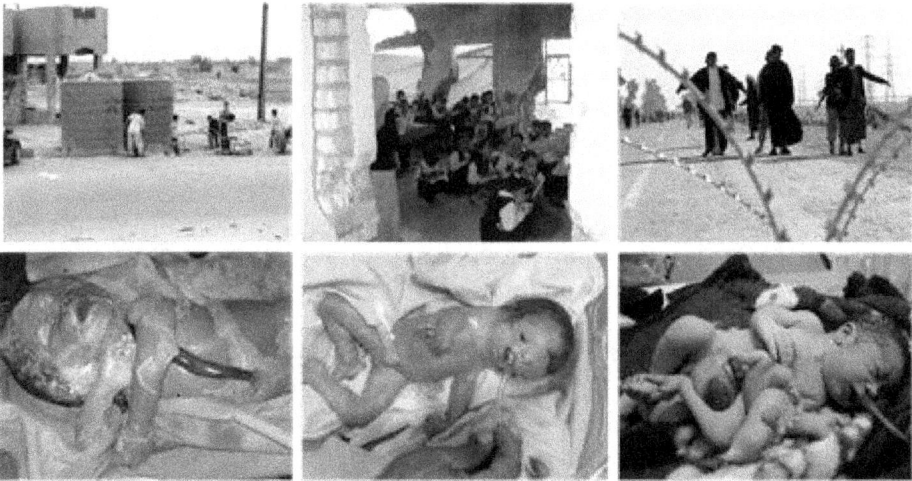

The Environmental Cause of the Cancer and Birth Defects in Fallujah

Christopher Busby

In Chapter 10 of this book you will read about the evidence of enormous and significant increases in cancer and birth defects in Fallujah after the battles of 2003. The effects in Fallujah are reported from all over Iraq in areas where there was fighting in 1991 and in 2003. I have been asked by the author, Muhamad Al-Darraji, to comment on the shrill and sometimes bewildering reports which have appeared on this issue.

I entered this area in 1998 as a result of my research into the health effects of Depleted Uranium. I visited Iraq in 2000 with Al Jazeera and went to the cancer hospitals and to the southern battlefields and tank cemeteries, taking sophisticated radiation measuring equipment. I also visited Kosovo with Nippon TV and later gave evidence to the Royal Society. I have become since then something of an international authority on the health effects of Uranium and was on the UK Government Depleted Uranium Oversight Board. Uranium binds to DNA and provides genetic damage through its amplification of natural background radiation as a result of photoelectron emission.

Depleted Uranium has a quite specific signature: its isotope ratio. This can be measured with sophisticated scientific instruments, and the sensitivity of these ICPMS machines have increased to an extraordinary level in the 20 years since the material DU was deployed in Iraq in 1991. But as detection ability has changed, the nature and type of the Uranium weapon has also changed as the military cover their tracks. We are finding natural or slightly enriched Uranium on battlefields. Uranium is being deployed in missiles and thermobaric weapons. There are new weapons of an entirely new type, which are believed to employ Uranium and heavy hydrogen, Deuterium and Tritium, to create a cold fusion nuclear bomb. Naturally, there is little information about this: but there are the traces left when this weapon is used, and we have measured these traces in Lebanon, in Gaza and in Fallujah, in the hair of the mothers of the children with birth defects. These were the test sites for these.

First I must say that I do not believe that White Phosphorus is a cause of genetic damage, cancer and birth defects in Fallujah. WP is a truly terrible weapon, and should not be employed, but Phosphorus is a natural substance which is used by the body, and white phosphorus burns to the pentoxide. There is no evidence from those who work with phosphorus of any genotoxicity which would lead to the kinds of cancer increases and extraordinary birth effects seen in Fallujah. Attempts to sell WP as the cause are, in my opinion, a smokescreen to divert attention from Uranium. The other possible cause, Mercury, which we also found in the hair of the mothers, can cause teratogenic effects, birth defects following the exposure of the fetes. But we are seeing in Fallujah effects which persist. This and the sex ratio effect point clearly to a genetic or genomic effect. And the only substance we found that could cause that is Uranium or radiation. Or some chemical weapon: but these chemical weapons like Lewisite, mustard gas, are easy to detected from the blisters they cause; nothing like that was reported.

The author, and others before him, present historic levels of cancer and birth defects and show that more recent measurements show large increases. It was this approach in the early 2000s that led to my entering this field. There is no doubt about large increases in cancer. But the fact is quite hard to obtain accurate or believable figures for cancer rates and congenital diseases in a third world country which has been battered by wars so that population data are hard to assemble. In a war, people move away, they flee. No one is collecting census figures. If a child dies shortly after birth, there is no time or technology to see if it was due to a congenital heart defect, or some other invisible cause. The child just fails to prosper, coughs a lot and dies. Often in areas where there is no hospital, nor any doctor. For this reason the recent questionnaire study by the Iraqi WHO is ridiculous. And the idea that the low pre-war cancer rate of 8 or 28 per 100,000 is true is also impossible. In the west, where there are good cancer registries, the crude cancer rate is about 400 per 100,000. In the 1950s it was less, but it has never been 28 or 8 per 100,000. You cannot compare crude cancer rates without a control population of the same ethnic origin and standardisation for age. So that is what we did in the now famous 2010 questionnaire study published in the International Journal of Environmental Research and Public Health. This compared, age for age and sex for sex the population of the Fallujah sample with a population on Egypt. This was the first, and is still the only study where this was done. And it showed (as you will read in Chapter 10) the highest levels of cancer in any population ever studied anywhere. In particular, and of enormous importance for childhood cancer and leukaemia research, it showed levels of these diseases which may go a long way to identifying the cause of child leukaemia in other populations. For example, those living near nuclear sites like Sellafield in the UK.

It is my belief that the cause of all these effects is Uranium, in the form of nanoparticles, produced by new Uranium weapons. It is not White Phosphorus: the suggestion is silly. It is not Mercury. We found significant excess Uranium in the hair of the mothers. We found enriched Uranium is a still fresh crater and in an ambulance air filter in the Lebanon. We found enriched Uranium in samples from an air filter in Gaza. And some radioactivity has been found in Fallujah according to the author, but I have not seen any details of measurements or identity of the radioactive isotopes.

What we did for cancer in the 2010 questionnaire study we then did with Dr Samira Al-Ani for the congenital malformations. The results were published in the Journal of the Islamic Medical Association of North America in 2012. The levels of births defects by type were listed there: top of the list is the congenital heart defects. These can only be diagnosed with ultrasound, and by experts. A child in a village with no access to a hospital will just die; no one will write "heart defect" on the certificate, assuming there is one.

It is my opinion that we have covered all we need to cover in this area. We made the epidemiology studies of the cancer, the birth defects, and the sex ratio. We measured the Uranium on the ground and in the parent's hair. And we have put our results in the peer-review literature. I have presented them at the Human Rights Council in Geneva twice. No one has put any results in the peer review literature showing any of this is wrong. They just ignore this, or criticize from the sidelines and write to the journal editors and my universities to have me thrown out. The Iraq WHO report was not peer reviewed and is not in the peer review literature. So the challenge stands: what is being done about it? Nothing!!

But something has been done about me. I have been much attacked and lampooned by those who are no-doubt employed by the nuclear industry and the military in some way or another. But as Joseph Conrad wrote: *after all the shouting is over, the grim silence of facts remain.* And the facts are indeed grim. The genotoxic effects in Fallujah, in Iraq, in all the places where these new Uranium weapons have been used speak for themselves. Similar effects are found in the veterans: There are reports in the literature of congenital birth defects in US veterans. I have been approached by many Gulf War veterans with cancer and leukaemia. But in the UK, the High Court has been persuaded by the UK Ministry of Defence that I cannot act as an Expert Witness any more in these cases because I am an "Activist". That is I write stuff about these hellish effects in magazines, on the internet in videos and appear on Russia Today and Al Jazeera and in newspapers.

I believe that the truth will eventually emerge. But only if we continue to fight this war for humanity, one of the battles of which is the battle of Fallujah, which is still being fought thanks to the perseverance and bravery of the author and his friends.

CHAPTER 11

Created Death Squads & Sectarian Strife in Iraq

11. 1. Reasons for the Salvadoran option

T he Western invasion of Iraq opened the door to many other hidden wars. Former US Secretary of Defense Donald Rumsfeld was optimistic about the "light footprint" of more than 140 thousand US soldiers. But in the end it turned into chaos that led him to submit his resignation in 2006. General David Petraeus replaced Rumsfeld to ask for more troops to pursue a counterinsurgency strategy in Iraq. President Obama was pushed to employ this strategy in the fight against the insurgency in Afghanistan too, but it proved a catastrophic failure there as well! This failure opened the way for new shadow wars, like drone attacks against suspected militants in Afghanistan, Pakistan and Yemen .[521]

The violence which began in Iraq 2003 came out of 3 types of conflicts. (1) First, was the military conflict that started with the initiation of occupation and its continuation. (2) Second, was the emergence of an armed popular rejection movement that attempted to expel the occupiers. (3) Third, were sectarian killing-some captured on film- that occurred from 2005 to 2007. Dr. Toby Dodge, an international political science professor at the University of Queen Mary, confirmed this in his analysis explaining that the actions of the Alliance forces (the occupation) led by America, helped either directly to increase violence or to cause its escalation because of political decisions that they imposed.[342]

Several Iraqi political parties that arose with the foreign occupation in Iraq concurred at their meeting with findings of a US military research group, [230] that the most important reasons for the lack of security after the entry of the occupation forces were:

1. Order No. 2 to disband the Iraqi army by the former Coalition Provisional Authority (CPA Order # 2);

2. Order No. 1 to implement De-Ba'athification by the Coalition Provisional Authority (CPA Order # 1);

3. The Consideration of US forces as occupiers, not as liberators;

4. The spread of looting and lawlessness;

5. The inability to control weapons and ammunition stockpiles;

6. The shooting of peaceful protesters in Fallujah.

Iraqi military officials themselves in 2004 acknowledged that US forces had been turning a blind eye to theft crimes, especially theft of stores of arms and ammunition by the lawlessness happening right in front of them. [230] In addition, borders were left open, confirming American's prior intention to make Iraq into an open battlefield across the arena occupied by opponents of the US occupation and politics. That made Iraq available to them with the easy availability of weapons, too. Making the wrong policy led to trouble at all levels and most influential was the military stalemate.

Local fighters fought a guerrilla war because of foreign presence on their land. They wanted no part of foreign occupation. Accordingly, they followed the approach of resisting the foreign occupation within a guerrilla strategy framework. David Kilcullen, an Australian military specialist on counter-terrorism, guerrilla warfare and international joint activities shared with the Pentagon from Australian counterparts their high expertise in counter-insurgency and terrorism. [498]

11. 1. 1. Military Stalemate

To know the truth about the US military stalemate in Iraq we need to consider, for example, the statistics of the US Army Medical Corps indicating that the number of their wounded who were treated in the 31st Combat Support Hospital in Baghdad alone exceeded 3,426 wounded for the period of December 2003 until the battle of Fallujah in November 2004. [214] Casualties after the first five years of the occupation reached 33,000, of which 29,000 had been wounded and more than 4,000 people were killed. [215] For this reason the US had been reducing the number of military forces, increasing the pace of operations, and using complicated weapons systems. These factors pushed the recruitment of mercenaries (contractors) to be used rather than members of the armed forces, according to the report of the US General Accounting Office issued on June 5, 2003. [115]

General Casey admitted in March 2005 that the militants operating from the Sunni areas had enough manpower, weapons, ammunition and money to launch between 50 and 60 attacks a day. [53] General Ricardo Sanchez described, when comparing Baghdad residents by sect, that the Sunnis are the most opposed to the occupation of US and coalition forces. [36] Given America's well known creation of death squads in Latin America, promoted under the pretext of freedom and democracy, it is no surprise that they fabricated lies to suppress resistance in the Sunni areas referred to as the Sunni Triangle. A Human rights report to UNAMI in the beginning of 2006 concluded that the US military operations, especially in Anbar province, raised concerns about the human rights situation, especially in the cities of Ramadi and Fallujah where there was the imposition of restrictions on movement freedom, and/or excessive use of force, abuse and robbery during raids on houses. [649] This suggests that the US started implementing a policy of revenge wreaked on civilians in those cities after the previous hard fought battles with them.

At the time the US Congress and State Department recognized the strong resistance (rebellion) of the Sunni mainstream, they admitted also the existence of Shiite militias according to the Commander of US Central Command CENTCOM), as early as August 2006. These militias are the largest contributors to the sectarian violence in Iraq. The Defense Ministry also reported in August 2006 that threat posed by Shiite militias was growing and posed a major challenge to the Iraqi government. Shiite militias that impact the security situation in most cases are the Mahdi Army and the Badr Brigade. [118] The author believes that this information represented an attempt to create confusion about which groups were resisting the occupation in contrast to other different groups deviating from their direction and goals.

After the killing of four security contractors in Fallujah on March 31, 2004, the Deputy Commander of military operations in Iraq, General Kimmitt, said a description that quipped about the difference between terrorists and insurgents, informing that the rebels may be from the former regime elements where they had received advanced training in the former Iraqi army, and that they were attacking his soldiers and police stations in Fallujah, while the terrorists are the ones who carry out amazing suicide attacks that targeted Iraqi army barracks, hotels, mosques and religious ceremonies in Karbala and Baghdad, with the participation of Al-Qaeda and Abu Musab al-Zarqawi. This suggests that the US military units did not record or note the presence of any foreigner fighter in those areas, believing that the attacks arose from internal armed organizations, according to journalist Robert Fisk. [506] For this, the guerrilla option and the creation of death squads is only fighting small wars in the midst of a big one as described by Australian and international terrorism expert officer David Kilcullen. [498]

11. 1. 2. Effect of Failed Foreign Mercenaries in Iraq

Death squads or murder gangs execute a terrorist strategy of mass murder, sometimes called the Salvadoran option because it was first implemented by the United States in El Salvador. The United States had supported militias that answered to El Salvador's dictator that had produced a series of murders of an estimated 75,000 victims. One American policy in Latin America was supporting and outsourcing the death squads to stop the feared Communist expansion there. In Argentina in the 1970s, and in Guatemala in the 1980s, soldiers dressed out of uniform and used unmarked cars in the night to kidnap and murder opponents of the regime or their suspected supporters

In September 2004, David Isenberg wrote to the British-American Security Information Council instructing them that the Pentagon's reliance on security contractors (PSPs) in Iraq was a bad solution that resulted from (1) the failure of the administration to provide adequate resources per international legal requirements for the occupation force; (2) the worsening security situation, [???*to avoid restrictions (selectors) of armed forces???*], and (3) the desire to employ the basic skills of contractors. as reasons driving the hiring contractors instead of existing members of the armed forces. [70]

Death squads and the explosion of the security situation limited press coverage and the freedom to work monitoring the daily violations and crimes. It was easier to punish pro national resistance zones where there was significant opposition to the presence of the occupation. Public Affairs Officer LTC James E. Hutton from III Corps and Fort Hood disclosed that the only factor causing deviation in media coverage in Iraq from what his administration had hoped for, was the presence of many organizations that check and collect daily statistics about victims with lots of photos and movies published by the press offices. [184] For this reason, vulnerable and unprotected journalists remained exposed in Iraq to ongoing murder in conditions that pushed Iraq to the forefront of countries most dangerous for journalists.

11. 2. The US Role

The Bush administration insisted that political power in the formation of the new Iraqi government after Bremer's rule must be on a sectarian and ethnic basis. It was a big mistake and this replicated exactly the formula that proved disastrous in Lebanon, a country that has remained mired in a bloody civil war for nearly two decades. [324]

The US Army Applied Guide (FM 31-20-3) applying to Foreign Internal Defense Tactics Techniques and Procedures for Special Forces in 2004, refers to the applied policy to support death squads and to support support corrupt governments in Latin America. It is the policy of the US Special Forces. [187] If we look back, we will find that the role of the CIA in creating al-Qaida followed an appeal by US President Carter to Muslims for jihad in Afghanistan during the Soviet occupation of Afghanistan (from December 1979 until the Soviet full withdrawal in 1989.) The support and US cooperation with Afghans and Arab fighters had grown increasingly. The National Security Advisor of former US President Carter, Zbigniew Brzezinski, also admitted and supported what the former US CIA Director Robert Gates revealed in his memoirs (From the Shadows). Both described how former US President Jimmy Carter signed a law authorizing the US intelligence apparatus to help the Mujahideen in Afghanistan following Soviet intervention in Afghanistan. This help fostered the emergence of Soviet intervention in Afghdstan. It was intended to give the Soviet Union a new war to fight, like the Vietnam War, for the US to strike back at them after the American defeat in Vietnam. The important thing to grasp is the trade-off was made to destroy the Soviet empire, to liberate Central Europe and to end the Cold War, in exchange for accepting invaluable support, and the emergence of the Taliban. [180]

[???MP for Texas] Charles Wilson expressed his support of US policy to help the Mujahideen in Afghanistan. He said that there were 58,000 US dead in Afghanistan, and we (the US) owed it to the Soviets to get a similar dose. He thought that the money spent in Afghanistan was the best thing used to hurt opponents. [431] This prompted the American writer William Blum, author of the Killing the Hope, a book that described and criticized the US intervention in Afghanistan (1979-1992) as "jihad the American way." [426]

It is well known that the occupation authorities had sponsored criminal militias and death squads before and after the occupation of Iraq. One of these forces, known as the Scorpions, had worked since the beginning of the occupation in secret. Its tasks before the war were penetration of Iraqi cities and sowing confusion and carrying out acts of sabotage to support the invasion. It was said that these units had entered the cities of Baghdad, Fallujah and Qaim, but the speed of the invasion's initial attack and occupation of Iraq made for rapid dispensing of their services. [455] But by the end of 2003, Washington had chosen a dirty war policy. It funded a new law recommended by the Pentagon, and approved by the US Congress in November 2003, to earmark $3 billion for Iraqi militias. [457] There were charges that in the city of Fallujah there was kidnapping, detention and killing of innocent people by the Iraqi army and the Public Order Brigade of the Ministry of Interior, that had entered after the second battle and under the supervision of US troops. [10 A]

After mid-2004, the occupation forces increased their reliance on irregular Iraqi forces, as well as special units set up under the nominal control of the Iraqi Interior Ministry. Pentagon sources spoke to reporters and news media about this policy as "the Salvadoran option," referring to the tactics of the United States in the fight against the insurgency in Central America in the early nineteen eighties. [458] Tjese comprised irregulars, new units set up in the Summer and Autumn of 2004, including the Hilla SWAT Team, the Iraqi Freedom Guard, the Amarah Brigade, and the Special forces police sometimes referred as the Wolf Brigade). [460] Many of the militias were trained and armed by the occupation forces. [461]

Many of the militias operated as death squads and carried out targeted assassinations. Many Iraqi leaders and former officers were vulnerable to assassination or targeting, especially after cleansing campaigns under the name of de-Baathification purges. [462] Meanwhile, Western journalists before the second battle in Fallujah were restrained from informing about the presence of spies for fear of being considered as conspiracy theorists. But spies and covert operations are not a conspiracy in Iraq, they are a daily reality! CIA Deputy Director James L Pavitt, said that "Baghdad is home to the largest CIA station since the Vietnam War" with 500-600 of their agents on the ground. Prime Minister Allawi then and throughout his life, spoke about working with MI6, the CIA and Iraqi intelligence service. [476]

The 2006 annual report of US Department of State on Iraq ,[229] revealed the true agenda of US policy as they started to foster sectarian tension. The report distinguishes groups strongly opposed to the Iraqi interim government as of May 2004 like Al'-Qaeda, scattered groups of the Baath party, and Sunni insurgents as waging guerrilla warfare. While they portrayed the sectarian and criminal violence by members of the security forces and sectarian militias as if it were individual behaviour in many cases, independent of government authority. It implied that the rebels' crimes were directly against the government, but the militias' crimes were merely acts committed by sectarians to hinder the government's work in the field of human rights. This gave a green light to help the militia continue their crimes. The same report speaks in detail of arbitrary or unlawful deprivation of life by the criminal activities of sectarian militias operating outside the control of the government without branding it " criminal." The report is in two parts, one pertaining to the Badr Brigades (the armed wing of the Supreme Council for Islamic Revolution, closely tied to to Iran), and the other the Mehdi Army militia of the Sadrist movement, which was established after the the occupation began.

The official US role in supporting liberation movements always depends on the US interest primarily, and not according to the right of self-defense and the right of armed resistance against foreign occupation as the simplest human rights recognized internationally. The role of the CIA in its relations with al-Qaeda in Afghanistan during the Soviet occupation of Afghanistan is the best proof of that. Before we address the death squad crimes, we will consider the most prominent players who emerged as supporters of the death squads in Iraq.

11. 2. 1. John Dimitri Negroponte

He was born in Britain to Greek parents, later gaining US citizenship. (He speaks five languages (English, Spanish, Greek, Vietnamese, and French)). The lowlights of his life and his deceptive and dirty role follow.

1. He was known during his stay as US Ambassador to Honduras (1981-1985) for helping to raise military aid to Honduras from $4 million to $77.4 million per year. The United States began to maintain a large military presence there in order to provide a bulwark against Sandinista revolutionary government in Nicaragua, as a left-wing party was struggling to expel dictator Somoza. The former US ambassador to Honduras, Jack Binns, appointed by President Jimmy Carter, had pointed out numerous complaints about human rights abuses by the Honduran military under the government of Policarpo Paz García. But after US President Ronald Reagan's inauguration, Binns was replaced by Negroponte, who denied knowledge of the commission of any offenses by the military forces of Honduras. Despite the subsequent confirmation of these violations, Negroponte did not demand that the US halt military aid to the Government of Honduras. [332] This, despite convincing evidence that emerged later to support the claim that Negroponte had been aware of serious human rights violations by the government of Honduras, nevertheless he did not recommend an end to US military aid to Honduras. In the early 1980s, the Reagan administration funded and supported the training of the Nicaraguan Contras militia in Nicaragua, but based in Honduras, in order to overthrow the

Sandinista government in Nicaragua. The United States supported the Contras militia using illegal US arms sales money obtained from Iran. This later became known as Iran-Gate, a major scandal of the Reagan administration. US Senator Christopher Dodd (Connecticut), on September 14, 2001, stated his objections and doubts on Negroponte's nomination for US Ambassador to the United Nations. [333] Democrats objected to his appointment because of his role in the cover-up and supporting the gangs despite their record of egregious violations of human rights in Honduras and Nicaragua. The US Congress quickly approved his appointment only four days after the September 11 attacks in 2001. American journalist Stephen Kinzer pointed out that Negroponte's appointment sent an insulting message to the UN, where he quoted a US State Department official as saying that "allowing for Negroponte this post is as a means of telling the United Nations, "We hate you". [334]

2. In his work as ambassador to the United Nations, Negroponte was instrumental in obtaining the unanimous approval by the Security Council of a resolution demanding that Saddam Hussein comply with the resolutions of the United Nations and disarm. [336] The facts refute all the lies told by US intelligence services about Iraq's continued possession of prohibited weapons. The lies could not cover up the catastrophic destruction of Iraq, the killing of hundreds of thousands of people, and the displacing of millions of people inside and outside Iraq.

3. On April 19, 2004, US President George W. Bush nominated Negroponte to be the US Ambassador to Iraq after the 30 June handover of alleged sovereignty. The US Senate ratified the appointment on May 6, 2004 by a vote of 95 to 3. He replaced Paul Bremer as the highest ranked US civilian employee in Iraq. He offered advice to the Bush administration that security was needed to reconstruct Iraq and to organize peaceful elections, as well as advice not welcome to Rumsfeld and the Democrats in Congress, that there is a need for commitment to a military presence in Iraq for a period of five years. [335] It was not surprising that death squads in Iraq started when US Ambassador Negroponte appeared in Iraq because of his experience handling such criminal operations. Professor Michel Chossudovsky from the American University of Ottawa confirms that the appointment of Ambassador Negroponte to Iraq in 2004 after he had been Director of US intelligence, was accompanied with the specific task of implementing the Salvador Option in Iraq. [326] On January 10, 2005 news leaked from US Department of Defense to Newsweek magazine that they were studying the formation of death squads of Kurds and Shiites for their targeting of the Iraqi insurgency leaders. This was a similar

implementation to the strategy of the US struggle against left-wing guerrillas in Central America 20 years earlier. [337] Negroponte worked on this project with his assistant in Iraq, Robert S. Ford, fluent in Arabic and Turkish languages, worked with the help of other people within their team for this enterprise, such as Ford's assistant Henry Ensher, the youngest officer in the political section of the embassy, and Jeffrey Beals who played an important role in the team because of his contacts with many Iraqi extremists. Also James Franklin Jeffrey, former US ambassador to Albania (2002-2004), joined this team. In addition, retired Colonel James Steele who was one of the assistants Negroponte during the mass killings in Honduras in 1980, was appointed by Negroponte as a consultant for new Iraqi security troops. Steele oversaw the selection and training of members of the Badr Brigade and some of the cells of Mahdi Army, the two largest Shiite militias in Iraq. These units were to target the leadership and support networks aiding the start-up of Sunni resistance. Whether planned or not, these death squads quickly escalated out of control, to become the leading cause of death and murder in Iraq. Dozens of bodies mutilated by torture by death squads began appear daily on the streets of Baghdad, by death squads existing thanks to Negroponte. This is the sectarian violence backed by the United States, that has led to a large extent to the hellish disaster that is Iraq today, according to US journalist Dahr Jamail.[338] Colonel Roberto Coates engaged in the training of Iraqi security forces, a former Special Forces Commander who brought experience from his death squad involvement in El Salvador during the civil war period.[19] Negroponte opened his ambassadorship unleashing a wave of targeted assasinations of civilians. Also targeted were engineers, doctors, scientists and intellectuals. The divide-and-conquer goal was to create divisions between the Sunnis, Kurds, Shiites and Christian factions, as well as to dispose of civilian support for the Iraqi resistance. The Christian community was one of the main military objectives of assassination. The goal of the Pentagon also consisted in training the Iraqi army and police and security forces to implement local procedures i.e. an unofficial "counter-insurgency" program on behalf of the United States. [337]

Negroponte was supervised by a group of US experts or consultants in every Iraqi ministry followed by the new Iraqi army under the control of the US military, while the new Iraqi intelligence entity took orders and was paid by the US Central Intelligence Agency. [463]

One of the Pentagon's initial proposals was sending teams of Special Forces to provide advice, support and training to Iraqi deaths squads, and to target Sunni insurgents and their sympathizers, even across the border into Syria, according to insiders in the US military. But it was not clear whether the processes that would be led by US special teams and carried out by the Iraqi paramilitary militias would include assassinations or kidnappings from foreign lands as reported by Newsweek January 8, 2005. [337] This dirty plan was under the pretext of supporting and assisting the government of Iyad Allawi, despite the refusal of the US Department of Defense to comment on the topic, but one of their employees told Newsweek, "which everybody agreed is that we can not continue only on what we are now. We have to find a way to take an offensive against the rebels. Now we play defense and we lose."

The US administration and the Iraqi government has repeatedly implicated the Syrian and Iranian roles in increasing violence and the flow of fighters and weapons into Iraq. Americans tried to reach a cooperative agreement with the Syrian regime to stop this interference in exchange for concessions to stop their accusations regarding the international investigation into the killing of former Lebanese Prime Minister Rafik al-Hariri. [503]

These initiatives, adjudged successes by some American politicians, led Negroponte to be chosen as the first candidate by President George W. Bush on March 17, 2005, to take over a new post as Director of National Intelligence (DNI). This new position was tasked to lead the US intelligence community and combine all agencies; and intelligence services' reports to give a unified report to the US President, the Senate and the US House of Representatives. The most important services and intelligence agencies under this new position were the Central intelligence agency (CIA), the multiple Intelligence Agencies in US Department of Defense, the National Security Agency (NSA), the National Reconnaissance Office (NRO), and the National-Geospatial Agency (NGA). [339]

11. 2. 2. General David Petraeus

Petraeus was viewed in the Pentagon as an an expert in the fight against resistance (or what they called " rebellion.") For this reason, he was sent to Iraq in mid-2004 under the pretext of training the Iraqi army and security forces. In June 2004, the Multi-National Security Transition Command Iraq (MNSTC) headed by General Petraeus was established. The MNSTC was an integral part of the "Salvador of Iraq" of the US Department of Defense, under the chairmanship of Ambassador John Negroponte. It was classified as an exercise in counterinsurgency. Petraeus had famously authored a textbook for the the US Army on how to deal with an armed resistance in enemy territory.

By the end of the Petraeus' tenure, MNSTC had increased to about 100,000 Iraqi security forces, police and a group of local military personnel to be used for targeting the Iraqi resistance, as well as civilian supporters. [337] While Petraeus admitted that his mission also included counterinsurgency, this, while trying to deny the existence of death squads, characterizing these killings as the crimes of individuals. Two months after Petraeus left Iraq, the Jadiriyah bunker was found. In it the bodies of 169 prisoners bore signs of torture, most victims were Sunni. [360] US General Karl Horst who found this bunker recognized that formations of the Iraqi Interior Ministry since 2005 have been infiltrated by sectarian militias, and that, at all levels. [357] These discrepancies in assertions indicate that Petraeus attempted to cover up the death squads that had been unleashed when he was in Iraq.

11. 2. 3. Colonel James Steele

He was one of well-known officers during the American dirty war to combat resistance (rebellion) in Latin America in the 1980s and had been appointed an adviser at the US Embassy after the occupation. He was seen as providing advice to the special units of the militias established by occupation forces. [459] The British channel, BBC, in collaboration with the British Guardian newspaper pursued over 15 months of investigation with officials, US and Iraqi witnesses and the victims, themselves. It unearthed the role of the US Pentagon to integrate the armed militias within the new security units to train them on ways to violate human rights, particularly torture, and how to cover up the death squad activities. BBC investigations revealed the following:

- There was a clear role for Gen. David Petraeus with the well known US intelligence officer Col. James Steele in the formation and training of death squads that participated in the dirty wars. These contributed significantly to the sectarian killing and torture from 2006 to 2008. This confirms the financing and supervision by the US government of these crimes.
- Army Col. (Retired) James Hoffman, and Col. Steele were always present in the secret detention centers funded by millions of US dollars. Hoffman was responsible to General David Petraeus after June 2004 to organize the new Iraqi security forces and their training. While Steele, who served in Iraq from 2003 to 2005, then returned in 2006, was directly responsible to Secretary of Defense Rumsfeld.
- After the Pentagon decided to cancel the ban on members of Shiite militias being incorporated into the security forces, armed Shiite

groups such as the Badr Brigade became elements of the Iraqi police commando units.

- For the first time the US advisors' involvement in human rights violations committed by Iraqi special police forces became known.
- All detention centers had their own committees to perform interrogationn. Each committee included an intelligence officer and eight investigators. These committees used all means of torture to force the detainee to confess, such as the use of electricity, or suspension by the legs, or gouging nails, and beating on sensitive areas of the body".
- Photographer Gilles Peres, on an assignment for the New York Times, met adviser Steele during a visit to one of the Iraqi police special force positions in the same library in the city of Samarra. Peres said, "We were inside a room in the library conducting an interview with Steele and I looked around and I saw blood everywhere."
- Journalist Peter Mass also prepared a report " There were scary cries of 'God, God, God!' But they were not cries having found religion or something like that but were cries of horror, pain".] These abusers seemingly followed the practices of documented abuses committed by torture squads, with advisers and funding coming from the United States in Central America during the 1980s and even before. Steele was head of a team of US special advisers who trained Salvadoran security forces to combat the armed movements. Petraeus had visited El Salvador in 1986 and became one of the biggest advocates of such methods to combat armed movements.
- Before Petraeus and Steele had left Iraq, Baqir Jabr Solagh was appointed the new Interior Minister. He was linked to the Badr Brigade militia and at one time to the accusations against the Iraqi police commando that they torture and the use brutal methods. It was believed widely that these units had turned into death squads as well.
- The Guardian newspaper learned that Petraeus received warnings from Iraqi officials working with the Americans after the invasion about the consequences of appointing Solag as Minister of the Interior, but their warnings did not receive a sympathetic ear. The result of funding and arming these special forces-launched sectarian militia killers who terrorized the Sunni. It also helped ignite a civil war that left tens of thousands dead. The Guardian noted that at the height of the sectarian conflict, 3000 bodies carpeted the streets of Iraq every month.

- The Guardian and the BBC Arabic news reported that after the deployment of the US troops, classified military documents exposed by WikiLeaks, recorded in detail hundreds of incidents of torture in the presence of American soldiers in the detention network of the special forces police across Iraq. [408,409,410]

11. 2. 4. Robert Fisk's Facts

The famous British journalist Robert Fisk revealed other facts confirming US involvement in the daily killings, car bombings and the killing of innocent civilians. In his article containing interviews with Iraqis fleeing Iraq that informed him about the previous unknown realities of Iraq, one person told him of his experiences as a member of the new Iraqi police. He described how he had been trained by the Americans to work as a policeman in Baghdad, where he spent 70% of his time learning to drive and 30% on how to use his weapon. Then they told him to get back to us after a week. When he returned a week later, they gave him a cellular mobile phone and asked him to drive his car into a densely populated area near a mosque. The policeman went to the specified place, but he was unable to communicate easily because of the weakness of the telephone signal. He left his car in another location to be able to achieve the best call connection, and when he connected to the Americans, his car exploded. There is another incident where a policeman trained by the US was ordered to go to a crowded site, told there were participants to contact. Upon arriving at the appointed place, he tried to contact them. However, his phone did not work properly. He left his car to reach his controllers by phone, telling them he had arrived. At that moment, his car exploded. [499] In another incident, residents in the Ghazaliya district of western Baghdad told Quds Press that the people had arrested Americans as they left their Caprice car near a residential neighborhood in the Ghazaliya district on Tuesday afternoon October 11, 2005. The local residents were suspicious, and the Americans were detained. Citizens restrained them before they could escape upon learning that they were Americans. Then the people called Iraqi police. [507]

In another television interview with Australia's Channel (ABC), the British journalist Robert Fisk said that the Iraqi community is not a sectarian society, but may be a somewhat tribal society, but there are those who want to ignite a civil war among them. Who are these people who are trying to provoke the civil war? Now the American government has suggested it's Al Qaeda, it's the Sunni insurgents, or Shiite death squads. But many of the death squads work for the Ministry of the Interior. Who runs the Ministry of Interior in Baghdad? Who pays the money to the Ministry of the Interior? Who pays the money to the militiamen who make up the death squads? The answer is, we do, the occupation authorities .[503] [not sure if this was a quote.??]

11. 3. The British Role

Before talking about the British role, we must take up the use of the criminal methods by the British government similar to the methods seen in Iraq. For example, the British people remember the shock that was received when they learned that one of the members of the unit of the IRA that had carried out the bombing in Omagh area on August 15, 1998 that killed 29 civilians was a double agent. He was originally a soldier in the British Army. Such use of double agents revealed how they used double agents to carry out terrorist acts to cover up their presence in the Irish Republican secret party. An abundance of evidence that emerged in 2002 on how the British Army had been using proxies embedded in terrorist organizations "to carry out assassinations on behalf of the British state." [502]

The US also carried out such activities but they were limted to areas where they were active, particularly in the province of Basra and in some other areas. The US troops carrying out similar activities in Iraq during the same time period suggests this criminal policy was shared between the US and Britain. The British conducted similar activities in Iraq as well. On September 19, 2005 the Associated Press published a story with supporting photos about the arrest of two British soldiers from the Elite Forces carrying different weapons and ammunition and wearing Arab clothing. On September 20, 2005 the BBC published a report about British forces attacking an Iraqi police station in the city of Basra in order to break out the two disguised soldiers from the jail. The governor of Basra, Mohammed al-Waeli, then announced that the arrest came after undercover soldiers opened fire upon the Iraqi police in an exchange leading to killing an Iraqi policeman and wounding another. Because of this attack, enraged citizens stoned British military vehicles. While Brigadier John Lorimer, a spokesman for the British Ministry of Defence, claimed the troops had broken into the police station learning about the intention at the police station to hand over those soldiers to the armed Shiite militia. The British claimed this forced them to intervene in order to save them. They claimed that Iraqi law requires the soldiers to be handed over to the occupation authorities and this was not happening. They found the two soldiers outside the police station in a house belonging to the militia. A spokesman for the British Ministry of Defence denied what Iraqis had told Associated Press, that more than 150 prisoners had escaped from the police station during the British attack. But British officials never made it known that the soldiers were carrying out their assignment garbed in local dress not uniform, although they were from the special force commandos or the so-called Unity of the Elite Special Forces, Marines Royal Marines (SAS). In that same period occurred the death of a security guard for US Diplomats, the killing of three American private contractors with a car bomb in Mosul, and the killing of four US Marines killed near the city of Ramadi. [500]

It is noteworthy that these two soldiers of British SAS troops, disguised in local Arab clothing, may have been planning to put bombs in the main square in the city of Basra during a religious event there. They were arrested on charges of seeking to carry out acts of sabotage and sedition among the city's population. The British government formally apologized to Iraq during the recent Basra events. A statement issued by the British consulate in Basra said the Government of London apologizes to the Iraqi people and the Iraqi government, and the people of Basra and the city and governorate councils and police forces on the errors committed by the British. This was reported as stated in a broadcast by Al-Alam Iranian television, and was also reported by the BBC. [507] It is noteworthy that Mr. Fattah al-Sheikh (representative of the Basra area in the Iraqi National Assembly formed by the occupation of the new constitution) stated that British troops had been charged to carry out terrorist acts against the people of Basra during an interview with Al-Jazeera on September 20, 2005. [508,502]

.

Then, in mysterious circumstances, Captain Ken Masters, a senior British police investigator in Basra was killed, according to a spokesman for the Ministry of Defence, who characterized his death as "not the result of hostile action", not of natural causes? Captain Masters was the Commanding Officer of the Special Investigations Branch of the Royal Military Police. It was said he was "responsible for the investigation of all serious accidents in the theater of operations, in addition to the investigations conducted by the general duties of the police component of the theatrical investigation team" (A statement from the British Ministry of Defence on October 16, 2005). In this capacity, Captain Masters had been responsible for investigating the circumstances of the arrest of the two undercover officers from the Elite SAS, in disguise in apostate's Arab clothing, by Iraqi police in Basra. (London Times, October 17, 2005). "The Ministry of Defence refused to disclose the details of his work but it is believed that he was involved in the investigation of the process of dramatic rescue of two of the SAS soldiers, which took place in a prison in Basra." (Daily Mail, October 16, 2005). They are "British Arabists soldiers", who were driving a car loaded with weapons and ammunition, and were later "rescued" by the British forces, in a major military assault on the building where they were being held by militias backed by the Iraqi police. [501]

11. 4. Iran - US cooperation and its impact on the deployment of death squads and sectarian killings in Iraq

"In fact, Tehran's support of terrorism includes both the sponsorship of Middle Eastern (and other) terrorist groups and acts of terrorism carried out by its own IRGC Qods Force" this according to Matthew Levitt (a Former-Wexler Fellow and Director of The Washington Institute's Stein Program on Counterterrorism and Intelligence). Levitt added, "World attention on Iran centers on the threats to international security posed by the country's nuclear program. As Iran presses on in its efforts to become a nuclear power, the regime in Tehran also employs an aggressive foreign policy that relies heavily on the deployment of clandestine assets abroad to collect intelligence and support foreign operations. The world's most active state sponsor of terrorism, Tehran relies on terrorism to further Iranian foreign policy interests." Levitt gave some examples about the terrorism role of Iran's regime:

1. Iran's propensity for sponsoring attacks abroad. Some were thwarted, including plots in Thailand, Bulgaria, Singapore, Kenya, Cyprus, and Azerbaijan. Others were not, including bombings in India and Georgia. Some of these operations were carried out by Iranian agents, others by Iran's primary proxy, Hezbollah.

2. A plot in Turkey involving four members of the Qods Force targeting diplomatic missions in Istanbul was reportedly foiled by Turkish security authorities in March 2012.

3. The plots in Azerbaijan leveraged relationships with local criminal networks to execute an attack.

4. The most brazen, and bizarre, was the October 2011 plot to assassinate the Saudi ambassador to Washington by Qods Force, as the Director General of MI5 Jonathan Evans told a crowd in June 2012.

5. Iran's record of supporting terrorist attacks includes the 1983 and 1984 bombings targeting U.S. and French forces in Beirut.

6. On June 1996 bombing of the Khobar Towers housing complex that was home to American, Saudi, French, and British service members in Saudi Arabia's Eastern Province. According to the testimony of a former CIA official, arrangements for the Khobar Towers attack began around 1994, including planning meetings likely held in Tehran and operational meetings held at the Iranian embassy in Damascus, Syria. It was in 1994, according to this account, that the Supreme Leader of Iran, Ayatollah Ali Khamenei, gave the order for the attack on the Khobar Towers complex.

7. 1994 attacks against Israeli interests in Argentina. Authorities came to the investigation into the 1994 bombing of the AMIA Jewish community center in Buenos Aires. Based on the testimony of Iranian intelligence defector Abolghasem Mesbahi, among others, prosecutors would ultimately conclude that Iran's Supreme National Security Council held a meeting in Mashhad on Saturday 14 August 1993, where senior Iranian leaders approved the bombing plot and selected the AMIA building as the target. The meeting, chaired by then-president Akbar Hashemi Rafsanjani. According to the FBI, around the time of this August meeting, intelligence reports indicated Hezbollah was "planning some sort of spectacular act against Western interests, probably Israeli but perhaps against the United States."

8. The U.S. government designated the Qods Force as a terrorist group in 2007 for providing material support to the Taliban, Iraqi Shia militants, and other terrorist organizations.

9. Most counterterrorism experts, expected that future acts of Iranian terrorism would occur in places like Europe, where Iranian agents have long targeted dissidents, and not in the United States, where carrying out an attack would risk severe countermeasures, including the possibility of a U.S. military reprisal, had the attack been successfully executed and linked back to Iran.

Before entering into Iranian involvement in sectarian killings and death squads in Iraq, we first consider the foundations of Iran - US cooperation, that was hidden and unspoken before the Western invasion of Iraq.

11. 4. 1. The Cooperation in the 1980s

Iran's strategic cooperation with the United States did not just start after occupation. It has deeper roots as military cooperation between Iran and the United States following the Iraqi - Iranian war. The Iran – Contra scandal revealed evidence of this the US - UK cooperation, and it was US President Reagen who agreed in 1980 to sell and supply Iran via Israel with modern weaponry during its war with Iraq (although there was no official embargo on the supply of weapons-this was to circumvent a Congress refusing to fund the Contras) in return for the release of five Americans kidnapped by Iranian militias in Lebanon. George H. W. Bush, father of President George W. Bush, made this agreement when he was vice-president under President Ronald Reagan (1981 to 1989). The agreement was made during a meeting with Iranian Prime Minister Abolhassan Bani-Sadr in Paris. This meeting was also attended by Commissioner for external "Mossad" "Israeli Intelligence, Ari Ben-Menashe, who had a major role in the transfer of these weapons from Israel to Iran. This cooperation was not a fluke but had been made through a prior agreement between the Iranians and the Israelis and the team of US presidential candidate Reagan before the election. They agreed not to release kidnapped Americans until just before one month after the end of the presidential election in November 1980. It was called the October Surprise and has been seen rightly by some Americans as an act of treason. It was intended to prevent the re-election of former President Jimmy Carter by denying him release of the hostages. It also provided Iran with military equipment worth $40 million. [489]

11. 4. 2. Primary Cooperation

Former Iraqi ambassador to Iran during the period before the occupation, Dr. Abdul Sattar al-Rawi, revealed many of the facts in his article titled (Documents of Iranian roles in the US war on Iraq). [13A] For the importance of his information and historical documentation, we review here the main points contained in this important document about the beginnings of the Iranian role in the war of occupation:

1. Before the occupation, Iran tried to make a deal with Iraq, to resolve the outstanding issues and to conduct a comprehensive settlement leading to a lasting, stable peace between the two countries. This would require that Iraq, in return, abandon Arabism in the Arabian Gulf and Arabstan (Emirate of occupied Ahwaz). [???I did not understand this section Iraq rejected this proposal pushing the Iranian officials to accommodate to American threats,

[207]

signalling to the US publicly and privately, first through the language of soft diplomacy and then by applying political pressure against the pro-parties to terrify civilians with terrorist attacks.???] Iraq's response made by Foreign Minister Naji Sabri in September 2002 was a critical and angry refusal to meet with the Iranian side. In February 2003, the Iranian newspaper Saast Rose (Politics Today) published that because of Iraq's refusal to alienate the Arab identity of the Gulf and the three UAE islands, this had caused Iran to increase its blackmail demands. Rafsanjani announced in a speech that Iraq must pay one billion dollars as compensation for war losses. This demand was then retracted the next day as the Iranian Foreign Ministry announced that the required amount to be paid was one hundred million dollars in reference to the impossible conditions demanded to establish a lasting peace with Iraq.

2. After Iraq's refusal, Iran tried to open the doors of cooperation with the US to topple the government in Iraq working through the Swiss as an intermediary, US Vice President Dick Cheney and Defense Secretary Donald Rumsfeld summarily rejected the Iranian support stating: "the US administration refuses to talk to the axis of evil." The administration also rebuked the Swiss mediator who conveyed the message. Hashemi Rafsanjani, the commander of the eight-year war, is known as one of the most extreme in his hostility to Iraq. This cunning fox was able to influence the Supreme Leader of the Islamic Revolution in Iran, Ali Khamenei, who had been undecided about cooperation. One possibility was that the war on Iraq was inevitable and lack of cooperation with America would give the US an excuse to wage war upon Iran after Iraq had been defeated. On the other hand, cooperation with the United States against Iraq would help America achieve its objectives with minimum loss and thereby improve chances for Iran to normalize relations with the US. At the same time, to avoid angering Arab public opinion, as they did regarding Afghanistan, the Iranian leader would continue criticizing the US, and keeping any cooperation secret.

3. The main lines of the new deal was the news circulating among the diplomatic corps in Tehran. It peaked on the opening day of Ahmad Chalabi's office on behalf of the Iraqi National Congress party in the center of the Iranian capital. This office turned over time into an operations room coordinating between the opposition parties from east and west and Iranian intelligence (Ettelaat). Through Ahmed Chalabi's efforts, it funded the Badr Corps forces and re-equipped it using US dollars under the law of the liberation of Iraq which the US Congress legitimized in 1999. The Iranian Foreign ministry denied the existence of such an office in response to a protest note brought by Iraq's ambassador Dr. Abdul Sattar al-Rawi. Meanwhile, the Iraqi embassy provided all their evidence and data on the presence of the office, and offered a list of the names of employees and visitors who pushed the Iranian Foreign to stay silent!

On September 27, 2003, Debka-net, an Israeli weekly magazine on military and intelligence affairs reported that a US delegation from the US National Council met with an Iranian delegation headed by Abbas Malki, Advisor to the Supreme Leader for International Relations. The American negotiator was Jonathan Smith Jr. (pseudonym, Tom Serkis who identified himself as serving in the US diplomatic corps in Kuwait). After months of difficult negotiations, the parties reached the following agreement: the co-operation against Iraq would be in put place between the Iranian and American sides as it was unified in opposition to the Taliban, al-Qaeda and Ansar al-Islam. The two sides signed confidentiality agreements that committed to the following parameters:

A. On the United States obligations:

1. The Iranian irregular forces will be accepted on the ground in the northern part of Iraq, now under the control of America and Turkey, and these forces will participate in the operations against the Baghdad government.

2. The United States and Iran will cooperate politically to form a new Iraq state offering an alternative to Saddam Hussein, and the Supreme Council for Islamic Revolution in Iraq will take part in the opposition and future state structure. An Interim National Council will meet in Arbil to declare an Iraqi National Council, then the Council will announce the dissolution of the Iraqi regime and the Baath party. This Council will require or ask the United States and England to help the Iraqi people to be saved from tyranny. America will be like an umbrella to protect the Shiites in the south, and they and another party in the north will participate in the upcoming Iraqi federal government.

3. The United States will provide protection for Iran if any territory came under attack from Iraq by conventional, chemical or biological weapons.

B. The Iranian delegation presented to their American counterpart the following pledges:

1) The Iranian regular troops would not enter Iraqi territory before or after the war.

2) Iran will not do any damage to stores of petroleum and petroleum installations.

3) The Iranian forces will not settle in Shiite areas and will not promote an anti-American line in Shiite areas during the time of war or thereafter.

4) Iran will not interfere in Iraqi internal affairs.

5) US Special Forces may enter Iranian territory with the participation of Iranian officers to track down al-Qaeda elements in the Afghan border.

4. To implement this Agreement, a team from the Badr Brigade and elements of specialized Revolutionary Guards against terrorism entered northern Iraq, accompanied by a team of US Special Forces and Turkish forces, then they traveled across the Iraqi city of Sulaimaniya to their assigned locations.

5. One month prior to the start of the war, Alexander Schwie unveiled one of the most important aspects of the secret agreement between Washington and Iran in his article published in Der Spiegel on March 9, 2003. Schwie wrote in substance that the Iranians met the Americans on January 28, 2003 in London, and that Deputy United States Secretary Richard Armitage had verified this information. It seemed that in this secret meeting, the Americans pressured the Iranians to pledge to accept the overthrow of Saddam Hussein. The parties agreed to the following mutual pledges:

> **A.** First, pledges of the Islamic Republic of Iran: 1. To provide the necessary security for American pilots if they were forced to land in Iranian territory. 2. To refuse to allow Saddam Hussein to flee across the Iranian territory. 3. To squelch any Iranian opposition to the new Iraqi state.

> **B.** Second, pledges of the United States: 1. To not make the new Iraq a departure point for action against Iran. 2. To give a role to the Shiite opposition in Iran in the future of Iraq after Saddam Hussein.

6. Iranian pledges showed immediate results: 1) In the Friday sermon on January 31, 2003 and after only four days after the secret meeting, Sheikh Hashemi Rafsanjani declared: (We agree to regime change in Iraq without agreeing to allowing American troops to enter the the region)! 2) Iranian

Foreign Minister Kamal Kharrazi announced that Iran will not reject the attack on Iraq if pursued within the aegis of the United Nations! 3) The Islamic Republic of Iran showed great cooperation with the United Nations inspectors, and Mohamed ElBaradei has made a successful visit to the city of Natanz without any problem. 4) The newspaper Ettelaat Strategy revealed on January 28, 2003 that Bayan Jabor, a Supreme Council leader, had disclosed that units of the Badr Corps equipped with heavy weapons crossed the Iranian border and settled these units in Iraqi Kurdistan in the headquarters of the (Kanechar) in northern Iraq, 35 miles south of Sulaymaniyah, and in other two locations under the control of the Patriotic Union of Kurdistan. This news was confirmed by the newspaper "Islamic Coup" on March 10, 2003, explaining that five thousand troops from Badr entered from Iran to Iraq and settled in a PUK camp, led by Jalal Talabani. 5) Representatives of velayat-e faqih flew to Salah al-Din, to attend the opposition conference under the auspices of Zalmay Khalilzad, representing President George W. Bush, accompanied by officials from the "CIA" and representatives from the foreign and defense ministries. Here, Iran decided that it was not sufficient to participate using agents from puppet parties, and proceeded to authorize official participation at the highest level by sending a delegation headed by Brigadier General Mohammad Jafari from the the leadership of the National Security Council in Iran. This entity had an intimate relationship with the opposition parties and the Kurds as well. Tehran confirmed again its partnership with Washington in their joint aggressive pursuit when it welcomed into its territory opponents who held their conference under the flag of the Islamic Republic, and in the capital of the velayat-e faqih. The distribution of roles among the parties involved was also finalized regarding forming the next government in Iraq and where it would be placed. Included the Conference were Massoud Barzani, Mohammed Baqir al-Hakim and Kosart Rasool representing Jalal Talabani, Ahmad Chalabi, Kanan Makiya, and leaders of the "Dawa" party and the Islamic Labour Organization. The political program of the conference manifested the highest levels of cooperation and partnership between Tehran and the White House.

7. Upcoming Cake: In the Iranian newspaper, Solidarity, on February 16, 2003, the Iranian writer Syed Mir Hossein Fazli called upon the government to ensure getting its share of Iraqi oil cake, maintaining that Iran should claim substantial damages as a result of its heavy losses caused by Saddam Hussein during the war of 1980-1988. Saeed Hajjarian, a representative of the reformist movement in Iran, published a study in "Iran Newspaper" on March 8, 2003 to discuss the Iraq war scenarios. Based on his vision which he called the Two Separated Steps Policy that sought to bite the entire Iraq "cake". The first step:

dictated by the interests of the Islamic Republic, was to remain neutral in full before and during the war, premised on that the logical diplomatic approach with Iraq should be based on confidence about resolving the Iraqi crisis. According to this perspective, not only is it right to welcome Naji Sabri, the Iraqi foreign minister, similarly, it is wrong to receive political opponents or support them in any way unless we discover that Saddam Hussein cannot use chemical or biological weapons or missiles against us. In this case, our position towards Iraq and the United States of America could change. The second step: to secure the infrastructure of Iran's influence in Iraq. Such include Iran's relationship with Iraqi Shiites and Kurds, the presence of Shiite leadership in Najaf, and prior knowledge of the Iraqi society and culture. Therefore, the most important factor in the formation of the Iranian role in Iraq's pending system, is not cooperating with the United States before or during the war. But the existence of the necessary infrastructure basis for influence in Iraq would force the White House to accept the Iranian political role there. It seems through these steps Policy Tehran would be protecting their interests under the current circumstances with the least amount of risk. [13A]

Therefore it is not surprising that Iranian, Mr. Ali Abtahi, at the end of the conference in Abu Dhabi in the United Arab Emirates, stated that his country had provided a lot of help to the Americans in their war against Afghanistan and Iraq, and Abtahi added: because of Iranian cooperation, Kabul and Baghdad fell so easily). [18A]

11. 4. 3. Iran's Relationship with Al Qaeda

US President George W Bush had called Iran part of an "Axis of evil," justified because of its presumed relationship with al-Qaeda. [633] But it will be difficult for some to believe that there is an alliance between Iran and al-Qaida and the Taliban. The two sides look at each other as enemies, although no there is no denying Iran's relationship with the Palestinian Sunni Hamas. But all signs point to al-Qaida's penetration of Iran e.g. there were a number of senior figures in al-Qaida in Iran, even if they were under house arrest or at least experienced some restrictions on their movements. Their story dates back to the final months of 2001, when the US forces and their Afghan allies in the Northern Alliance, headed towards Kabul for the overthrow of the Taliban government. The Iranian government tolerated the presence of US troops on its doorstep,on its eastern border. President Mohammad sent emissaries to Kandahar, the Taliban stronghold, to open a line of communication and provide some help. The Taliban did not need weapons or money but needed a safe way out of Afghanistan, and Iran agreed to provide it. In November 2001, a television network correspondent working for CNN, reported when visiting an Afghan refugee camp, about a free region of people located beyond the Iranian border inside Iran. During this period, Iran allowed hundreds of dignitaries from the Taliban, including the family of Osama bin Laden's members. One family of his wives included at least two of his sons, Khalid, who was killed with bin Laden in 2011 in a raid by United States on Abbottabad, and other son, Saad, who was killed in 2009. It also included a daughter, Eman.

Other dignitaries from Al-Qaeda who entered Iran, according to US journalist's correspondence are:

- Suleiman Abu Ghaith, a Kuwaiti citizen and son-in-law of bin Laden, who fled to Turkey later.

- Saif al-Adel, an Egyptian citizen and head of the Security Committee of al-Qaeda.

- Mohammed al-Masri, who is said to be the mastermind behind the 1998 bombing against the US embassies in East Africa. [Killed recently?]

But they all found themselves hostages of the Iranian government, which decided to put most of them under house arrest, and others in prison in southern Iran. Iran had changed its tone, and was looking at its hostages as a bargaining chip. There is ample evidence that Iran has continued to still hold some hostages to this day, despite many hostages having been handed over either to their country of origin or simply being allowed to leave the country. In 2003, it was reported that Iran had offered a deal to the US administration. It was ready, the report said, to exchange some of these prominent figures in al-Qaida for imprisoned leaders of the Iranian armed opposition group in Iraq, the Mojahedin Organization (MKO). In 2010, Bin Laden's teenaged daughter escaped from house arrest in Tehran, successfully seeking refuge in the Saudi embassy. She was finally allowed to leave Iran, but not before the regime learned that Iranian diplomat Heshmatullah Attar-zadeh Niaki who was kidnaped in Pakistan had been freed. According to all stories, there are still a number of senior figures in al-Qaeda in Iran today. [511] According to the United States, the Saif al-Adel (Mustafa Hamed) was the link between al-Qaeda and the Iranian government following the fall of the Taliban. [512]

The start of cooperation between Iran and al-Qaeda preceded the beginning of the war by the United States-led forces in Afghanistan. The US administration had information about significant Iranian cooperation with al-Qaeda and the Taliban to gain a foothold on a relationship. According to the New York Times, US Special Forces around Herat noted that Iranian agents had threatened or offered a bribe to tribal leaders to undermine the programs that the United States supported. That is why President George W. Bush warned Iran at the beginning of January 2002 of instability in Afghanistan. He also said Washington expects Tehran to hand over any of the members of Al-Qaeda who may have fled across the border from Afghanistan. [524]

The US Ambassador to Afghanistan, Ambassador Zalmay Khalilzad, in February 2002 provided the American evidence of this cooperation, saying we have provided them with the information we have with respect to what we believe is happening, especially with regard to the presence of al-Qaeda in Iran and their movement across Iran. Mr. Khalilzad said that he believed that some elements of the Revolutionary Guards had a relatively long-term relationship with al-Qaeda and helped a member of the group escape from Afghanistan to Iran. Some members of al-Qaeda, as he claimed, had allowed them to travel to other destinations. He added that Washington is confident that Taliban officials also received assistance in crossing the border into Iran. [523]

In August 2002, a spokesman for the Iranian Foreign Ministry, Hamid Reza Asefi, asserted that his country had handed over 16 suspects as evidence of his country's cooperation with the United Nations campaign against terrorism, and he added that other suspects have been handed over to other countries. The 16 men, all Saudi citizens, had taken refuge in Iran in the wake of US military operations in Afghanistan. While American Senator Fred Thompson (Senate Intelligence Committee) on television accused Iran of having helped al-Qaeda in the past. This prompted the Bush administration to consider Iran as part of the axis of evil, as well as North Korea and Iraq. [522]

Canadian officials said in April 2013 that they had foiled an attack that was planned with the support of al-Qaeda operatives in Iran, despite Iranian denials of any link to the two men who were arrested in Canada on suspicion of planning an attack on a train. The Royal Canadian Mounted Police said the two men, who were not Canadian citizens, had plans to derail a train operated by the railway company, VIA, and thus "kill and hurt people." The Royal Canadian Mounted Police Chief Supervisor, Jennifer Strachan, said the attack was "definitely in the planning stage, but not imminent." Note that this process was foiled in cooperation and coordination with the US FBI. [512] In September 2012, Canada severed all diplomatic relations with Iran, closed its embassy in Tehran and expelled all remaining Iranian diplomats from Canada. At that time, Foreign Minister John Baird said that Canada considers Iran "as the most important threat to international peace and security in the world today." The Canadian Minister referred to Iran's support for the regime of Bashar al-Assad's controversial nuclear program and the continued   human rights violations as the reasons behind his decision sever diplomatic ties with Tehran. [519]

These facts confirmed what was said by one Iraqis politician previously, Adnan al-Dulaimi the parliamentary bloc leader, in previous press statements, that al-Qaida in Iraq are three independent groups, the first is associated with the international al-Qaeda, the second is connected to Iran, and the third is related to the United States.

11. 4. 4. Signs of Iranian Aggression Against Iraqi People (2003-2015)

Iran's move to extend Iranian influence in Iraq and the Middle East did not end after the eight-year war and its catastrophic losses and costs, but it was the beginning of a 3 decades-long project to expand its influence.[633] Iran's role in Iraq during American - British occupation was based on an open-door policy that supports groups of resistance in order to reach the key persons to negotiate with and to deliver it. [635] In February 2004, John Berry performed an analysis for the Department of Civil Occupation Authority (CPA) in Iraq, warning of Iranian involvement, arguing that Iran is keen to divide Iraq into three semi-autonomous regions. This in turn would weaken Iraq's old enemy, ensure control of the holy cities with income from the pilgrims, and build prestige for them again in the same orbit of Qom. In March 2004, Mike Gfoeller of the authority of the CPA South Central Region said that "the Iranians and, in particular, the Revolutionary Guards (IRGC) and the Iranian Ministry of Intelligence (MOIS) are working with three opposition groups, the Supreme Council, the Dawa Party, and the Organization of Moqtada al-Sadr, while we seek to help the Iraqis achieve a democratic future." [236] Iran's Revolutionary Guards also were accused of being behind the kidnapping of four British persons on   May 1, 2007. One of the kidnapped was a British computer expert, Peter Moore, and the three bodyguards with him. A monument to the program would be to show how the transfer of a huge amount of international aid to Iran's militias in Iraq was executed. This kidnapping operation was coordinated by the Assaib militia (League of the Righteous) that had split from the Mahdi Army and was led by (Qais Al-Kazalli), and the Qods Force of the Iranian Revolutionary Guards. The kidnapping investigation, according to the British newspaper, The Guardian,   revealed that the reason for increased oversight of the financial system is the disappearance of $18 billion in the [Lost and Found counter???]. [406]

Iran's role in the training of militias and gangs in making bombs and improvised explosive devices (IEDs) was documented by US intelligence reports. [183] In 2008, commander of US forces and allied forces in Iraq (Multi-National Force-Iraq) General David H. Petraeus, admitted in his report of the Commission of the US Congress, that what threatens the security in Iraq were two sides, al-Qaeda, and extremist elements groups. Stating further that Iran has played a destructive role by funding, arming, training and directing these groups, especially the so-called Special Groups, and Special Groups pose the greatest long-term threat to the survival of a democratic Iraq. He added, if we look at al-Qaida, we find that its role has been greatly diminished in Iraq after the fight by the Awakening Councils, despite his acknowledging the great Syrian role in helping al-Qaida. The other extremist groups, especially these special groups created by the government of Iran over Iran's Qods Force activities, are run by trained and funded with the help of the Lebanese Hezbollah. These special groups working as dormant cells activate when necessary or according to an agenda prepared for supporting sides. They pushed General Petraeus, forcing him to admit that Iran had fueled the violence in Iraq. [323]

In January 2007 five leaders from the Iranian Revolutionary Guards were arrested in Sulaymaniyah city. The official spokesman for US forces in Iraq, Maj. Gen. Kevin Bergner, disclosed that, one of the five elements of the Revolutionary Guards, is Mahmoud Farhadi, a Captain in the Zafar force, one of the three Subordinate to Ramazan Corps from the Revolutionary Guards in Iraq. Farhadi was responsible for all operations of the Quds Force in northern and central Iraq. These operations included the transfer of weapons, people and money across the border. He has a long history in operations inside Iraq, and many sources assert the involvement of Farhadi in providing weapons for Iraqi criminal groups and its spies from Iran. He added that we also know that for more than a decade, he was involved in Iranian intelligence operations in Iraq. Colonel David Bacon, head of strategic plans and communications, in the US forces in Iraq, added Farhadi is one of the most senior officers in the Quds in Iraq. Col. Bacon also stated also that the newly manufactured weapons and evidence from fighters of Force of Iran who were arrested captured from the Qods Force, Lebanese Hezbollah, and Iraqi Special Groups support Iran's direct involvement in supporting Shia terror networks inside Iraq. [656]

Evidence has also emerged about Iran's support to Shiite death squads and al-Qaeda at the end of December 2006, when US forces arrested two Iranian agents from the Qods Force in the Supreme Council compound in Baghdad. The Iraqi government was angered by the arrests. The Iranians were part of a diplomatic mission in Iraq and later were released and deported to Iran.[657] The Washington Post reported that these two Iranian Intelligence agents upon arrest possessed lists of weapons and documents related to arms shipments to Iraq, organizational charts, and phone logs, maps and information among other sensitive intelligence ... [and] information about modern imports, especially improvised explosive devices in Iraq. "One of those arrested was the third-highest official in the Quds Force of the Iranian Revolutionary Guards." [658] While another US newspaper, the New York Sun, described these documents found with the two officers of the Revolutionary Guards as showing how the Quds Force, an arm of the Iranian Revolutionary Guard which supports Hezbollah, the Shiite and Sunni Hamas and Shiite death squads, also works with groups affiliated to al-Qaeda in Iraq and Ansar al-Sunna individuals according to the intelligence official, whom the newspaper interviewed. [659]

On February 4, 2009, Lieutenant General Lloyd Austin, Deputy Commander of US forces in Iraq said that Iran continues the arming, funding and training of special groups and munitions manufactured in Iran are still being discovered in Iraq, which leads us to believe that the activity of supporting Iran continues.
[661]

11. 4. 5. The Role of the Iranian Revolutionary Guards & Gen. Qassem Soleimani

The Iraqi government and the US military said several times that Iran has supported various Shiite terrorist groups inside Iraq, including elements of the Mahdi Army. Although the Iranian government has denied the accusations, the Iraqi and US forces arrested dozens of officers and elements of the Iranian Quds Force, and also arrested several leaders of the Shiite terrorists operating under Iranian leadership, and found numerous documents confirming that Iran had provided them with weapons of Iranian manufacture. [661]

General Qassem Soleimani joined the Iranian Revolutionary Guards in 1979. He was appointmented Commander of the Qods Force of the Iranian Revolutionary Guard a few months before the invasion of Iraq. In this role, he became responsible for the Iraqi file as commissioned by Iran's Supreme Leader Khamenei. As the International Herald Tribune newspaper sreported, he is the mastermind behind the expansion of Iranian influence in Iraq's political affairs and the provision of military support to the Syrian regime of Bashar al-Assad. US Commander General Petraeus was briefed closely during his work in Iraq concerning the influence of Soleimani, describing in his letters to the US Secretary of Defense at the time, Robert Gates, that Soleimani was really an evil person and his direct intervention in the Iraqi political intrigues was widespread. While former US Ambassador Ryan Crocker said that the Iran-Iraq war from 1980 to 1988 had informed Soleimani's opinion of Iraq, and that this war was not over for him. The strategic goal was to achieve complete victory in Iraq, and if this was not possible, a weak Iraq must be created vulnerable to Iran's exercised influence. Meanwhile, an Iranian researcher recognized that the Qods Force had seen its golden opportunity and was continuing and enhancing the preoccupation of the Americans in Iraq by creating chaos there as much as possible. In further support, Jalal Talabani characterized Qassem Soleimani as saying that he had hundreds of spies in Iraq. When the Qods Force was arming and training Shiite militias, it was at the same time dealing diplomatically with Iraqi politicians. Soleimani was fueling violence thereafter intending to intervene and mediate to end the conflict, making himself indispensable to all sides. [631]

After General Petraeus was appointed CIA Director, he talked about an incident that occurred with Soleimani in early 2008, during battles between the US and the Iraqi army together against Shiite militia. Petraeus received a phone text message from Soleimani in Arabic that an Iraqi general read for him that said: "General Petraeus, you should know that I, Qassem Suleimani, control the policy for Iran with respect to Iraq, Lebanon, Gaza, and Afghanistan. And indeed, the Ambassador in Baghdad is a Quds Force member. The individual who's going to replace him is a Quds Force member." But in spite of Petraeus' recognition that Soleimani was the maker of problems and the fighting between Shiite militias and US forces, he did not present the realities of the crimes that confirm the existence of aggressive war crimes carried out by the Iranian Quds Force. As stated, Soleimani has strong relationships with many Shiite politicians who refuse to discuss within the Iraqi parliament the existence of any Iranian role in the Iraqi conflict! [632] Mowaffak Rubaie disclosed to a Middle East newspaper: "He is the most powerful man in Iraq without question" and nothing is done without him. [19A] Muqtada al-Sadr re-confirmed Soleimani's control of decision making in Iraq through a statement to the Lebanese Hayat newspaper saying that Qassem Soleimani, Commander Iranian Guard is the most powerful man in Iraq.) [20A]

During the Iraq - Iran war, Soleimani was responsible for coordinating Iran's Revolutionary Guards with the Iraqi militias that had been battling with the Iranian army against their own country, Iraq, and especially with the militia of the Badr Brigade. He was the coordinator of Iranian interference with these militias during the 1991 Gulf war. They burned and destroyed government departments, and killed or executed members of the Iraqi army as they retreated from Kuwait. Two of the officers who were officially employed with him as officers in the Iranian Revolutionary Guards are both members of the Iraqi parliament for Maliki's party (Dawa). The first is Abu Mahdi, an engineer, and the second is the former Minister of Transport from the Badr Brigade Hadi al-Amiri. [638] This longstanding penetration of politicians, their parties and militias supported by Iran, allowed Soleimani to control the reins of power in Iraq, the large US presence notwithstanding.

During the sectarian fighting in 2006, after the Samarra bombings, Soleimani secretly visited Iraq and was walking around the campsites without a personal escort. Americans did not know that he had been in the capital until he returned to Iran. they were furious knowing that their arch-enemy had been among them. The US official senior spokesperson that week said, "No one knows about his past and that the same person, it's all over the place and there is a specific place". Although the US official description of Soleimani was: "He is indeed like Keyser Söze," but they let him have control of the Iraqi political file. One of the Iraqi senior politicians was the second Deputy of Prime Minister al-Maliki (in the first government), disclosed that Soleimani was present at a meeting in Damascus where the the second Iraqi government was formed. It was at this meeting of many leaders from Syria, Turkey, Iran and Hezbollah that Soleimani exerted his power"and forced them all to change their minds and approve the appointment of Maliki as a leader for a second term."[632]

Soleimani' role was not limited to the engineered intervention to form the Iraqi second government of Maliki. But his role has become more commanding, greatly supporting the survival of Bashar al-Assad's regime in Syria, which was also revealed by former Syrian Prime Minister Riad Hijab. [635] This role caused American journalist Dexter Filkins to describe him as an Iranian factor that is reshaping the Middle East, and he has directed Assad's war in Syria. Filkins describes Soleimani's policy in reshaping the Middle East in Iran's favour. His tools were the power of his work as a mediator, and by all means military power including assassinating his opponents, arming its allies, and for a decade, directing a network of militant groups that have killed hundreds of Americans in Iraq. The US Treasury Department recognized the key role of

Soleimani in support of the Assad regime, and incitement of terrorism. John Maguire, a US intelligence officer, describing Soleimani stating "Soleimani is the most powerful factor in the Middle East today." [633] One of his sources of strength and his leadership of the Shiite militias in Iraq was his personal involvement in arranging a cease-fire between Maliki forces and the Mahdi Army of Moqtada al-Sadr in March 2008.[634] After this agreement, Muqtada announced the dismantling of the al-Mahdi Army and its entrance into the political process. This step prompted one faction, the League of the Righteous, Alasaib, to separate and become independent from his decision, thereby continuing Iran's support for them at all levels. [661]

As a result of the large role played by the leadership of the Iranian Revolutionary Guard in providing support equipment to help the Syrian regime in suppressing protests in Syria, he was put on the European sanctions list on June 24, 2011.[636] The blockade and the prohibition against Soleimani were adopted also by the Swiss government in September 2011 for the same reasons cited by the former European Union.[637] The United States considers him as a terrorist and prohibits its citizens from working with him. [639] However, the significant role he plays in Iraq underscores the complicity of the US in allowing the expansion of Iranian influence in Iraq and Syria, despite the US placing the Iranian Revolutionary Guards on the list of terrorist organizations where it has remained since 2007. [686]

11. 4. 5. 1. Special Groups and the Involvement of the Lebanese Hezbollah

Iraqi groups such as the "Dawa" party collaborated with Hezbollah in conducting terrorism and political violence in support of their own interests and Irans's interests. They have done so on their own initiative and also in collaboration with the Iranian "Quds Force". In fact Hezbollah created a new organizational form,"Unity 3800," dedicated to helping the Shiite insurgency in Iraq. Iraq has become the core for Hezbollah not because it has any relationship to Lebanon, but because they have gained influence in Iraq, and hegemony in the region is critical for the Iranian guardians of Hezbollah.[686]

In May 2005, Musa Daqduq,Commander of the Special Operations Unit of Hezbollah and the supervisor of security measures to protect the party's leader, Hassan Nasrallah, traveled with Yusuf Hashim (head of the Lebanese Hezbollah operations in Iraq) to Tehran for a meeting with the Deputy Commander of the Foreign Operations Branch of the Iranian Quds force, an elite Iranian special operations group in charge of the deployment of the

Iranian theocracy to neighboring countries. Daqduq also made four trips to Iraq in 2006, where he personally witnessed the operations of Special Groups that are formed by both Special Forces from the Mahdi Army and the League of the Righteous, Alasaib, a faction that rebelled against the Mahdi army, as well as Iraqi Hezbollah. Upon his return from Iran, Dayduq was assigned to organize those Special Groups similarly to the organization of the Hezbollah militia. In a July 2007 press conference, Brigadier General Keven Bergne explained the system of Special Groups. He said that Daqduq started training Iraqis inside Iran to carry out terrorist attacks in their own country. It had trained groups of 20 to 60 recruits in the use of bombs, explosive armor-piercing shells and mortars, rockets and sniper rifles, and created instructions on how to conduct intelligence operations and kidnapping. Bergner added that "these special groups are extremist militias, funding, training and arming of external sources, specifically by elements of Qods Force of the Iranian Revolutionary Guard, and without this support, these special groups have difficulty conducting their operations in Iraq." [465]

The most prominent criminal group in Iraq, that has trained, funded and supervised the operations by the Iranian Quds force, was the League of the Righteous (Alasaib), which merged with Special Groups. Both are dissidents from Moqtada al-Sadr's Mahdi Army. Included were Qais al-Khazali, who led the Alasaib militia, who was arrested on March 20, 2007 by the US forces in the city of Basra in Iraq with Ali Musa Daqduq, along with his brother, Laith al-Khazali. The three who had been arrested were accused of participating in the kidnapping and killing of five US soldiers in Karbala in January 2007. Qais al-Khazali and his brother Laith were released in December 2009 in exchange for the release of the British hostage Peter Moore who had been kidnapped by the Alasaib militia, as reported by Army officers and intelligence to the US newspaper, the Long War Journal. While other US military officers criticized releasing al-Khazali, observing that we let go a very dangerous man and his hands are stained with the blood of Iraqis and Americans, and adding, we're going to pay for that in the future. [Is the preceding a direct quote?] Nevertheless, the Maliki government has said that the release of these men came within the national reconciliation plan. In contrast, an official in US military intelligence said "the official announcement said it was the release of al-Khazali for national reconciliation, but in fact this was the exchange of prisoners of war," and he warned that the Group will return to terrorism. The kidnapping was of a British computer systems expert Moore with four of his bodyguards while working in the Ministry of Finance in Baghdad in May 2007. [Earlier you state 3 bodyguards.??]The Alasaib militia executed the four guards, while giving up the British expert in exchange for the al-Khazali brothers. This spurred an American officer to opine that this was a deal sealed and signed by British and American blood, we have released their leaders and members of their organization, and they killed the hostages and sent their bodies in body bags, and are we supposed to be so happy! [655] In mid-October 2007, the United States released more than 100 members of the Alasaib militia. More than a month after the release of Laith al-Khazali and his brother, along with many of his followers, in January 2010, the Alasaib kidnapped an American civilian contractor working in Iraq, Issa T. Salomi. Americans considered the abduction of this contractor as proof that Alasaib has no real intentions of reconciliation as falsely claimed, and will continue to use violence to achieve their ends. [661]

A spokesman for US forces in Iraq, Maj. Gen. Kevin Bergner had said that a majority of 27 high-ranking leaders in secret cells, or in Shiite terrorist Special Groups fighting in the streets of Iraq, had been arrested. Three were killed. He added that many of the documents seized with them, including a 22-page document showing the planning of Lebanese Ali Daqduq and the rest of the other elements, along with interrogation information confirmed the Qods Corps network's details and role in the establishment of Shiite terrorist cells inside Iraq. He added, "What we have learned from Ali Musa Daqduq and Qais al-Khazali and other members of the special groups expands our understanding of how the Iranian Qods Force agents were training, funding and arming the Iraqi special groups. It shows how the Iranian logic works in using the Lebanese Hezbollah alternatives in creating such capabilities." Brigadier General Bergner revealed that they had identified three training camps for "special groups" inside Iran. US satellite images identified mockups of the headquarters of their troops, called in short, PJCC, as if they were in Karbala, but they actually existed inside Iran! This facility has been used to train the al-Khazali network to attack in Karbala. Brig. Gen. Bergner said that Iran's top leadership was aware of the Quds Force's activities inside Iraq. "Our intelligence has revealed that the senior leadership in Iran is aware of this activity." Bergner explained further that, "it would be difficult to imagine" that Ayatollah Ali Khamenei, Supreme Leader of Iran, would not be aware of the role of the Qods Force in bringing violence inside Iraq. Especially, since the Quds Force reports directly to Ayatollah Ali Khamenei. Bergner had explained that these "special groups" and "secret cells" had been targeted dramatically since Petraeus' conference about Khazali and the Shibani networks on April 26, 2007, and that US forces had killed at least 91 members of these secret cells and had arrested 113 since April 27, 2007. [660]

The release of Daqduq, Khazali and others demonstrated America's complicity with the death squads. The US forces had transferred Daqduq to an Iraqi prison operated under Maliki's government, then the United States returned and asked Iraq to hand over Daqduq so that his trial might be held in a US federal court. But an Iraqi court blocked his extradition to the United States. It was the US Department of Justice's intention to prosecute Daqduq in a US court, but Republican senators opposed his transfer to US territory for trial. Some of them wanted to try him before a military tribunal at Guantanamo, however, the Obama administration refused to allow the transfer of Daqdouq to prison, and instead it claimed that it is seeking to close that prison! The United States also released a number of senior officers of Iran's Qods Force, including Mahmoud Farhadi, the Zafr Force Commander. This is one of three units of a subsidiary of Ramadan Corps. Farhadi was among five Iranians handed over to al-Maliki's government, which in turn handed returned him to Iran in July 2007. [656]

Armed Shiite militias like the Mahdi Army, a force of 50,000 fighters, and its personnel receive a weekly salary of an estimated $300 US. [346] Although the Commander of the militia, Muqtada al-Sadr, has expelled many of his army commanders who violated his orders or committed other violations, some those expelled leaders have taken with them the combat groups that followed them, so are no longer under the control of Muqtada. [347] After the rejection by Moqtada al-Sadr of the security agreement between Iraq and United States, Moqtada established a secret militia called The Promise Day Brigade. According to US and Iraqi intelligence sources, the Promised Day Brigade (PDB) is a terrorist organization sponsored by Iran, in addition to the Hezbollah Brigades, which have been active in and around Baghdad since 2007. [661] Although Muqtada al-Sadr had made several calls for a truce, the majority of the violence and killings in Baghdad and its outskirts were attributed to him. [348]

It is known that the number of Shiite militias after a fatwa on Jihad by cleric Ali al-Sistani in 2014, under the pretext of fighting the organization of the Islamic State (IS), has increased to more than forty Shiite militias, with arms and funding mostly from Iran. Many films documenting the terrible abuses and arbitrary killings for sectarian reasons and beheadings by members of these militias have been published. Some horrifying propaganda videos have shown people being burned to death, or suffering agonizing deaths by knife.

[223]

11. 5. Some of the Most Influential Activities of Death Squads:

11. 5. 1. Assassination of Dr. Mejbel Sheikh Issa

He was a member of the Constitution Drafting Committee. He was one of the most prominent figures assassinated by death squads. This act had a special effect upon the political events in Iraq and impacted the form of the new constitution, written under the occupation. On July 19, 2005, masked gunmen in a civilian car stopped outside a restaurant in a street near the Conference Palace in Baghdad, adjacent to the Green Zone. They killed two Sunni members of the Committee writing the new constitution representing the Sunnis in Iraq. Those two victims were Dr. Majbel Al- Sheik Essa and Mr. Kamel Ubaidi. In addition there was a third victim, a nephew of Dr. Essa. I had met with Dr. Mejbel just days before his killing. He was leading the group that rejects the idea of writing a section pertaining to a federal system within the new constitution for fear of this leading to an eventual division of Iraq later. He told me that he had received death threats from two major political groups warning him to give up his opposition to federalization. Essa had informed both the UNAMI and some people close to him about these threats, according to what he told me in our last meeting. Creating more doubt is that the restaurant where he was assassinated was on a street located between two Iraqi security checkpoints on both sides of the street. Tellingly, neither checkpoint's personnel intervened in the attack. The United Nations was called upon to investigate the crime, but the Jaafari government did not push for something to happen. It has claimed only regret for what happened, as did the US embassy in response to this assassination and political murder. The assassination was terrorism directed at any party who rejects the agenda prepared in advance by the new Iraq under the US - British - Iranian tutelage. The assassinations served two purposes: (1) eliminating political opponents, and (2) forcing the drafters of the new constitution to follow the dictates of the occupation as to its political agenda.

11. 5. 2. The Samarra Bombing and the Beginning of Iranian Sectarian Genocide in Iraq

Bayan Jabor, Iraqi Interior Minister, made remarks at the time indicating that fighters from the al-Qaeda had stormed the shrines in Samarra, disarmed and tied up the guards, then planted containers inside the shrines, to detonate at 9:00 AM on February 22, 2006; the shrines blew up as intended. Many witnesses who live near the shrines had testified that US forces had accompanied Iraqi men who had surrounded the shrines from midnight until six o'clock in the morning, and then pulled out of the place. Witnesses, in documented testimony, added that they had seen the US forces directing firing over anyone who tried to look at the troops while they were in place in the shrines. The results of the investigations were reported by the Intergovernmental Committee formed after this incident. They stated that booby-trapping the shrine would have taken at least 15 hours. This directly contradicts the testimony of Interior Minister Jabr that al-Qaeda fighters were able to complete the booby-trapping in less than 3 hours!

After the bombings, "religious" statements inciting violence and sectarian revenge were promulgated by several religious figures, while some condemned this crime. The Civil War continued for more than a year, claiming tens of thousands of lives of innocent people who were killed merely because of their identity. At the same time, the new Iraqi army and police exhibited disgraceful behaviour, by joining with criminal militias rather than doing their patriotic duty to protect lives of all parties and to impose security and law for everyone. The High Commissioner for Refugees estimated that sectarian violence had displaced some 730,000 people in the period between February 2006 and March 2007. [630] Because of death squads, killings spread widely after the bombings; the number of Iraqi refugees and displaced people numbered more than 4 million refugees outside Iraq, with more than 2 million Iraqi refugees displaced internally (UNHCR September, 2007).

Admissions in a book by David Kilcullen, an Australian advisor on counter insurgency during this period and a former aide to Gen. Petraeus, although condoning the action, described the details of the bombings and the Iranian role. The most important of these follow: [498]

1. Bombings occurred in the last period of rule by the transitional government of Ibrahim al-Jaafari, and bombings had pushed Shiite groups to kill Sunni civilians. [640] During a one month period, from February 22 to the end of March 2005, 600 bodies of Sunni civilians were strewn on the streets of Baghdad, with most of them children and adolescents showing signs of having been brutally tortured before being executed. [641]

2. Although the Iraqi staff at the US embassy in the Green Zone were too terrified to go to their homes for fear of sectarian killings, [642] US staff and officers at the headquarters of Multinational Forces (MNF-I) perceived it as not

that bad ! Kilcullen opined that a few days later, he discovered that the impact of the bombing had not yet sunk into the perceptions of military officers or civilian officials in MNF-I headquarters . This evidence should not be interpreted as showing a lack of interest, quite the opposite, it was the start of the Salvadoran option.

3. At the end of February 2006 there was a regular meeting of American officers with Rubaie's office and officers and representatives of the Iraqi National Security Agency. Kilcullen described the meeting in his book as seeming like a dialogue of the deaf. Americans were offering to provide security and reconstruction, while Iraq's national security agency staff saw the question as about the primacy of the security of Shiite citizens who needed protection from Sunni terrorism! Kilcullen added that the Americans looked bored, giving the impression that they were humoring the Iraqis, rather than being straight with them. [643]

4. Admissions and warnings were made by Iraqi politicians to US leaders, purporting that Samarra was a disaster that had fundamentally and irrevocably altered the nature of the war, [644] were not taken seriously by the US. This was especially evident during the Battlefield Update Analysis given daily to the Commander at the time (of MNF-I), General George W. Casey, over the four and a half months from the day of the Samarra bombing until mid-June 2006. There was not any mention during daily discussions about the existence of a civil war, according to what was said, although the Iraqi officers had told him then, that this concerned all Iraqis. The daily update was limited to the official deliberations about the most important of the priorities of their forces, and what the US embassy staff thought under the leadership of Ambassador Zalmay Khalilzad. [645]

5. US policy at the time, and until the end of 2007 was concentrated on the principle of solving problems using a top-down model and starting over to determine how to transform al-Maliki's state into a modern government that might reduce domestic violence. The US sent a prestigious political crew to help under the leadership of Tom Warrick, who had opposed Kilcullen about the involvement of the new Iraqi cabinet. But after more than five months, they were convinced that forming a new government would not help in reducing violence.

6. The Numbers of daily killings increased greatly during that period with the arrival of a new military command under General David Petraeus, and the new US Ambassador Crocker. This duo advocated for the US embassy to change its

policy to a bottom-up policy, i.e. securing residential complexes first, and then breaking the cycle of violence in the launch areas instead of waiting for help from Iraqi politicians.

The most important lesson in Kilcullen's book showing the consequences of this domestic violence for US troops, was how to change US military policy from a pariah occupation force, unwanted by the citizens, viewing all of the Iraqi civilians as a threat, to a new policy requiring them to be closer to Iraqi civilians, to try to protect them from the rebels!

The writer's recognition that the increase in US troops after President Bush's speech on January 10, 2007 by sending in 28,500 US troops was accompanied by a change in the nature of their tasks. These additional forces started working with the police and army in each region in order to stop the violence! (646)

7. After the Samarra bombings, one started to see terminology that increased the sectarian strife in Iraq. Groups that killed Sunni civilians were innocuously referred to as Shi'a Communitarian Militia, while those who were killing Shiite civilians were labelled al-Qaeda (AQI) or Sunni insurgents. The first were killed by terrorist attacks by the second, while the second citizens were being killed in retaliation by the first militias!

8. Between September 2006 and January 2007, between 2,700 and 3,800 civilians were being killed every month. The worst month was December 2006, when an average of 125 civilian victims per night were slain, more than half of them in the city of Baghdad. (647)

9. The other important recognition by this Australian officer that it was likely that the cause of this increase in the murder rate happened because of the severe penetration of government institutions by Shi'a sectarian extremists, and their deployment in most of the security checkpoints in the streets of the capital Baghdad. He added that the current policy changed by trying to put the issue of protecting Iraqi citizens in the hands of the Iraqi government. But the data shows that killings increased because the Iraqi government had become a Sectarian Combatant in the civil war; it was not an honest broker and did not care for all its citizens equally. (648)

10. US attention was focused on the transition process but not with an eye to restoring peace to all Iraqis. This was evidenced by the US increasing aid to the sectarian government under the pretext of accelerating the transition of

responsibilities, but the actual intent was increasing sectarian violence. The Australian observer admitted that the situation was similar to horrific, a near - genocidal cycle of violence due to ill - judged intervention.

11. He revealed that some 50% of the fighting in Iraq in 2006 was in Baghdad alone. This confirms the freedom of movement allowed to the criminal militias in the capital despite the government and foreign military presence.

Al-Arabiya correspondent Atwar Bahjat al-Samarrai was killed with her team and media workers, only one escaping. The reason for this killing was because they were in Samarra after the bombing documenting the arrest of an Iranian visitor near the shrine during the bombings. Reports noted that the sole survivor of Al-Arabiya team said that the execution of his team may have been caused by their documenting Iranian involvement in the bombing drawing the ire of Iraqi security control. [??Did I get this right?]

The US position on this issue was summarized by President George W. Bush. He flatly rejected that this was a civil war, calling it mere attempts at destabilization. He stressed that al-Qaeda was behind them! Gen. Abu Zeid stated that "Iraq is very far from civil war." Gen. Mark Kimmitt also described the situation saying "civil war begins when the army and the government are divided along ethnic or sectarian lines, saying that what's happening is a sectarian violence." But the United Nations had a different view from the US, and a more honest and accurate one. Secretary-General Kofi Annan said, "What is happening in Iraq is much worse than a civil war!"

Actually, the war and bloodshed were neglected while the US was preoccupied with characterizing (wordsmithing) the events, and disputing the choice of terms! Ellen Knickmeyer ,a political analyst, in a Washington Post article published on February 28, 2006 opined that, "at a time when the Americans deny the civil war in Iraq, many of the experts and political analysts and even ordinary people in the Middle East believe that this war really existed." [673] But Joost Hiltermann, expert at the International Crisis Group, offered, "We're not talking about just a full-scale civil war. This would be a failed-state situation with fighting among various groups," growing into a regional conflict." [675] Matt Lauer from NBC TV conducted long discussions with a number of specialists, strategists, political and military analysts including a military expert, Barry McCaffrey, on this question: Do you classify what is happening in Iraq as part of a civil war or not? Finally, NBC started characterizing the Iraqi conflict as "civil war" directly repudiating Bush's evasive terminology. [676] The same term was adopted by the Los Angeles Times newspaper, Newsweek magazine, the

Associated Press Agency and others. Monica Duffy, Toft Professor at Harvard University, adds that "the civil war actually located in Iraq." For hProfessot Toft, key questions regarding what sort of war were:

1. Is the focus of the war control over which group governs the political unit?
2. Are there at least two groups of organized combatants?
3. Is the state one of the combatants?
4. Are there at least 1,000 battle deaths per year on average?
5. Is the ratio of total deaths at least 95 percent to 5 percent? In other words, has the stronger side suffered at least 5 percent of the casualties?
6. Is the war occurring within the boundaries of an internationally recognized state or entity? [674]

In 2006, the total number of civilians violently killed was 34,452, 16,867 from the Medical Legal Institute in Baghdad (unidentified bodies) and 17,585 from hospitals (operation center) throughout Iraq.The yearly average was an astonishing average of 94 civilians killed every single day, while the number of wounded civilians was 36,685 also in 2006, including 2,222 women and 777 children. At least 470,094 people have been forcibly internally displaced since the bombing in Samarra on February 22, 2006. Baghdad alone hosts 38,766 displaced individuals.[687] The United Nations High Commissioner for Refugees (UNHCR) estimated that as of December [year? 2006??] there were over 4.4 million displaced Iraqis worldwide, including some 2.5 million inside Iraq and about 1.9 million in neighboring countries. [688] According to the periodic reports of the UN mission in Iraq, the Maliki government had declined to give any statistics on the number of civilian casualties in 2007, while announcing at the end of 2008, that the total number of Iraqi civilian deaths in the whole of 2008 amounted to 6,787 civilians, while 20,178 were injured. The government did not disclose details on the numbers of women and children among the victims. While in 2009, it announced that the total number of civilian victims was 4,068 killed, and 15,935 wounded.

11. 5. 2. 1. Who are the Parties to the Terrorist Bombings of Samarra's Shrine?

[?? This para seems a different font, Arial?] Iraqi Major General Ghazi Khader Aziza (Operations Commander in the Interior Ministry from 2003 to 2008), in an interview on the Al-Arabiya Channel, admitted that in 2005 that they had arrested 22 Iranians in Samarra city carrying explosives. He explained that they confessed that they had orders from Iran to bomb religious shrines in Samarra. The accused Iranians were released after a month, and turned over to Iran without trial. Actually, they had blown up the religious shrines after spending one year in the city! [22A] The US military commander and former Commander of US forces, General George Casey, told the annual conference of the Council of Iranian Resistance (MKO) in France on June 23, 2013, that the killing of thousands of Iraqis was Iran's doing. Iran was responsible for the bombing of the Al-Askary shrine in Iraq, thereby fueling the sectarian conflict, to weaken and destroy Iraq as a state. Casey added: Maliki told me and he is a partner with Iran and that the majority of bombings that targeted civilians were the responsibility of Iranian Revolutionary Guards, and the militias in Iraq that have received all their support from the Iranian Revolutionary Guard).[487] This recognition demonstrated that these organized crime militias had arisen under the eyes and awareness of the US forces and government!

According to Casey's revelations, the parties to this crime, are as follows: first, the Iranians bear the main responsibility for operational and logistical support to those who carried out the bombings, or widely distributed sectarian killings following this crime; second, it was the American President Bush and his administration, including Casey, who knew and covered up who the offenders were; third, Prime Minister Nuri al-Maliki was personally involved as Casey said that he had told al-Maliki that the available evidence suggests the involvement of Iran and allied militia behind the Samarra bombings and most of the bombings in Iraq. However, Maliki did not conduct the basic investigations honestly, and he contributed to the crime; fourth, the instigators, especially some Shiite clerics and militia officials, were known to be loyal to Iran, as were all those who contributed to inciting murder and sabotage; fifth, al-Qaida was a party, because it falsely claimed a terrorist attack that it did not do, thereby helping to distract and relieve suspicion from the real villains.

11. 5. 2. 2. Indications of a Scheme to Commit Genocide After the Samarra Bombing in Reports from the Human Rights Office (UNAMI)

These reports have a particular importance because they reveal part of the truth from an international perspective, independent from the parties of conflict. UNAMI recognized the following and important facts about this crime and the emergence of death squads.

1. The last UNAMI report of 2005 (covering November - December), highlighted profiles of the perpetrators of the bombings in Samarra and the sectarian killings. There were also reports of an increasing number of people abducted in

Basra, Baghdad, Mosul and other parts of Iraq. It is often the case that the perpetrators are individuals in the armed militias linked to political factions or criminal gangs, or criminals wearing uniforms and posing as security forces. They continued the bombing operations and repeated killings that targeted civilians, clerics and mosques in order to weaken community ties ... and in spite of the significant increase in such attacks during the past few months, it seemed confined to specific areas .... for example, the Chief of the Sunni Bata clan, Sheikh Kazem Srhid Alhmam, was killed in Baghdad on November 23, 2005. Three of his children and his brother in law were killed with him. The report added that there was an organized threat operation against Sunni citizens in Abu Khsib and Zubair that were mainly Sunni). In the same report came the information about the Medico-Legal Institute in Baghdad's receiving at the Institute, 886 bodies in November 2005. Significantly, 555 had lethal gunshot wounds. Also brought to the Institute in December were 787 dead, of whom 479 were killed by gunshot. [650]

2. In the monthly report for January-February 2006, the first report after the Samarra bombing, (see paragraph 6) it was reported that in response to the Samarra bombings, there have been large numbers of Sunni mosques that were attacked, sabotaged and even destroyed. Many of the imams of the attacked mosques are among those who have faced assassinations. It is clear that these attacks were not random, but rather to the contrary, there was revealed a high degree of organization, and it was apparent that the perpetrators of such acts have the ability, and potential to obtain resources and equipment used to carry out these actions with ease. This recognition was not only about the involvement of the Jaafari government but also clearly concerned US complicity, especially with the presence of tens of thousands of US soldiers, particularly in Baghdad. This observation, confirmed by events (see paragraph 7) also came at a time early on, when violence was targeting only Sunni Arabs, because of their alleged (unproven) relationship with destruction of the al-Askari shrine. This violence adversely affected much of Iraqi society with a wave of violence and revenge attacks as well. There is no longer any way to accurately assess the number of people injured or to know the fate of missing persons or the number of persons arrested. The absence of records here demonstrates just how large was the terrorist plot to commit destruction and genocide and the breadth and complicity in the attempt to hide these crimes.

3. From the same report, evidence was presented about the involvement of the largest government security services in the systematic extermination operations. The report (see paragraph 8) emphasizes the reporting of numerous serious abuses in Basra, including killings and attacks on mosques. In one incident on February 22, 2006, the Sunni men detained on charges of terrorism were killed execution-style by a group of 70 armed men wearing protective lead shields, despite having been captured far away from alleged Shia victims. The Islamic Party headquarters in Basra was attacked by militias and two were injured defending the headquarters. During the treatment of these wounded men in the hospital, armed militia arrived and killed both wounded persons. UNAMI (see paragraph 9) expressed concern about reports that militias and agents from the Interior Ministry were implicated in violence against civilians, or that they do not do their duty to curb further bloodshed. The report (see paragraph 10) notes information about incorporating militia elements into the security forces and forming secret parallel structures while retaining their loyalty to their own parties. At the same time, the US military revealed without formal announcement that probable death squads are active at least within the framework of the Ministry of Interior; they had arrested 22 men dressed in uniforms of the Interior commandos assisted by a person who seems to have been to be executed. Although the Ministry of Interior of the Jaafari government announced that it would investigate this incident, for every incident that comes without an announcement of the investigation, results are forgotten. According to the Ministry of Interior itself (see paragraph 17 of the same report), they recognized the deaths of 249 people between February 22 and February 25. This indicated again the absence of the necessary right to life and protection that prevails in Iraq. The report (see paragraph 18) also referred to the continued killing and displacement as a threat to minorities, especially the Palestinians residing in Iraq (all are Sunnis) and states that they were victims of human rights violatons. The same threats were also made on the Christian minority in Iraq (see paragraph 19) trying to displace them, too.

4. The report recognized the increase in the number of random arrests as one of the most disturbing aspects. This is understandable with more than 29,000 detainees in Iraqi, with more than 14,000 of them in US prisons, while more than 8,000 were held at the Ministry of Justice, up to 500 boys were kept prisoner at the Ministry of Social Affairs, as many as 6,000 people were detained by the Ministry of Interior, and 460 had been imprisoned at the Ministry of Defence as of February 28, 2006. The report finally noted (see paragraph 28) concerns about the delay in announcing the results of the investigation of brutal torture in the Jadiriyah shelter. A representative of the Secretary-General of the United Nations in Iraq sent a message about the UN's concern about the delay in announcing the results of the investigation, and the need to bring to justice those responsible for such violations. Such justice has not been achieved thus far despite all the years that have passed since that crime because of the cover up by the three governments of Jaafari and Maliki that prevented our knowing the results of the investigation.

11. 5. 2. 3. Murders of scientists and national competencies and opponents

Although the international and local reports confirm that the planned extermination of Iraqi scientists and competencies behind it some anti-Iraq international and regional intelligence, but the terrorist militias have played an important role in helping this agenda. This may explain a little bit the growing roles of the militias and their access to be sometimes having first decision in front the inability of the security and military government authorities.

In beginning of 2005, Isam Al-Rawi, a geologist at Baghdad University and head of the Association of University Lecturers, says about 300 academics and university administrators have been assassinated in a mysterious wave of murders since the American occupation of Iraq began in 2003. About 2,000 others, he says, have fled the country in fear for their lives (In 2 years only). At the Ministry of Education, Abdul Rahman Hamid al-Husseini documents cases of murdered and intimidated academics. He said "Extortion is another motive of criminal gangs have kidnapped academics and other wealthy Iraqis for ransom and have threatened others. But, some of the killings are designed to weaken Iraq by forcing its scientists and academics out of the country". He added, "We think it's politically motivated of the murder campaign for depriving the country of its sharpest thinkers [701].

Natures' journal confirmed in a scientific research (2006) that violence is common currency in Iraq, but one group is increasingly and persistently singled out — academics. Each week brings reports from Iraq of assassinations or kidnappings of scientists, academics and intellectuals, in what many argue is a systematic effort to eliminate or exile a group crucial to the country's reconstruction [702]. In January 2007, BBC Radio confirmed the targeting of Iraqi academics by militias, where hundreds of academics, doctors and other specialists killed in Iraq since the invasion led by the United States in 2003 [703]. Assassinations of Iraqi academics. Over 500 professors have been killed, a number that continues to grow [704]. Maliki during his first government seeks to sectarian devote inside Iraq exclusion and killed, where he managed teams to the killing and arrests obeys his orders, and established a series of secret prisons run by the Shiite militias has caused the deaths of 75 thousand including 350 scientists and 80 pilots over the information provided by al-Maliki of the Israelian Mossad and the Iranian Revolutionary Guards [23A].

11. 5. 2. 4. Sectarian Killings and Genocide under the Pretext of Fighting Terrorism, (2014-2015)

On July 13, 2014, Human Rights Watch (HRW) confirmed that the Mailiki government-backed militias had been kidnapping and killing Sunni civilians throughout Baghdad, Diyala, and Hilla Iraq provinces over five months, and that this marked a serious escalation in sectarian violence. Human Rights Watch documented the killings of 61 Sunni men between June 1 and July 9, 2014, and the killing of at least 48 Sunni men in March and April in villages and towns around Baghdad referred to as the "Baghdad Belt." Witnesses, medical and government sources said that militias were responsible in each case. Witnesses for the most part identified the main militia as Asa'ib Ahl al-Haqq (League of the Righteous). HRW found that Prime Minister al-Maliki had been forming a new security force, consisting of three militias to police Baghdad: Asa'ib, Kita'ib Hezbollah, and the Badr Brigades. A government official from Mailiki's office told Human Rights Watch that while Asa'ib fighters "take orders" from their leader, Qais al-Khalazy, "ultimately they're loyal to Maliki, who gives Qais orders." [695]

On October 14, 2014, Amnesty International reported (the report titled, Absolute Impunity: Militia Rule in Iraq) that Shi'a militias, supported and armed by the government of Iraq, have abducted and killed scores of Sunni civilians in recent months and enjoy total impunity for these war crimes. The report provides harrowing details of sectarian attacks carried out by increasingly powerful Shi'a militias in Baghdad, Samarra and Kirkuk, apparently in revenge for attacks by the armed group of IS. Scores of unidentified bodies had been discovered across the country, handcuffed and with gunshot wounds to the head, indicating a pattern of deliberate execution-style killings. "By granting its blessing to militias who routinely commit such abhorrent abuses, the Iraqi government is sanctioning war crimes and fuelling a dangerous cycle of sectarian violence that is tearing the country apart. Iraqi government support for militia rule must end now!" [696]

It is known now that the number of Shiite militias after a fatwa competence Jihad by cleric Ali al-Sistani in 2014, under the pretext of fighting the Islamic State (IS), has increased to approximately 50 Shiite militia arms, funded, and claiming allegiance to Iran. Many films have documented the war crimes, terrible abuses, beheadings and arbitrary killings for sectarian reasons by members of these militias. The worst show people being burned to death or being cut to pieces!

America's top military official, Chairman of the Joint Chiefs of Staff, Martin Dempsey, repeatedly warned Iraqi leaders about the conduct of both the Iraqi military and the the militias that fight alongside them, a senior U.S. official told ABC News. The State Department spokesperson, Jen Psaki, said the images amounted to "disturbing and serious allegations." Sen. Patrick Leahy, D-Vermont, along with international human rights advocates and military experts, called the photos evidence of Iraqi "war crimes." [691]

Philip Smyth of the Washington Institute said evidence pointed to the authenticity of the film, and that it was one of hundreds of videos distributed by the militias, rivalling footage distributed by Islamic State (Isis) for its brutality. A video distributed earlier this year allegedly showed militia members roasting a man alive over an open pit, said Smyth. Another, which emerged in March, showed militia members shooting dead a child accused of being a supporter of IS, while photographs allegedly showed a Sunni civilian being beheaded. "There are tons that have not even hit the mainstream," said Smyth. "There are videos that go up, there are photos that go up on official [Shia militia] Facebook pages of really nasty stuff." [692]

Foreign Policy analysts have criticized Iran's Shiite militias fighting with the Abadi' government, as Iran's Shiite militias aren't a whole lot better than the Islamic State for being committed to sectarian cleansing crimes in Sunni areas, and have condemned the US government for providing air cover for the crimes of these militias. [693]

Human Rights Watch reported that Iraqi government-backed militias carried out widespread destruction of homes and shops around the city of Tikrit in March and April 2015 in violation of the laws of war. Militiamen deliberately destroyed several hundred civilian buildings with no apparent military reason after the withdrawal of the extremist armed group of ISIS from the area. The 60-page report, "Ruinous Aftermath: Militia Abuses Following Iraq's Recapture of Tikrit," uses satellite imagery to corroborate accounts of witnesses that the damage to homes and shops in Tikrit, and the towns of al-Bu 'Ajil, al-Alam, and al-Dur covered entire neighborhoods. After ISIS fled, Hezbollah Battalions and League of Righteous forces (Asa'ib Ahl al-Haq), two of the largely Shia pro-government militias, abducted more than 200 Sunni residents, including children, near al-Dur, south of Tikrit. Ominously, at least 160 of those abducted remain unaccounted for. [694]

On June 10, 2015, Amnesty published two briefings, reporting its findings on two massacres carried out on January 26, 2015. They were motivated apparently to avenge IS crimes: one massacre of at least 56 Sunni Arab men, possibly more than 70, was carried out in Barwana, a village in Diyala province, by Shi'a militiamen and government forces as execution-style summary killings, amounting to war crimes. A second massacre reported was the killing of 21 Sunni Arab villagers in the Sinjar region by members of a Yezidi militia. Donatella Rovera, Amnesty International's Senior Crisis Advisor, who has spent much of the past year in Iraq documenting war crimes and other gross violations of human rights, said "With perpetrators from the IS and from powerful Shi'a militias mostly out of reach of the law, civilians have no one to turn to for protection and victims have no access to justice." [697]

11. 6. Death Squads Inside Iraqi Government Institutions

11. 6. 1. Ministry of Interior

Here we highlight Bayan Jabor, one of the most important leaders of a militia, the Badr Brigade, formed by Iran of groups of Iraqis fleeing to Iran. He has held the Ministries' positions of Interior and then of Finance during the occupation, and he is one of the most important leaders engaged in death squads in Iraq during the era of sectarian killings after the shrines' bombings in Samarra, according to testimony of many international sources. The United States Institute of Peace in its special report on the Iraqi Federal Police created under US supervision, quoting a US official and military sources also recognizes that the former interior minister in the government of al-Jaafari ,Bayan Jabor, in 2005, had helped its militias and police commando and special units to participate in the kidnapping, torture, and killing of Sunnis in Iraq. It described the attempt by US forces, launched in late 2006 by a reformist unit's commandos, [??involved program in these crimes in order to re-qualify,?? Not clear what is meant] then followed in 2007 attempts of the Interior Minister Jawad al-Bolani to purge the police force of killers and death squads .[340]

Al-Bolani did not give any details about the trial, or acknowledge whether or how they might have been engaged in these crimes or were simply expeled or exempted from service for other reasons. Suffice it to note also that the US General Karl Horst has admitted that Bayan Jabr converted his Badr Brigade militia units to be complete units within the Ministry of the Interior to implement his agenda. [357]

A lot of important evidence has also been related by John P. Pace, Chief of the Human Rights Office of UNAMI, who held this position from August 2004 to February 2006. He revealed some of the facts about the death squads pervasive in the security systems. [46] John Bashi [?? Who is that?] said that the Transitional Assembly had failed to provide proper administration, especially as to security. This failure is reflected by the deterioration of the economy and rising unemployment due to the free expansion of criminal elements. The Ministry of the Interior made the bad situation even worse by politicizing the police force when it introduced elements of armed militias from those parties making up the Government. Consequently, several serious attacks on civilians have been attributed to these units, so that the police force rather than providing protection, perpetrates violence against civilians although the units were supposed to have been set up to protect them). [46]

The lack of internal accountability mechanisms in the Ministry of Interior, despite the intended function of the Office of the so-called "Human Rights and Public Inspectorate," gave freedom to the violations and crimes to be continued by pervasive militia elements because of the integration of militias reflecting their own political party's policies inside the government police. [46] It was known in late 2005, that US forces raided an Interior Ministry basement and found 169 detainees, mostly Sunnis, who had suffered brutal torture. Investigations announced by the former Prime Minister, Ibrahim al-Jaafari, as well as investigations of other imprisonment sites, illegally detaining thousands, were found later. All of these investigations are still without declaration of the results so far so it's no surprise there have been no consequences for the captors. [357,345,46]

Although the Special Representative of the Secretary-General, and the High Commissioner for Human Rights of UN have offered to provide international support to help the Iraqi government to carry out such investigations to address the illegal detention there has been no such success by the Iraqi government . The official opinion was that they could carry out implementing their basic obligation to protect their citizens against arbitrary arrest, detention and torture. But the protection of the right to life has not been evident given the increasing reports of mass executions without trial. In fact, the Minister of the Interior, Bayan Jabor, who himself was a militia commander, never provided the required assistance. At this time, Iraq experiences a real schizoid existence, where there is a continuous political dialogue, but the situation in the streets continues to deteriorate, prompting much speculation about a civil war. [46]

British journalist Deborah Davies in 2007 documented in film a confirmation of the UN and NGO's reports on the nasty work of death squads in the Iraqi Ministry of Interior. Torture and slaughter of Iraqi civilians reached unprecedented levels, with estimates of up to 655,000 casualties as of early 2007. Night after night, the death squads rampage through the major cities of Iraq. In Baghdad, a hundred bodies a day were seen tossed like garbage into the streets. In many cases, they had been tortured with electric drills. While they exercise the daily killing, they are working little toward defeating al-Qaeda and Sunni insurgents.

The majority of killings were conducted by Shiite death squads that hope to turn Iraq into a Shiite state of Iran. Davies' documentary film investigated the links between the Shiite death squads and high-ranking politicians. She revealed how the Shiite militias that control those politicians may systematically infiltrate and seize police units, potentially all government ministries. The documentary film shows the investigations that link these units to the death squads. In fact, they often comprise the death squads themselves. These killers went unpunished with little investigation into their activities.
(358,359)

Harper's Magazine published in mid-2006, an investigation from reliable sources, describing the Shiite militias killing hundreds of people from the Iraqi Sunni majority, then throwing their bodies in the streets of Baghdad. The victims were blindfolded, handcuffed, and their bodies showed signs of torture, broken skulls, signs of burning, and eyes engraved by electric drill. There were 500 such tortured bodies in October 2006 in Baghdad alone. A month later, US forces reported discovering a secret prison in the Iraqi Interior Ministry. This lock up held 160 Detainees showing signs of beating and starvation. They were mostly Sunni. Since then, Shiite militias have become integrated with security services in the Iraqi government, which even organizes their work methodology and targeting. They are usually referred to in Iraq (and in the American media) by their proper description, as death squads. The death squads expanded their area of operation from the capital to most parts of the country, thereby killing even more civilians in Iraq. Iraq is in a state of civil war, and some of the most murderous fighters who do not respect the law are members of the Governmental Special Security Unit. According to official sources, the rise of the death squads in Iraq corresponds almost exactly to the April 2005 appointment of Bayan Jabor as Interior Minister in the Iraqi Transitional Government. He soon expeled the Sunnis staff of the ministry and brought in members of his militia, the Badr Brigade. Jabor a member of the the

Coordinating Committee of the Conference of the Iraqi opposition. This meeting was held in London in December 2002, just three months before the US-British invasion. People at the meeting supported the invasion. According to former US Ambassador to Iraq, Zalmay Khalilzad, the Iraqi former Interior Minister reported that Bayan Jabr had told him that he had ordered the arrest of 16 Sunni men who were captured, then executed later. The US officers sought to remove him from the Interior Ministry because of its association with death squad militias. It was thought by US personel and intelligence officers that as Minister of Housing during the reign of Paul Bremer, Jabr had been unusually corrupt and thuggish. Such sentiments pushed Bremer to dismiss him in April 2004, two months before the end Bremer's power and the formation of the first transitional Iraqi government, this, despite Bremer's doubts about the involvement of Jabr militias in political assassinations. Two other ministers who served with Jabr were also accused of sectarian killings, former Health Minister, Abdul Muttalib Mohammed Ali, and former Transport Minister, Salam al-Maliki. [324,344] The spread of corruption in the Iraqi Interior Ministry, led by Solagh was referred to in a report of the US Congress in 2006, which acknowledged the existence of investigations of corruption-related issues that numbered 790 cases in 2005 alone. [341]

American journalist Robert Fisk posed logical questions about who runs death squads and criminal militias that kill hundreds a day, and kill thousands a month. Although he agreed with the report published by the Washington Post about the continuation of the massacres perpetrated by the militias linked to Iran, he asked, who is running Ministry of Interior? Who pays for insurgents dressing in black leather, and who are working in the Interior Ministry? He replied to his rhetorical question, that the occupation force pays them and the Iraqi government is run by occupation. He reasoned that this government cannot write a constitution or perform any work without the presence of the US and British ambassadors, therefore the sectarian killings could not happen without the consent or assistance of the occupation authorities. Fisk further added that the Iraqis are not suicidal people who would blow themselves up to kill others. [503]

11. 6. 2. The Role of the Dawa Governments (Jaffari and Maliki)

On May 22, 2005, former Prime Minister Ibrahim al-Jaafari issued decree No. (1), (Q6 / 4214) which provided for the cessation of all legal proceedings against all detained Iranians on charges of committing various crimes. Later it became evident that the decision was to further the Iranian interference in Iraq, especially since most of the Iranian prisoners were Iranian intelligence officers who committed terrorist acts in Iraq. Almost one year later, on May 10, 2006, Iraqi President Jalal Talabani's office issued a statement which referred to the death toll resulting from the sectarian killing. An official report from the Forensic Medicine Department (mortuary) of Baghdad identified 1,091 citizens killed in April 2006 alone.

On July 15, 2006, Ministry of Interior forces associated with militias attacked the headquarters of the Iraqi Olympic Committee and abducted more than 50 members, including its Chairman, Dr. Ahmed Abdul Ghafur al-Samarrai. This operation took more than an hour, with the presence of police cars and checkpoints of the Iraqi army surrounding the scene. In November 2006, some militias wearing Iraqi police uniforms, driving government vehicles, abducted more than 100 civil visitors at the Scholarships Department of the Ministry of Higher Education and Scientific Research. They took their kidnap victims by a road leading to Sadr City, the center of the biggest Shiite militia in Baghdad. According to some of the abducted people released later, that day had been planned for graduate students and professors to handle security requests from universities and staff in the Sunni provinces of Anbar, Salahuddin and Nineveh. The meeting had been aimed at arranging transactions to get scholarships abroad. Some of those victims who were released by the Mahdi Army militia, were released because they are Shiites while the rest who remained kidnaped were Sunnis, taken to Sadr City. The murder of these people whose bodies showed different signs of torture was painful in itself, but the pain was heightened by the statement made by Iraqi Prime Minister Nuri al-Maliki, who in describing the kidnaping, said, "it's not terrorism; it's just a conflict between militias!"

In December 2006, gunmen wearing police uniforms kidnaped dozens of people from the headquarters of the Iraqi Red Crescent Society building in Baghdad. There are official witnesses confirming others, that the armed forces attacked the office in the Karrada area using trucks. They separated the men from the women, then abducted approximately 10-20 men and then left. According to eyewitnesses and Reuters News Agency, Baghdad was witnessing daily kidnappings that were criminal or political. The participation of the armed forces was weak, while they kidnaped about 30 people from the industrial area in central Baghdad, they released most of them within hours.

In December 2006, terrorist militias supported by units of the Iraqi police and army in the third Hurria area in Baghdad, under US air cover, attacked the area, killing 23 men and displacing more than 140 families who fled mostly to schools and mosques near the neighborhood of Addel (Justice).

In a severe step in the escalation of sectarian war by the Maliki government, in December 2006, during a conference held in Baghdad for national reconciliation, al-Maliki called upon former army leaders to return to the new army and announced a new plan to grant pensions to all those who held the rank of colonel and above. As a result, 20 of the high-ranking officers went to a bank near their homes in Kazemih to receive their salaries and benefits al-Malaki guaranteed earlier. But militias accompanied by members of the Ministry of Interior in collaboration with some of the bank's employees kidnaped these former officers. The next day the bodies of 18 of them were found with signs they had been tortured prior to their execution.

The broadcast on a British television channel (BBC), in mid-September 2005, about the arrest of two British soldiers, reported that the Iraqi police had handed them over to the Shiite militia. This deal between militia and Iraqi police prompted the British army to attack the prison to release their soldiers by force. The National Security Adviser in the Iraqi government at the time, Rubaie, said that the Iraqi security forces had been attacked by gunmen! Rubaie stressed that he did not know the seriousness of these violations, saying, "I must admit that the Iraqi security forces in general and the police of Basra in particular, have been infiltrated by armed militia even before the emergence of the terrorists." He also criticized the British army for using force instead of negotiations to free the two British soldiers held in Basra. Meanwhile, the Interior Minister (Bayan) told a story contradicting that version announced by the British army in mid-September 2005. "The two British detainees at the Iraqi police in Basra are still in prison and they did not hand over to the militias" acccording to Bayan's statement to radio BBC.

A report by the British newspaper, the Guardian, on March 2, 2006, revealed that the director of the morgue in Baghdad fled from Iraq because his life had been threatened after the former United Nations official for human rights in Iraq, John Pace, said that death squads killed more than 7,000 people in the last months of 2005, taking into account that in 2005 the death of more than 15,000 civilian victims of all ages had occurred. Iraqi Al-Sabah newspaper also published on June 30, 2006, the statement of Dr. Adel Muhsin Abdullah Inspector General in the Ministry of Health disclosing that: "the morgue received 8,000 bodies during the first half of 2006." The refrigeration is limited in the number of bodies it can preserve, especially in times of escalated acts of terrorism. There were more than 100 bodies outside the refrigerators. Between 30 and 50 bodies were received daily on average and sometimes number is up to 150 bodies if there are armed operations." [I changed this to make it proper grammar. Maybe you should not quote this last part if it's a direct ungrammatical quote?]

On March 26, 2006, Iraqi officials in the Ministry of Interior said that the authorities had arrested a police officer, Arkan al-Bawi, who works in Diyala. They accused him of involvement in specialized assassination brigades led by his brother-in from the Diyala police station.

On March 27, 2006, members of Interior Ministry forces attacked an Iraqi company, Al Saeed Import and Export, based in the Mansour district of Baghdad. These forces traveled in three cars, of Nissan Patrol model, with three other Chevrolet cars, with a lot of armed men wearing official badges of the Interior Ministry. They also bore an official letter from the Ministry of Interior. Forces came from the police station in front of the company's headquarters, where the police station offered protection to the attackers and facilitated their mission to kidnap all the employees of this company. A day later, the Ministry of Interior replaced all the former officers from the police station with new police. All 18 employees had been working in civil commercial matters exclusively. Later, 6 were released because they were "Shiites." They emphasized that the remaining 12 prisoners, had been subjected to ill-treatment, including all kinds of brutal torture, because they were citizens of Fallujah, Samarra and other Sunni cities. It was revealing that although the Interior Ministry claimed that these employees had been kidnaped by unknown groups, every single eyewitness confirmed that the forces that attacked the company were linked to the Ministry of Interior.

In November 2006, the Iraqi Interior Minister, Jawad al-Bolani, announced the expulsion of about three thousand from his ministry staff after confirming their involvement in sectarian killings, and administrative corruption and looting. But oddly, this expulsion of employees was done without presenting them to the specialized courts in order to punish them for their crimes! This, even though the UN mission (UNAMI) had demanded that the Interior Minister explain the reasons for expelling such a large number of staff!

In the first months of 2006, in the midst of the growing spread of death squad crimes in Iraq, the US warned of the penetration by armed militias, backed by Iran, inside the ministries of Defense, Interior, and warned of Iran's deployment of death squads against Sunnis in Iraq. [412] In April 2006, US

Ambassador in Baghdad, Zalmay Khalilzad, said after the killing and kidnapping of more than 1,000 people in one month, mostly attributed to Shiite militias, that the presence of a lot of armed militias are the infrastructure of civil war, and more Iraqis are dying from militia violence than violence coming from the terrorists. [413]

After the outbreak of sectarian war brought by criminal death squads, the government of Nouri al-Maliki failed from the beginning to take appropriate steps against the militias and criminals. US officers, Lieut. Gen. Peter Chiarelli and Major Gen. James Thurman, in a 2006 Guardian interview, told the Guardian that the Maliki government, because of a lack of real interest in ending the violence, failed to take serious steps to put an end to the militias guilty of criminal offenses or its control that rivals Iraqi police control in the streets. The number of victims had reached 7,000 people in just two months. [411]

The former Iraqi Intelligence Director, Mohammed Shahwani, exposed the role of al-Maliki in overlooking initial security warnings about bombings, and preventing him from taking appropriate measures, thus al-Makiki facilitated daily bombings that claimed the lives of thousands of dead and wounded Iraqi civilians. [16A]

Maliki's government banned the Ministry of Health from giving statistics of the monthly civilian casualties of the dead and wounded to the UN office in Iraq. Its hiding these statistics thereby facilitated genocide. This ban caused a representative of the Secretary General of the United Nations in Iraq, Ashraf Qazi, to become very angry. The United Nations had tried to exert pressure by producing comprehensive statistics on the number of Iraqi civilian deaths. From August 2005, to March 2007, UNAMI released a series of quarterly reports on human rights in Iraq. These included sections on casualties of Iraqi civilians. On April 25, 2007, the Iraqi government announced its intention to stop providing civilian casualty figures to the United Nations. Ivana Vuco from the Human Rights office of UNAMI said, "Iraqi government officials have made it clear during the discussions that they believe that the disclosure of the fact that casualty figures make it more difficult to suppress unrest! [327] A UNAMI report on Human Rights (issued on October 11, 2007 for the period between April to June 2007,) expressed regret that "during this reporting period, [UNAMI] was again unable to persuade the Iraqi government to release the number of casualties data between civilians and collected by the Ministry of

Health and other institutions. The mission continues pressure to this public data be available to serve the public interest." [328]

Regardless, the government covered up the crimes of militias, the influence of death squad militias and that its control had reached to Iraqi hospitals. A US TV network (CBS), upon visiting Iraq, confirmed that the hospitals had become the headquarters and control center of the Mehdi Army, describing how Sunni patients were killed or dragged from their beds. The militia conducted hostage-taking in some hospitals, torturing and killing targeted victims. Militias also used ambulances to transfer the hostages with their illegal weapons, and even in some cases helped them to escape from US forces. [361]

In an interview with Boston Globe, Admiral Gregory Smith of US military, said that the Iraqi Ministry of Health indicated an increase in estimates from a low level of 568 dead in December 2007 and 541 people dead in January 2008, to 721 people dead in February 2008, and 1,082 in March 2008. "This meant that there is an increase of 25 or 30% in the number of civilian casualties looking at the month of March compared with February" Smith added, despite all of this, figures are still far away from what it was last summer. [329] The New York Times has reported on Iraqi Ministry of Health reports that listed 865 civilian deaths for July 2008 and death of 975 during June 2008. [330] So the conclusion is inescapable that this was a true civil war measured by its destructive power, number of victims and the level of vandalism.

The Dawa Party engaged in several bombings and assassinations before the US occupation. Violence then spread widely and continuously to the point of car bombs and assassinations becoming common. Perhaps the most prominent of those crimes were:

1) A car bomb was used to attack the Ibn al-Bitar hospital in Baghdad in the spring of 1987. The armed car was parked next to Ibn al-Bitar hospital of Cardiac Surgery in Baghdad, and the bombing caused loss of life and property.

2) On January 5, 1985 the Deputy Cultural Representative at the Iraqi embassy in Kuwait, Mr. Hadi Awad Saeed, and his eldest son, were assassinated at their home in Kuwait. The killer, who used a silenced gun, was arrested and found to be Member of the Dawa Party.

3) In June 1982, the Dawa party announced its bombing of the Ministry of Planning building in the heart of Baghdad. The car had been driven by a suicide bomber, Abu Bilal, a member of the military line of the Dawa party. That crime killed dozens of civilian men and women.

4) On January 15,1981 agents of the Dawa party stormed the Iraqi Embassy building in a car bomb suicide attack. This attack collapsed the whole building, and killed a large number of auditors and staff, including Iraqi Ambassador Abdul Razak Lefta, and Ms. Balqis Al-Rawi, wife of poet Nizar Qabbani. It also destroyed the area in the vicinity of the embassy buildings. After less than a month, security services provided the details that the operation conducted by Abu Mariam, had been ordered by the leadership of the Dawa Party in the Syrian capital Damascus. Iranian intelligence funded the operation, while Syrian intelligence developed the key logistics requirements.

Perhaps one of the most prominent leaders in the Dawa Party who was notorious for his bomb making expertise – this led them to call him "the Engineer" - is a member of the Iraqi Parliament, Jamal Jaafar Mohammed (Abu Mahdi Mohandes). That he was Iranian, and had been accused of involvement in several terror cases, aroused considerable controversy within the corridors of the House of Representatives. The United States announced that it included the name of the terrorist, Abu Mahdi Mohandes, on its wanted list, on charges of terrorism. Relevant was his role as advisor to the Qods Force of Iran's Revolutionary Guards, given the financial sanctions imposed on them for their relationship with the Lebanese Hezbollah, and their role in the terrorist attacks in Iraq. The US State Department classified the Hezbollah Brigades with foreign terrorist organizations because they had committed or posed a significant risk of committing acts of terrorism. They declared that Mohandes and the Hezbollah Brigades had carried out many terrorist acts in Iraq and abroad.

11. 6. 3. Supporting Terrorism

The spread of organized crime and government corruption to very high levels encouraged terrorism, whether backed by government institutions or local government. The President of the Iraqi Integrity Commission, Judge Radhi al-Radhi, escaped to the United States. then testified before the US Congress in 2007. He recognized that 31 investigators from his staff had been murdered after they had discovered and accused Iraqi officials of stealing and smuggling $18 billion. Radhi described in his testimony, how he had found the father of one of the investigators had been executed by attack dogs, and that Radi's family had faced an attack with mortars. But the most significant testimony was documentation of the secret orders signed by the head of al-Maliki's office, prohibiting the investigation of crimes of senior officials including the

Prime Minister Maliki himself! Radi also explained the incriminating evidence about the Ministries of Defence, Electricity and Labor hatching schemes to steal hundreds of millions of dollars. Radi acknowledged too that the Oil Ministry now funded terrorism effectively, and al-Maliki personally closed the investigation of corruption against his cousin and former transport minister, Salam al-Maliki. [679] The US silence on these matters despite these admissions, betrays their involvement in this corruption and its giving license to support terrorism, that reached the highest level of executive authority in Iraq after the occupation.

One of the most prominent evidences of the Al-Maliki government's involvement in supporting terrorism is how it aided the smuggling of dangerous prisoners and re-forming terrorist cells to serve political objectives. The former Justice Minister, Hassan Shammari (for the Virtue Party) in Maliki's government, admitted that the smuggling of hundreds of prisoners accused of terrorism from the prisons Taji and Abu Ghraib were accomplished through a security breach from the outside and complicity from within the government systems. They had withdrawn the security forces, a brigade and regiment for protecting the prison. This confirms the existence of a conspiracy! As this incident was timed with the imminent issuance of the US Congress's decision to attack Bashar al-Assad regime. Congress stopped the issuance under the pretext of the growing role of al-Qaeda in Syria!

11. 6. 4. Arming Shiaa Militias:

In addition to considering the confessions about the Iranian and American roles in arming the Iraqi militias alluded to above, it is necessary to go back to the beginnings of the government-armed militias. One of these was through a deal contracted by the government of Iyad Allawi with the Government of Bosnia, through order and coordination across the United States, for import of 200,000 Kalashnikov rifles (AK-47) with their equipment. Amnesty International stressed in its report issued on May 12, 2006 that these weapons have been lost during shipping from Bosnia to Iraq. This was what US officers alleged in Iraq. They flatly denied all knowledge of the purpose of the shipment, although they are responsible for arming the Iraqi police and army. On May 13, 2006, an official statement by the Bosnian Minister of Defense, Nicola Radovanovik, issued his response to the accusations made by Amnesty International that accused the Bosnian government of lacking transparency about the transaction referred to above, and that a portion of those weapons had not reached Iraqi security forces as had been agreed. The Bosnian Minister said that all the weapons agreed to by the new Iraqi government may have received by the Jaafari government, and the delivery of arms to Iraq was legal. One must take into consideration about the transparency issue, that those weapons were supposed to have been destroyed and eliminated by a European organization created by the European Union to get rid of weapons in Balkan countries. Parties related to some militias had accused the Defense Minister in Allawi's government of stealing the weapons and selling them to his own advantage.

The second deal was intended to provide the Iraqi police with 20,000 pistols of Brita type produced by the British Bristol factory. In fact, these British arms got into the hands of militias across groups affiliated with the Iraqi police. A lot of young people, and even some older ones, were carrying these weapons in demonstrations such as those held in Sadr City after the execution of the former Iraqi President Saddam Hussein.

On October 9, 2015, the former Prime Minister, Iyad Allawi, announced the disappearance of 76 armored vehicles, airlifted to the Baghdad airport after being donated by a Gulf Arab state. They seemed to have disappeared as soon as they arrived. In response, Iraqi military sources suggested that one of Shiite militias in the popular crowd had captured them at the airport. (Note that the Minister of Transport is Bayan Solagh from the Badr militias of Iran.) A parliamentary committee announced opening an investigation about this case to see which militias captured it at the airport! [21A]

The former Iraqi Prime Minister, Nuri al-Maliki, admitted in a television interview that he many times had opened the army stores to supply militias, under the pretext of fighting terrorism. This confirmed his involvement in the creation of militias and death squads engaging in war crimes. It is reported that Shiite militias were organized into military parades in the Shiite areas of Baghdad or Basra or other cities in southern Iraq to show off various weapons including heavy ordinance like cannon, armored vehicles, and tanks.

11. 6. 5. Results of the Shiaa Militia Terrorism:

1. Ninty percent of all IDPs [Define acronym] in the Middle East and North Africa live in Iraq and Syria, and Iraq ranks the third in number of IDPs in the world, according to Jan Egeland, the Secretary General of The Internal Displacement Monitoring Centre (IDMC). He added that, "Global diplomats, UN resolutions, peace talks and ceasefire agreements have lost the battle against ruthless armed militiamen who are driven by political or religious interests rather than human

imperatives." Egeland also stated that, "this report should be a tremendous wake-up call. We must break this trend where millions of men, women and children are becoming trapped in conflict zones around the world). [677]

2. Assassination were one of the disastrous results of death squads' crimes in Iraq as cited by an English newspaper that published official statistics on civilian casualties in Iraq. In support, The *New England Journal of Medicine* reported that close scrutiny of the cause of death for 60,481 civilians Iraqis who were killed violently during the first five years of the Iraq occupation, showed the opposite of the contention that most of the victims were killed in car bombings! This study showed that most of those killed had been executed by gun and not by bombings. Researchers have found that 33% of the victims were killed execution-style after they had been arrested or abducted. And 29% of these victims were found with physical signs of torture and burns, while those killed by suicide car bombs or on foot had increased by only 14%. Also the study found the death toll due to US air strikes was 4% of the total victims! [651]

3. Financing of militias and armed groups is one of the greatest threats to society because it enables the threatening of internal security, stability and the economy. These criminal organizations and militias have political and financial agendas. The most prominent mechanisms to fund and provide the necessary resources include theft, diversion and smuggling of oil, the kidnapping of people for ransom or killing them after receiving the ransom, extortion, drug and cocaine trafficking, robberies of banks, historical relics, women and cars, and finally, the government corruption between organized crime and political elites. Each type of offense depends on their goals. For example, a war of control for resources among the Shiite parties in Basra led to the imposition of an illicit tax on the export of oil, or stolen oil as was revealed by one of the parliamentary committees in 2011. The committee found an absence of statistics on the number of barrels exported daily since the beginning of occupation in 2003. This allowed opportunities for oil theft according to illicit cooperation and agreements between those parties and the political militias. Other crimes with financial or sectarian goals were the kidnappings and displacement of Sunnis from multiple areas in Baghdad, Basra and Diyala by the Mahdi Army. [678]

4. Prisons are workshops of terrorism and crime. Prison administration in Iraq has been controlled by militias of sectarian parties under the rampant corruption inside the prison.   This put many innocent prisoners in the hands of criminal militants or extremists in prison. The majority of prisoners have lost confidence in the judicial system and justice in Iraq, hoping to avenge their rights, usurpted because of the sectarianism and corruption that helped to form extremist cells. Seeking revenge and retribution, these prisoners become ready to cooperate with any party with terrorist militias, and other armed groups operating outside the prison. The situation made governmental prisons incubators for creating criminals rather than repairing those unjustly imprisoned, and intensified their developing desire for revenge. This desire was heightened by the torture practiced largely against the Sunni community. The development of this criminality was managed ad implemented because the system was controlled by militias.

5. Demographic change. The control by criminal militias of areas of Baghdad with a Shiite majority led to intimidation, kidnapping and killing of many people of other ethnicities, especially Sunnis and Christians. Terror militias helped to spread sectarian division between the various mixed areas in Baghdad, threatening the unity of Iraqi society and weakening its security and safety.

Chapter 12

The Role of International Law Towards Invasion' Crimes

12. 1. Occupation of Iraq and Aggression Crime

Before to address the legal position of occupation crimes in Fallujah and other crimes connected with it, come back as a reminder to the recognition of the former UN Secretary General Kofi Annan of (the crime of aggression on a sovereign state such as Iraq is a violation of the Charter of the United Nations and international humanitarian law which requires punishment by the Security Council). According to the first paragraph in first article of the UN Charter stipulates on the responsibility for the United Nations to maintain international peace and security, and to do this mission, the UN body should take effective and collective measures to prevent threats to peace or remove it, and the suppression of acts of aggression or other breaches of the peace, and to bring about the peaceful means, according to the principles of justice and international law, to resolve international disputes which may lead to a breach of the peace or to be settled [8A]. *Der Spiegel*, German newspaper wrote "that in this war, America has broken international law, and defamed allies and made the United Nations an object of ridicule" scandal of torture at Abu Ghraib prison damaged reputation moral of the United States which is proud of its democracy, and US soldiers who believed they liberators became perceived as occupiers, as well to mention that this war has thrown Iraq into chaos and civil war that cost hundreds of thousands of victims [521].

The political pressures and the exchange of the higher interests of the five permanent members of the Security Council members prevent of conviction to the invasion and the recognition of only the existence of the occupation as a fait accompli. Then they did a series of subsequent resolutions, trying to lend a false kind of international legitimacy to the presence of international forces, including the territories to avoid legal punishment for war aggressive crime. Even if you look at the wording of Security Council resolutions after its first

[251]

resolution to recognize the status of Iraq under the occupation of America and Britain, we will see that the mandate given by the multinational allied forces Security Council with US forces imposed on them to abide by international laws and the Geneva Conventions because they are not authorized to such a war, but the Council had hoped to end the occupation and bring peace and the return of international legitimacy while giving UN role in this process, which did not happen. That's why these forces have a legal responsibility with the emergence of evidence of violations of international law and the magnitude of the human suffering caused to Iraqi people.

The article of an American professor in International Law FRANCIS A. BOYLE had formed a great incentive and helped my idea for writing this book. He pointed that Article 6 (b) of the Nuremberg Charter 1945 and defined the Nuremberg war crime in the special segment (.... its deliberate destruction of cities, towns or villages ....) On this basis of final definition, which trailed and executed because of it the Nazi leaders despite not having weapons of mass destruction, there is no doubt that Bush and Tony Blair are war criminals after the deliberate destruction of Iraq and what happened in Fallujah is evidence[18]. Foreign policies of former US President Bush and former British Prime Minister Tony Blair are criminal policies in accordance with the principles of international law and, in particular, the Nuremberg Charter, rule, and the principles. For this reason, it was not strange that occupation and its clients in a blur of war crimes in Fallujah [18].

Despite this appeal of Prof. Boyle in order to be regarded as the Bush administration pose an ongoing criminal conspiracy under international criminal law through the violation of the Nuremberg Charter, sentenced, and the principles and is caused the aggressive war that are closer legally to those committed by the Nazi regime. Hence the importance of the international pressure for the trial of those guilty politicians to activate the role of international law which was founded by the civilized world, and to return of the most basic rights of the victims of war. In addition to ward off the risk of a third world war which has led by who take those politician roles as a model to him and trying to walk on their approach.

It will make any liberated reader agrees with Prof. Boyle is that a result of these reckless governments with the blood of innocent people in occupied Iraq as start now shows with revelations days of murder for their entertainment acknowledged even by senior leaders such as Gen. Mattis, and went to the extent of Iraqi bloodshed by even their mercenaries security [73]. Armed conflict in accordance with international law, and in particular with the section of military occupation that applies to the case of Iraq, it also was recognition by one of US Congress report for 2005[86]. This means that this situation requires the application of the four Geneva Conventions 1949, as well as the Hague Regulations and other international agreements governing the status of foreign occupation. According to the rules of international law, the war crime is the crimes committed by soldiers against civilians and prisoners of war [387].

Prior to assessing the crime of Fallujah according to the principles of international law, we should remember some of the facts relating to the status of international attitude toward accounting the invasion or occupation. The secretary-general of the United Nations, Mr. Kofi Annan in his interview with the BBC to confirm the fact that the United Nations Charter had been violated and that he has not been punished this invasion by the Security Council)[48]. While all the evidence in the previous book chapters emphasize the size of the disaster of occupation and the war crimes committed and the necessity to trial George Bush and Tony Blair for war crimes and genocide in accordance of international law [404]. It is what we are trying to confirm it here in accordance with the irrefutable evidence of such crimes.

It should also mention some of the legal aspects about the occurrence' time of crimes in Iraq under the shadow of foreign occupation, including:

1) Iraqi courts had been prevented from promoting any transaction complaint against any member of the occupation forces according to orders of the civilian administrator of the occupation and US law that protects soldiers in combat missions outside the USA. This legislation continued especially after the signing of the cooperation security and military treaty between Iraq and America, known Sofa Treaty.

2) The systematic killings and violence emphasizes the eligibility of the trial of top official criminals who gave orders before demanding the trial of the soldier who carried out these orders that violated the rules of the Geneva Conventions.

3) Allegations that the return of Iraqi sovereignty after the withdrawal of occupation forces means at least a repeal of laws and orders issued by the occupation and which prevented the promotion of such justice and allow the return of the Iraqi judiciary authority over all crimes committed inside the Iraqi courts administration.

The battles of Fallujah alone were committing more than 70 violations of international humanitarian law [35]. The joint report with the US Attorney Karen Parker [246], look at the overall violations of rules of humanitarian law which governs modern basic rules in the course of the fighting, we will find that they violated the most taboo in this law, such as:

1. Prohibition of attacks on centers of defenseless civilian population in housing or buildings or schools or hospitals...

2. Prohibit the use of tactics to intimidate the civilian population and hostage-taking and prevent orders not to leave survivors (not to maintain any living persons)

3. Prevention of military operations that lead to civilian casualties unwarranted.

4. Prevent military operations of facilities that may create a danger to the lives of the civilian population, such as power plants or food, water and electricity sources.

5. Prohibition of indiscriminate and retaliatory military tactics against civilians such as starvation of civilians.

6. Ban preventing civilians from access to food, water and medicine necessary to sustain their lives.

7. Prohibit the use of military means and ways that affect the natural environment.

American Professor Larry May from the University of Washington St. Louis in his book "crimes against humanity" confirmed that the Charter of the Nuremberg Tribunal in 1945 identified three categories of international crimes: crime against peace, war crime, crime against humanity. Then after 50 years, has identified the Rome Statute of 1998 of the International Criminal Court (ICC) to list of four categories of crime: genocide, crimes against humanity, war crimes, the crime of aggression. Although the "crimes against peace" in Nuremberg Charter are pretty much the same specifications for "the crime of aggression" in the Rome Statute of the treaty system, but the war crimes and crimes against humanity are remaining the main crimes that threaten international peace and security [387].

12. 2. International Criminal Court ICC

The occupation war of Iraq has all the international standards of an aggression war, making it a crime of aggression because of the explicit recognition of the Security Council of foreign invasion. This meaning the applicability of the descriptions of this crime within the scope of the International Criminal Court (ICC), but unfortunately, the court did not consider so far in this genre of crimes, although it is within the terms of its articles of agreement. When the announcement of the Rome Convention for the International Criminal Court in 1998 this crime was within paragraph 1 of Article 5, which had to accept any State Party to the Statute to accept the Court's jurisdiction in this type of crime. But the dispute over the definition of the crime and the conditions for the Court to exercise its jurisdiction to make the participants in the founding conference put paragraph 2 of Article 5, which does not allow this Court to exercise jurisdiction in this type of crime so as to solve these differences. The International participants at the Review Conference 2010 agreed through the resolution (No. RC / Res.6), for their definition the crime and the adoption of its conditions for the exercise of court' jurisdiction according to the Articles 121 and 123 of ICC convention. Court has become a right of jurisdiction of the crime of aggression on a country that has ratified a year after the deposit of the instrument of ratification that it enters into force after 1st January 2017, after decision of ratification taken by two-thirds 2/3 to adoption of the amendment!! [416]. Then came the aggression crime definition in Article 8 as follows:

1. The crime of aggression means the planning, preparation and implementation or attempted, by a person in a position to exercise control over or to direct the political or military action of a State, for an act of aggression which, gravity, and the nature and scale, constitutes a clear violation of the Charter of the United Nations.

2. For the purpose of paragraph 1, "act of aggression" means the use of armed force by a State against the sovereignty and territory integrity or political independence of another State, or in any other manner inconsistent with the Charter of the United Nations. Any of the following acts, regardless of a declaration of war, according to the United Nations General Assembly resolution 3314 (XXIX) of 14 December 1974, and described as an act of aggression as following:

(A) The invasion or attack by the armed forces of a State on the territory of another State, or any military occupation even was temporary, resulting from such invasion or attack, or any annexation by the use of force to the territory of another state or any part thereof;

(B) Bombardment by the armed forces of a State against the territory of another State or the use of any weapons by a State against the territory of another State;

(C) The blockade of the ports or coasts of a State by the armed forces of another State;

(D) An attack by the armed forces of a State on the land, sea or air or marine and air fleets of another state forces;

(E) The use of the armed forces of one country, which is within the territory of another State with the consent of the hosting State, in contravention of the conditions set forth in the agreement or any extension of their presence in this region beyond the termination of the agreement;

(F) The state of allowing the use of its territory, which put at the disposal of another State, that other State to commit an act of aggression against a third State;

(G) They sending gangs or irregular armed groups or mercenaries by or on behalf of the State, which carry out acts of armed force against another State of such gravity as to amount to the acts listed above, or its substantial involvement therein.

According to this detailed definition and clear conditions, it shows that countries which provided facilities for the invasion of Iraq is also involved the crime of aggression on the state and people of Iraq.

Under the statute of ICC and the conditions for the exercise of jurisdiction for "the crime of aggression" by the court, the court may exercise its jurisdiction over the "crime of aggression" in the case of: 1) A referral by the State party to the Convention, or 2) The referral by the Security Council of UN under Chapter VII of the Charter of the United Nations, 3) Prosecutor of the Court starts investigation in respect of such a crime in accordance with article 15[415], knowing that the prosecutor's office in the International Criminal Court allows him to carry out investigations in following cases:

[256]

1. Found a reasonable basis to believe that he was committing a crime within the jurisdiction of the Court or are still being committed

2. Determine the admissibility of the case or report (gravity and complimentarily)

3. Considerations intervene in the interests of justice [(418)].

The deal way of prosecutor's office of ICC with complaints and information that claims for crimes falling within the jurisdiction of the Court is include following phases:

- Phase 1, The Office conducts a preliminary assessment of information about all the alleged crimes listed under Article 15 ("Article 15 communications"), to filter the information from the crimes that are not within the jurisdiction of the court.

- Phase 2, Analyzes all the information about the alleged contained or collected to determine if its meet to the prior exercise of jurisdiction under the terms of Article 12 and whether there is a reasonable basis to believe that the alleged crimes fall within the jurisdiction of the tribunal crimes.

- Phase 3, Analyzes the admissibility in terms of integration and gravity.

- Phase 4, After the conclusion of the preliminary study that the case is accepted, it will be considered in the interests of justice. Note that the recommendation that an investigation would not serve the interests of justice only in very exceptional circumstances [(422)].

In case that the state are exposed to the crime of aggression is not a party to ICC statute, the Court shall not exercise its jurisdiction over the crime of aggression when committed by citizens of that state or on its territory. But if the Prosecutor office of the Court concludes that there is a reasonable basis to proceed with an investigation with respect to the crime of aggression. The office must first make sure whether the Security Council passed a resolution to confirm it as an act of aggression committed by the state concerned. The Prosecutor shall notify the Secretary-General of the United Nations of the situation before the trial, including sending any information and relevant documents. Security Council that issuance of such a decision helps Prosecutor to proceed with the investigation in respect of the crime of aggression. If such a decision was not issued within six months from the date of notification, can the prosecutor to proceed to investigate the crime of aggression by provided permission from the office of Pre-Trial Division to begin the investigation with respect to the crime of aggression in accordance with the procedures set out in Article 15 of its statute and the Security Council does not mind in accordance with Article 16 [415].

The US position on the Statute of the Court, according to Harold Hongju Koh, legal adviser at the State Department in the era Secretary of State Hillary Clinton has said about the outcome of the Review Conference of the Convention for 2010, saying (the United States considers the definition of aggression is defective but has been adopted a number of important safeguards. They adopted the understandings to make a more precise definition, to ensure that the application of the only crime to the circumstances of the most egregious. While we believe that the final decision takes into account the insufficient role of the Security Council devoted to the definition of aggression, states parties rejected the solutions presented to the Court's jurisdiction without Security Council approval or the basis is clear. We hope that this crime is getting better in the future, we will continue to interact for this goal to the end) [417]. Former US President Bill Clinton signed the Convention on the court in 2000 but has not ratified it, and after him President W. Bush in 2002 came to the Secretary General of the United Nations ad told him that his country does not want to remain a party to the Convention.

The Britain has signed a court agreement in 1998 and ratified in late 2001, but they made reservations and did not ratify the crime of aggression, while Poland was that participated a few troops are also in crime occupation has signed the convention in 1999 and ratified in 2001, too. Australia, which has supported the crime of aggression on Iraq and some troops involved had signed the Convention in 1998 and ratified by mid-2002[419]. While the countries that have agreed and ratified the amendments on the crime of aggression in the Rome Statute of ICC is only five countries (Estonia, Liechtenstein, Luxembourg, Samoa, and Trinidad and Tobago).

With regard to the crimes in Iraq, the Prosecutor of ICC had announced in writing answer in response to the 240 complaints reached him from individuals and organizations concerning the situation of the occupation of Iraq and human losses due to military operations in a timely manner. Prosecutor' message dated 9 February 2006 was explained the responsibility and the possibility of commencement of preliminary investigation, according to his power in paragraph 15 of the court system, and in case that received information have a large amount of efficiency that give an integrated and enhanced case supported by evidence from all aspects as stated in Paragraph 1 of Article 53 items ((1) (a) - (c)). The Prosecutor pointed out in his reply to several important points on the way to achieving a new claim, including:

1. In accordance with Article 12 of the Statute of the Court can not accept the case of a complaint of a citizen from the country that has not signed or accepted the jurisdiction of the court, but in the case that the accused person is from the nationality of a certification system ICC countries, and as in the case of Fallujah, it applies to the British participation.

2. The validity of the court before the Review Conference of the court held in 2010 was only examine evidence that confirms the existence of violations during the conflict and not from who made a decision about the war. But after this conference and put the basis for the definition of the crime of aggression, it is likely that he has become the prosecutor the right to investigate the crime of aggression.

3. lack of evidence and information provided at the time to confirm the existence of the crime of genocide or a crime against humanity, which requires evidence more on targeting the occupation forces total destruction or part, a national group, ethnic, range itself (Article 6) definition of the crime of genocide. There was no evidence of any widespread or systematic attack directed against any civilian population (Article 7) of the requirements of a crime against humanity. But the evidence that we have here, I think, is enough now to confirm this crime.

4. According to international humanitarian law and the Rome Statute, the killing of some civilians during the military conflict is not a war crime because it allows attacks disproportionately against military targets, even if it included civilian casualties, but the war crime will be possible if there was a deliberate attack against civilians (the principle of distinction) (Article 8 (2) (b) (i)) or in the event of an attack on a military target, with the knowledge that the incidental civilian injuries would be clearly excessive in relation to the anticipated military advantage (principle of proportionality) (Article 8 (2) (b) (iv), which criminalizes: (Intentionally launching an attack in the knowledge that such attack will cause the consequences of loss of life or injury to civilians or damage to civilian objects or widespread, long-term and severe natural environment which would be excessive damage clearly with respect to the achievement of military very unexpected. Article 8 (2) (b) (iv) refers to the principles coming in Article 51 (5) (b) of the First Additional Protocol 1977 of Geneva Conventions 1949, but it restricts the criminal prohibition to cases that is "clearly" excessive.

The application of Article 8 (2) (b) (iv) requires many things for evaluation, namely:

(A) The expected damage from the destruction or injuring civilians

(B) The expected military advantage

(C) What had happened (a) Does the "excessive" relate (b).

In addition to meet the elements of this crime, information should be required to show the involvement of the citizens of a state party to the Statute of the crime within the jurisdiction of the Court.

1. Cluster munitions are not on the list of weapons that are prohibited for use in itself (Article 8 (2) (b) (XVII) - (XX) ((Article 8 (2) (b) (xvii) - (xx)), but the analysis of the allegations relating to the use of cluster munitions is in accordance with Article 8 (2) (b) (i) and (iv) (Article 8 (2) (b) (i) and (iv)) (the targeting of civilians or excessive and obvious attacks)

2. Most of the military operations have been carried out by non-States Parties to the Rome Statute, and reports indicate that 94-96% of the sorties carried out by non-States Parties. This claims that British, Australian and Polish Air Force constitute only 8.4% of Air Force fighting during that period!!

3. Proportion of precision-guided weapons have been used in Iraq, compared with the total of other weapons is 66%, while British Defence Secretary announced that 85% of the weapons fired from his aircraft warships were precision-guided bombs, to prove their efforts to reduce the civilian casualties!!

4. With regard to the allegations of murder or inhumane treatment of civilians, has concluded that there is a reasonable basis to believe that crimes within the Court's jurisdiction have been committed, such as murder and inhumane treatment. Information available at this time to support a reasonable basis for an investigation includes between 4-12

victims of murder and a limited number of victims of inhuman treatment, totaling in all persons less than 20.

5. Although Article 8 (1), which states that "the Court shall have jurisdiction in respect of war crimes in particular when committed as part of a plan or policy or as part of a large-scale commission of such crimes." But the cases to which they believed a reasonable basis to believe that a crime has been committed, and this is not enough to proceed with an investigation by the International Criminal Court, because the Statute of the Court requires the admissibility before the court under the seriousness of the crimes and the integration of national systems (for example, the start of the local courts to conduct investigations, which does not allow this in Iraq about this type of crime). After the availability requirements of Article 8 (1), it will be necessary to look at the general gravity condition under Article 53 (1) (b). The Office of the Prosecutor supports various factors in assessing gravity, and most important of these factors is the number of victims of serious crimes in particular [420].

From this information above, it is clear to us and after such a long period of exposure to a lot of new and important facts, it is possible to introduce new complaints to the Prosecutor of the Court with respect to the crimes that Britain, Australia and Poland is a party or shared even by overseeing or participating planning. The most important of these crimes is the crime of aggression and war crimes through the first and second battles of Fallujah followed by similar crimes in other cities.

It is worth mentioning that Iraq at the time of the interim government of Iyad Allawi formed by occupation, was signed in February of 2005, the Statute of the Court and declared its readiness for approval also to be a party to the ICC treaty for a couple of days [423]. But US pressure on this government (as confirmed to me personally by a senior staff of the United Nations) made Allawi withdraw the signature after only 4 days of signing the pretext of the absence of a strong judicial system in Iraq to engage within the Convention and to fulfill its obligations [424]. This excuse is still so far to confirm the fact laid allegations the rule of law and respect for human rights in all government agencies and bodies set up by the occupation and so far.

12. 3. International Court of Justice

The court may accept two types of lawsuits: legal disputes often provided by one of the two conflicting states (contentious cases), or by requesting them considered for providing an advisory opinion (advisory proceedings) on legal issues from the specialized United Nations agencies and bodies. Because of the lack of a national Iraqi government have independent decision and under control to the foreign occupation, making the first option almost impossible proceedings at the present time for the Iraqi government filed a lawsuit against the aggression crime and accompanied it from various war crimes and crimes against humanity and grave violations against the Iraqi people. This remains the second option in an attempt to obtain an advisory opinion from the ICJ to recognize the aggressive war crime in Iraq in 2003 by the occupation forces. The attempt may seem to many as fantasy, but in practical way and in accordance with the powers of this court and some of the cases that occurred previously, I am sure the potential success of this step in case proper authorities and international instruments chosen for the start of the claim.

The goal should be is to get through one of the international bodies authorized to put two questions to ask the opinion of this court about:

1. The range of violating international law by the resolutions of Security Council which authorized the international forces in Iraq despite the fact that the Council's recognition of these forces is occupation forces??

2. Is invasion of Iraq by the US and the UK considered as a crime of aggression and a crime against peace and sovereign of the state as well to violating the UN Charter? Have Iraqi people the right to demand full legal and physical appropriate compensation as a result of this aggression war?

Any decisions will be issued and confirm these facts and rights, it will be considered as international instruments for help Iraqi people to recover claims about his rights and compensation for all the violations and crimes.

12. 4. Foreign occupation crimes in Fallujah

12. 4. 1. Destruction and Deliberate Bombing Operations of Civilian Areas

Occupation forces during the air and ground intensified bombardment and for long periods on these cities, caused destroying thousands of homes, shops, mosques, clinics and schools, and without doubt, it resulted in the death and injury of many civilians [564]. Indiscriminate shelling with large-scale strategy, before the ground attacks, has reduced the number of victims of the occupation forces but has heavy cost in lives and injuries to the rest of the residents of Iraqi cities.

The Washington Post reported what described by official in Falluja, who spoke on condition of anonymity, "that 12 hours of raids by US helicopter overnight, with the bombing of bombers fighter jets and artillery field and tanks as a process (shaping operations). The use of a military commanders term to reduce the time in the preparation of the battlefield, combat operations specifically intended to remove strong enemy points in early time of the attack" [565]. In the second attack on Fallujah, the air strikes began on 15 October, the first day during Ramadan the holy month for Muslims, and lasted for three weeks before the official attack on 7 November 2004. In Najaf, the US Marines bombed a cemetery near famous Imam Ali Shrine as well as a lot of the city center, in a massive attack with the support of aircraft and tanks. In Ramadi, US forces carried out intensive bombardment, targeting the city's power plants, water treatment facilities, and water pipes, leaving many destroyed houses and civilian services do not work [566].

The US military bombardment destroyed large areas of cities and reports have confirmed that entire neighborhoods have been razed buildings and other buildings remained only as columns. The *Independent* newspaper of London said that "Those who witnessed US aircraft fired missiles on human packed houses in Sadr City have been suspended and saw the result from that massacre, claims handling precision strikes were faced deep suspect" [567].

Air raids and artillery shelling usually indiscriminate and according to a study prepared by a group Iraq Body Count about the different types of weapons and aircraft attacks have been responsible for the largest proportion of children who were killed [568]. In addition to the massive bombardment with high explosives, and there is clear evidence of the use of indiscriminate weapons, especially harmful and particular incendiary in this relentlessly violent campaigns [569].

12. 4. 2. Urban Assault And Snipers' Crimes

Occupation forces were bombing widespread deliberately in some Iraqi cities, in addition to the columns shot fired by tanks and other armored vehicles.

Heavy explosions because of tank fire destroyed several structures and expanded havoc in urban areas.

It was a crime to give orders to Americans snipers in order to hit a moving object during the battles of Fallujah is clear evidence without doubt about the violation commitment of the occupying forces about the need to distinguish between civilians and combatants, and thus confirms the occurrence of another war crime.

The troops seize remaining buildings and then conducting house searches in those remains structures. Soldiers often used violent methods to enter the home, such as placing explosives or demolition of part of the front wall with a military vehicle [570]. The US military has increasingly relied on snipers to back up protection for infantry patrols. Usually, leaders give a vision about the snipers are more accurate way to avoid civilian casualties, but in fact sniper teams open fire on anyone who often moves in the streets, in parks or even inside buildings. It is dealt with everyone in besieged cities as an enemy. The use of night goggles and special high-power scopes, the snipers shoot at any moving object, which may be civilians out of their desperate search for food or water, or access to medical care, or fleeing from the building collapsed, or trying to leave the city. During the siege of Fallujah in April 2004, the *Guardian* newspaper reported that US snipers opened fire on the ambulance, and an old woman carrying a white flag, as well as against one aid workers as he tried to deliver medical supplies on foot [571]. The United Nations has reported that in August 2006, the snipers in Ramadi killed three civilians were ten of those who violated the curfew, which resulted in the deaths of seven people and wounded six in just one district of the city [572].

12. 4. 3. Targeting Medical Facilities And Preventing Humanitarian Aid

It is one of the crimes that meet the definition of the crime of genocide, which means that it whole or in part destruction of a national, intended or ethnic, racial or religious group. If we look at crime of hit health centers and civilian ambulance cars in Fallujah by US forces will find it with three recipes in violation of the law of war, as the targeting and attacks on medical jobs is part of a large-scale attack on civilians. After the occupation of Iraq (April 2003), the crisis of Fallujah became the first massive humanitarian crisis in an urban area in Iraq and, unfortunately, no one is ready to respond to it [219].

These attacks on civilians have been in order to achieve the military advantage and the attackers did not respect the moral duty towards health professionals and the provision of care for patients. This means that the World Health Organization needs a strong leadership with systematic documentation of these violations and the need for the medical community to take the necessary steps to improve compliance and protection and accountability [218].

US occupation to the main hospital of the city of Fallujah which outside the city to prevent medical staff to provide treatment for the sick and wounded inside city is contrary to the Geneva conventions, and also between human rights and health coordinator at Amnesty International in London Jim Welsh (can not prevent the medical staff to provide health assistance which they believe is part of their responsibilities) [166]. While the bombing of a medical clinic is a process of killing the sick and wounded people as well to the medical staff as a war crime as long as did not provide evidence of use it for military purposes.

Despite the fact that hospitals and medical clinics under the protection of international law during the war, but invasion forces occupied the main public hospital in Fallujah outside the city, and did not allow them to provide any therapeutic role for people in need of treatment of all parties, whether civilians or other, after they occupied the hospital and arrest all from the first moments of the storming of Fallujah [100,230,219,101]. They even have arbitrary detention for each male aged between 18-50 years [219].

The occupation forces were targeted for many times medical facilities during the attacks in urban areas, and destroyed and confiscated ambulances, making it almost impossible to care in emergency time. In Fallujah, US forces were "destroyed small civilian hospital in a massive air raid, after they captured the main hospital and prevents the use of ambulances" [573]. They arrested all individuals working in the medical services and patients were removed [574]. Similarly, as well as the United States forces launched a major attack on Najaf, al-Hakim Hospital had been "seized by military forces as a base, and is out of use and serve of civilians [475]."

In summer 2006, and during an attack against the city of Ramadi, the occupation forces cordoned off the public hospital in the city and became the delivery of health care to patients impossible [576]. According to the UN source, the US forces occupied a specialized hospital in the city on 5 July and remained in it for more than a week until 13 July, after that time they withdrew but set up a patrol outside [577]. Other reports of the United Nations spoke about the US troops stationed snipers on the roof of Ramadi General Hospital, in addition to troops stationed in the hospital garden, and this made residents avoid going to the hospital because of fear from attack [578]. In Tal Afar, the UN reported that the city hospital had become "occupied" by the occupation forces for a period of six months [579, 650].

The US troops prevented the convoys of humanitarian and medical aids from reaching inside during its attempt to enter the cities, and obstructing the work of humanitarian agencies in an effort to assess needs, and to provide relief supplies and provide emergency aid to the population [580]. In Samarra in March 2006, US forces attributed (prevent) convoys of aid to the Committee of Iraqi Red Crescent, leaving hundreds of families, including children, without medical assistance and basic necessities [581]. Top health official in Najaf city Falah Al-Mahani said that the attack cause "a real disaster" for local health services" and prevented ambulances from reaching the wounded" and added that "our team is not able to reach hospitals, we are living with paralysis" [582]. As a result, it has led to a much higher proportion of dead or wounded civilians with serious physical harm than if medical care was available, which contributed to the high mortality rate in Iraq.

The Fourth Geneva Convention states that "occupying force has duty to ensure food and medical supplies of the population," and the Additional First Protocol came to broaden the scope of this provision by adding more commitment also to include "the provision of clothing, bedding, means of shelter and other essential to the survival of the civilian population in the occupied territories and things supplies necessary for religious worship "[367].

Despite this explicit provision in the Geneva Convention, but the tactics of blockade and seek to punish the population because of the presumption of sympathy with the local fighters, to force the fighters to leave the city, and to pressure on the civilian fighters to surrender. In some cases, coalition forces used the siege officially as a bargaining tool. In Ramadi, the US and Iraqi forces announced that the population would not get water, electricity and telephone services and other services again unless they handed over what it calls "terrorists" [557]. According to Lieutenant Colonel Hassan al-Medan spokesman for the Iraqi forces in Najaf, he had said at that time, "If we allow the entry of food and medicines to the city we just offer food to the rebels" This is despite the presence of thousands of civilians in the region [558]. During the second battle of Fallujah (November 2004), it has been cut off electricity and water before the start of military operations, in spite of the presence of nearly 50,000 civilians [197]. It is noted that the Special Rapporteur of the United Nations on the right to food, Jean Ziegler has condemned such practices in its annual report to the Commission of Human Rights in March 2005 [559]. Ziegler said later at a press conference that "the coalition forces are using hunger and deprivation of water as a weapon of war against the civilian population", describing such acts as "a flagrant violation of international humanitarian law" [560].

The occupation forces were trapped and prevented journalists from covering major events before the attacks, in order to keep the perceptions of international public opinion about what is happening on the battlefield under full control. In US military operations in Najaf on August 2004, the Iraqi police cordoned off a hotel where journalists lives, and asked them to leave the city and threatened to arrest all those who will not leave [561]. While police claimed that the ban was based on concerns about the safety of journalists, police officers said they will take all mobile phones, cameras [562]. In Fallujah, the US military ban all journalists non-embedded from the city. Reports have said that the journalists were arrested and Photography crews and their equipment confiscated, without explanation, before being released later without charge [563]. Reporters Without Borders (RSF), in referring to Najaf, condemned the "unacceptable foreclosing on a ban on the release of information" and insisted that "the presence of journalists on the spot is indispensable, as is always the worst atrocities committed in the absence of witnesses" [564].

12. 4. 4. The Use of Forbidden & Excessive Conventional Weapons

The use of weapons is in accordance with the general rules of international humanitarian law on the conduct of hostilities. These rules limit the right of conflict' parties in the use of methods and means of warfare of their choice. These include the well-established rules on *proportionality*, *preventive* and *discrimination*, as well as *banning* the use of weapons and the means and methods of warfare of a nature to cause superfluous injury or suffering unnecessary [401]. According to a study prepared by American lawyer Karen Parker, the basic rules governing the use of banned weapons are: 1) not to be present within the legal field of battle, 2) can not be activated or not used only when you place the war ended, 3) It do not cause damage or unnecessary pains, 4) It does not cause undue harm to the natural environment. And special weapons such specifications are nuclear weapons, bacteriological, biological, chemical, toxic, and weapons of excessive and indiscriminate damage. Usually, it refers to The Hague law, which controls the progress of the fighting and weapons because of a large number of international treaties organized in this direction. While it referred to the international humanitarian law as the

Geneva law as refer to the Geneva Conventions. Both laws governing the status of foreign military occupation, as happened in Iraq. International humanitarian law, which governing the use of weapons to The Hague law, Geneva, and customary international law and numerous treaties prohibiting specific weapons [256].

US lawyer Parker adds that according to the Geneva, Hague Conventions the and international humanitarian customary law, it becomes automatically of war crimes include: willful killing, torture or inhuman treatment, willfully causing great suffering or serious injury to body or health, or of prisoners of war and pain to civilian; illegal detention and the deportation or transfer of civilian, illegal-transfer for prisoner of war, and prevent fair trial rights of civilians or prisoners; hostage-taking, and wanton destruction of property and taking it [246].

Geneva Convention 1925 confirmed the prohibition of using toxic and suffocating gasses in addition to bacteriological weapons. Article 35 (paragraph 1) of the first additional protocol 1977 of Geneva Conventions of 1949, stated (in any armed conflict, the right of parties to the conflict to choose methods or means of warfare is not really open at all).

The Section I of Part IV of the first additional protocol defines the mechanisms for the protection of the civilian population from the effects of the fighting [205]. Article 48 obliges the need to distinguish between military targets and civilian places, and, therefore, directing operations only to military targets. Article 52 prohibits indiscriminate attacks. Paragraphs 54 and 55 also prohibit officers from starving to discount the civilian population or destroy the places which are not indispensable to their survival or causes seriously, widespread and long-term damage to the natural environment. Paragraphs 86 and 87 determined the direct responsibility of military leaders to ensure compliance with these rules.

The customary international law includes all the agreements on the use of gas weapons and gas, biological weapons, and chemical weapons. International Humanitarian Law responsible to the management of the affairs of the armed conflict and seeks to achieve a balance and concern for the humanitarian problems with respect for the military action requirements [38]. This applies equally to all parties in an armed conflict [11], and this is independent of whether the use of legal force or not in the framework of the common law to declare a just war, as it stated in the Geneva conventions 1949 and the two additional protocols of 1977, which regulates the situation during armed conflicts under military occupation or international or local conflicts. That is why the four Geneva Conventions of 1949 apply except first additional protocol which Iraq and the United States is still not part of it. However, the four Geneva Conventions focused on the protection of persons in the hands of the enemy. And the air strikes are subject to Customary International law and the first additional protocol, which provides the principle of discrimination (Article 48) and includes:

1. Prohibition the direct targeting civilians and civilian objects (Article 51, paragraph 2, Article 52, paragraph 1).

2. Prohibition of indiscriminate attacks, including those that may be expected to cause excessive incidental civilian casualties and damage (principle of proportionality) (Article 51, paragraph 4 and 5).

3. Prohibition hit property necessary to sustain the life of population centers (stations of filtered water and electricity) (Article 54).

4. Prohibition hit of cultural property (Article 53)

5. Commitment snapped a caution during the attacks (Article 57)

6. Obligation to take preventive measures against attacks (Article 58)

7. Prohibition of the use of human shields (Article 51, paragraph 7)

In addition to the rules contained in the regulations of IV Hague Regulations 1907, which reflects the customary law of war on the ground and apply all of the specifications of the war that took place in Iraq.

12. 4. 4. 1. The Use of Nuclear Weapons

The action of nations in times of war is governed by regulations of international law which change with the continuity of progress in weapons technology. Geneva Conventions 1949 set the rules for the protection of the population during periods of armed conflict. It requires a distinction between civilians and soldiers and prohibits indiscriminate methods of attack which are not directed at a specific military objective. Like the weapons conventions that prohibit to causing unnecessarily damage and those cause long-term and severe environmental damage. The use of depleted uranium weapons in the American aggression on Iraq clearly violates international humanitarian law with regard to the armed conflict.

In accordance with Article 65, paragraph 1, of its statute, the International Court of Justice issued on 8 July 1996 Advisory Opinion decision [9] on the threat or use of nuclear weapons in armed conflict, at the request of opinion submitted by the General Assembly of the UN United (paragraph 4 of resolution 49/75 K on 15 December 1994). It says in the text of its resolution: (the realization that the continued presence or development of nuclear weapons pose a significant threat to humanity, Bearing in mind that States have an obligation under the UN Charter to refrain from the threat or use of nuclear force against the territorial integrity or political independence of any State). The Court pointed to previous General Assembly resolutions (resolution XVI 1653 on 24 November 1961, resolution 33/71 B in 14 December 1978, resolution 34/83 G in 11 December 1979, resolution 351152D in 12 December 1980, resolution 361921 in 9 December 1981, resolution 45/59 B on 4 December 1990, resolution 46/37D on 6 December 1991, which It recognizes that the use of nuclear weapons would constitute a violation of the UN Charter and a crime against humanity. The importance of this decision coming from the mechanism of action of the United Nations Charter in keeping peace and security, including the principles governing disarmament and arms regulation and progressive development of international law. Most importantly, in this UN resolution it is referring to paragraph 25 of the Covenant on Civil and Political Rights and the International Covenant which confirms that these rights do not stop in a time of war. Also it condemned the use of depleted uranium weapons by the Sub-Committee at the United Nations for the Prevention of Discrimination and Protection of Minorities (UN Subcommission on prevention of discrimination and protection of minorities) through its decision, which condemns the use of depleted uranium and certain other weapons during its 48 August 1996, and endorsed a complete ban on the production, marketing and use of such weapons, and urged States that have not yet done so to sign and ratify the conventional weapons and protocols thereto [402].

Advocates of nuclear disarmament confirm that based on this judgment of the International Court of Justice, the threat to use nuclear weapons in violation of United States law, as well as international law. Article VI of the United States Constitution states "All signed treaties that must be made, under the authority of the United States, shall be the supreme law of the country." The threat or use of nuclear weapons constitutes a violation of international treaties signed by the United States and ratified it (for example, Geneva Convention), and then use or threat of use of these weapons should be illegal.

According to recent scientific evidence supported by researchers and official bodies, it has shown the use of radioactive uranium weapons in Fallujah 2004 after finding remnants of weapons containing very high radioactive in some areas of Fallujah enrichment level [5,190]. As well it has been used at the beginning of the occupation battles of Iraq also [468]. This confirms that governments of W. Bush and Tony Blair committed a crime against humanity and a violation of the UN Charter. Accordingly, it is the right of victims to raise collective complaints to the International Court of Justice, through official channels to demand compensation suit the size of the damage and not less than the size of the compensation paid by the Iraqi people to affected civilians of Americans and Kuwaitis previously.

It is worth mentioning, that since the issuance of this opinion decision by the International Court of Justice in 1996, some international courts recognized some requests to opponents of the presence of nuclear bases, carriers have under this decision. In October 1999, a Scottish judge has rejected a lawsuit against three women who had caused the damage to the base, which was part of the defense Trident nuclear submarine program. The judge referred to the opinion of the International Court of Justice, he claimed that women justified in their work because they were trying to foil the use of illegal weapons. In June 1999, a jury in Washington state found four activists as innocent after they charged with obstruction of traffic in the Trident nuclear submarine base. The Court relied on international law, including the opinion of the International Court of Justice.

12. 4. 4. 2. Cluster Munitions

In 1996, a decision issued by the UN Sub-Commission on Prevention of Discrimination and Protection of Minorities, which was considered under which the production and use of cluster bombs is compatible with human rights and international humanitarian law [43]. Because the effect of its use in residential areas or civilian is not limited as permitted militarily destroyed or civilians, as stated in the issue (pro-rata) of paragraph 2 of Article 51 of the first additional protocol of the international humanitarian law, but also to the indiscriminate targeting of people with the potential rates of high failure in fission submunitions in addition to the long-term consequences for human health and the environment.

The use of cluster munitions is a violation of the international humanitarian law because of the prohibition of indiscriminate strikes that result from the explosion of the ammunition [38]. The United States and British governments had been used nearly 13 million units of cluster bombs during the first Gulf war in 1991 [38]. So the risk of contamination remains a large and threatening the lives of Iraqis in areas where these units did not explode. While British forces acknowledged by dropping 70 cluster bomb type (RBL 755) and especially on the outskirts of the city of Baghdad, while fired nearly 2,000 cluster munitions type (L20A1) on the Basra area and its edges [39]. As well as the US forces admitted firing at least 1,200 cluster bombs divided as follows: 818 bomb of the type (CBU-103s), 182 bomb of the type (CBU-99s), 118 bomb of the type (CBU-87s), and 88 bomb Type (CBU-105s). In addition to the use of various artillery shells including cluster shell (MLRS) [40].

European Parliament had passed a resolution in 2001 it provides for the (announcement of the immediate halt to the pending negotiation of an international agreement on the regulation, restriction or prohibition of the use or production and transfer of cluster munitions within the framework of the Convention, including cluster bombs dropped by warplanes or small units which launches across artillery or rockets or mortars) [41].

The problem here is not only in the use of cluster munitions and cause heavy casualties among civilians only, but also not to give any real assessment of the humanitarian situation after the use of these munitions in terms of percentages of failure in the blast between small units of ammunition and which will threaten the lives of civilians later. The amended Protocol II provides for strict obligations to provide ratios of failure small self-destruction of ammunition and mines that have not bombed during the fighting. For example, the British government's recognition of the working paper submitted to the group of regulate Convention the use of Conventional Weapons (CCW) that cluster bombs (BL755) (MLRS) dropped by aircraft during the Kosovo fighting resulted in high failure rates is unacceptable [38].

It was a shameful international silence toward the occupation forces to use these munitions in its attacks against Fallujah without even demanding the occupying forces any details or claim to respect international humanitarian law. This is what happened after the Fallujah fighting, especially after the first battle in which these munitions were used extensively [42].

In 2008, a new convention added to the international humanitarian law and international humanitarian customary law, which applies to all states, an agreement to ban the use of cluster munitions (Convention on Cluster Munitions) and signed by 107 States is bound under the Convention on the prohibition of the use, development, production, acquisition, stockpiling or transfer of such weapons [45]. On the basis of this agreement, cluster munitions will be considered like weapons of expanding and explosive bullets, chemical and biological weapons, anti-personnel mines, weapons that use fragments undetectable and blinding laser weapons, as are all banned weapons in accordance with international humanitarian law. Other international sources confirmed the use of cluster bombs occupation states during military operations in Iraq [469].

12. 4. 4. 3. Use of Chemical Weapons (WP) and firebombs (napalm)

The use of napalm start with the Second World War, and the US continued to use it on a large scale during Vietnam War, which led to a public outcry and international refusal overwhelming for such weapons because of the resulting severe damage (cruel) random and wounded (indiscriminate).

While the First World War (1914) witnessed the beginnings of the use of chemical weapons, where the story was initiated with the use of France cartridges (rounds) 26 mm caliber rifle containing 35 g of tear gas (ethyl bromoacetate), but its impact was minimal against German soldiers. While the Germans tried to increase the impact of fragmentation shells (shrapnel shells) caliber 10.5 cm by adding a source of a chemical called nuisance (dianisidine chlorosulfonate), who did not notice its effects when used against British troops in October (1914) in Neuve Chapelle area. Then the Germans developed their shells to affect the largest cross-providing them with tear gas such as benzyl bromide or xylyl bromide [472].

US law for the implementation of the CWC (Chemical Weapons Convention Implementation Act of 1998), which called a brief (18 USC § 229F), which contains the definition of chemical weapons as follows [270]:

1) Toxic chemicals and derivatives, which excluded the materials prepared for purposes not prohibited under this chapter as long as the type and quantity consistent with that purpose.

2) Ammunition or devices designed specifically to cause death or other harm through toxic properties of toxic chemicals specified in above paragraph (1), which will work as a result of such employment for such ammunition or devices.

3) Any equipment specifically designed for use directly in connection with the work of these munitions or devices specified in subparagraph (2).

In order to clarify more about what the laws and agreements that violated through the use of chemical weapons in the battles of Fallujah, which was mostly talking about the violation of the international chemical weapons treaty and customary law. According to the legal study researcher Roman Reyhani, Article 38, paragraph 1, of the Statute of the International Court of Justice have availability of resources that can be relied upon that prove the violation of the International Convention for the Prohibition of Chemical Weapons (CWC) and customary law which prohibit the use of chemical weapons [303].

To expose the double standard in US policy in this area, on 5 February 2003 (the same day that the US Secretary of State Colin Powell, speaking before the United Nations criticizing the Iraqi deception in the chemical weapons program) [271], and Secretary of Defense Donald Rumsfeld appeared in front of the House Arms Committee, he said that the absence of presidential waiver led that the US forces will not be able to use Riot Control Agents (RCAs) in the fighting: "In many cases allow our forces to launch fire on one and kill him, but they are not allowed to use RCAs non-lethal under the law [272]. In April 2003, US President Bush was allowed to the American army to use tear gas in Iraq [273]. Therefore, on 30 April 2003 start the US Department of Defense' officials interpretation of the Chemical Weapons Convention as a means to allow the use of chemicals to control the Iraqis, "for their own safety or for the defense of the American forces [274].

As the American legal scholar Roman Rihani expanded in his article on the illegality of the use of white phosphorus as a weapon in Fallujah, and on the basis of all the evidence (see Chapters 6 and 8), which emphasizes the use of this weapon during the two battles, he pointed out that clear fact now is [303]:

1. The evidence of use a WP weapon during my battle of Fallujah in 2004.

2. Proven firing of white phosphorus on suspected insurgents in Fallujah sites in order to evict them and kill them with severe explosives.

3. Marines often do not realize the goals that have been bombarded, or what is the damage that gets because of it

4. Although they were not intentionally targeting non-combatants, but the difficulty in distinguish them from fighters in urban areas, and lack of control over the random effects of white phosphorus to make non-combatants from civilians suffering from the effects of the attacks and are vulnerable to the effects of such weapons.

This study important adds also that Article 1 of the ((Convention on the Prohibition of the Development, Production, Stockpiling and Use of Chemical Weapons and on Their Destruction)) (CWC), and monitors the application of the Convention by the Organisation for the Prohibition of Chemical Weapons (OPCW) motivate the States parties for not to use any chemical weapons under any circumstances, and not to develop, produce, acquire, stockpile chemical weapons or retain or direct transfer or indirectly to any person, or "assist, encourage or induce, in any way, anyone to engage in any activity prohibited to a State Party under this Convention, and destroy any stocks has of these chemical weapons or any facilities exist produces components such weapons [320]. Any look to pledge formula, will find prohibitive and obligating saying (never under any circumstances) without any excuse for interpretation or questioning for secondary purposes possible that the use of this type of weapon. Its wording came to emphasize not to allow reservations to its provisions, and its emphasis on inclusiveness in the international and local conflicts of the States parties, with the need for a domestic legislation to enforce this agreement and extend to all persons under the legal authority and its territory [321] . Before the battles of Fallujah take placed, the United States and Britain are both signed and authenticated to the International Convention on the prohibition of the use of chemical weapons.

It is worth mentioning that the US military had issued a combat guide in 1999 which came to emphasize that (the use of white phosphorus against personal goals is contrary to the law of land warfare and violates international law [179,127,195]. In 1980, the media publish pictures of naked and wounded Vietnamese girl during the Vietnam War 1968. These photos caused a great shock to the civilized world and led the United Nations to prohibit the use of napalm weapon against civilians. The United States has not ratified the Convention, which is among the few countries in the world that still use this deadly weapon. In 2012, four countries officially recognized to possess chemical weapons, the United States, Russia, North Korea and Syria [470].

The Chemical Weapons Convention (CWC) in addition to the Executive Law of the Chemical Weapons Convention (CWCIA) of 1998 gave unequivocal definition of chemical weapons include the "toxic chemicals and their derivatives (precursors), except where intended for purposes not prohibited under this Convention, as long as the types and quantities are consistent with such purposes. In paragraph 2 of Article 2 from the chemical weapons convention, definite the toxic chemicals as (any chemical which through its chemical action on life processes can cause death, temporary incapacitation or permanent human or animal damage to occur. This includes all these chemicals, regardless of their origin or method of production, and regardless of whether they are produced in mass (facilities) or ammunition or anywhere else). The paragraph 9 of Article 2 provides a list of purposes non-prohibited, which include military purposes unrelated with the use of chemical weapons and not dependent on the use of the toxic properties of chemicals as a means of war. In both conventions (CWC and CWCIA) they distinguish knowing the use of toxic chemicals as a means of war against human as the use of an illegal chemical weapon.

If we look to the United States Code, we will find in the Chemical Weapons Convention Implementation Act of 1998 in paragraph (7) (C*) of section F229 of Chapter 11B of Part I of Title 18, where this paragraph specifies purposes that not prohibited to the United States in use for military purposes and which does not allow the use of chemical weapons, or the use of weapons that do not rely on the use of its toxic properties or suffocating as a chemical weapon in order to cause death or harm "[270].

C*) "Unrelated military purposes.— Any military purpose of the United States that is not connected with the use of a chemical weapon or that is not dependent on the use of the toxic or poisonous properties of the chemical weapon to cause death or other harm"

This means that US military during the battles of Fallujah (2004) violated even the US law to use the same lethal properties of white phosphorus. Although the United States it has denied the use of napalm during the occupation operations of Iraq in 2003 [58], but the Pentagon is back and admitted in the month of August 2003 by using a Mark-77 bombs, which is the development of napalm [465]. Despite the US denial was based on an attempt to differentiate or claim that the fact that the Mark-77 bombs are a type of napalm bombs, as the only difference between them is the type of fuel used within it to make a huge flame ignition [473]. But in the end, the Pentagon admitted that Both weapons are remarkably similar [465]. The United States is the country most frequently used napalm weapons in armed conflicts [95].

The United States has jurisdiction when chemical weapons used outside the United States, committed by one of its citizens, the criminal punishment includes a fine or imprisonment, and in the case of the use of chemical weapons resulted in the death of another person, and the punishment will be the death penalty or life imprisonment. And such a punishment will also allow for civil penalties to prove the violation through the multitude of evidence.

[276]

Under US federal law, the members of the US military outside of the United States is not exempt and are not allowed to use chemical weapons or toxic chemicals or suffocating that cause death or injury to humans [248]. Britain had signe the Convention on the CWC in 1993 and ratified it in 1996 [471].

In spite of the prohibition of chemical weapons like the mustard gas and nerve gas and napalm by the International Convention since s1980. But the main justification made by the United States, British and Australian governments on March 2003 for their invasion of Iraq under the pretext that Iraq possessed stockpiles of these banned weapons and was preparing to use over the Al Qaeda terrorist network to attack them !!!. The most cynical and lying event is that the use of US troops to chemical weapons against the Iraqi people before, during and after the battles of Fallujah, but this use did not prevent the issuance of a US intelligence report warns of the potential of various chemical warfare and fear of the components of these weapons including in the hands of terrorist groups, according to a report threats issued after the Fallujah fighting by Department of Defense Intelligence Document in 2005 and in cooperation with the three US specialized intelligence agencies [185].

For more analysis of the legal implications of the examples given for the use of white phosphorus, we should look to:

12. 4. 4. 3. 1. The General Principles of International Humanitarian Law and Defense Necessities.

After the battles of Fallujah, a White House spokesman said the WP is not forbidden weapon, while one of US intelligence CIA documents on the use of these weapons against the Kurds in northern Iraq to be regarded and considered WP as chemical weapon [178]. WP is an incendiary and toxic weapon at the same time.

Despite the Pentagon's confession during the occupation of Iraq war that it had destroyed its stockpile of incendiary weapons in 2001, but a spokesman for the Marines reiterated using Mark 77 firebombs. Therefore, John Pike a defense analyst with the group research organization called the International Security (GlobalSecurity.org) pointed on the nomination of the bombs (Mark 77) saying (you can name it something other than napalm, but it remains Napalm). While Robert Musil, executive director of Physicians for Social Responsibility, based in Washington, and opposes the use of weapons of mass destruction, when asked about discrimination of Pentagon between napalm and Mark 77, he said (this outrageous discrimination (deeply flawed) because these incendiary weapons produces burns difficult to treat) [95]. The more accuracy in the description of this weapon as one of napalm was recognition by British Defense Minister Adam Ingram and British secretary of defense affairs of state John Reid When asked by the British Parliament (on Tuesday 11 January 2005) on the use of this weapon in Iraq, as reported (the United States confirmed to us that they did not use a weapon Mark 77, which is essentially napalm bombs) [98], but both came back later and apologized because they gave inaccurate information because of the lie of the United States in this matter [97].

White phosphorus is an example of a chemical "dual-use". As is the case with most dual-use chemicals, and there are legitimate and prohibited purposes. It is especially from the legal unstable due to the presence of chemicals on both legitimate and potentially military purposes be improper [266].

Joseph D. Tessier, US former military participated in the occupation of Iraq (Operation Iraqi Freedom II) and graduate from Fort Sill US military school - Field Artillery (2002), and by the help of two US laws experts, he wrote a great article entitled "Shake & Bake: Dual-Use Chemicals, Contexts, and the Illegality of American White Phosphorus Attacks in Iraq" [248]. He describes the violation of US forces Principles of international humanitarian law by 3 clear violations as following: First, the principle of distinction, which requires the use of weapons in a way distinguish between civilians and fighters, secondly that the weapons should not be used to hold such a way causing unnecessary suffering, and thirdly the prohibition of the use of the weapons have advantages or asphyxiating gas. As indicated in paragraph 22 of the Statute concerning the Laws and Customs of War on Land: (the right of belligerents to adopt means of injuring the enemy is not unlimited (not open)). Paragraph 23 also refers to the same system of banning the use of gas weapons or employ weapons or materials which may cause injury or unnecessary suffering.

Hague Gas Declaration of 1899 Also confirms and recognizes that the use of projectiles that cause severe or harmful gasses would be illegal under international law [249]. If the effect is common between gasses and shrapnel, it must be the biggest impact of the shells caused by shrapnel to achieve the legitimate use.

In 1925 a new international protocol text that prohibition during the war any use of asphyxiating, poisonous or other gases or liquids or materials and equipment near these specifications, and the public opinion of the civilized world must be acceptable to have this prohibition as part of international law.

[278]

It is noted here the evolution of international law to include any material or equipment and not just projectiles. US President Ford was ratified to this Convention in 1975 [250].

The purpose of the use of arms is the one who determines the legitimacy and in accordance with Article 36 of the additional protocol of Geneva Conventions (12 August 1949). The Field Guide to the US military to fight in urban areas warns clearly that the chemicals are lawfully possessed such as ammonia, chlorine, sulfur; phosphoric acids toxic may pose a threat to both governmental and non-governmental actors in that places [269].

12. 4. 4. 3. 2. Convention on the Prohibition of Chemical Weapons and the Executive Law to the Chemical Weapons Convention of 1998.

Chemical weapons in accordance with the definition of the International Convention on the Prohibition of Use of Chemical Weapons (CWC) is (a) toxic chemicals and their derivatives, except where intended for purposes not prohibited under this Convention, as long as the types and quantities are consistent with such purposes; (b) munitions designed specifically to cause death or that harm through toxic properties of toxic chemicals specified in subparagraph a, which will be launched as a result of or incidental to such munitions; (c) any equipment specifically designed for use directly with respect to the employment specified ammunition in subparagraph (b).

This agreement also give a clear definition of chemicals banned use during military conflict, in the second paragraph of Article II (2): any chemical which its chemical action on life processes can cause death, temporary incapacitation or permanent human or animal damage. This includes all such chemicals, regardless of their origin or method of production, regardless of whether they are produced in facilities or munitions or anywhere else.

As a result of these definitions, it became possible to know the material their use leads to murder or injury of permanent or temporary harming human beings or animals. But you should pay attention for two important issues. Firstly, there is intention for using the toxic properties of this type of gear, so it causes the murder or temporary incapacitation or permanent harm. For this, researcher Rihani recognized of violating the United States of its obligations under the Chemical Weapons Convention (CWC), and adds that the use of the toxic properties of white phosphorus in Fallujah is similar to previous criticism by the international community about the United States using tear gas (riot control agent (RCA as a means of warfare in Vietnam in order to mislead Vietnamese and attacking them after with killer gun.

The use of white phosphorus as camouflage is permitted in accordance with international agreements. Article 1 of Protocol III of the Convention on Certain Conventional Weapons knows incendiary weapon as "any weapon or ammunition primarily designed to set fire to objects or to cause burns to people through the flames and heat, or a combination thereof, caused by a chemical reaction of a substance went on goal" The same protocol also prohibits the use of incendiary weapons against civilians (prohibited under the Geneva Conventions), or against military targets close to civilians or civilian property. This protocol is binding only on those who signed it, and the United States, have not signed it in the third protocol.

However, regardless of whether any country or territory has signed or agreed to be bound by the third Protocol of CWC convention and the use of white phosphorus incendiary weapon against military targets that are not in close proximity to civilians or civilian property is completely illegal.

The III Protocol of the International Convention on conventional weapons prohibits the use of incendiary weapons against civilian targets or against civilians, where states (prohibited in all circumstances to make any military objective located within the gathering of civilians as object of attack by incendiary weapons launched from the air). Although the United States is not a signatory to the Protocol shall not affect legally by this agreement, but the British forces that were operating within the joint command with the leadership of US forces and participation during this massacre is considered legally responsible as the perpetrator of this crime as Britain signed and authenticated on this Protocol. Although the British Defence Secretary had provided misleading information during the response to a British parliamentary question on 6 December 2004, when asked about the use of napalm, and the minister answers in the negative absolute for using these bombs!! [54].

For your information, the official response of the United States of America to the third Protocol (Protocol III) to prevent and restrict the use of incendiary weapons of United Nations Convention on Certain Conventional Weapons of 1980 came as follows (the United States, with reference to Article 2, paragraphs 2 and 3, reserves the right to use incendiary weapons against military targets located in civilian populated areas, where they are judged on such use including causes less of the victims and a number / or lower side of the alternative weapons damage, but will not use it unless it is taken all possible precautions in order to minimize the incidental effects on the military objective, to avoid or minimize loss of civilian life, injury to civilians and damage to civilian places [96].

The prohibition of the use of white phosphorus as a weapon chemical according to the Chemical Weapons Convention known as (CWC) is used when toxic and harmful merits, and not for the smoke composition or lighting at night on the battlefield. Any chemicals may be used against human or animals and cause injury or death due to toxic chemical specifications are considered chemical weapons and prohibits their use.

In Article II paragraph 2, says a definition of chemical weapons as any chemicals do its chemical effect on life-processes to cause death. This was confirmed by Peter Kaiser of the Organization for the Prohibition of Chemical Weapons which he added (that white phosphorus is often compared to napalm because both burn directly when exposed to oxygen and then burn the body start of the skin until the bones) [127]. This refutes US allegations about the fact that WP is not a chemical weapon, although the official documents of 1991 confirm it ranked as a chemical weapon [93]. These International Convention are which forbids states member to use any chemicals may be used advantages deadly as chemical lethal weapons under no circumstances prevent the use as stated in the first paragraph of the first article. While paragraph 5 of the first article deprive the member states of the Convention by using Riot as a means of warfare agents [269]. Unlike the Law of Land Warfare, this international convention prohibits its use forbidden and not allow under any circumstances and without any exceptions for military imperatives. On this basis, the use of a toxic chemical as a means of war are considered prohibited under the treaty, even if there is a necessary defense under the laws of war.

Joseph D. Tessier explained the hard facts in the battle of Fallujah are [248]: 1) the use of WP in the Shake & Bake strategy to expel the Fallujah fighters from their dungeon and kill them traditional weapons [34], 2) the direct use of illuminated WP mortar against human targets [265], 3) use of improved white phosphorus bombs in order to expel local fighters from buildings [266].

David P. Fidler, US law professor had written an important article on the site of the American Society of International Law about the use of his country's troops to white phosphorus munitions in Iraq, calling for independent investigations on the use of these weapons, indicating that the use of White phosphorus munitions in Fallujah has violated many international legal prohibitions through the violation of these laws [253]:

1. Prohibit The Use of Chemical Weapons in Armed Conflict

Both the Geneva Protocol of 1925 on the use of chemical toxic gases and the Chemical Weapons Convention of 1993 (CWC) prohibits the use of chemical weapons in armed conflict [280], and the United States and Britain, both two parties in both of these treaties. According to the Convention on the CWC, white phosphorus munitions allows its uses for purposes not rely on the use of the toxic properties of chemicals as a means of war in accordance with Article numbered (Article II.9 (c)), and as long as the types and quantities used them proportionate with this non-purpose combat (Article II .1 (a)). To prove the use of banned WP munitions according to the Chemical Weapons Convention, it is essential to prove first that white phosphorus munitions had been used toxic chemical properties or one of its derivatives toxic, and secondly to prove use for the purposes banned by the Convention on the Prohibition of Chemical Weapons . It is well known that the US had used in battles in Iraq, chemical weapons of white phosphorus [467]. White phosphorus has been used against ground targets in densely populated civilian areas [468].

2. Prohibit The Use of Riot Control Agents As a Method of Warfare

It is also evidence that the US use of white phosphorus munitions in violation of the Chemical Weapons Convention is based on the ban also be on the use of riot control agents (RCAs) as a means of war (Article I. Paragraph 5). How to match the Chemical Weapons Convention with the use of riot control agents RCAs was a source of disagreement between the United States and other international parties in the CWC agreement. Many US officials have stated that RCAs are not toxic chemicals under the Chemical Weapons Convention (and thus can not be chemical weapons) and regulated by banning the use of RCAs as a method of warfare. Position of the United States means that the WP munitions will be subject to the rules of RCAs even if WP is not a toxic chemical as defined by the Chemical Weapons Convention. Many acceding States Parties to the Chemical Weapons Convention considers that RCAs are toxic chemicals as such are subject to the rules of the Chemical Weapons Convention. Material or factors of RCA supposed to cause irritation or raised temporary disability and disappear after a period of time (Article II Paragraph 7). While in the WP munitions possible cause more than that, especially if fired in places closed and not open, as it was the main purpose is in the process of shake and bake.

3. Prohibit The Use of Incendiary Weapons Against Military Objectives Located Within a Populations of Civilians

US Marine Colonel Randolph Alles, commander Air Group 11 within the Marines forces admits that the napalm also raised psychological grave, where he confessed to using napalm when the bombing of the two sides of the bridges on the river Saddam Canal during the invasion Iraq in 2003, and confirmed the burning of people on both sides of the bridges ugly manner [465,58]. It is well known that the US may use one kind of modified incendiary bombs from napalm called MK-77 [466].

The use of WP munitions in Fallujah was as a violation of the Third Protocol to the Convention on Prohibitions or Restrictions on the Use of Certain Conventional Weapons. III Protocol deals with the prohibition or restriction of the use of incendiary weapons. The United States, however, is not a party to III Protocol. Thus, this offense does not apply to the use of the United States of white phosphorus munitions, unless it can be regarded as customary rules in III Protocol within the binding international law on the United States. To implement this vision, it is applied to each of Protocol III of customary international law on the use of WP munitions in Fallujah.

Protocol III is prohibited in all circumstances: (1) making the civilian population and civilian personnel, and civilian objects of attack with weapons of petrol, and (2) any military objective located within the gathering of civilians as object of attack by air incendiary weapons (Articles 2.1 and 2.2).

According to the International Committee of the Red Cross (ICRC): When it use of incendiary weapons "must take special care to avoid, and in any event to minimizing, incidental loss of civilian life, injury to civilians and damage to civilian buildings."

4. Prohibit The Use of Weapons Indiscriminately in Areas Where Civilians Exist

International humanitarian law prohibits (1) the use of weapons that are inherently indiscriminate; and (2) the indiscriminate use of other weapons. Some believe that the US use of white phosphorus munitions in Fallujah confirm that US military forces have used these munitions and other weapons, random ways that led to the death on a large scale with the suffering of civilians.

The large-scale damage of US attack on Fallujah raises questions, however, about how the US military used a variety of weapons. In order to conclude whether the United States violate this aspect of international humanitarian law during the attack on Fallujah.

5. Prohibit The Use of Weapons That Cause Superfluous Injury or Suffering Unnecessary

Italian television documentary of RAInews24 channel which display bodies' images burns by WP munitions as weapons abhorrent because of the way that burns through the skin and tissues in the human body. This photograph raises questions under international humanitarian law prohibition on the use of weapons that cause excessive pain or unnecessary.

The problem with the use of WP munitions in Fallujah and violations of this prohibition is that the use of such munitions to cause such potential effects on the human body. The banned use of weapons in a way produces excessive pain or unnecessary may apply more directly if WP munitions were used for a specific purpose such as the killing and wounding of combatant enemies.

WP was not classified as a chemical weapon, but the chemicals have been coverage of the third protocol of the 1980 Convention on the use of conventional weapons, where Protocol III forbids the use of incendiary weapons against military forces in civilian areas within uninhabited or where civilians are concentrated (which gives the right to use it against the military nor entitled to use against civilians).

From all these facts and the evidence shows that banning the use of incendiary bombs had been coming through the prohibition of use in populated areas, as confirmed by Protocol III of the UN Convention on Certain Weapons 1980, because it caused excessively injurious and indiscriminate effects. In addition to the prohibition of international customary law for any possible indiscriminate attacks that unwarranted injuries or serious injuries occur. Therefore, the use of white phosphorus as a chemical weapon is a violation of international humanitarian law.

12. 4. 4. 3. 3. Similar International Situations

The WP weapon was banned its use in the US Army in 1975 during the reign of former President Gerald Ford, as approved by his administration within the executive order No. (EO 11850) after scandals of use CS gas in Vietnam, and gave one exception only for restricted use of RCA in the case of defense to save lives only [303].

On 22 March 2003, *Sydney Morning Herald* and CNN channel [54, 58] announcement reports that US forces had used napalm near the Iraqi border with Kuwait in Tel Safwan area, where fired helicopter missiles (Hellfire) while the cannons (howitzers) of the US Navy with attribution of US Navy aircraft to throw up to 40,000 pounds of heavy bombs and napalm explosion, according to a US officer told this newspaper. At first, the United States has denied the allegations but later acknowledged use of incendiary bombs Marc -77. Marc - 77 bombs differ from napalm only its proximity to aircraft benzine instead of the normal gasoline bombs in napalm and both cause terrible burns [54]. It is worth mentioning that the United States had claimed to have all their content from napalm bombs have been destroyed on the grounds that Marc -77 not including, but at the same time refers to properties similar to napalm, yet it has sent 2,000 pounds to participate in the first Gulf War in 1991 [59]. While another US source pointed out that the bombing only Safwan area have been using the one-ton satellite-guided bombs 18) [95].

Actually, the historical lessons are very important because it shows the major need to assess the legality of weapons or methods of warfare in the context in which they are being applied. The evaluation of chemicals as a weapon depends on what capabilities holdings of toxic or suffocating. Here are other historical examples for mention:

12. 4. 4. 3. 3. 1. Hydrocyanic Acid Case (Zyklon B) [248]

During II World War, has been shipping large quantities of Zyklon B gas to German detention camps for health purposes include disinfection of buildings and the extermination of lice in clothes of detainees prisoners. On the one hand, this chemical is the main material toxic causing the systematically exterminat for six million approximately, and four and a half million of them were exterminated through the use of Zyklon B gas in just one camp, known as Auschwitz / Birkenau .

In the case of the use of Zyklon B gas as a brutality crime, has proceeded a British military court on a charge of three Germans businessmen were Bruno

Tesch, Joachim Drosihn, and Karl Weinbacher on charges of war crime, claiming that they are in the city of Hamburg, Germany may be used for the period between the first of January 1941 to 31 March 1945 in violation of the laws of war and usages did not use gas supplies poison to exterminate the citizens of the allied nations persons in detention camps with knowledge that gas was used to it . The prosecutor presented evidence about the request of first accused (Bruno Tesch) in order to exterminate the Jews by this gas in the indoor perish as insects, despite the fact that three businessmen said they are not guilty.

The defense lawyer of Bruno Tesch provide documents as following (1: Bruno was not aware of the killing of people by this gas, 2: Sending the gas was only for the natural purposes of sterilization and medical purposes, 3: The sale of parts of the gas rooms was for the purpose of extermination of insects, 4: The concentrations and quantities of gas obtained by the camps were naturally according to the proportion of the population, 5: Training sessions were held only in accordance with the laws and relevant regulations on how to exterminate insects through the use of this gas). While the defense of the remaining two (Weinbacher and Drosihn) denied knowledge of their clients using this gas in the killing of human beings until the end of the war, they did not have any reason to believe that by using this gas is killing insects tasks, and insisted that this gas was not a weapon and are not aware of context in which it is being used.

But the judge argued lawyers to deliver judgment against the defendants, because the court shall make sure of three facts, first that the peoples of the Allied states who had been poisoned with this gas, secondly it is ascertained the fact that this gas has been equipped by the accused (Tesch and Stabenow), thirdly that the accused had prior knowledge the fact that this gas will be used to kill human beings. Despite this, the court found both Tesch and Weinbacher guilty of relying on test three facts, while Drosihn position as chief responsible did not have knowledge of the way in which the gas is used in these prisons. Despite the lack of evidence for the tribunal to have knowingly and Weinbacher prove non-use project for the gas, but the court thought that he had reason to know depending on his career in the company's processed gas [267]. Dual-use chemicals were just a ploy used by the Germans to avoid international criticism and responsibility for war crimes. Although the German minister of armament Albert Speer recognition after the end of II World War and during the Nuremberg trials that the main reason for not using Germany's massive stockpile of toxic gases like Sarin and Tabun, not only to fear of reaction act against the German people after losing the war, but not to allow to happen war crime may accused the German people for international crimes after losing the war. Despite the care of the Nazis for not to use massive amounts of known chemical weapons, but they have used lawful chemicals gas such as carbon monoxide (Death Vans) and insecticide (Zyklon B) in the killing of human beings.

12. 4. 4. 3. 3. 2. Halabja case

The Iraqi city of Halabja was attacked with chemical weapons during the fierce battle between Iraqi and Iran armies on 16 March 1988 in an incident similar to what happened in Fallujah, which claimed the lives of more than 5,000 Kurdish martyrs from all ages, not to mention the 10,000 victims who were blind and physical deformities [493]. Despite the clear evidence and confessions of official US military using chemical weapons (WP) in Fallujah and what show later in the subsequent trials, but many of the supposed international organizations being neutral has not issued any statement of claim or denounce an international investigation similar to what happened in Fallujah. Human Rights Watch has published a report on what it called the same allegations on the use of chemical weapons against Iraqi civilians during the years 1991 to 1992 [57]. But on the other hand, it turned a blind eye and did not try to issue any report in front of the confessions of US military their use chemical weapons against civilians in Fallujah [34]. We have seen all of the Iraqi criminal court trials of staff and officers of the former Iraqi army and Iraqi government officials before the occupation, and although the stories and the evidence offered. The point of view of one side has highlighted the things Iran and US administration wants at this particular time. While withheld a lot of evidence of opposite side for their opinion. Although the former US President Bush used to justify it for the invasion of Iraq about the argument to use chemical weapons in the Iraqi Kurdish city of Halabja (March 1988), but the most surprising is the indifference of any of the independent international human rights organizations, not even the Americans political opponents of the war to demand an investigation about the confessions were released before including the facts and documents are following:

1. The US expert and university professor Stephen C. Pelletiere, a senior US Central Intelligence Officers (CIA). He pointed out serious facts virtue of his work as a Central Intelligence Agency's senior political analysis focused on the issue of Iraq during the Iraq-Iran' war in addition to his work as a professor in the Faculty of US military war from 1988 until 2000. During his leadership of the military commission of inquiry in 1991 on how you can fight Iraqis in the

war against the United States. He has frequently briefed on the battle of Halabja, which acknowledged that the Iraqi army had used the details of the chemical weapons against the Iranian army, which occupied the town of Halabja at the time and which is also has used another type of chemical weapons. Unfortunately, the Kurds and Iraqi civilians trapped in the city were the victims of an exchange between the two armies in this battle, not the main objective of targeting by the Iraqi army. The officer of CIA pointed to the Defense Intelligence Agency (DIA) to conduct a direct investigation after the battle and distributed copies of the results of the investigation among Americans intelligence personnel in order to know. The important fact that in the report of investigation, according to this official was referring to Iran's gas used in the battle is the killing factor of Iraqi Kurds and not the gas used by the Iraqi army!!

Both parties have used chemical weapons during their battle on the outskirts of the city of Halabja. The bodies of Iraqi civilians Kurds pointed to kill her with a gas works in the presence of Blood Agent like a Cyanide gas, which are known to be used by Iran during its war with Iraq, and because Iraq is known to use mustard in that battle and it is not possible possession of gas that causes blood agents at the time, according to US intelligence expert [56].

2. CIA report admitted as following: (Most of the casualties in Halabja were reportedly caused by cyanogen chloride. This agent has never been used by Iraq, but Iran has shown interest in it. Mustard gas casualties in the town were probably caused by Iraqi weapons because Iran has never been noted using that agent. [495]

3. Professor Stephen C. Pelletiere confirmed through a university seminar, to be a battle between two armies in Halabja was not the purpose of which is ethnic cleansing against the Kurds as rumored before, especially since the information to the US agencies confirm that the group Talabani has helped the Iranians on the entry of Halabja before get them out by the Iraqi army [494].

These facts have been obscured by Iran's allies in some areas of northern Iraq because of cooperation and Iranian influence there [175], as well as by the US administration in an attempt to make the justification for military action is coming to the occupation of Iraq with Iran accepting the role of partner and assistant in it. Any deep vision in the Halabja case will give the right to victims in Halabja accordance with international laws in front of these facts that demands Iran also compensation, in addition to demanding foreign companies that provided these chemical weapons to Iraq and Iran in order to pay other compensation to victims of Iraqi Kurds in Halabja, In parallel with similar international cases.

12. 4. 5. Genocide of Civilians

Military operations US-led in populated areas caused to fall dozens of dead and wounded civilians. Civilians killed by ammunition explosions, collapsing buildings, fires, snipers targeting and many other violent causes. While the occupation forces claim that most of those killed in the attacks are men in military age, and credible reports indicate that many, if not most of the victims in these operations were non-combatants. A report issued by the UNAMI in 2005 concluded: "the United Nations was not able to get accurate figures on civilian casualties after such operations but reports from civil society organizations, medical sources, and other government agencies indicate that they include a lot of women and children" [583]. During the first week of the attack on Fallujah in April 2004, the manager of General Hospital in the city Dr. Issawi said that more than 600 people have killed, most of them women, children and elderly [584]. In Najaf, also, "the killing number was 570 with 785 wounded. These statistics were taken from local hospitals, and not included the bodies buried in homes or elsewhere during the fighting" [585]. Using information from tribal leaders, and medical personnel and witnesses, and local, the Washington Post estimated that "Operation Steel Curtain," of US assault in November 2005, included bombings that killed 97 civilians in Husaybah and 80 to 90 in the city of Qaim and 18 children in Ramadi, and many other civilians in other towns and villages [586]. Amnesty International and other human rights organizations have expressed concern about the growing number of civilian casualties due to the very violent processes in the counter-insurgency forces of the United States [587]. The increasing use of air strikes, which have increased five-fold in 2005, that greatly increased the likelihood of more civilians killed in the fighting in urban areas [588].

Despite the attempts of US leaders and military courts in the description of horribly murders by US forces against civilians as it were individual cases, but recurrence and brutally biggest reveals the truth about a systematic culture of excessive violence to criminality extent which is often overlooked by field commanders. We can mention some of these crimes like:

1. Haditha massacre. 19 November 2005, a squad of US Marines went in a rampage after a roadside bomb on the road killed one of their group. Firstly the division commander was killed five unarmed young men who were their presence on the scene in a taxi. Then the Marines raided nearby houses and shot and killed freely civilians, including women and children. Twenty-four Iraqis killed in the accident, including ten women and children and an elderly man in a wheelchair [610]. Marines announced they were under a concerted attack of the insurgents, and their lawyers said also that their work justified in using lethal force [611]". But most of the evidence and testimony Court indicate that civilians were not armed and that the Marines killed Iraqis in cold blood, then tried to eliminate the adverse evidence, including crime place and record video from unmanned aircraft.

2. Mahmoudiya massacre. On 12 March 2006, four soldiers from the US military were drunk during their mission in area stationed at a checkpoint south of Baghdad. Then they changed their clothes to civilian and walked to the home of an Iraqi house of al-Janabi family. They were left one soldier out of the house to guard the door, and the rest entered and killed father, mother and daughter at the age of five years. Two of the soldiers raping Iraqi girl aged 14 years, called Abeer Qassim al-Janabi, and then murdered her. The girl's body was found naked and partly burned, for the destruction of criminal evidence [603]. Although the perpetrators were more than one, but one of them confessed to the crime, a soldier named James Barker, and after the defendant confessed to being guilty, he was sentenced to 90 years in prison. Parker said in the court: "I love my friends, my fellow soldiers, and my leaders, but I began to hate everyone else in Iraq" [604,605]. (The soldier James Baker committed suicide on 20 February 2014 in the Arizona prison where he was serving a life imprisonment).

3. Ishhaqi massacre. The massacre took place just three days after the massacre of Mahmudiyah, On 15 March 2006, the US Marine attacked ranch, eight miles to the north of the city of Balad, it is clear that the gunman was inside. US helicopters fired missiles at the house in order to support its soldier's attackers on this house. According to a report by the Joint Coordination Centre for Iraqi police, and based on the report submitted after an investigation by local police, US troops entered the home and gathered the family members in one room and executed 11 people, including five children and four women and two men, then they bombed the house, burned three vehicles and killed their animals" [606]. Among those who killed a woman aged 75 years and a child aged six months.

4. Hamdaniya murder. On 26 April 2006, a squad of seven Marines and one sailor apparently attacked the innocent, unarmed Iraqi and disabled Hashim Ibrahim Awad in his home, tied his hands and feet, and shot him repeatedly at close range [607]. The band was in ambush for someone else, and when that person did not come and put their plan to kill any Iraqi instead [608]. The men entered Awad's house, and dragged him out and shot him repeatedly in the head and chest, then staged the scene to make it look as Awad may be attacked by gunmen. These men accused in the 21 June 2006 of murder, kidnapping, conspiracy and making false statements to investigators. One of the participants was Petty Officer Nelson Bacos, who testified against the others in the trial, saying "I did not think they will do such a plan, there was no justification, I knew that what we were doing was wrong" [609].

These incidents led to the disclosure of the atrocities which turned out to be part of a pattern of extreme violence and unrestricted, which was more common among the occupation forces.

12. 4. 6. Mass Destruction

Heavy shelling during the military operations of the occupation forces had caused great destruction in the cities that have been attacked, including historical and religious sites, as well as water, electricity and sewage networks. US forces have bombed leveling many buildings, either as part of the attacks or reprisals against civilians who did not give information about the rebels [589].

In Fallujah, Phantom Fury operation left the city in ruins state, described as a "ghost town", while reports talked that the attack resulted in the destruction of 70% of the buildings and houses and shops [590]. At a news conference on the scale of the destruction in Najaf, Minister of State Kassem Daoud said, "It is terrible and it is hard to know where to begin" [591]. Officials in Najaf told IRIN that "a total of 72 shops and 50 hotels, and 90 houses, three schools and dozens of cars were destroyed in the fighting" [592]. They said, "There was also a widespread destruction of the old historic part of the city, and some are impossible to fix it" [593].

In the military operation against the city of Ramadi in 2006 "rather than continuing to fight for the downtown, or rebuild it," according to *The New York Times*, the occupation army said "we're going to get rid of it, or at least a very large part of it" [594]. Journal of the American Department of Defense (*Stars and Stripes*) stating in their reports that at least eight blocks of buildings have been destroyed "We are used to taking down walls, doors, and windows, but eight blocks is something new for us." according to Marine 1st Lieutenant Ben Klay who admitted of those who participated in the demolition work in Ramadi [595].

12. 4. 7. War Crime of Using Mercenaries of Security and Military Companies

Use the mercenaries of military and security companies had a major role in the violations and the harm caused to the Iraqis in general and the people of Fallujah in particular, and in order to give the international legal dimension in that direction, we will see the internationally recognized about the criminalization of using mercenaries as a means of violating human rights and impeding the exercise of the right of peoples to self-determination. It is known that each person is located in the hands of the enemy during the war and under international law he should be: either have as prisoner of war and protected by the Third Geneva Convention, or civilian protected by the Fourth Geneva Convention, or medical staff of the armed forces and who are protected by the Convention in the first one. There is no an intermediate state, and there is no one in the hands of the enemy could be outside the scope of this law [82].

According to the Swiss researcher Lindsey Cameron of the University of Geneva [79], Article 47 (paragraph 2) of I Additional Protocol of international humanitarian law (IHL) defines mercenary across from carrying characters as:

1) He was recruited from the inside or abroad, in order to participate in an armed conflict

2) He already participated in hostile acts such as:

a. To be motivated to take part in the hostilities essentially by the desire for personal gain, with promises by or on behalf of a party to the conflict, with material damages far greater than that promised or given to fighters of the same rank or function in the armed forces of that party.

b. It is not a citizen of any party to neither the conflict nor a resident in the territory controlled by the party to the conflict.

c. Not a member of the armed forces of a part to the conflict.

d. It is not sent to the conflict by the State which is not a party to the conflict on official duty as a member of its armed forces.

Lindsey explains [79] that in spite of the need to provide the above criteria combined to launch a recipe mercenary on the person, but many believe that this is unworkable definition, because anyone can shoot and next to his lawyer to save him because of the lack of all the above conditions !!! In the first paragraph of Article 47 states (not permissible for a mercenary to have a right to be a combatant or a prisoner of war), and with this, the first protocol stipulates that even if someone from unlawfully in hostilities participated, then did not have the right to be a prisoner of war, he takes advantage of the protection provided by Article 75 of the I Protocol as a fundamental guarantees.

Due to the fact that the I Additional Protocol is not sufficient in this area, it has two international treaties introduced for banned and criminalize mercenary, International Convention against the Recruitment, Use, Financing and Training of Mercenaries [83] and Convention for the Elimination of Mercenarism in Africa [84]. Both explained the people who are criminalized after that apply to the person specification definition as a mercenary, participated in the hostilities, or even tried to participate in hostilities under Convention of the United Nations. Because the second paragraph is considered the person who recruits, uses, financed and trained mercenaries who commits a crime even if he not present at the attack scene. On this basis, the staff from South Africa who had been working as a protection in Paul Bremer's office apply to the paragraph 47 of I Protocol, and they are paid 1,500 $ per day and have the freedom to shoot the Iraqi resistance targeted Paul Bremer. African Union Convention repeats literally the definition of Article 47 of I Protocol [79].

United Nations Convention is attempt to curb the use of mercenaries through consider it as crimes, with extradition procedures in the event of committing violations, especially the mercenaries who are being recruited to participate in the overthrow of a legitimate government or undermining the authority of the state [70]. The United Nations Convention against mercenaries entered into force in 2001 but ratified by only 28 countries until 7 September 2006. While the African Union Convention entered into force in 1985 and ratified by only one country.

The United States tried to evade the provisions of this Convention for prevention regarded his contractors by virtue of mercenaries by the claim that their duties are not hostile or to fight, but only within the personal security provision and physical has a defensive nature of the tasks, but the fact of the matter and also agreed with US military study (Kevin Collins, 2006), the United

States you set security and military contractors specifications and powers of the combatants [70,110]. As well as to the hostile, the brutal, and repressive nature and deliberate killing of innocents by mercenaries of Blackwater according to the complaint by US constitutional freedoms Center [288]. But continued declaration of the United States as non-combatants put them under the protection of prisoners of war in any armed conflict. It is also the biggest disadvantages of using private military contractors companies, is that employees will not be held liable for the same legal acts or violations that they do compare with the regular army soldiers [150].

Opinion and Analysis of International Organizations About Using Mercenaries:

12. 4. 7. 1. United Nations

In a press release issued on 27 October 2003 [126] Special Rapporteur on the prevention of the use of mercenaries, Mr. Enrique Bernales Ballesteros announced that the United Nations to respond effectively to the use of mercenaries in armed conflicts and illicit trafficking and other crimes, through the amendment of the legal definition of mercenaries to include countries complicit in the activities of mercenaries, because of the participation of mercenaries in a wide range of criminal activities. He said during a meeting of the Social, Humanitarian and Cultural Committee considering the right of peoples to self-determination and the elimination of racism and racial discrimination. He pointed out that the use of mercenaries as elements of a criminal does not only prevent the right of peoples to self-determination, but it also was a way for the violation of fundamental human rights, because of the absence of laws to combat mercenary activities, and was often mercenaries away from the trial, which helped to impunity.

On the sidelines of UN meetings on human rights, and in the press release issued on 7 November 2007, the UN team Working Group on the use of mercenaries said that the number of methods of private security companies operating in conflict such as Iraq and Afghanistan regions is a new form of mercenary activities, warning that countries that employ them can be held responsible for human rights violations committed by their employees [121]. The team explained that the prosecutor at these companies that their employees are not civilians or fighters, is a new form of mercenary (similar irregular fighters), which is in itself a concept is not clear, and warning the exporting countries to those employees to avoid granting them immunity from the judiciary. The team at the same time complained of the lack of transparency and accountability with regard to the work of these companies, and the lack of an international regulatory framework for monitoring their activities.

In its report for 2011, the same team pointed the seriously feel concerned the lack of judicial matter for the violations committed by mercenaries of private security companies in Iraq 2003-2009. The victims of such violations and their families are still waiting for justice. With reference to the Status of Forces Agreement between Iraq and the occupying power (the United States) called SOFA is not clear with respect to lift the immunity of security fighters if it includes all the contractors types with the US government, and whether the application will be in Iraqi courts, and considering clarify this issue as priority [122].

It is worth mentioning that this team in its report on 13 September 2006 revealed something important and serious at the same time [123]. They pointed out that the US personnel in the security and military companies, which two special charged atrocities in the torture at Abu Ghraib prison have been subjected to an internal investigation only by their companies and have not been investigated by any other party, that is other than those pledged by the United States government. In the report of the High Commissioner for Human Rights at the United Nations on the situation in Iraq (E / CN.4 / 2005/4), drew the High Commissioner attention of the United States of America to the fact employed for very large numbers of private security companies, which raises questions about what the system Legal which applies to them and what are their duties, was the response of the United States government that this private security staff are under the supervision of the occupying forces (Alliance) and subject to the jurisdiction of the federal criminal courts in the United States !!!!! This incident shows two important things, the first is a recognition of the US government direct to contractors under its supervision of private security companies work (and this is important condition helps in this regard the work of private security companies as companies mercenaries with the responsibility of the US government for accounting of violations). The second thing that was confirmed is the US government lied in the subordination of violations of employees of private security companies in front of the jurisdiction of the federal courts of America, not only in the case of torture of Abu Ghraib crimes but even in the murders of civilians, such as the crime of 17 Iraqi civilians killed in the Eagles Square in Baghdad in 2007.

12. 4. 7. 2. International Committee of the Red Cross (ICRC)

The rules of the International Committee of the Red Cross in the interpretation of the Geneva Convention relative to the mercenaries, require the presence of the country's leadership of mercenaries, not lead them by their company, and that the United States is trying to claim that those mercenaries are outside authorities and orders of US military to prevent the responsibility of the US government on their actions. For the US government organized many laws to allow practicing the work of these security companies, including International Traffic in Arms Regulations (ITAR) which began within the Arms Export Control Act. Note that US security companies want to market their services outside the United States, it must register with State Department's Office of Munitions Control, with submission of annual reports on their activities and overall returns them in accordance with the law [111].

Accounting the violations of mercenaries of private military and security companies follow the contracted side. If they contracted by the US Department of Defense (DoD) to providers of security services, it means they would be subject to Justice Act outside the territory (MEJA) of 2000. For that carries this law, criminal responsibility only on civilian contractors with the Ministry of Defence in the event of committing a violation against United States military facilities abroad or within the control of US military commanders in case there was no agreement between these forces. While this law does not prosecute violations of the security services contractors with the State Department or the CIA. In addition to that the main problem lies in the application of legal procedures even with them applies the law of MEJA. They work in Iraq as more than 20,000 contractors with the Department of Defense and although there are many proven violations cases, but we have not seen the trial of a single contractor in accordance with this law.

Despite the growing interest in the need for services of mercenaries and as stated in the draft defense appropriations Act for fiscal year 2005, which also stipulates that the US Department of Defense obligates for tighten restrictions on the providers of security services (PSPs). Therefore, it's began Ronald W. Reagan National Defense Authorization Act, where the language of the law refers to the discomfort by Congress of the dark legal status from the use of PSPs operating in Iraq. For this reason, Congress requests the Minister of defense to make a report on the following points with respect to contractors working with the military:

1. Provide a description of the entire chain of command and control mechanisms that are out there, to ensure the leadership and supervision of contractor personnel in security critical times.

2. Provide a description of the sanctions imposed on the contractor employee's if failure to comply with the law or regulation or participated in the misconduct.

3. Provide a description of the disciplinary and criminal proceedings brought against a contractor employee during the period of 1 May 2003 until the issuance of this law.

4. Provide interpretation of the legal status of employees and contractors involved in the security tasks in Iraq after the alleged transfer of sovereignty on 28 June 2004 [112].

In addition to the legal issues, the Congress has demanded from the defense minister a report on the death toll of contractors due to hostile fire!!!, and the number of accidents by hostile fire, and the types of tasks in which the gunmen Contractors works, and what are the plans that have been developed to ensure knowledge of military commanders with full information about the contractor's activities.

But what surprised from this information are two things, first was a request from Congress to Minister of Defense to make available some requirements pertaining to the work of contractors, which shows the lack or absence of it before, or lack of coordination as required before this Act. They asked follows:

1. Provide a quick way to identify and distinguish members of PSP by members of the armed forces.

2. Provide a means for the exchange of relevant information to threaten members of PSP.

3. Provide assistance to members of PSP in the event clashed with hostile forces.

4. Investigate the background and qualifications of workers in PSP.

5. Development of rules for using force by PSP and to ensure appropriate training in accordance with the rules of the use of force.

6. Functions of security, intelligence, law enforcement and criminal justice functions are inherently governmental functions, and should not be performed by individual contractors.

7. Establishing procedures to identify any security, legal and intelligence functions and enforcement of justice that will be implemented by military personnel from that will be performed by a private company.

8. Calling the minister constitutional authority as commander in chief of the armed forces to supervise the unitary executive branch.

But former President George W. Bush objected many of these requirements imposed for the Defense Authorization Act of 2005 which was the second thing I surprised. President Bush is well aware that these requirements would give the US government direct supervision to the work of contractors and thus help to the applicability of the recipe as mercenaries on security and military contractor Americans.

In May 2005, the US Department of Defense deploys a new set of regulations for contractors in the Defense Federal Acquisition Regulation Supplement. These regulations revealed the real status of the work and the behavior problems of contractors between them and US military. For this, the regulations represent an attempt to improve coordination between contractors on the one hand and military, on the other hand, through the publication and the tightening of restrictions on the activities of the contractor. The regulations asking of contractors to comply with all the laws of the United States and the host country and orders issued by the combatant commander and require the contractor to conduct medical and security screenings on his staff, and granting of the contracting officer the authority to remove the contractor employees who offer their troops at risk or overlap with the job is done. Also its prevent contractors to wear a military uniform unless authorized by the military commander (and provided that they are uniform and clearly distinguish Contractor personnel of military personnel). The regulations also stipulate that the military commander to provide force protection for all individuals and equipment Contractor (but do not include regulations provide protection for contractors with destinations outside the Ministry of Defence) (70).

These regulations indicate without any doubt that the opposite of these instructions is what prevailed prior to the issuance of these regulations, which means that the mercenary security companies incidents before the first battle, and during the second battle was a mess law of the jungle in an occupied country!! There was a lack of clarity in the relationship between the tasks of contractors and the military personnel. This means that their actions, garments, powers or their mission is the reason led to the targeting of combatants before the first battle of Fallujah.

Major Kevin Collins (2006) recognizes that the introductory language in the regulations confuse the legal status of the contractors and its failing to clarify of many task of PSPs, which states that they are not combatants and not taking any such assignment, such as the use of force, or exposing their risk. Especially regulations that prevent contractors of direct participation in any actions that may cause damage to the enemy armed forces. This means that regulations language has not only failed in recognition of the role PSPs, but also ignored the nature of the enemy in the contemporary work environment. The officer Collins also recognizes that growing the security problem because of the increased resistance that prompted Paul Bremer (led occupation authority) to increase its reliance on PSPs in the implementation of security tasks!! The Memorandum of Understanding between the US Ministries of Defense and Foreign give Ambassador Paul Bremer, the responsibility for the security of all executive officers and employees of the Department of Defense, or submission direct support allocated to the Ministry of Foreign [70].

Coordination problems in the cooperation between the military authorities and civilian contractors caused deep hostile between them, because of some incidents by contractors against military people, as well to the sensitivity of the difference salary. PSP employee paid salary could be up to two thousand dollars per day compared with the various military ranks that charge between 25-100 $ per day, and PSP staff working within a legal vacuum because of the lack of clarity jurisdiction if they committed violations [116,70].

The families of Americans four contractors who were killed in Fallujah (2004) filed a lawsuit in North Carolina for wrongful death against Blackwater, then addressed the US Congress on this issue in the discussions. It was promulgated in 2007 National Defense Authorization Act, which gave the right to prosecute private security companies working with the United States within the external emergency operations in accordance with the Uniform Code of Military Justice [216]

.

On 25 August 2008, the report of the US Congress [85] admit the existence of several fears and concern about the transparency of the work of US security contractors in Iraq and the issue of the lack of measures in order to hold them accountable about any violation they did under US court or even foreign judiciary. There is no complete information about the terms of the contract, including cost and standards that govern the recruitment and performance making it difficult to assess their effectiveness. Although the report mentions that contractors are non - combatants and do not have the protection of the fighter under international law in the event participated hostilities. But they come back and they say that section 552 of John Warner National Defense Authorization Act for FY2007 which known simply (PL 109-364) makes military contractors follow the authority of military courts. But because of constitutional concerns, it seems likely that contractors who commit crimes in Iraq will be prosecuted under criminal laws that apply outside the territory or within the regional maritime jurisdiction of the United States of America, or through the Military Extraterritorial Jurisdiction Act (MEJA). Same report admits that Iraqi courts without owning for any authority or jurisdiction to prosecute security contractors prior permission of a member country of the relevant part of the coalition occupying forces because of the continuation in force of civil administrator Bremer authority orders of the occupation called CPA, which prohibits any Judicial mandate of the state to Iraqi courts (which means that the criminal jurisdiction must be via sending to the country of contractor mercenaries). The most dangerous notice in this report is that some contractors, including those working with the Ministry of Foreign Affairs, may remain outside US jurisdiction, whether civil or military for improper conduct in Iraq!! This report recognition that does not includes private contractors who are working to gather intelligence information from prisoners, even though they also armed contractors. Another American recognition according to the report of the US Congressional Budget Office (2003-2007), the number of private contractors of US Contracting in Iraq until the beginning of 2008, they were up to 190,000 thousand, of whom 40% of the staff of private contractors were Iraqis, and 20% of them were Americans nationality, which means that the remaining 40% are from the third nationality (38,700 US citizenship, and 70,500 from the local nationality of the country (Iraq), and 81,000 of the third nationality). It is sufficient to note that this government report has confirmed the use of the US government to private contractors in military operations in Iraq by more than 2.5 times what they used previously, especially in the last Balkan War 1990 (where they used 20 000 militaries compared to 20 000 civilian contractors, while in Iraq were 200 000 fighters compared to 190 000 of civilian contractors) [287].

The torture crimes of mercenary contractors against Iraqis civilian's detainees is an explicit violation of the provisions of the four Geneva Conventions of 1949. Hague Regulations define the status of detainees, and the responsibility of the state in their treatment. Also, the International Covenant on Civil and Political Rights prohibit cruel and inhuman or degrading. Torture cases violating the United Nations Declaration of Human Rights and the UN Convention Against Torture. In addition to violating US federal laws for War Crimes Act of 1996, and for the Torture Victim Protection Act [86].

The lack of application and the existence of procedures and regulations is the main reason to prevent the establishment of lawsuits against Americans contractors or US military personnel who have committed crimes of torture, which keeps thousands of Iraqi victims who were affected by the arbitrary arrest and without charge, and released Iraqi victims without any compensation for physical or even psychological rehabilitation to helps them for cross these crimes. This impunity gave an important corner in order to establish an international criminal court for Iraqi victims of the US occupation.

The United States has expanded the task work of mercenaries accompanying its occupation forces to include combat missions for the second's army in contravention of the Geneva Conventions of 1949. That is why we see the US confessions in recent research confirms and asking the prior coordination of the role between security contractors with Joint Task Forces will ease the burden of combat missions for the US Army [77,78]. Another evidence of the ability of mercenary security companies in impunity, we see the US military investigation has proven after finding a video depicting the rape cases to Bosnian women by civilian contractors for the company (DynCorp) in one of the US military bases in Bosnia in 1999, but they were able to evade justice because they are subject to the accounting by the Uniform Code of Military Justice and not able to punish them because the local Bosnian judiciary is inactivated like that of Iraqi. But the US Congress tried to give a new image arose, expanding the powers of law (UCMJ) in the fall of 2007 within the scope of contingency operations or during the period of declared wars. US Sen. Lindsey Graham which urged that this amendment and said that this amendment will give US commanders greater justice and means to bring civilians contractors in front of military courts [164].

It is the duty of states to prosecute perpetrators of war crimes in its own courts and it is also committed countries to punish the perpetrators of war crimes, regardless of their nationality or where the crime was committed. Regardless of the level of individual responsibility, the state and its authorities remain legally responsible under international law to prosecute and prevent impunity [71]. The United States has violated its international obligations binding due account of the treatment of prisoners, especially with the lack of any direct charge them for the entire period of their detention in the prisons of the occupation, which give eligibility to claim damages appropriate and parallel for psychological and physical damage that they have suffered.

Civilians and military contractors enjoyed the American legal protection and immunity from prosecution under Iraqi law in accordance with resolution No. 17 of the civil governor of the occupation authority called (CPA). Because this situation is consistent with the powers of the United States as an occupying power under the Hague Regulations of 1907 and the Geneva Conventions [70]. Unfortunately, this immunity continued even after the transfer of alleged sovereignty and authority as we saw in the massacre of the Eagles Square in Baghdad and killed 17 Iraqi civilians by mercenaries of Blackwater company. But this type of serious crime as war crimes and torture is possible to be dubbing under the International "universal jurisdiction" and any state have it can be prosecution and they will not be protected by immunity agreements [71].

In the beginning, the Memorandum No. 17 had prevented the security contractors from participating in military operations or law enforcement operations, with restrained from acquiring heavy weapons and weapon limited to 7.62 mm or less. But at the same time they follow the same rules and behavior of the occupation forces in use of force [70], and this making them particularly as mercenaries!!!.

According to the Geneva Conventions of 1949, which distinguishes between members of the armed forces (fighters) and civilians who are allowed to accompany these forces only for the purpose of providing civil and humanitarian assistance without participating in military actions because that will fall down on their international protection in accordance with these agreements.

12. 4. 7. 3. Human Rights Watch

The trial of American civilians involved with war crimes and torture in Iraq are also possible in the United States courts, because the trial in US military courts can not be unless the crime occurred during the period of declared war (US Uniform Code of Military Justice). Note that the security company contractor is responsible for the crimes of the security contractor, and not an occupying army administration [71].

1. In accordance with Federal Law of US, there is US War Crimes Act of 1996 (18 USC 2441), under which the US Contractor security can be sued in US courts if committed a war crimes such as any grave breach of the Geneva Conventions 1949 (such as torture and inhuman treatment) or any violation of article 3 common to all the Geneva Conventions (which includes not only torture, but also the outrages upon personal dignity, or humiliating and degrading treatment). Sanctions in US law include fines or imprisonment for life or any term of imprisonment, or the death penalty in the case resulted in the death of the victim because of torture or degrading treatment.

2. Civilian contractors working in military interrogators can be prosecuted under the federal anti-torture statute (18 USC 2340), which prohibits torture by any person who commits an act of torture outside the United States. It can jail any contractor convicted of torture to a sentence of up to 20 years or even death in a case of torture leading to the death of the victim.

3. Contractors work for the US Defense Department can accounting under the Military Extraterritorial Jurisdiction Act of 2000 (Public Law 106-778) called briefly (MEJA), which gives the Justice Department the power to bring American civilians contractors in front of the US civil justice in the event of committing crimes outside the United States [164]. Despite that this law was issued in order to protect American soldiers and their families at US bases after they had been subjected to crimes by contractors military personnel have immunity from prosecution. This law allows the lifting of lawsuits in federal courts of the United States of civilians who were accompanied by US troops abroad about the commission of certain crimes (a federal crime) is punishable by imprisonment for more than one year. This law authorizes the US Secretary of Defense for Law Enforcement on the ministry's staff and the arrest of the suspects and bring them to the United States, provided that the prosecutions will be under the Military Extraterritorial Jurisdiction Act by federal civil authorities because the Defense Ministry has not issued executive regulations required by the law. However, two cases at least bring under the authority of law MEJA before being minimized on 29 September 2004. In July 2004, the dropping of the charge before the jury for the pair of air sergeant who stabbed his wife to death at a US base in Turkey. The second case was charged with the contractor David Passaro who worked for the Central Intelligence Agency for committing acts of torture by the risk of a weapon in the Asadabad base in

Afghanistan. Although the law MEJA does not provide jurisdiction over non-contractors with the US Department of Defense, the US State Government confirmed jurisdiction under Title 18 of section 7 (9) (A) of the code of the United States of America, which expands federal jurisdiction to the diplomatic and consular missions and military of the United States abroad [70]. But the problem, according to Peter Singer specialist mercenary affairs of security and private companies, from the US Department of Justice did not use this law or working on applied only rarely, while Proffessional Services Council preferred to expand MEJA law instead of expanding the UCMJ law [164].

From the standpoint of Human Rights Watch believes it is possible to sue the other contractors in the US federal courts, on the grounds that the alleged act took place in the US military base abroad, and because in Iraq was and stayed many of the contractors who do not work with US Department of defense, but with the Ministry of Interior [70].

12. 4. 7. 4. Center For Constitutional Rights

In his complaint submitted on behalf of one Iraqi civilian victim in front of US courts [288], the lawyer of center explained that members of the US Blackwater may have committed a violation of US law itself, by committing the following acts:

1) It's work in accordance with the pattern of recklessness in the use of deadly force.

2) They are not only working on the creation or strengthening of a culture of excessive use of deadly force, but they had not to investigate crimes as well as to take sanctions on violators of their employees.

3) It sent routinely heavily-armed shooters to the streets of Baghdad, and they know that some of these shooters are under the chemical influence of steroids or other stimulant elements.

4) They know that 25% or more of the shooters taking a chemical steroids but failed to take effective steps to stop the abuse of these drug.

5) They did not hold any drug-testing to these shooters before sending them equipped in these tasks.

6) US lieutenant colonel served in Iraq, confirm describe during a press statement with the correspondent of *Washington Post* newspaper that the

Blackwater mercenaries are archers immature, and have fingers pushing too fast on the trigger, for this tend to shoot first and then ask questions later. Another US military commander told the same newspaper, that these shooters are acting as shepherds of oxen, and they have a record of recklessness.

7) Black Company provided data to the Commission on Oversight and Government Reform of US Congress about the occurrence of 437 internally incidents occurred in Iraq, which reveals the use of mercenaries of this company to excessive force and unnecessary constantly, which resulted in deaths and injuries and damage to property is unnecessary.

8) Interference of Blackwater' mercenaries' in the work as preemptive, offensive and used deadly force instead to be as defense. According to internal reports of the company, 84% of the accidents were mercenaries of the company begin the fire without justification.

9) The incidents of September 2007 has shown that the fatal shooting of innocent civilians was accompanied by the fire of helicopter own mercenaries also causing in one week injuring 43 innocent civilians, and killed 21 from them. Another incidents covered by *The New York Times* was killing of one of the bodyguards of Iraqi politicians by one of the mercenaries of Blackwater named Andrew J. Moonen by firing the pistol Glock type 9mm and injury in the face of the victim from very close range. As well as on 25 June 2005, Blackwater mercenaries opened fire on the chest of an innocent person was standing on the street and shot him to die and the victim was a father of six children, and Blackwater was not succeeded in documenting the incident at first but tried to cover up it later.

10) Blackwater attempt to cover up the killing of many innocent civilians by their shooters mercenaries without reason, by providing modest sums of money to the families of the Iraqi victims.

11) The company submitted to the US Congress committee reports revealed that the company's archers were open fire constantly at moving vehicles while wandering without stopping to see if there were casualties or not. As it revealed these reports about mercenaries company failed to document incidents of non legal use of force, and permanent lying about the use of excessive force.

12) From the logical conclusion to company reports submitted to the Committee of US Congress is to give non-real data for the entire incidents committed by a mercenary of the company in Iraq. According to two former company employees stated to *Washington Post*, in confirmation of one of these two ex-shooters of the company, his team of 20-mercenary was committing 4-5 shooting incidents a week, for example, which confirms the lack of credibility of the total number submitted by the company to congressional committee about the overall accidents in Iraq.

13) Financial gain of Blackwater Company was derived from the pattern and practice of abuse of deadly force.

14) No one killed of US government officer or employee was under the protection of Blackwater' mercenaries, which shows that they have the desire to kill innocent people to be strategy and advantage for the company distinguishes them from the rest of the other security companies. This leads to the conclusion the most dangerous fact that this company' mercenaries is ready to kill innocent bystanders in order to keep statistics without killing any government employee under its protection for propaganda purposes among market security companies. On this basis, it is financially benefit of killing bystanders innocent.

15) In addition to use of mercenaries known to their use of stimulants and drugs, it also hired mercenaries from former military officials, although they may have been involved in human rights abuses in Chile, and this leads to the logical conclusion that Blackwater recruited mercenaries from special Chilean troops who were granted amnesty from punishment in exchange for not engaging again in any military or security activities in Chile.

16) Logical conclusion is likely that Blackwater had contracted with mercenaries from the Philippines, Chile, Nepal, Colombia, Ecuador, El Salvador, Honduras, Panama, Peru, Bulgaria, Poland, Romania, Jordan and perhaps also from South Africa. This makes the company hired with this violation of the laws of these countries that prevent work as mercenaries.

17) Blackwater holds a sufficient number of mercenaries to be able to provide a private army for any buyer needs this army. In 2003, the President of the Blackwater (Gary Jackson) declaring the operation vision for this company, saying (I would like to be our company as the largest and most professional private army in the world). At a conference in the Jordanian capital Amman in

March 2003, said Executive Director of the Company (Blackwater able to deploy a special brigade-sized force in any conflict area).

18) The company itself initiated an internal investigation about the involvement in the smuggling arms into Iraq and into the hands of groups is considered terrorist, according to the US government.

19) Although the Blackwater have got more than a billion US dollars from the US government during the period between 2001 to 2006, but it failed repeatedly and continually violate the law of war, or the laws of the United States of America, or international law.

20) The recognition that US government paid all these amounts of money for the Blackwater company in order to be able to act and provide services legally, but the fact that it was acting outside the scope of the law and provide mercenaries heavily armed and who are working to break the laws of the United States and the host country (Iraq).

21) The Blackwater does not have the valid formula contract legally with the US government because of the presence of two laws (The Anti-Pinkerton Act, and 5 USC § 1803), which prevented and attend the US government from contracting with the people employed by Pinkerton Detective Agency and similar organizations, and here applies to the Blackwater similarity with such institutions, which means any mercenary or similar institutions of mercenaries. On this basis, it lacks a valid legal relationship with the United States Government.

22) According to the American law called Alien Tort Statute, or what is also called (28 USC § 1350) [289] or request foreign compensation law, the crimes of Blackwater' mercenaries in killing and wounding of innocent civilians in a deliberate, brutal, malicious and oppressive are signs on the occurrence of a war crimes.

At 27 June 2011, the Supreme Court in the United States rejected to listen to lawsuits by a group of 250 Iraqis who want to sue the two contractors of international CACI and Titan Corp. (now a subsidiary of L-3 Communications co.) on allegations of ill-treatment by investigators and translators at Abu Ghraib prison during 2003 and 2004 (file a lawsuit in the question of whether private contractors hired by the US military to perform services in a war zone may be held accountable on charges of participating in acts of torture and other war crimes). Suits were rejected by a majority of three judges (two-for-one) on the basic of what happened is an activity serves the armed forces in what is known "battlefield preemption". The Court of Appeal also ruled that Iraqi detainees were not applicable to their situation with Alien Tort Statute to file a lawsuit in a US court seeking to impose a violation of the law of nations. The judges said that although torture committed by the government is a violation of international rules, but the same act by a private contractor is not!! The difference between the three judges was clear, One judges refused to accept the case Laurence Silberman, claiming that the US Congress when make this law was established for residents of the United States to sue foreign governments in the event of committing the crime of torture, and that the federal law has ruled out the possibility of bringing a similar suit against American military officials in abroad, or individuals working with the United States government abroad. While the judge of Court of Appeal that willing to accept the case Merrick Garland, saying "there is no law in Congress not previously required by the terms of judicial prosecutors in the prosecution of contractors from the private sector - whether they were soldiers or civilian government employees" [527].

This incident and the unequal resolution confirms the presence of two parties of the conflict within the US court with the presence of these loopholes that give the right of victims to sue foreign mercenaries and US security and military companies. Here it will highlight the urgent need for the two important issues:

1. The importance of large legal experience in the promotion of the US justice party sympathetic to consider and accept the cases of violations.

2. The importance of adopting long self policy across the US and try to all possible options and no matter how long time need.

In order to understand deeply the fact that justice and courts applications in United States with respect to the Iraqi people victims of war will show what happened in some examples of cases of killing of prisoners of Fallujah and killed unarmed civilians in Haditha.

12. 4. 8. War Crimes In The Killing Of Prisoners And Civilians During Armed Conflicts

12. 4. 8. 1. War Crime Of Killing Prisoners Of Fallujah City

Although the Former sergeant Jose L. Nazario Jr. is accused of slaughtering two of four Iraqi detainees on the second day of the second battle of Fallujah, and he was supposed to faces up to 10 years in prison by a federal court because he no longer works in the US Marine Corps, and thus no longer subject to the Uniform Code of Military Justice [72]. But on 28 August 2008, federal court in California found after six hours of deliberations, to declare the jury of his innocence of the charge of unlawfully killed, or that he had ordered members of his team to kill the four detainees [92]. The other Marines soldiers participants in the crime and who are still in the military service, refused to give their testimony in this case despite the immunity that they enjoy, and although federal judge considered that they had contempt court via their refusal to testify [92].

In 7 December 2007, US Marines resubmitted accused of murder and dereliction of duty against Sgt. Jermaine Nelson (continued in military service), who was accused of participating in the murder of one of the four detainees in Fallujah in case of Nazario. He faces a sentence of up to life in prison if found guilty, after the US Marine Corps had the charge of murder to Nelson since September 2007, but Lt. Gen. James Mattis and military band Camp Pendleton ordered to withdraw the charge against Jermaine for re-investigation!! It is noted that the charge of negligence was for violating the rules concerning the treatment of prisoners of an enemy and the laws of armed conflict [72].

The trial of US soldiers for their crimes in Fallujah raises many legal issues. One of the soldiers tried in front of a civilian court while the other in front of a military court, and both accusing acts basically the same, but the penalties they would face radically different in the case have been convicted !!!

This crime and other crime of execution of the wounded prisoner in a mosque of Fallujah were war crimes because of their sequence with a lot of other crimes. Also, the execution of combatants and wounded unarmed violates Article III of the treatment of prisoners of war, the Geneva Convention, which states in part that "persons taking no active part in the hostilities, including members of armed forces have handed over their weapons, or those placed hors de combat by sickness or wounds, detention, or any other cause, shall in all circumstances be treated humanely. More seriously, what revealed by US journalists (Evan Wright) that found that the training of US Marines involved in one of his lessons combat the execution of wounded fighters in accordance with what they call in their training dead-checking [109].

12. 4. 8. 2. War Crime In The Killing Of Civilians In Haditha

The results of US military investigations have indicated that Staff Sgt. Frank Wuterich had fired on a white civilian car type White Sedan, and killing Ahmed Kutar (Fenr) Museleh, Wagdi Aida Alzawi, Kaled Aida Alzawi, Mohmed Tbal Ahmed and Akram Hamid Flaeh. Also, Sergeant Frank Wuterich had given orders to his soldiers before housebreaking civilians to deal with this house as a hostile and that shoots first and then asks questions later!!! Sgt. Salinas was first to burst into the home and shot first, killing Khamisa Tuema Ali, while Lance Cpl. Mendoza saw Abdul Hameed Hussin Ali moves in the room and he shot and killed him. All the Serg. Salinas, Corporal Tatum and Serg. Frank Wuterich were still in the salon of house, they hear noise coming from one of the rooms on the left. Serg. Salinas and Serg. Wuterich may be thought that the sound of AK-47 weapons and has been prepared to fire (and Serg. Tatum agreed with them to identify the sound type). So, the Corporal Tatum and Serg. Salinas threw grenades inside the room, and went immediately inside and began shooting inside the room, and the result was killing Guhid Abdalhamid Hasan, Abdullah Waleed Abdul Hameed, Ali Abdul Hameed Husin and Asmaa Salman Rasif. While wounded of Eman Waleed Abd Al Hameed and Abd Al-Rahman Waleed Al Hameed. After the shooting stopped, one of the Marines shouted that there is running out, the serg Wuterich commanded his soldiers get out of this house and follow this galloping person. Prosecution team went towards the second house that took on all sides, one of the Marines knock the door, and the person was coming to door is Yunis Salim Rasif. So, the MP Serg. Mendoza shooting him from behind the door and before he open the door and fell killed. Then arrive to the house both Corporal Mendoza and Sgt Wuterich as well to other soldiers. The Serg. Wuterich ordering of Lance Corporal Tatum that frag adjacent to the kitchen room, and actually corporal Tatum took grenade from his colleague Serg. Salinas and delivered to the room to break down the bathroom pipes. They did not know that at the end of the room that destroyed there two women in scalped angle with six children. The Sergeant Wuterich gave order for continued clean (murder) of the house. The final outcome was the killing victims in the second home like Aida Yasin Ahmed, Mohomed Yunis Salim, Aisha Unes Salim, Zainab Unes Salim, Sena Yunis Salim, Noor Salim Rasif, and Yuda Hasin Ahmed. In the same testimonies that were given to the Committee on the military investigation, MP Serg. Mendoza said that he had told corporal Tatum that he found in the back room for a second house contain only women with children, and Tatum replied that kill them, Mendoza returned clarify they're just kids with women in the room, then left and took his position in the kitchen. MP Corporal Tatum had denied this conversation He said that Mendoza did not know whom inside of the room. While only survivor witnessed of the massacre, was Iraqi victim Safah Yunis Salim Rasif said that the American soldiers had thrown a hand grenade in the room but it did not explode, leading him with others of his family to rush to the corner of the room. Then the aunt screaming for help, but the Marines continued shooting at everyone in the corner of the room [74].

The recognition of US troops that 24 people (men, women, and children) were killed in the Iraqi Haditha city on 19 November 2005, after an improvised explosive device in the road led to the destruction of US Humvee and killing of lance Corporal Sharratt and wounding two others from the US Marines. The convicted persons of killing Iraqi civilians were Lt. Col. Jeffrey Chessani, Lance Cpl. Stephen Tatum and maybe have been joined by the commander of forces in Haditha at the time Sergeant Frank Wuterich who was recommending his trial on seven counts of murder as a result of negligent homicide. Lt. Col. Jeffrey Chessani accused of failing to accurately report and investigate a possible violation of the laws of war by the Marine Corps, which was under his leadership (he is the holder of a medal bronze star faces a prison sentence to period up to 30 months in prison and dismissal in case of his conviction). American politicians confirmed this crime, and US Rep. John Murtha after popping the entire incident information said (it seems that the Marines had killed civilians in cold blood, and their leader tried to hide this crime, we believe that some of the officers adult Marine has influenced the course of the investigation and the way that has reached now) [72].

Although the lawyer of Chessani has told the court that their client was not the only one who did not order an investigation into the recent murder victims, as the commander of US Marines in Iraq at the time, Maj. Gen. Richard Huck has testified that reports he received also from a series of references confirmed that the civilians were killed from collateral damage resulting from the fighting. Corporal Stephen Tatum, face charges of involuntary manslaughter, aggravated assault and the exposure to reckless endangerment. He may face a sentence of up to to 19 years in prison with discharged from military service in case of his conviction. It is one of four people accused of the incident of the killing of civilians in the town of Haditha. He was charge for unpremeditated murder and four cases of death as a negligent homicide, but reduced the charges after the military hearing under Article 32 on the grounds that there was insufficient evidence!! [295].

On 9 Monday January 2012, the Western Judicial Military Circuit Court at Camp Pendleton listening sessions are open to the testimonies in the case of the killing of 24 Iraqi civilians in Haditha city in November 2005. The Serg. Wuterich accused of voluntary manslaughter and aggravated assault, and reckless endangerment, dereliction of duty, and obstruction of justice with respect to the murder. Although he had no previous combat experience, after a roadside bomb on the side of the road ordered his men shoot first and ask questions later, during looking to militants. They killed many Iraqi civilians include 10 women and children, have been killed at point-blank range. Although the investigation has accused the seven US military personnel, but subsequent investigations have dropped charges against six of them, sparking the anger of the Iraqi authorities. The Serg. Wuterich stayed as the only one of Marines who faces accusations, although Major General Eldon Bargewell has found the phenomenon of serious misconduct on all the chain of command levels in the Marine Corps during the investigation [294]. After five years of investigations and on Monday 23 January 2012, Serg. Wuterich admitted pleaded guilty as a result of negligence and during duty in exchange for dropping all charges remaining with him (such as murder, aggravated assault and exposure to dangerous reckless, and obstruction of justice) [629].

12. 4. 9. Torture As War Crime

The international law absolutely prohibits torture and cruel, inhuman or humiliating. This means that, unlike other important criteria, it is not allowed to countries touch this right or equilibrates with other values or rights, not even in emergency case. Moreover, the world agreed for a long broad consensus time regarding the absolute prohibition of torture and abuse which is a customary rule, that is valid in legal terms for each country, organization or person where, and about their business in every place on earth, without relationship of the application of any international document like this or that.

The Universal Declaration of Human Rights of the United Nations in 10 December 1948 in the fifth paragraph provides for (a person should not be subject to torture or to cruel, inhuman treatment or punishment) [145]. Torture and ill-treatment were widespread and systematic, according to the policy and pattern of exercise because of the permission of US government in spite of the absolute prohibition on its use set forth in US law or US military regulations [131], in stark contrast to the powers granted to them. The Third Geneva Convention about the treatment of prisoners of war, prevent the practice of torture, whether physical or moral coercion on any prisoners of war to secure information from them. The United States, Britain and Iraq are signatories and members of the Convention against Torture of the United Nations and the third and fourth Geneva Conventions. The Convention against Torture defines torture (Article 1) in the following terms: any act by which severe pain or suffering, whether physical or mental, is intentionally inflicted on a person for such purposes as obtaining from him information or a confession, punishing him for an act he has committed or is suspected of having committed , or intimidating or coercing him.

It's funny that the Coalition Provisional Authority has issued a number 7 on 9 June 2003, to repair the Iraqi Penal Code, where it stopped execution penalty and banned torture and cruel, inhuman or cruel, inhuman or degrading treatment, as well as banned discrimination treatment [366]. But the formal confessions about systematic torture and inhumane practices of detainees were one of the high points of confessions and compelling. We see the recognition of the US and the former defense minister James Schlesinger in his report (the abuse of detainees was widespread and not just the failure of some individuals to the followers of known standards, there is a personal responsibility and institutional in high levels in Command) [132]. Major General Antonio Taguba, who led the official investigation into the US Army about the torture at Abu Ghraib prison scandal and testified in front of US Congress in May 2004 on the investigation findings, he admit and said (there is no longer any doubt As committed by the administration (Bush) are war crimes, and the question, which is expected to answer whether there is provision for accountability for those who gave the orders to torture) [133].

Despite the government reports that demonstrate the use of torture and inhumane treatment of detainees in Afghanistan and Iraq, yet there was no comprehensive criminal investigation in policies and practices. Moreover, it has been the rejection of all the civil lawsuit filed by the victim or the survivors of torture programs to the United States without any judicial decision on the merits of claims.

Although prosecutions highly publicized on low-level members of the military such as Lynndie England and reservists in the other ear army practiced torture and ill-treatment of some detainees in Iraq [138]. It has not been any criminal charge to any senior member of the US military for their role in the coordination or condoning torture and inhumane treatment of detainees in Iraq and Afghanistan [140].

To confirm shake confidence in achieving justice in US courts, whether federal or military ones, the US military court acquitted on 28 August 2007, the only officer accused in the famous case of ill-treatment and torture of Iraqi prisoners at Abu Ghraib - Baghdad prison. After a series of prosecutions, which lasted for three years, Court consisting of nine leaders of Military colonel rank (Colonels), and one rank of one-star General, decided that the accused Lt. Col. Steven L. Jordan (51 years old and was director of Joint Interrogation Debriefing Center at Abu Ghraib prison), he is innocent of the charges, which include responsibility for the supervision and training of soldiers convicted of abusing detainees in prison, and acquitted also of the charge of abuse of prisoners by personally supervising the use of naked force and the use of military dogs to intimidate detainees during interrogations in late 2003. Although he found disobedience in deliberate Maj. Gen. George Fay, who asked him not to contact with soldiers at Abu Prison during his investigation, but Gordon is back and contacts them. This provision means that the responsibility of any US officer at Abu Ghraib, to keep the sanctions prosecute only 11 soldiers and small ranks and the ones shown in the photo scandal, which emerged at the end of the month of April of 2004. While the year after the scandal, a military intelligence officer who ran the prison, Col. Thomas M. Pappas said statements about the use of dogs to intimidate detainees. Brig. Gen. Janis Karpinski military police commander faced administrative penalty demoted because of the failure of leadership, not because of the direct link of torture and ill-treatment!!! The scandal led to many internal and Limited US investigation, while the US Congress was busy for developing laws relating to the treatment of detainees in the United States, without the development of laws that prevent impunity in blatant state of covered up. US human rights organizations denounced the policy of impunity administered by the US administration. John Sifton researcher at Human Rights Watch described and saying (the army is interested in seeking the real issue, they have shown themselves only committed in the development of they are behind the Abu Ghraib scandal). Elisa Massimino head of Human Rights First said (there is not a criminal court achieved in leadership, which has developed methods of harsh interrogation, although there are many investigations series military, while the Ministry of Justice investigations did not lead to charges against civilians investigators contractor), which was awaited by everyone, and the judgment of the Court which proved the existence of a huge gap, a fact she has disappeared entirely). The Gordon trial is revealed similarities in methods of investigation and interrogation of Abu Ghraib prison and the US detention camp at Guantanamo in Cuba. The court did not investigate how and why the transfer of interrogation techniques from Guantanamo to Iraq. US military police soldiers said they had received guidance in the use of these techniques by investigators and civilian contractors for use in section A of the Abu Ghraib prison. The detained was prisoners with high intelligence value, but this attack took place there. The soldiers received prison sentences and were the most for 10 years against Cpl. Charles A. Graner Jr. It also mentions that the officer Gordon had previously told *The Washington Post* (by accusing the US military to use it as a scapegoat, but not in order to put an officer in the trial) [139].

In European courts, for the first time on the history of international justice, it recognizes the crime of torture by the CIA. European Court of Human Rights issued on 13 December 2012 decision of requires that the German citizen Khaled el-Masri had been tortured at the hands of CIA agents. European Court of Human Rights said in a landmark ruling that US intelligence officers may have tortured Khaled el-Masri, through the practice of sodomy, and shackling, beatings, as Macedonian police considered guilty also on charges of torture, and abuse abusing, and confinement in secret for Khaled el-Masri, under the pretext of its association with illegal terrorist organizations. Masri was abducted in Macedonia in December 2003 and handed over to the CIA "Rendition team" in Skopje airport and flown secretly to Afghanistan [528].

Although the renditions, under which CIA arrests any suspects and moving to secret detention centers affiliate, is contrary to the laws of European human rights, but the most dangerous are recently discovered about this program, is a new report for 2013 by US organization Open Society Justice Initiative. They reveal the involvement of UK with 24 other European governments of collaborators in the global kidnapping, detention and torture, leaving them vulnerable to the issue in front of the European Court of Human Rights. According to the Human Rights organization documented the secret support all over the world for this program. At least 54 different governments - more than a quarter of the world's total - had been working secretly with the global kidnapping, detention and torture program [529]. It is being sued now against Poland, Lithuania and Romania after allowing for the CIA run secret prisons on its territory. Italy faces the same procedures in the European Court about the involvement of the state in the abduction of a Muslim cleric (Imam Abu Omar), who was kidnapped in Milan and flown to Egypt by the CIA to be tortured there [530]. On 2010 and after years of procrastination, Poland acknowledged officially in participating in this illegal program and contrary to the human rights. It was the station for the transfer of high-ranking people from suspects in terrorism from Iraq and Afghanistan, and at a rate six times the transfer of at least between February and September 2003 [531].

12. 5. Britain's Role in Fallujah Crimes

Britain's role was not hidden in the first battle, according to a testimony of Gen Sanchez in his book. In January 2005, the British defense minister in Workers Party government Adam Ingram denied that US troops were used in Iraq, a new generation of incendiary weapons codenamed (MK77) during the second battle of Fallujah.

But he came back and admitted in a private letter to Labour MP Harry Cohen obtained by the British newspaper *The Independent* (he did not mislead Parliament on purpose because the erroneous information was from the United States. "The United States confirmed to our officials that they did not use MK77s in Iraq at any time, and this was the basis of my answer to you, "he added Mr. Cohen." I regret to say that I have discovered that this is not the case now, and must correct the situation" Ingram confirm the use of 30 incendiary bomb from MK77 type by 1st Marine Expeditionary Force during the invasion of Iraq between 31 March and 2 April 2003 [225]. But unfortunately, the British minister remained silent about these facts for several months and then his confession only came after the general elections are over in Britain at the time.

The United Kingdom is a party to the Certain Conventional Weapons (CCW) that prohibits the use of these weapons (MK 77) against civilian targets and allow for use against military targets just as incendiary weapons and internationally reviled weapons. But in the battles of Fallujah it may have caused harm to civilians in Iraq, and the United Kingdom forces are part of the occupation forces did not comply with the internationally agreed standards of the war in the first battle of Fallujah and second [54]. Even if the US side has been misled British ministers about the use of bombs, MK 77 in Fallujah, this does not exempt it from legal liability as a party to the International Convention. Former British minister of defence Adam Ingram was not interested even in explaining to a member of parliament (who asked about the use of these Forbidden weapons) about why did the US officers lying in this regard [225]. But the most scandal is that this incident has revealed that the international coalition that multinational coalition in Iraq has proved and controlled and run by US officers and other officials only without genuine consultation with its partners, or even the international community. This denies to this coalition any recipe representation of the international community or even work to the Geneva Conventions approved and ratified by the occupation states itself.

Britain's role in the subscription offense of second battle was clearly known from the government's decision of Tony Blair in moving 5,000 troops from Black Watch Battalion from Basra to the outskirts of Baghdad near Fallujah, in order to provide support for the Marines as they entered the city, as announced later. Despite the denial of British Secretary of State for Defence and his confirmation that there were no British military units in Fallujah during the question in front of the British Parliament [98]. But soon it initiated the massacre subscription Facts appear realistic over time after the occupation forces leaders felt reassured of impunity in international courts with the happiness of empty victory. The international coalition forces in Iraq (MNC-I), which gave order No. 15 about the storming of Fallujah and was commander Assistant of this forces is a British General Andrew Farquhar. This means that Britain's participation in deciding the storming of Fallujah and the process of planning and implementation of a process. On 7 October 2004, leadership of MNC-I met with Colonel John Ballard, Lieutenant Colonel Mike Paulk and Lieutenant Colonel Kevin Hansen in order to show the results of a joint meeting to multiple destinations (Marine Expeditionary Force (MEF), Civil Affairs Group (CAG), Marine Air Wing (MAW), Force Service Support Group (FSSG), and Division planners in the base of operations in the city of Ramadi (Camp Blue Diamond). This meeting focused on the final phase requirements before the start of attack [193]. British joint forces within the supported forces in the process had reached to the area to join to US Marine Corps on 27 October 2004, and were 1st Battalion of The Black Watch Regiment, in order to help forming bigger and stronger collar around the Fallujah area to prevent any aid or free press from entering [203].

British forces participate in war crimes during the first and the second massacre of Fallujah has proved, according to different sources:

1. Lt. Gen. Ricardo S. Sanchez (general commander of the occupation forces (Alliance joint) from the period June 2003 to June 2004) in his book (WISER IN BATTLE, A Soldier's Story), admitted that during the first battle in Fallujah, about the role and participation of British officers and other leaders of the coalition forces in the battle of the first massacre in Fallujah through subscription plan after the first days of the battle over, saying in chapter twenty in page 389 ((In addition to Bremer, coalition member nations were putting tremendous pressure on us to stop the fighting. In the early days of the Fallujah offensive, it became very apparent that the U.S. government had not cleared the decision to launch with the political leadership of the coalition nations. And the leaders of these nations were upset about it. My British

deputy commanding general had been involved in all of the internal planning, and all of our coalition commanders were full partners in the execution of our offensive plan. The British three-star general on the CJTF-7 staff participated in all our planning sessions and communicated our intentions to London on a daily basis. Consistently, he voiced his government's concern about our planned offensive, and I'm certain that lively discussions took place between the White House and 10 Downing Street. London believed that we were being far too heavy handed, but President Bush still gave the order to launch)) [36].

The seriousness of this recognition is not only the involvement of British troops with the occupation forces (US, Australian, and Polish), but also to participate of the others (international forces leaders that joined the occupation forces later under the name of multinational forces (Multi-National Forces), which It existed in Iraq during a first battle of Fallujah, a Republic of Dominic, Honduras, Philippines, Thailand, New Zealand, Portugal, Netherlands, Hungary, Norway, Italy, Lithuania, Slovakia, Romania, El Salvador, Estonia, Bulgaria, Moldova, Albania, Denmark, Ukraine , Czech Republic, South Korea, Japan, Tonga, Azerbaijan, Singapore, Bosnia and Herzegovina, Macedonia, Latvia, Kazakhstan, Armenia, Mongolia, Georgia). The importance of this international involvement in genocide crime during the first battle in Fallujah, focusing especially on what the role of European forces [276]. Especially as it was before the advent of the NATO mission that requested by the interim government of Iyad Allawi and incomplete sovereignty in order to train the Iraqi army and security forces after the first battle in Fallujah [275]. This mission, which came after the issuance of UN Security Council resolution No. 1546 dated 8 June 2004 and in which it welcomed the decision of the occupation forces to work for end the occupation and the formation of a multinational force with welcoming the forming of an interim Iraqi government and not elected, headed by Allawi [277].

2. Although the Ministry of Defence has ruled out British forces joining any Fallujah attack, shadow defence secretary Nicholas Soames said UK commanders must be fully involved in the planning as British troops could still face reprisals if it went wrong [297,238].

3. In the diary of Rumsfeld said that (Sattler still needed a dependable outfit to patrol the main highways to the east. On April, the insurgents had almost cut off Baghdad. This time, Mattis called on the British as the force with the right skills. Turning aside protests in Parliament, Prime Minister Blair approved the temporary shift of the Black Watch Battalion to the Fallujah region—a move that was criticized in the United Kingdom as "politicized) [88].

4. The *Daily Telegraph* correspondent in Fallujah Toby Harnden pointed to the presence of British forces and their proliferation at the southern part of Fallujah to prevent the escape of militants and halt their supply lines, as well as the reporter saw of using white phosphorus munitions in this battle, said (The 1st American Cavalry Division provided a blocking force to the south, preventing insurgents from fleeing along "rat lines". The Black Watch has also been deployed to the south to block fleeing enemy fighters and supply lines. White phosphorus shells lit up the sky as armour drove through the breach and sent flaming material on to suspect insurgent haunts. Soldiers expressed the fear that with so much firepower the biggest danger was friendly fire [69].

5. The site of one former US military veterans (Talking Proud Archiv / US Military), which draws its information from various US military sources, that the units of the British Air Force had led a good role in the second battle in Fallujah, as said (The stacks consisted of Navy carrier-launched, land-based Marine and land-based USAF fighter aircraft. AC-130 gunships were also there. We also understand British air units were used as well) [67].

6. US commander Gen. Ballard was mentioned in his book (*The fight for Fallujah*) the role of British forces in that battle pp. 53-75 [193].

7. US retired Lieutenant Colonel Kenneth W. Estes explained the arrival of British reinforcements (The first of these reinforcements reported to the 1st Marine Division on 27 October when it received tactical control of the 1st Battalion, The Black Watch Regiment (UK). The logistics base supporting Baghdad, Logistics Support Area Dogwood, initially served as the arrival and assembly area for the British Army unit, which reported to Colonel Johnson's 24th MEU to assist in its mis-sion of securing northern Babel Province and the vital main service routes running south of Baghdad) [203]. US forces recognition that Square military air operations over Fallujah, called the military high-density air in the region and identified through a diameter of 30 nautical miles area (55.56 km) [68], which Its means the occurrence of some areas of the presence of British troops in the area of these military operations.

8. Near Baghdad, the British Black Watch Regiment relieved American forces preparing for the operation [62].

9. A study prepared by US Institute For Defense Analysis depending on the orders from two US military sides, are Fallujah Battle Reconstruction (JFCOMJCOA) with help provided by the Joint Center for Operational Analysis

(JCOA) of Joint Forces Command (JFCOM). This study recognize with the participation of British troops in the second military operation in Fallujah (Dawn) after the approval of British Parliament about the transfer of military units of their forces from Basra to Fallujah (The United Kingdom, which had disagreed with the Coalition's approach to VIGILANT RESOLVE and what it considered America's heavy-handed tactics, also voiced reservations over AL FAJR. However, the MNF-I's request to move the UK Black Watch unit to the Fallujah area to support the operation required the approval of UK Parliamentary. Request and approval ensured that any reservations the United Kingdom might have had were reconciled before the battle. That said, there was still reluctance, albeit unofficial, within the UK ranks) [230]. This study is one of many American military studies interested to draw the lessons from the battles of Fallujah.

10. Report of the US Congress had confirmed and acknowledged this role by the co-British battalion in the massacre of the storming of Fallujah [87].

11. GEN Casey, the MNF-I commander, had ordered a British battalion from Basra to guard the road leading out of Fallujah, silencing much of the coalition "back-biting" that had occurred for "Fallujah I" (West 2005) [63].

These recognitions and evidences of leaders and officers from the forces participated in crimes of massacres in Fallujah. The British journalist George Monbiot described the use of white phosphorus as incendiary weapon against Fallujah a war crime because they did not use it to enlighten the battlefield, but as a weapon to push the Fallujah fighters outside their buildings. This description came in his article (the United States used chemical weapons in Iraq, and then lie about it) in *The Guardian* UK newspaper [127].

The irony historical exotic as the policy of double standards and duplication of US policy, US President Ronald Reagan was at the beginning of 1980, condemns the atrocities of the former Soviet Union through its spraying chemicals called yellow rain over specific parts of South Asia which caused the deaths of thousands of people. According to the information of Washington, there were 3042 people have been killed in 47 sporadic incidents in Afghanistan alone. These crimes have made President Reagan denounces 15 times in sporadic speeches about the brutality of the Soviet Union to use these chemicals for the killing of innocent [29]. While his predecessor presidents Bush father and son came to use not only chemical weapons but even depleted uranium and radioactive weapons together against the Iraqi people in front of international sneaky and shameful silence, especially by the UN agencies and the international community.

12. 6. Evidence Cover-ups Policy

In most cases of serious misconduct and murder, the involved soldiers in these crimes have tried directly to cover up the crimes. Often the leaders are ignoring the evidence, and fail to actively even the most serious cases and making public statements exonerate criminals seeking. In the case of the Haditha massacre, the Marine Corps issued a press release the next day claiming that many Iraqis have killed as a result of an insurgent' bomb. Although of many Iraqi victims, but the company commander did not visit the incident site, and preferred to rely on the report of the soldiers involved. Later, investigators found pages were missing from the company's notebook and a video from unmanned aircraft flying over the incident has disappeared!! Apparently, those who were perpetrators or their accomplices may have destroyed or withheld evidence [612]. Involved soldiers in the incident apparently also gave misleading statements to investigators. Marine investigation determined that "some officers gave false information to their superiors" in the initial follow-up to this issue [613]. In a subsequent report, he Major General Eldon A. Bargewell found "willful neglect between naval officers and their attempts to hide criminal behavior" and added: Indicators showed to ignore serious misconduct, perhaps to avoid conducting the investigation and the possibility of negative effects on themselves prove or pedestrian their marine "[614].

In case of Mahmudiya' crime also soldiers tried to hide the evidence of the rape and murder of a teenage girl and her family [615], or in Hamdania' crime where soldiers put a gun mechanism AK- 47 besides the man who had killed him [616], and those involved in crime of Ishaqi massacre murder when called air support to bomb the house, and they were apparently hoping that the evidence of the crime will disappear under the rubble [617]. US soldiers cleared it at first, saying that three civilians were killed as a result of exchange of fire in a military operation and also because of the collapse of the house, which took place during the fighting. They determine the number of civilian killed to be "unintentional," and it was said that the US forces involved in the incident had "followed the rules of engagement"!! [618]. But neighbors and local leaders complained to police that the soldiers entered the house while it was still standing. Police opened an investigation, using the criminal investigation team which trained by the United States and they collect all evidence from the house collapsed [619]. After examining the bodies with restrictive hands and all victims were in one room with bullet holes in the head as execution-style and examination found nearby the US military cartridges, therefore, investigators concluded that people had been killed in cold blood. They were 11 victims and not three after found other dead under the rubble [620]. Autopsies in Tikrit hospital confirmed and said that all victims had been shot in the head [621]. The *BBC* showed video by a photographer of Associated Press, which documented immediately after the incident, and this provides strong evidence of the terrible crime [622]. However, the US military has refused to open a case or further investigation!!

In the case of the killing the Italian intelligence officer Nicola Calipari Also, the Italian government criticized in its report issued on 3 May 2005 the way in which disappeared shooting guide. There was no way to keep the scene to investigate, and US military unit has destroyed records that fired on the car of Nicolas in the next day of the submission their question for investigation. This proves at least a decadent style in the obstruction of justice and covers up the crime [623].

A mental health study of the Pentagon confirmed that their soldiers in Iraq, "less than half of them (soldiers and Marines) have unethical behavior", such as failure to follow general orders, a violation of the rules of engagement, and abuse or killing of civilians [624]. This prompted the US military authorities, who felt embarrassed in front of these terrible crimes, and have been launched to give justifications of the facts, insisting that the victims killed as one of the collateral damage in military operations. This cover-up of some cases in front of the public for reduces the strength of the evidence against the perpetrators of crimes in trials.

12. 7. Impunity

As it is known, the war crimes require proof of knowledge of accused individuals to their actions against of international law [44]. The works of the US military justice system in very rare cases punish cases of murder and atrocities. Most of these cases never reach the formal charge. The cases are rejected usually in the initial stage of the administrative court or in self-defense stage. Or they have been settled at any stage with a very light punishment or reprimand. It included a very small number of charges of murder, even in such terrible incidents in the massacre of as Haditha city.

In late August 2006, the *Washington Post* reviewed military cases in the period of June 2003 to February 2006. The newspaper found that while thousands of Iraqis have been killed by US soldiers in dubious circumstances, but the military justice system have not tried only "part small of these incidents" [625]. There were no trials as a result of homicides in all of the shootings at checkpoints, but to charge to a very small number of senior officers.

Leaders who were supposed to take the decision to begin a criminal investigation against their subordinates, they often failed to investigate the killing of Iraqi civilians. They prefer to be called as a result of unintended during combat operations, and order the administrative or non-judicial punishments instead. Gary Solis, a former prosecutor in the US Navy said, "I think there are a number of cases that do not reach the stage of submission of the reports, so there was a reluctance to pursue them vigorously," and added "There have been fewer prosecutions in Iraq than might be expected One" [626]. The *Washington Post* according to US Major army saying, "I think there are many other clashes, which should have been investigated, but certainly no one wants to be seen or reported, it's just the way things work" [627].

War resolutions or declaration of military operations against the city of Fallujah and civilians in twice carries a lot of important evidence. The decision to mass punishment of the city and the resulting tragedies during the first battle was a US decision merely whether politically or military [36]. While the second battle decision was a pretext give it up and authorization by the Iraqi prime minister which was inaugurated by the occupation [99]. It is not legally to the occupation for entitled the fate of the occupied people or coercing a report on the political process under occupation. From here the decision of storming was not based on legal basic because it was not issued by the legitimate and elected government in independent country, and that this government has failed in the first elections under the protection of the occupation.

The authority of the appointed and interim prime minister without election (Iyad Allawi) are under the occupation authority, and his decision in 7th November 2004 to make all regions of Iraq (with the exception of Kurdistan) under martial law authority and prevent any demonstrations or protest marches (to prevent the popular cohesion against the occupation as in the first fight), as well as the continuation of the curfew in Fallujah all 24 hours with the exception of the occupation forces (which makes any citizen outside their buildings as target of the free shooting). This confirmed also by one of Marine commanders (Colonel Michael Shupp) told in his interview with Agence France

Presse (AFP) when he said in a 7th November 2004 (I told the forces in Fallujah to open the fire on any Iraqi civilian raise his hands and tried to approach them because it might be a suicide!!!).

12. 8. Compensation

One of the biggest lies promoted by the occupation is the existence of a fully sovereign government after the formation of Allawi's interim government on 30 June 2004, despite the recognition of non- authorized the power to amend the Transitional Administrative Law that issued by the occupation governer Bremer [7A]. While all the facts and events were asserts control of occupation forces on the reality status of Iraq, especially the legal side and neutralize the Iraqi judiciary authority. For briefing the legal aspects against crimes of occupation forces in Iraq, it has found that limited to the following sides:

12. 8. 1. Iraqi Courts

In the first issue from the newspaper (*Al-Waqaih Al-Iraqia ,The facts of Iraq*) was released after the occupation [23 A], which is the Official Gazette of the Republic of Iraq (No. 3979 dated 17 June 2003), Paul Bremer the director of Provisional Authority occupation issued a regulation and regulatory No.1. The text in its second part ((remaining laws that was applicable in Iraq as of 16 April 2003)) in effect, unless the Coalition Provisional authority decided to suspend or replace them with other, or if it is canceled, and the adoption of other legislation replaced by ....).

As is known, the Iraqi courts were prevented from promoting any transaction complaint against any member of the occupation forces on the instructions of civilian administrator of the occupation and according to US law protects soldiers in combat missions outside the home. On this basis, the allegations of the return of Iraqi sovereignty after the withdrawal of occupation forces means at least a repeal of laws and orders issued by the occupation and which prevented the promotion of such issues and allow the return of the Iraqi judiciary authority over all crimes committed within the Iraqi courts administration by the retroactively. And, unfortunately, it did not take any action by government agencies or political involvement because of the Iraqi security agreement with US government, under which exempt US forces from any legal consequences as a result of their practices and their movements and committed inside Iraq. To know the real political situation beyond the so-called transfer of full sovereignty, the Satellite TV released a video for a murder crime committed by US troops in the New Baghdad district of the capital Baghdad, in

2007. The Chairman of Legal Committee in the Iraqi Parliament (Bahaa al-Araji) issued a statement calls for adoption of suits complaints of the victims with prosecutor!!(1A). This call was without talking about the issue a decision or an Act of Parliament allowed the Iraqi judiciary to consider these crimes as a sovereign right of the Iraqi people, or take practical action to save the right of victims within the new legislation, but it remained within mere media statements to absorb the anger of the Iraqi street. The second incident was killing 17 Iraqi civilians in Baghdad on Aviation Square in 16 September 2007 by mercenaries US security company Blackwater.

12. 8. 2. The US Courts

The Penal Code and the military compensation of US states that during the presence of the occupation forces in Iraq, which authorizes compensation for the Iraqi human being 2,500 US$ only in accordance with the law of foreign Compensation called (Foreign Claims Act), which was an insult to the Iraqi civilian victims and a reason plus in fueling anger against US troops [279]. United States has issued a law requiring troops to pay $ 2,500 in compensation for every citizen to kill him by mistake without charging or punish the killer or loaded any legal responsibility and during times when not have the presence of an armed clash. Therefore, the horrific massacre that took place against civilians during the first battle in Fallujah, have not compensated the civilian victims (both of them killed or wounded or who have damaged their property). This law has another problem that excludes those affected victims before the end of military operations in 16 April 2003 and this injustice and prejudice to the right of many citizens who bombed their homes and killed their loved ones during the military operations [A1, A4].

Some other US laws allow a kind of compensation according to the special circumstances, as following:

a) Alien Tort Statute: It's called also as (28 USC § 1350) and allows foreigners to request compensation from the abuses carried out the US by the United States government or one of its employees. This law grants US district courts (shall have original jurisdiction) of any civil action by an alien for the damage committed against him because of a violation of Public international law or international treaty to which the United States is a party. This statute of United States courts allows listening to complaints of human rights cases brought by foreign citizens for conduct committed outside the United States [289].

b) Military Extraterritorial Jurisdiction Act: In accordance with the law and in a case similar to cases happened in Iraq, but in Afghanistan, it has been sentenced to two Blackwater mercenaries workers in Afghanistan called Justin Cannon sentenced to 30 months (after admitting that 80% of the responsibility for his crime is due to post-traumatic stress disorder and traumatic brain injury as a result of previous military service. In addition to judging on Christopher Drotleff that jailed for 37 months because of a shooting on 5 May 2009 on the unarmed civilians in the capital Kabul and killed in a war zone and they were under the influence of intoxicated, and they have avoided during trial any charge conviction of murder and they were sentenced to the crime of manslaughter [290,293].

A judge Royce Lamberth for the US District Court for the District of Columbia on Monday 13 April 2015 sentenced a former Blackwater security contractor to life in prison and three others to 30 years for the killing of unarmed Iraqi civilians in 2007. Nicholas Slatten, a former Army sniper, was found guilty of murder for firing the first fatal shots. According to the court documents that the convicted before the accident he showed his desire to "kill as many Iraqis" in retaliation for the attacks of 11 September 2001 !! The other three men, Dustin Heard, Evan Liberty and Paul Slough, were found guilty of manslaughter, attempted manslaughter and use of a machine gun in a violent crime. While in court for their sentencing, the men maintained their innocence and claimed that the shootings were justified. The 2007 shooting ultimately ended in killed 17 Iraqi civilians, according to Iraqi investigators, and 14 by American interrogators. The incident also led to the injury of 17 others. [681].

c) The US Law For Regulate The Implementation Of The Chemical Weapons Convention of 1998 [270]

The US is party and stated the Prohibition of development, production, stockpiling and use of chemical weapons and compel it to destroy those weapons, in accordance with US Code in Article 18 thereof, which also regulate the work of international chemical weapons convention CWC, and Article 7 of which belong to explain non-prohibited purposes to use of chemicals, we will find the following paragraphs:

(A) The peaceful purposes - any peaceful purposes relating to aspects of industrial, agricultural, research, medical or pharmacological activity or any other activity.

(B) Protective purposes - any purpose connected directly to the prevention of toxic chemicals and protection against chemical weapons.

(C) Not connected military purposes - any military purpose of the United States which is not linked with the use of chemical weapons or that it does not rely on the use of toxic properties of chemical weapons to cause death or other damages.

(D) For law enforcement purposes - any purpose for law enforcement, including any domestic riot and it's purpose of controlling and imposing order.

12. 8. 3. British Courts

It does not accept public complaints against the British government's policy of occupation crimes, but agreed to consider the issues of victims affected because of violations committed by the British Ministry of Defense or any other ministry without allowing the lifting of a personal complaint against the prime minister or the government as a whole. But the decision of the European Court of Human Rights, issued in 2001, which was considered the presence of British troops in Iraq as occupation forces for the period of May 2003 to June 2004, has assumed the legal authority and responsibility to maintain security with US forces. In these exceptional circumstances, and the presence of a judicial link between Kingdom United and individual Iraqis who were killed during security operations carried out by the British forces, so it must oblige to investigate the cases of killings of Iraqi civilians and compensation.This European decision was in the case of Baha Daoud Mousa from Basra city, who was arrested by British troops killed with five other detainees as a result of torture during detention which left 93 injured on his body [282]. This case by the families of the victim Bahaa with others six against the Secretary of State for Defence was filed the existence of judicial outlet for Iraqi victims proved of transition of power from occupation to Allawi's government on 30 June 2004. The victims of Fallujah during the first battle and prior violations are also included in this decision. Crime of torture by British forces committed several terms of the agreement to the European human rights and have been violated (the right to life (Article 2), the right not to be subjected to torture (Article 3)). British legal status before the issuance of this resolution, allows only the Iraqi victims of the British courts according to the Human Rights Act 1998 (HRA). According to this Act, English Appeal Court decided to evidence insufficient against the British commitments of the British Human Rights Act. This decision of the European disclosed that the Chapter VII of the UN Security Council resolutions gave the right to arrest for British and US forces as occupation power responsible for maintaining order in occupied Iraq, but did not go beyond the right to life and the right not to be subjected to torture or any other cruel and degrading treatment or inhuman. The other thing that the actions of British troops due to the responsibility of the British government because of failure these forces or international troops joined later to follow supervision of Chapter VII of the UN Security Council resolutions [283]. The other important, the British courts criminalize any whatever office employees in the event of proving lie or defrauding lead to crime. The lies of former Prime Minister Tony Blair is considered with evidence about a lie to justify the involvement of his country's troops in both, the war on Iraq or his war crimes occurred in the battles of Fallujah. Seeking to condemn Tony Blair as employee and not as a former PMs of government is possible through the pursuit in the British courts, as well as to the possibility of accountable under international courts for violating international conventions.

This legal status confirmed by the event took place with me. On March 2008, Italian journalist Maurizio Torrealta (director of the documentary film "Fallujah Hidden massacre, 2005"), told me that he would go to London to present his film inside the British High Court for terrorism in London as a witness in the case of British Muslims on terrorism charges (due to their release and demanding phrases vows to fight the British and US forces during the collecting donations for the people of Fallujah during the second battle of Fallujah). Torrealta asked me that join him as an additional witness, because Mr. Iqbal Ahmed solicitor representing 5 of the Defendants Muslims (CoSolicitors office) and the barrister Thomas Mackinnon have asked the two Marines testimonies in the film with my testimony in order to clarify crimes that took place in Fallujah, and justify a state of anger and frenzy among the defendants, which led them to launch such statements.

I agreed to travel and continued with Mr. Ahmed Iqbal to organize my visa from the British Embassy in Rome in two days, and I sent to him my testimony about what happened in Fallujah. In addition, I wrote my evidence about Blair accused of lying and causing a second war crime war in Fallujah and prevent the peace chance. The day before the travel, I surprised that the journalist Torrealta apologized for going because of the advice from his channel director that not to participate in this case. On the day of travel and before traveling hours from Fiumicino Airport of Rome, I was surprised to postpone all flights to Heathrow Airport in London because of a strong storm there. I stayed at the airport for the night hoping to travel the next day, and here came the second surprise. Mr. Iqbal call me at ninth p.m. GMT of Italy to inform me that he apologized for cancelling of my travel to them because the judge of trial after

[328]

he read the text of my testimony has decided refuse it and not allow me even to enter the courtroom because my testimony may help the defendants and gets the innocence of the charge, as well as to open the biggest political case about the role of Blair, which they are not prepared it!!

In August 2012, I began contacts with a famous French lawyer William Bourdon, a specialist of genocide and crimes against humanity. He was already the director of the Human Rights Watch organization in America and owns a law firm in Paris (Cabinet BOURDON-VOITURIEZ et Associés). Initially, he did not show interest in the financial side, but after seeing the entire evidence, and after making sure that there is sufficient evidence to convict Tony Blair and Britain's violation of international treaties. Then, Bodron ascertain the adequacy of the evidence, and request to discuss in wages before starting any analysis of case, because he needed to at least two associates and a firsy payment of 30 000 euros. Although I told him at the beginning of the communications that I do not have a high financial possibility!!

12. 8. 4. The International Courts

1. The International Court of Justice is the court to consider disputes between countries and governments, and it has repeatedly stressed the ban on the use of force by one State against another as part of the international customary law. The case of the dispute between the United States and Nicaragua in 1986, which is more than a somewhat similar example to the issue of Iraq. Paragraph 4 approval in relevant part that "the United States of America, through some of the attacks on the territory of Nicaragua, which involve the use of force, has acted against the Republic of Nicaragua, in breach of its obligation under the international customary law and not to use force against another state." It will be recalled, the United States had agreed in the end to pay compensation in kind [285].

2. The International Criminal Court, which is entitled to those affected by the crimes of genocide, crimes against humanity, war crimes, and aggression war of resorting to it (in case of the state was a member signed and ratified the Convention or not). As is known, the United States and Iraq are not members to the International Criminal Court treaty, especially the Government of Iraq has given the signature in 2005 by Prime Minister Iyad Allawi and then after just four days he

withdrawn his signature under US pressure [2A]. While the United States signed the Convention but did not ratify it so far, and then returned to announce its withdrawal altogether!!

3. For starting the universal jurisdiction and looking to any violation of international human rights instruments, it requires the fulfillment of certain conditions before being seen by the international supervisory body according to laws set. These requirements include the fulfillment of prescribed inputs on the admissibility of personal jurisdiction, admissibility of the decade, the admissibility of the subject and the spatial jurisdiction. Then the supervisory body to start universal jurisdiction of request or complaint [247]. For example, the Statute of the Inter-American Commission states that the Commission is a body of the Organization of the American States, which was created to encourage and monitor the defense of human rights. While most of the European courts, which consider the external complaints within the international jurisdiction put impossible conditions to prevent raising lawsuits against leaders of the occupation. The application of universal jurisdiction limit the powers sometimes through the local laws of each country, as an example of the requirement for a victim should be from that country to accept the crime occurred outside the country and by criminals are not from their country.

Iraqis government and parliament had agreed to compensate victims of US civilians affected psychologically during the second Gulf War by an amount of 400 million US dollars for forty American people of all ages, and most bizarre that based on the decision of a US judge and trial in a timely manner in spite of the absence of any Iraqi representation of government during trial, thus losing credibility and justice of this trial. The Maliki government's decision to approve the compensation is the strangest decisions, due to be implemented by the caretaker government not to sign the powers of such a huge financial burden. It is also no bilateral agreement between the two countries for judicial enforcement of judicial rulings, and Iraq is not obliged to implement the decisions of the US courts, which also confirms the subordination of the interests of the occupier!!.

If we look to the issue of Kuwaiti reparations after the entry of Iraqi forces into Kuwait, we will find that the Kuwaiti government are taken on the responsibility of preparing the Kuwaiti victims' files as a result of the second Gulf War in 1991 and the pursuit of internationally through the UN Security

Council to issue a resolution 687 of 1991 to regulate the development of the compensation stated in paragraph 18 of resolution through the establishment of compensation fund from Iraqi funds to Kuwaiti victims [278]. While in the case of Iraqi victims were Iraqi government absent from this role due to give immunity for US troops and prevent the promotion of compensation transactions for Iraqi victims because of crime and violence and violations of the occupation forces (continuation of the Governor's decision former civil occupation, Paul Bremer, to assure the continuing occupation and dependency).

After the second battle of Fallujah (November 2004) compensate damage estimated of civilian housing amounting to 2,500 dwelling only and the amount of total costs up to four hundred and ninety-two million US dollars (492 million US $) [230]. This amount of money is not equivalent to the size of the damage and casualties of the city has a population 300,000 people, who have been displaced from their homes and became refugees displaced by the military operations, as well as to mention the human and material losses and destruction of property. While the government of Nouri al-Maliki and later the Iraqi parliament had agreed in 2011 to pay compensation to those affected Americans within financial settlements file before agreeing to a US withdrawal from Iraq, which included compensation to the amount of US $ 400 million had been decided by a US judge as a result of psychological damage that suffered of 40 American civilian who had been detained in the Iraqi presidential palaces during the second Gulf War in 1991!!

The question that arises then is how to reconcile the occupier commitment to the application of human rights - which may mean in some cases, legal reforms - with the principle of continuity of the domestic legal system. For which extent is the implementation of reforms compatible with the rules set forth in Article 43 of Hague Regulations and article 64 of the Fourth Geneva Convention? The caution and deliberation required here to prevent slipping, which can result from pretext the occupier's fulfillment and its international obligations cover, and the occupier can be implementation of structural transformations in the occupied country without a democratic consultation with the concerned people. This is the biggest risk with respect to economic, social and cultural rights, and the rules set out in this area are inaccurate in some cases and subject to irregular interpretations [367].

The Iraqi land use as garbage illegally, or leave some hazardous materials at home without taking into account safety and health rules, inflicted the heaviest damage to Iraq's resources and its environment and the pollution of land, and perhaps that alone is a crime against humanity, after the crime of the occupation and the violation of the rights of Iraqi people as a whole. Pollution crime is from class of international crimes that should compel the United States, companies and individuals contractors of international legal responsibility, and claim all of these entities to pay compensation for all what happened to Iraq as moral and material losses due to these inhumane practices and contrary to legal and ethical considerations. The signature of Baghdad on Iraqi - American agreement of security in late 2008 prevent Iraq from claim Washington to compensation for all what happened to Iraqi people from injustice and damage under UN resolution 1483 issued in 22 May 2003, which admitted the occupation and apply the Geneva Conventions of 1949 and first and second additional protocols of 1977 according to the rules of international humanitarian law [19A].

Obliterating Fallujah: A Nazi War Crime

By Professor FRANCIS A. BOYLE

Law Building
504 E. Pennsylvania Ave.
Champaign, IL 61820 USA

[332]

Article 6(b) of the 1945 Nuremberg Charter defines a Nuremberg War Crime in relevant part as the: ". . . wanton destruction of cities, towns or villages, or devastation not justified by military necessity." According to this definitive definition, the Bush Jr. administration's wanton destruction of Fallujah constituted a Nuremberg war crime for which Nazis were tried and executed at Nuremberg. To be sure, I oppose the death penalty for any reason.

Since the Bush Jr. administration's installation in power by the United States Supreme Court in January of 2001, the peoples of the world witnessed a government in the United States of America that demonstrated little if any respect for fundamental considerations of international law, international organizations, and human rights, let alone appreciation of the requirements for maintaining international peace and security. What the world watched instead was a comprehensive and malicious assault upon the integrity of the international legal order by a group of men and women who were thoroughly Machiavellian in their perception of international relations and in their conduct of both foreign policy and domestic affairs. This is not simply a question of giving or withholding the benefit of the doubt when it came to complicated matters of foreign affairs and defense policies to a U.S. government charged with the security of both its own citizens and those of its allies in Europe, the Western Hemisphere, and the Pacific. Rather, the Bush Jr. administration's foreign policy constituted ongoing criminal activity under well-recognized principles of both international law and U.S. domestic law, and in particular and especially the Nuremberg Charter (1945), the Nuremberg Judgment (1946), and the Nuremberg Principles (1950).

In international legal terms, the Bush Jr. administration itself should be viewed as an ongoing criminal conspiracy under international criminal law in violation of the Nuremberg Charter, the Nuremberg Judgment, and the Nuremberg Principles, because of its formulation and undertaking of aggressive war policies that were legally akin to those perpetrated by the Nazi regime. Their obliteration of Fallujah was emblematic of their genocidal destruction of Iraq and their wholesale extermination of the Iraqis. This American Nazi Project against Iraq and the Iraqis continues today as this book goes into print. Every citizen of the world community should read this book and then act upon its knowledge in accordance with his or her own conscience.

CHAPTER 13

The United Nations and human rights violations:

Paradoxes of human rights and humanity

13. 1. Effects of Occupation and Destruction of Iraq

International silence about what happened in Fallujah is the epitome of international cowardice and a failure of humanity to Commenting on the lack of respect for human rights in the modern era, Bill Henderson, an American journalist, criticized the silence of the press about the crimes of his country's troops in Fallujah. After the hit on the city there was a humanitarian disaster and the comprehensive destruction of the health of the people, as well as severe environmental consequences, and while the press criticized the doctors' mistakes or the neglect of some patients, they were silent about the crime against humanity in which thousands were affected. [386].

In the event of large international conflicts like an invasion of a country like Iraq there are international commitments that international officials and non-governmental organizations are required to respect. The failure to take necessary and agreed steps to punish crimes and violations of human rights in Fallujah is a serious indication of the great imbalance in the work of these international institutions. Conflict management including punishment for crimes requires a united effort of all the international organizations and institutions under the auspices of the United Nations and the Security Council.

In 1998, the International Criminal Court was established to deal with individuals who commit international crimes. It was agreed that four types of crimes should be punished - war crimes and crimes against humanity, the crime of genocide and the crime of aggression through war. But unfortunately in the end only the first three crimes were recognised, while the court cannot work on acts of aggression so far, because only four small island states were signatories who have a fear of foreign invasion. Although the United Kingdom is a party and ratified the convention, the United States has signed but not ratified it fearing, most recently, prosecution of its leaders for war crimes committed in Iraq. Article 8 of the Court's Act recognizes as a crime the act of causing collateral damage from launching an attack by invasion (and, as happened in Iraq). The United States put civilians at risk by the use of cluster bombs and depleted uranium, thus being liable to prosecution [404]. However, bringing any one of these criminals in front of this Court is difficult. The introduction of the terms of this agreement intothe domestic laws of these countries, and allowing universal jurisdiction, might result in an international police warrant and allow any one of the perpetrators to be arrested when they visit these countries.

The analysis here of the consequences of foreign occupation in Iraq will also give a clear road map of the public role that should be played by the international community in the case of this kind of aggression and show why and how it should assume its responsibilities in disasters like this. For example, there is an international study prepared by the Global Policy Forum with the participation of 31 international organizations that identified the most prominent crimes perpetrated during the occupation. They are: [425]

1. The destruction of the Iraqi state with all its institutions left to looters and arsonists, , and the demobilization of all military and security system personnel, destroying very forces able to maintain national security and law and order.

2. The destruction of cultural heritage, as the United States and its allies did not listen to all the appeals and warnings launched by international organizations for the need to preserve cultural heritage in Iraq, including museums, libraries and many archaeological sites, which are considered the wealth of human civilization.

3. The use of indiscriminate weapons by the US forces and allies, especially exceptionally harmful ones prohibited under international convention because they are not acceptable or humanitarian. Incendiary weapons, including a type of napalm, as well as white phosphorus munitions were used against ground targets in densely populated urban areas. During the 2003 invasion of Iraq, the United States of America and its alliance also used depleted uranium munitions and cluster bombs that all violate the ban on weapons that cause unnecessary suffering with indiscriminate harm as well as their use being a crime against the humanity.

4. Detention and imprisonment, where the US and coalition forces with their Iraqi governments detained a large number of Iraqi citizens in "security and

secret detention centres" without charge or trial, in direct violation of international law. There is no Iraqi who is safe from arbitrary arrest, with a vast increase in the number of prisoners after 2003. More than 30,000 Iraqi detainees lack basic rights and are retained in deplorable physical conditions, often for long periods. US commanders have taken thousands of detainees to Iraqi authorities whose prisons seriously violate all human rights standards.

5. Prisoner abuse and torture, in which US troops abused and tortured a large numbers of Iraqi prisoners, most of them suffering grievously from this inhuman treatment and some of them having died as a direct result. The torture was in all central prisons and investigation centres, and now also continues to increase in Iraqi prisons with US awareness and complicity.

6. Attacks on cities, in which US coalition forces attacked several important cities on the pretext that they were insurgent strongholds, the attacks leading to a mass exodus of people with large losses of civilian lives and many casualties and massive destruction of infrastructure. In addition to Fallujah, there were dozens of towns such as Qaim and Tal Afar, Samarra, Ramadi, Haditha, Najaf and Sader city. Attacks included heavy shelling from the air and ground weapons with the intention of cutting electricity, water, food and medicines. These attacks left hundreds of thousands of people homeless and in camps for displaced people.

7. Killing civilians, murder and atrocities, in which the US forces and allied leaders created permissive rules of engagement to allow the use of lethal force against any conceivable threat. That is why the United States and its allies regularly killed Iraqi civilians at checkpoints and during military operations, purely on the basis of suspicion. Among the horrific crimes that came to light is the massacre of civilians in the town of Haditha.

8. Displacement and mortality, in which from April 2007, displaced persons and refugees including an estimated 1.9 million Iraqis have been displaced within the country and about 2.2 million refugees abroad. The Iraqi government estimates that 50,000 people are leaving their homes every month. The size of problem and difficulty of reaching the displaced people put the crisis over the provision of relief beyond the capacity of the international system. A lot of people were killed. The death rate for Iraqis killed under occupation has risen sharply, in that in addition to the deaths caused by the fighting, it is now known that coalition forces killed many Iraqi civilians. Iraqis were also killed because of the disintegration of the health care system, as well as in the

[337]

violence perpetrated by militias, gangs, death squads, and terrorists. A study conducted in 2006 estimated more than half a million deaths "an increasing excess" since 2003.

9. Corruption, fraud and gross malfeasance, in which under the control or influence of US authorities, the public funds in Iraq have been drained because of rampant corruption and looted oil, leaving the country unable to provide basic services and unable to engage in re construction of the country. Billions of dollars have disappeared. To avoid accountability, the United States and the United Kingdom have reduced or undercut the Council Commissioner of Surveillance and Consultation by the United Nations. Iraq has suffered from stolen cash, padded contracts, cronyism, bribery and kickbacks, waste and incompetence, as well as the shoddy and inadequate contract performance. Main contractors are most likely politically engaged, with US companies, and worked up to make billions of profit.

10. Long-term rule and embassy compound, in which the United States has been pressing towards the construction of several very large and expensive military bases and for a long stay in Iraq as well as the massive embassy compound and the new size in Baghdad. Construction projects this is controversial too. Iraqis overwhelmingly oppose the bases, as many opinion polls have shown, and in the United States Congress have also refused to spend money on the basis of a "permanent presence" in Iraq. Despite the opposition there is large scale construction at the embassy, a sign that the United States is planning to extend its massive military and political influence in Iraq for many years to come.

11. The cost of the war and occupation, in which Iraq incurred exorbitant costs, including financial destruction and widespread loss of life and debilitating injuries and trauma, as well as lost economic output and lost oil revenues. The United States has spent about USD 400 billion of government direct funds in the conflict as of December 2006, where US has doubled the cost of the federal budget of USD 4 billion per month in 2003 to more than USD 8 billion a month in late 2006. Total costs of the United States, including spending estimates in the future, and interest on the national debt, medical costs for veterans and other factors, has already reached two trillion dollars.

At the meeting of the 24th session of the Human Rights Council of UN which was held on 9 September 2013, International Youth and Student Movement for the United Nations provided and issued a joint statement with several non-governmental international organizations about the impact of 10 years of occupation on Iraqi children. They pointed to the catastrophic situation of Iraqi children from 2003 - 2013, and this has also been acknowledged by the United Nations Children's Fund (UNICEF), in which a report stated that 3.5 million children are living below the poverty line and 1.5 million under the age of five suffer from malnutrition and 100 infants die every day, in addition to the killing of thousands of children during the occupation and the invasion of Iraq. This confirms that there were egregious violations by the occupation forces and the Iraqi authorities of the Fourth Geneva Convention and the UN Convention on Children's Rights [538].

One of the political ironies that the international permit for the first interim Iraqi government formed under occupation in 2004 was recognize the existence and the spread of the phenomenon of children's psychological trauma as a result of successive wars unexplained constant bombardment on the residential neighbourhoods and civilians especially the children, women and elderly. Those politicians formed by the occupation forgot that the invasion had used the policy of shock and horror and had used the most terrifying and deadly weapons since the 1991 Gulf War, continuing even after the official announcement by President Bush that the task of the occupation of Iraq was completed in 2003.

13. 2. Security Council' Stance

The resolutions of the UN Security Council after this aggressive war of US - British military occupation, contain double standards within the folds of their decisions. In the Gulf War of 1991 the entry of the Iraqi army into Kuwait was considered internationally as an invasion and military occupation. This military action put Iraq under Chapter VII of the UN Charter, which imposes a package of measures to be taken against a country that threatens international peace and security and leads to the occurrence of aggression. This step was not taken the states of US and Britain when they occupied Iraq) [9A].

A look at the relevant paragraphs of Chapter VII shows clearly the difference and duplicity of the UN Security Council resolution dealing with the occupation of Iraq, in which these paragraphs were not applied to the invasion of Iraq, which if it had been so applied would have confirmed the illegitimacy of the presence of any troops that later joined the occupation forces under the name of the international coalition. The paragraphs of the seventh Chapter are:

- Article 39, which stipulates that the Security Council is to decide whether any threat to the peace or breach of it was an act of aggression and shall make recommendations, or decide what measures, shall be taken in accordance with the provisions of Articles 41 and 42 to maintain international peace and security or return it.

- Article 40, which states that in order to prevent aggravation of the situation, the Security Council has the right before making the recommendations or deciding upon the measures provided for in Article 39, to calls both disputants to take necessary or desirable interim measures without prejudice to the disputants' rights and demands, or positions. In the event of failure to solve the dispute the Security Council must take these temporary measures.

- Article 41, which states that the Security Council may decide what measures to take, not involving the use of armed forces to implement its decisions, and it may call United Nations members to apply these measures, including the interruption of economic relations and rail, sea, air, postal, telegraphic, radio and other means of communication, and partially or completely severing diplomatic relations.

- Article 42 stipulates that should the Security Council consider that measures provided for in Article 41 would be inadequate or have proved to be inadequate, it may take such action by air, sea, or land forces as may be necessary to maintain international peace and security or to return it. This act may include such actions such as demonstrations, blockades, and other operations by air, sea, or land forces by members of the United Nations.

- Article 43, states that if the Security Council requested international forces with all the facilities, then these should be placed at the disposal of the Council for the preservation of international peace and

- Article 44 states that if the Security Council decided to use force, it shall before calling a member not represented in it to provide armed forces in fulfilment of the obligations stipulated in Article 43, call this member to be involved if willing, in the decisions of Security Council concerning the employment of contingents from that member's armed forces).

- Article 45 stipulates that in order to enable the United Nations to take urgent military measures, members shall have air units that can be used immediately for the work of the Joint International repression. The Security Council determines the forces of these units and their degree of readiness and plans for their combined action, with the assistance of the Military

Staff Committee and within the limits set out in the special agreement or agreements referred to in Article 43.

- Article 46 provides for plans necessary for the use of armed force to be set by the Security Council with the assistance of the Military Staff Committee.
- Article 47provides for :

1. Forming a committee of the Military Staff and its mission to advise and aid the Security Council and cooperation in all matters relating to military requirements for the maintenance of international peace and security, and to use the established forces at his disposal and its leadership and regulation of armaments and disarmament to the extent possible.

2. Constituting the Military Staff Committee from the Chiefs of Military Staff of the permanent Security Council members or their deputies The Committee may invite any member of the United Nations of members that are permanently represented to oversee the work as necessary on behalf of the Committee and carry out its responsibilities

3. The Military Staff Committee to be responsible under the Security Council for the strategic direction of any armed forces placed at the disposal of the Council.

4. The Military Staff Committee may set up sub-regional authorization of the Security Council after consultation with appropriate regional agencies.

- Article 48 states that:

1. Necessary actions for the implementation of Security Council resolutions to maintain international peace and security, shall be carried out by all the United Nations members or some of them, as determined by the Council.

2. The United Nations members should implement advanced decisions directly and through their own actions in the appropriate international agencies of which they are members

- Article 49 provides that United Nations' members shall unite in affording mutual assistance in carrying out the measures decided upon by the Security Council.

- Article 50 states that if the Security Council adopted preventive or enforcement measures against any state, then any other state - whether they are United Nations members or were not - confronted with special economic problems arising from the implementation of these measures, shall have the right to consult with Security Council with regard to a solution to these problems.

- Article 51 states that nothing in the present Charter shall impair the inherent right of individual or groups to self-defense if an armed attack occurs against a United Nations member, until the Security Council has taken measures necessary to maintain international peace and security measures, and the measures taken by the Members in the exercise of the right of self-defense shall be informed immediately to the Council. Those measures do not affect in any way the Council's authority under the continuing provisions of this Charter and its responsibilities and the right to take at any time such action as it deems necessary to maintain international peace and security or return to it.

UN Security Council Resolution No. 1546 [277] welcomed the steps of the invasion governments in ending the occupation on 30 June 2004, and preparing for democratic elections, with an emphasis on the right of the Iraqi people to determine their political future and control their own natural resources. The occupation forces ended the Iraqi Governing Council that they had formed and the Security Council greeted the progress made in the implementation of the arrangements under resolution 1511 (2003). In the preamble to the resolution the Security Council welcomed the role played by the United Nations Mission in Iraq (UNAMI) and the international community to help secure the future of the country in accordance with resolutions 1483 and 1511. This decision does not give legal status to the elimination of the occupation, but simply welcomes it with hope of ending the foreign occupation of Iraq in exchange for the implementation of the promises to return the sovereignty and authority to over the country to the Iraqi people. Moreover, the Iraqi interim government has asked foreign troops in Iraq to stay, despite the fact that this situation is a continuing threat to international peace and security [277].

On 19 September 2012, the Security Council adopted a resolution condemning strongly the violations of international law against children in armed conflict, calling states to bring the perpetrators of the continuing violations to justice, stressing its readiness to take targeted measures against these barbarians [538]. But in spite of all the evidence that declared an ongoing crime of genocide against the newborns in Iraq, including Fallujah and Basra because of pollution

[342]

by forbidden weapons, the Security Council is unable to implement its decisions.

The main reason for the inability to bring actions against any side, despite the killing and suffering from battles, is that in order to assess the humanitarian impact of the conflict in Fallujah, there is a need for data about the casualties, and this data is lacking. [35]. I found that unfortunately, most of the Western writers are not interested in justice for Iraqi victims nor do they even respect their western readers by stating the truth. Some of them tried to show only the part that politicians want to show.

The foreign policies of former US President W Bush are criminal policies according to the principles of international law, in particular, the Charter and principles of Nuremberg, and for this reason was it not strange to cover up the war crimes in Fallujah [18]?

The American international lawyer Francis Boyle made an appeal to consider the what the Bush administration did as constituting a criminal conspiracy under international criminal law, by way of the violation of the Charter, rule and principles of Nuremberg, in that it entered into an aggressive war similar as far as its legality was concerned to what the Nazi regime did. But we must not forget the Blair government's participation in this crime. Hence the importance of calling upon the international will and the Security Council of the UN to prosecute these international criminals and do justice to their victims to ward off the risk of the same countries and their leaders trying to continue on the same path with continued global impunity.

Even the US military court's decision which blamed the massacre in November (2005) on a minor military officer (Serg. Wuterich) and punished him with three months imprisonment has not been implemented for technical reasons, although this crime left 24 civilians dead including women and children. Therefore, it's impossible for us to wait for any hope of justice from the US courts and instead our mission should be focused on getting justice through specific international bodies.

The US forces considered the Iraqi fighters as terrorists in order to justify mass punishment for crimes that are, in fact, crimes of state terrorism. The American army itself admits that it was legitimate for the fighters to resist and defend themselves in the first battle of Fallujah, and they negotiated with two local delegations of the city in order to cease fire after they announced the cessation of military operations on their side. Marines only decided to carry out mass punishment in operations named as operations against terrorism after they shifted their position and decided that cooperation between civilians and fighters was a threat to the safety of US troops. Suddenly it was as if Iraqis were the occupiers of their own country and that it was not the opposite that is true!!

The concept of state terrorism was clear and supported by a lot of evidence as presented in previous chapters of this book, and its humanitarian cost was huge. It destroyed the life of hundreds of thousands of people who were left to suffer so far without any compensation that fits the size of the brutal damage they suffered.

13. 3. The Reasons For The UN's Failure In Iraq:

The occupation forces and their policies were the first beneficiary of the bombing of the UN headquarters building in Baghdad (18 August, 2003) and the killing of the Representative of the Secretary General of the United Nations, Sergio Vieira de Mello (Brazilian-born) along with 15 another employees and staff of international organizations and the wounding of dozens more [170]. This incident caused the suspension of the real and required role of the UN in occupied Iraq, especially regarding the application of the Geneva Conventions, and thus curtailed their role through the transfer of their offices outside Iraq, leaving the occupation unsupervised.

The second cause that triggered this war of aggression and occupation of Iraq was the human rights situation in Iraq. Although there was a position of Special Rapporteur of Human Rights in Iraq, which was chaired for last time by Mr. Andreas Mavrommatis (a Cypriot citizen who held this position between the period of December 1999 until mid-2004) but he presented his latest report on the situation of human rights on 9 June 2004 and did not renew his mandate thereafter and so did not continue his work [364]. While the United Nations continued to issue reports on the human rights situation in Kuwait by its Special Rapporteur of Human Rights there until 1992 although the Iraqi army had withdrawn from Kuwait [365]. This internationalist position to protect and monitor the human rights situation in Iraq stopped after one year of the occupation in Iraq, while it had continued for two years in the case of Kuwait.

13. 3. 1. High Commissioner Office For Human Rights (OHCHR)

The activity of this office was such an important influence for me as an activist and defender of human rights in Iraq. I participated and trained with this office in many activities that opened to me this volunteer field of learning and training that I had chosen during the occupation period and continued so far. At a joint seminar with the Special Rapporteur of UN for protection of human rights defenders Ms. Hania Gilani during a seminar hosted by the Human Rights Office of UNAMI in Amman 2005, we discovered that the human rights office in UNAMI is part of the development and training department in OHCHR!!! This means that it is not interested in monitoring and documenting the violations of human rights in Iraq and is without a supervisory role. When this problem was discovered it outraged most of the participants, and after long discussions that lasted for months they finally agreed to support the proposed project by our NGOs for establishing a Monitoring Net of Human Rights in Iraq (MHRI), for the purpose of ensuring the preservation and continued application of the findings of the reports which were issued before by the Special Rapporteur of Human Rights in Iraq. After the issuance of the first report of the Iraqi Net MHRI, the human rights office in UNAMI has also begun to issue periodic reports to inform the international community about the human rights situation in Iraq.

Highlights of the gaps that accompanied the work of the Human Rights Office of UNAMI. These may be summed up in the following points:

1. Despite the massive destruction and huge numbers of victims because of the military operations of the occupation forces or militias that were established under occupation, no international action to investigate when there is information about serious violations and war crimes or mass punishment and destruction or genocide was taken. The first of these procedures is to inform the Security Council of UN in order to send a fact-finding mission. Sadly it is known that the occupation governments who are the same ones who sit on the Security Council may even be preventing discussion of sectarian killings and genocide, mass displacement. It is all left in the hands of the US-UK governments, as if Iraq is a US territory!!!

2. The Office of Human Rights in UNAMI is a branch of the Department of Training and Development for the Promotion of Human Rights, and it is not a monitoring mechanism, which explains why some of their employees in their organization said they were unable to work more against violations. It was against their mandate!! At the same time they know that the size of the crimes and violations are such that the UN mandate itself needs to change to

accommodate the size and type of violations and genocide that violate the most basic of human rights as is the case in Iraq, which is the right to live. But the political agenda that controls the decision inside the United Nations prevented it from changing the mandate and giving a green light for investigating and punishing continuing violations and major crimes.

3. Anyone who has followed the reports on human rights violations by UNAMI will see clearly the US pressure to curb its oversight role. First of all UNAMI only released their reports of human rights in Iraq because of the pressure of the release of periodic monitoring reports on Iraq by Iraqi net of human rights in Iraq –MHRI. After that in mid-2005 UNAMI began to issue reports every two months. But instead of issuing these reports every two months as they did until the end of 2006, the United Nations bowed to the political pressure of US and some Iraqi officials involved in serious violations against human rights and the internationali reports began to be issued only every six months. There were also delays in issuance and whether on time or not they are without effect due to the events that are accelerating in Iraq. To illustrate the importance of these disruptions and delays, I would like point out that if grave events were taking place and they become known only after two months the impact of the information will have a lower value because the news gets restricted to only the worst of the crimes. The delay means the report looses its importance as a means to arouse world public opinion, and this is the reason for making the reports semi-annually. The delayin issuing the reports is evidence of the cover up of the crimes by the occupation forces that were sitting inside the United Nations office.

a. In 2006, they issued 6 periodic reports and each report covered the events of just two months.

b. In 2007, only 3 reports were issued and each report covers the events of 4 months

c. In 2008 and 2009 they issued semi-annual reports, and each covered the events of six months

d. In 2010 and 2011 they issued an annual report covering the whole year only!!

e. In 2012 and 2013, the mission returned to issuing semi-annual reports covering the events of six months, but just for the second half of the year without any report at all on the first six months of 2012 and 2013!!

f. In 2014, they released a report for just the first six months and then stopped the periodical reports altogether. In the second half of the year they released 2 specific reports about protection of civilians and one about the death penalty!!

g. In 2015, they released one specific report covering the first 5 months about protection of civilians in armed conflict in Iraq.

4. The main problem is not only the delay in issuing of reports and thus making them ineffectual, but also the political pressure on of the human rights office of UNAMI. The most dangerous changes are in the language inside the report, which is political rather than juridical. Each accident or a crime is personalized to the type of violation. The second dangerous thing is that they cancelled two paragraphs in the regular reports about arrests, rule of law and government corruption, which are in fact the most serious violations going on that have encouraged violence and terrorism.

5. The strangest thing in the language of the reports is that they try to make a parallel and make equal the sectarian militias' crimes to highlight the problem as sectarian, but without any reference to the size of its penetration in the military and security systems of government. And this penetration has happened despite the fact that those systems were formed under the auspices of the international community during the period when Iraq was under Chapter VII of the UN Charter. The reports are like an official recognition for the fact that now militias follow the government or politicians and parties; while they describe the rest of the armed groups of the opposition as divided between terrorists or unknown groups!!! This kind of description is not the work of a professional and non-independent agency nor is it based on the principles of an international organization interested in human rights.

6. The human rights office issued periodic reports more regularly during the one year when it was working outside Iraq (Jordan), while after coming back to Baghdad the reports became annual or semi-annual. This proves that it is bowing to political pressure that is preventing the fact of crimes taking place in Iraq bring made public.

7. These doubts are also raised when it turned out that they did not publish some of these periodic reports in the Arabic language, thus depriving Iraqis who do not speak English of taking advantage of them. And this also deprived many activists and defenders of human rights in Iraq from the opportunity to interact and engage with the international reports and it has increased the distance between the UN office and Iraqi people who see the UN as linked with the corrupt political class.

8. The fear of opening investigations about the crimes of occupation forces has made OHCHR give up any real role in stopping the violations and protecting the victims. To emphasize this point, I will remind the reader that e two incidents have confirmed this fact. The first event was with Mr. John Pace chief of Human Rights office in the UNAMI mission. They did not renew his position because he was sending reports condemning the crimes of the occupation in Iraq. In the last meeting with the High Commissioner of Human Rights in UN (Louise Arbour) in Geneva on 2006, she had asked him to stop sending reports like these because they do not want problems with Americans!! Note that the most prominent periodic reports of his office are a condemnation of death squads of Shiaa militias that were trained and equipped by the occupation who gloss over their crimes and escape from accountability. After Pace was sure of their decision to deport him from the office he called the Guardian newspaper to expose to them the death squads against Sunnis inside the Interior Ministry [682]. I have been personally informed by him in the last meeting with Pace that I had in the Jordanian capital Amman in 2006 that it was his intention to spread all his information in reaction to what they did with him.

The second event related to the reports of our monitoring net of human rights organizations (MHRI) specifically after the issuance of our first report under the supervision of Pace's office and after it was sent to the High Commissioner's office in Geneva. Their reaction was to send two employees to gather information about who the members of our monitor net are and any party they belong to! The UNAMI office recommended telling them that those organizations were trainees of the mission. Then Mr. Frej Fenniche, Senior Human Rights in OHCHR sent a letter of thanks to our net and demanded more professional and discreet reporting. Actually, we sent three other reports as well as individual reports about the war crimes in Fallujah, the Ishaqi massacre, and death squads of Shiite militia's parties. Unfortunately, we did not get any response to the attached recommendations and not even the condemnation of the High Commissioner for each of those serious crimes. Therefore, I went in 2010 to Geneva for a meeting with the High Commissioner's office and to ask why they had not investigated anyone for those crimes before. The answer was that some of their employees had hidden that evidence and that it had not arrived in the Geneva office!! But they evaded taking full documentation of these crimes that I had brought on 2 CDs along with printed reports. The most mysterious of this is their unwillingness to investigate who was behind the attempt to hide the evidence of the Fallujah' crime and prevent it being displayed in Geneva, and all this confirms that all these arguments were fake and the evidence had really arrived with them, but a political decision prevented the investigation.

13. 3. 2. The International Committee of Red Cross (ICRC)

ICRC is one of the most relevant institutions within the United Nations' for dealing with armed crises and is considered a bodyguard to monitor the application of the four Geneva conventions during armed conflicts. The powers of this international organization' work compared with the nature of the crimes committed in Fallujah, will confirm that this organization evaded its responsibilities, at least in bringing the perpetrators of war crimes and major crimes in front of international courts, and this in spite of the various reports of local organizations and testimonies of the victims published across different media. We did not see any real action by this organization for the victims of the many grievous human rights violations except providing medical and food aid and projects to help the disabled and water purification stations ... etc. The required role of bringing to justice those who committed flagrant violations of the Geneva Conventions during the battles of Fallujah has been absent for unknown reasons and raised a lot of question marks??

One of the organization's activities is to address the effects of weapons pollution and they used the term Weapon Contamination, which covers assistance operations to reduce the negative effects on civilians due to the pollution by these weapons. ICRC in one of its bulletins (4022/002 01.2010) recognizes that the real nature of the potential threat by these weapons varies and depends on the nature of the conflict and the nature of the weapons used in it. But the desired action is not taken to follow up on all the facts of the crimes and violations of human rights due to the serious pollution in Fallujah, despite the fact that one party to a conflict in the case of Fallujah, and the main perpetrator of pollution by its weapons, are the states of US and UK.

The official website of the organization in Arabic speaks about the nature of the four Geneva conventions and its Protocols saying that these are conventions and protocols calling for actions to be taken in order to prevent all violations or put an end to them, including enforcing strict rules to deal with what is known as "grave violations", and to find all the persons responsible for "grave violations" and bring them to justice, or extradite them, irrespective of their nationality. [205], and this is what ICRC have not done whether with respect to destruction, punishment, murder, or torture which happened under the occupation in Fallujah before, during, and after the battles crimes. If we agree on the existence of political pressure to prevent ICRC to present the war criminals and the violations that took place in Fallujah to international courts, then the other question arises as to , why did they not provide the assistance required for civilians or others to get to know the weapons used in Fallujah battles, and put an international program in place to reduce the use of such devastating types and their effects which appear in the form birth defects and the growing percentages of cancers. Their omissions confirm that ICRC is afraid to talk about its failure in Fallujah crimes. I was on a visit to Geneva in September 2010 to listen to the discussions of the regular meeting of the human rights council of the UN, and we met the Director of the Middle East and North Africa in ICRC Ms. Silvana Mutti (who is of Italian origin from Milan). The meeting included also the former Iraqi diplomat Naji Haraj and famous British physicist Christopher Busby, where we raised the issues of Fallujah from both the health and human rights side. Ms. Silvana explained health and medical projects that have been previously submitted by ICRC in Fallujah, but unfortunately she ended the meeting immediately without even giving a refund of ticket costs when my question was about their supposed role in bringing the perpetrators of crimes in Fallujah in front of international courts!!

The ICRC recognizes in one of its reports about the relationship between the occupation and the law of economic, social and cultural rights of peoples under occupation, that the occupying power is obliged to ensure the proper functioning of the medical institutions, hospitals and health services, as well having the responsibility to take the necessary measures to combat infectious diseases and epidemics [367]. But unfortunately, they did not say anything during the siege by American marines and British forces of the General Hospital of Fallujah and the prevention of the delivery of humanitarian services to civilians remaining inside the city. This international silence remained even after the appearance of cancers and birth defects that started during the occupation period in Iraq. Unfortunately, the position of the organization was to not even encourage the call for banning the use of depleted-uranium munitions, which was launched in 28 January 2001, under the pretext that there was insufficient evidence on allegations of high destruction [398]. Although the European Council demanded through its statement on 24 January to stop the use of this type of weapon [399], and although there was also the decision of the European Parliament on 17 January to invite the member states which are also members of the North Atlantic Treaty Organization to propose calls to stop the use of depleted uranium weapons in accordance with the principle of Hedge, and then the re-launch of this appeal three more times [400], in spite of all the published research and evidence, ICRC issued a book in 2005 called Weapon Contamination Environment, in which they explained the hazardous nature of depleted uranium weapon, but claimed that there is disagreement about the health effects of depleted uranium. And it called for nothing more than not to walk in the vicinity of the armoured vehicles that were destroyed or near the bunkers / infrastructure destroyed by this weapon [401]!!

As a sponsor of the Geneva Conventions, ICRC failed to protect medical institutions and civilians in Fallujah during the military conflict and during the deployment of the terrorism initiated by the former Iraqi Prime Minister Maliki and continued by his successor Abadi since the 1st January 2014 till now. The government forces and government-backed Shiite militias bombed Fallujah Hospital 39 times, including 5 times by attacking it with explosive barrels and using various other weapons, including indiscriminate targeting which is banned internationally in urban or residential areas. As a result of these sectarian crimes against civilians in Fallujah, the number of civilian casualties since the beginning on 1st January 2014 until 20 October 2015 reached 5530 wounded, including 688 women and 799 children who were injured, while the number of the martyrs of civilians is 3366 martyrs, including 305 princes martyred and 465 children, according to statistics provided by the hospital.

One of the unforgettable events was the silence and inaction of ICRC in its duty to protect up lifters of the white banner during the Iraqi army's withdrawal from Kuwait in 1991, and its inaction regarding the war crime of killing Iraqi army soldiers, after the US Navy commander gave the order to attack them, and he has remained so far without punishment despite the fact that his order violates the Geneva conventions and international law [427]. It is important now to put pressure on the UN and the international community in order to create new mechanisms to monitor more stringently the application of the Geneva Conventions and their Protocols and dealing with ICRC now that it is apparent that they chose to play a very limited role and failed in many cases.

13. 3. 3. The World Health Organization (WHO)

The Charter of the WHO emphasizes many responsibilities towards pollution issues as stated in the constitution of its work (Article 2), including the directing and coordinating of the international health work authority (paragraph a), proposing agreements and approvals and regulation (paragraph k), reporting on the administrative and social techniques that affect the public health both preventive and curative (paragraph p), and taking all the necessary action to achieve the objectives of the organization (paragraph v). This means taking moral and professional responsibility for the environmental pollution suffered in Iraq, including the tragic situation of risk in Fallujah especially and Anbar province generally.

 The real problem now for health destruction due to environmental pollution is not only in the need to train more medical staff to work against the growing cancers and deformities, but they should also help in the fight against pollution and its causes, through spreading the knowledge of the type and the role of pollutants that is increasing the burden of surgeons, and bringing to the world's attention the need to find a ways of protecting humans from carcinogenic effects [207]. But we have not heard so far any serious claims or applications or demands to fund international programs by this organization, nor to address the problems or put in place the foundations for addressing the issue of genetic destruction and the spread of cancers and birth defects, which is very high and has reached very scary proportions.

In 2012, WHO launched a joint study with the Iraqi Ministry of Health to investigate the phenomenon of a large number of distortions and deformities that abounded throughout Anbar province and especially in Fallujah city. But the report, which it was hoped would be issued at the end of February 2013, has not been issued so far for political reasons, and only the summary of the study were announced by the Iraqi ministry of health.

The importance of the role of UN agencies and the international community comes from the fact that if there is a suspicion that there will be a pollution disaster from forbidden weapons like depleted and irradiated uranium and WP, linked in previously unknown ways to the emergence of serious diseases, it is their responsibility to prepare civilians to the huge and almost daily problems among civilians that result, especially in areas where military operations are most intense such as Fallujah and the city of Basra. Today scientists and doctors assert a correlation between contamination by depleted uranium todiseases like congenital birth defects, and the emergence of new diseases in the kidneys, lungs, and liver, as well as immune system collapse. There is also the sharp rise in leukemia and anemia cases especially amongthe children. Reported cases across many Iraqi provinces confirmed a huge jump in cases of miscarriages and premature births among Iraqi women [384].

13. 3. 4. United Nations Environment Programme (UNEP)

In April of 2003, UNEP announced his intention to send a team of scientific experts to study the effects of Depleted Uranium, in order to address people's fears that depleted uranium leaves fatal traces, according to spokesman for the program [354]. On 20 October 2003, UNEP issued an assessment report of the environmental situation in Iraq, noting the need for environmental assessment of contaminated sites identified in order to determine the risks to human health and livelihoods, and to initiate urgent risk reduction measures [356]. However, all efforts were focused only on capacity-building projects through UNAMI with the Iraqi ministry of environment in order to tackle risks of pollution by depleted uranium weapons [355]. This effort was without reference to the size of the environmental pollution and risks at the current time and in the future. Only training Iraqi local staff does not begin to arrive at the size and nature of the contamination that exists in Iraq.

From the period after the Gulf War 1991 until 1999, the United States completed the registration and physical examination of nearly 100,000 veterans of the Battle of the Gulf, within more than 145 projects [391]. Despite the fact that the disaster during the occupation war of Iraq till 2003 was biggest, we did not see or hear of such research projects for the protection of humans or the environment in Iraq. UNEP presented in 2012 a proposed new resolution issued by the General Assembly of United Nations (non-obligating) calling for the precautionary approach toward depleted uranium weapons [392]. The international community was deaf towards these reports that reported using these weapons in Iraq and the emergence of disastrous consequences. Unfortunately, the UNEP did not demand at least research projects in Iraq similar to what the United States has done with its troops after the Gulf War 1991, despite the availability of Iraqi financial resources.

After years of war UNEP released a report in 2007 on the post-Israeli attacks in the Lebanon war (July / August 2006), including the supposed activity of UNEP in areas of conflict. UNEP experts studied specifically the possibility of the use of munitions containing depleted uranium. They visited thirty-two sites south and north of the Litani River and more than fifty samples were taken for laboratory analysis. The samples of dust and soil were analyzed using highly sensitive equipment with the latest technology It did not find any evidence of the use of depleted uranium [394]. And yet despite the fact that in the case of Iraq where there is sufficient and more scientific and official evidences on the use of nuclear weapons, especially those that contain depleted uranium, they never once addressed or answered the question as what are the scientific and practical steps that must be taken by the international community and the Iraqi authorities in the face of such a disaster???

UNEP opened a new section for Disasters and Conflicts, and continues to work in Iraq after the US and British occupation 2003, but its activity is limited to just evaluation studies of environmental pollution and training of Iraqi capabilities in the analysis of results of the samples the last report coming out in 2007 [397]. The Department of disasters and conflicts as advertised on their website (http://www.unep.org/disastersandconflicts/) is divided into four sub-sections complementary to each other's work as following:

1. Post-Crisis Environmental Assessment, has its task to work on the establishment of global advocacy to help the affected areas, create partnerships for environment and disaster risk reduction through the promotion of sustainable methods for the management of ecosystems as a key strategy for reduction of disaster risk and adaptation to climate change, capacity development and technical assistance, and building the knowledge products. They say it is important to develop and build the knowledge base based on the ecosystem to reduce environmental disaster risks.

2. Post-Crisis Environmental Recovery, is about how after any crisis, UNEP implements programs for the rehabilitation of the environment through field projects to support the long-term stability and sustainable development in countries affected by disasters and conflicts, according to country-specific needs.

3. Environmental Cooperation for Peace building aims to use environmental cooperation to transform the risk of conflict into resources and opportunities for achieving stability and peace-building in war-torn societies or fragile communities. Therefore, one of its functions is conflict prevention, peace-building and natural resources, the development of greening peacekeeping operations, environmental diplomacy and mediation to assist the parties in the conflict in the creation of opportunities for cooperation and building confidence and ending the conflict by addressing common issues of environmental and natural resources, legal protection of the environments that are victim of armed conflict, especially the direct and indirect

environmental damage and the collapse of the institutions that possible threaten people's health and livelihood, security and undermines peace-building after conflicts, as happened with the 600 burning oil wells in Kuwait and the destruction of forests in Vietnam.

4. Disaster Risk Reduction, by working to prevent and reduce the effects of natural hazards on vulnerable communities and countries through the sustainable management of natural resources, and these functions correspond to the tasks of assessing post-conflict environment.

A simple look at the action of these sections of UNEP and its mentioned action in Iraq, shows that the internationalist program has neglected for unknown reasons to do three important tasks, such as 1) Creating a global advocacy to help the Iraqi people stricken by contamination of depleted uranium weapons and other weapons used using the same international approach taken toward environmental pollution due to the burning Kuwaiti oil wells, 2) The failure to provide the international legal protection to the polluted or endangered environment, 3) addressing the environment through field projects to revive the environment, as happened in Kuwait after the Gulf war 1991, through the many activities about which reports have been published

13. 3. 5. The Political Failure Of the UN Toward The Military Operations Of Invasion

US commanders tried to give the impression that the military operations against Iraqi cities were a joint operation between US and Iraqi forces. This disinformation was in order to make the siege operations against cities more acceptable to Iraqi and international public opinion. Although US forces are the only side that have the power to move Iraqi troops in joint operations. Observers argue that the United States always take the lead. In fact, sometimes the Iraqi government authorities condemn the operations and the behaviour of US troops.

After a week of heavy fighting in Najaf on August 2004, the interim Vice President Ibrahim al-Jaafari "called on US forces to leave Najaf and let only Iraqi forces remain there" [596]. The Deputy Governor of Najaf, Jawdat Kadhim Najim Quraishi, resigned and 16 of the total 30 members of the Najaf Province Council followed him to protest against the abuses being perpetrated in Najaf [597]. In the attacks of the occupation forces on Fallujah, the feelings of all Iraqis rose up and stunned the occupation leaders. A number of members of the Iraqi Governing Council (which was formed by the occupation) criticized the attacks and threatened to resign if US commanders did not stop the offensive operations. Adnan Pachachi a senior member of the Iraqi Governing Council called the operation "illegal and totally unacceptable" [598]. While Ghazi al-Yawar who was president of the Governing Council in Iraq at the time, said "How can a superpower like the United States put itself in a state of war with a small city like Falluja?" [599]. In a statement to government television on August 2006, former Prime Minister Nuri al-Maliki sharply criticized US-Iraqi raids in Baghdad's Sadr City, saying that such operations "violate the rights of citizens," and added "the use of such weapons in this process are unreasonable to detain someone – like using planes " he said, "firstly I want to apologize to the Iraqi people, and this will not happen again" [600]. These public statements are signals of serious problems between the Americans military leaders and their allied Iraqi politicians, and show how weak the Iraqi government control of its sovereignty is, although they claim to be elected.

The killing of civilians by US forces triggered angry resentment among the Iraqi population and led to strong statements from Iraqi officials that reveal the true lack of Iraqi sovereignty and revealed that an occupying power was staying in order to ensure that immunity was granted to the members of these forces. After the massacre in the town of Haditha, former Prime Minister Nuri al-Maliki described this violation as "totally unacceptable", and violence against civilians by members of the United States qualified as a "daily phenomenon" in Iraq. He added that "coalition forces do not respect the Iraqi people" [628]. After the announcement of the results of US investigations that found US troops not guilty of the Ishaqi massacre, the reaction of the Iraqi government was pure confirmation of its total lack of sovereignty when Adnan al-Kazimi, deputy of PM Nuri al-Maliki, said the government would seek an apology from the United States and compensation for the victims in a some cases [629].

Before the attack on Fallujah in November 2004, the General Secretary of the United Nations Kofi Annan wrote an open letter to US President W. Bush and UK PM Blair, expressing "particular concern about the safety and protection of civilians. He continued: "battles are mostly likely to take place in densely populated urban areas, and with a clear risk of civilian casualties ... " [601]. Shortly thereafter, the siege on Fallujah continued, and the High Commissioner for Human Rights Louise Arbour invited an investigation into possible war crimes [602]. The United States and its allies ignore all warnings of risk to civilians and war crimes and continued their attack. International law sets clear standards for the conduct of military operations. The Geneva Conventions prohibit attacks which do not distinguish clearly between military targets and

[356]

civilians, or have a disproportionate impact on civilians. Coalition military operations clearly violated these laws, with massive population displacement, and indiscriminate killing of civilians, and the widespread destruction of housing and urban infrastructure, including historic buildings and religious sites. Occupation forces violated yet more provisions of the conventions through the deliberate targeting against hospitals and emergency medical care to stop and prevent the arrival of humanitarian aid. In further violation of the prohibition of "siege tactics", it deprived civilians of food, water, electricity and medical supplies and vital services. These practices of collective punishment were inflicted on the Iraqis. All of these violations represent a serious violation of international humanitarian law.

During a seminar organized by UNDP and UNOPS in 2006, to discuss the results of the elections that took place in four Arabian countries including Iraq, one of the most important persons in attendance was Mr. Boutros-Ghali (former General Secretary of the United Nations), and I asked him personally during a break about the most important thing that was in my mind after seeing the mechanisms of the United Nations work in the follow-up to major crimes. I asked him for a few minute of advice: "During your time as General Secretary of the United Nations, you succeeded in forming an international criminal court against genocide crimes in Rwanda, and in Fallujah there is a genocide that took place and banned weapons have been used and we have evidence to prove it, so can you advise us how to reach a new UN resolution to form an international criminal court against the US - UK occupation crimes in Fallujah??". The man smiled and he said "it's difficult my son, it's impossible that Americans will accept or allow, I was SG of UN and our work of Rwanda Tribunal, but the Americans frowned and told me that you exceeded the red lines" then added "for this they did not like me to stay in my position!!" .

13. 3. 6. UN' Steps Required To Develop Its Mechanisms

Through the above we report the most important negatives that we've seen through our work with UN agencies, and the necessary change that needs to follow to prevent the imbalance in the UN missions for maintaining international peace and security. The international crisis is growing and there are a large number of victims in conflict areas to the extent of it reaching a level of World War victims. Thus there is clearly a need to develop the existing international mechanisms because of their inadequacy in the current circumstances. The following needs to be done:

1) OHCHR:

i) The establishment of better control mechanisms than what there are in Iraq to protect human rights, such as putting in back in position the Special Rapporteur on the situation of human rights in Iraq, authorized to open the most comprehensive investigations of huge violations relevant to the entire group of agencies and bodies inside OHCHR.

ii) To establish strict amendments to the international conventions that have been violated and failed to stop such violations or bring perpetrators to account for crimes such as the use of banned weapons.

iii) The formation of a special office for complaints of victims and activists and NGOs after a failure of the urgent action procedure and because of the lack of coordination between them and their mission in Iraq, and the creation and continuation of safe electronic means of communication.

2) ICRC:

i) The establishment of a special criminal court for war crimes and violations of international humanitarian law, including the Geneva Conventions, and court covering the cases that are difficult to prosecute locally or internationally and where the violation of Geneva Conventions is proven, in order to prevent impunity globally.

ii) The formation of new or additional monitoring mechanisms on the four Geneva Conventions given that the ICRC has failed in its mission to document many of these international violations or bring the perpetrators to justice. A solution could be to invite and involve the Prosecutor' office of the International Criminal Court.

3) WHO:

i) Putting a newly obligatory paragraph in its convention for a mission to set up an investigate office for complaints supported by scientific evidence about environmental and health pollution in areas of armed conflict crimes.

ii) To work for establishing a new international convention to criminalize any person or side causing health disasters, whether by

[358]

armed conflicts or economic or political local and governmental entities, such as pharmaceutical companies.

4) UNEP:

i) To establish a special department for investigating scientifically how forbidden weapons threaten the environment and public health, even if that State did not ask for this assistance.

ii) The development of a professional mechanism that works to identify in the event the presence of environmental contamination that is otherwise outside the purview of the program, and to prevent discrimination on political grounds in environmental pollution issues.

5) The Political Office of UN:

i) The right of veto in the Security Council is sometimes used to prevent accountability for major international crimes, and to stop this obstacle the rules of the UN must be modified in order to give the right to the General Assembly for issuing a resolution for establishing Special Criminal Courts on the crimes for which the UN Security Council fails to hold them accountable after taking a vote and getting the support of more than half of the members of the General Assembly.

ii) The development of a new paragraph in the UN Charter to consider any providing of help to secure impunity for major international crimes as a threat to international peace and security, in order to prevent domestic legislation that protects state terrorism or major crimes against one of its communities.

13. 4. Policy of Prevent Genocide

Polish jurist Raphael Lemkin, credited with coining the term "genocide" (he first formally used it in his 1944 work Axis Rule in Occupied Europe), and mounted a life-long campaign to have it legally considered an international crime. Many of his recommendations are found in the language of the final UN Genocide Convention. The UN Convention on the Prevention and Punishment of the Crime of Genocide defines this term as "acts committed with the intent to destroy, in whole or in part, a national, ethnical, racial or religious group." Such acts include systematically killing members of a group and creating conditions that would lead to its destruction, such as forced starvation policies.

The difficulty of determining the responsibility has also hampered effective action, especially when it comes to genocide. According to Ernesto Verdeja, an assistant professor at the University of Notre Dame: "Different communities and different interlocutors are using the same term for slightly different purposes". Verdeja added that the concept of intent, which distinguishes genocide from other mass atrocity crimes, needs revisiting. We need to move away from a situation where "one has to prove that the perpetrator had not only knowledge that his or her policies and actions would lead to the destruction of the group, but also specifically intended that the group be destroyed," because this is almost impossible while a conflict is taking place. "Normally, you don't see a case where you have the perpetrator saying, 'We intentionally aim to destroy this group" he pointed out.

In fact, the word genocide has spread recently in the context of the crisis in the Central African Republic and is being used by France, the United States, and the United Nations, in the context of an imminent risk, with little or no discussion of the defining characteristic of intent.

During three months (April - July) of 1994 five hundred to eight hundred people were the victims of sectarian violence in Rwanda, and two million people were displaced and fled to neighbouring countries. With the collapse of the legitimate institutions and governance there was widespread suffering and mass displacement of the population. All of these cases require a range of responses from the international community, including intensive diplomatic efforts to resolve the conflict, and disciplinary procedures of the United Nations, and the provision of humanitarian bilateral and multilateral assistance by public and private entities. The international response to the crime of genocide in Rwanda can be divided into the following stages:

1. The international community's responses to the civil war and the civil violence that preceded the crisis of April–July 1994;

2. The early warning information available to the international community about a likely genocide and reactions to such warnings;

3. The international responses to the genocide that started after the 6 April 1994 shooting down of President Habyarimana's plane;

4. The international humanitarian assistance to the survivors inside Rwanda and to the huge refugee communities in neighbouring countries;

[360]

5. The international assistance for repatriation and rehabilitation of refugees and displaced persons, and to recovery and reconstruction of the Rwandese government and society after the upheaval [539].

The Rwanda crisis is replete with instances of violation of international law by some member states as well as derelictions of responsibility of others to champion action directed at violators. The types of international law that were violated fall into three broad categories:

- First and foremost is The Convention on the Prevention and Punishment of the Crime of Genocide, adopted by the General Assembly on 9 December 1948. The perpetrators of genocide in Rwanda clearly stand guilty of violating the Convention. The rest of the international community violated the spirit if not the letter of Article VIII of the Convention, which states that "Any contracting Party may call upon the competent organs of the United Nations to take such action under the Charter of the United Nations as they consider appropriate for the prevention and suppression of acts of genocide or any of the other acts enumerated in Article III". ?

- Second is International Humanitarian Law, in particular, the Geneva Conventions of 1949 and their additional Protocols of 1977. Member states have an obligation to disseminate knowledge of international humanitarian law as widely as possible and to adopt any national measures and enact any legislation to provide for effective implementation of international humanitarian law. [539]

- Third are international norms, particularly well–developed in African regional international law, regarding the rights of refugees to repatriate and stability of relations among states. Member states must take invasions across borders seriously, initially at sub-regional and regional levels, to defuse and contain the resulting conflict. The international community must also support states most directly concerned to ensure that refugees are not left in limbo, but within a reasonable time obtain secure membership in a state. Had effective and prompt action successfully addressed these issues involving Rwanda and Uganda in the 1980s and in 1990, the tragedies of the ensuing years could have been averted.

[361]

The editors of the book "Responding to Genocide: The Politics of International Action", Adam Lupel and Ernesto Verdeja, argue that a lack of political will and an overly stringent definition of genocide are major challenges to preventing, intervening and stopping mass atrocities and genocide. "International responses, time and again, we found, come up against the problems of political will and political division as the principal problems to timely, effective action," Lupel, senior fellow at the International Peace Institute, said at a recent event in London. "You see this in cases of Bosnia, Rwanda, Darfur and, currently, Syria". During the 1994 Rwanda genocide, some of the reluctance to commit peacekeepers can be traced back to the deaths of 18 US soldiers in Somalia in 1993. [540,542].

Kofi Annan, then director of UN Peacekeeping, notes in his 2012 book Interventions: A Life in War and Peace, that while there were requests for a bigger contingent in Rwanda, "in the post-Somalia international climate, there was no appetite in the international community for taking even the slightest risks with the lives of peacekeepers, certainly not in the United States."
But four mechanisms - creating common interest, generating incentives, using responsible leadership and furthering international norms - can lead to conditions for consistent political will to tackle these crimes, Lupel argues: 1. Creating common interest; 2. Generating incentives; 3. Using responsible leadership; and 4. Furthering international norms.

"We can make the moral claim as much as we want, but the truth is that states tend to act when it is in their national interest," he said. Therefore, focusing on these common interests is likely to be more effective. "Mass violence against civilians causes refugee problems; it can cross international borders, fuel regional instability and damage transnational economies," Lupel noted. "It is not something that can be contained in one country." It "can undermine the whole international system of collective security by calling into question the ability of the UN Security Council to live up to its responsibility as the authority [tasked] by law with the maintenance of international peace and security," he said. [540].

13. 5. Promoting Global Standards through Civil Society

While the international laws compelling states to intervene in mass atrocities have not been applied consistently or regularly, they nonetheless are crucial in preventing mass crimes. Iavor Rangelov a research fellow at London School of Economics, said "These rules and tools are extremely important because they do shape the terms of the debate and also the range of options which are considered appropriate and legitimate in the face of any particular crisis," [540]. For example, there is broad agreement on the content and substance of the 2005 Responsibility to Protect (R2P) norm, but it is weakened by serious division over how to apply its provisions, particularly the elements about the use of force. [541].

Rangelov believes that if civil society is used to push for the creation of new norms, it can help generate the political will needed to limit mass atrocities. He said people need to think of civil society "less as a whistleblower in a particular crisis and more as an agent of normative change in relation to genocide and other large-scale human rights violations.". Indeed, civil society individuals have at different points in history, been indispensable to the furthering of laws on mass crimes. In lobbying governments to intervene in individual crises, civil society campaigns are likely to fall short. This, Rangelov argues, is because transnational civil society is not a single, uniform entity but is fraught with division, contradiction and contestation. "Very much like political actors, they are also competing," he noted. [540].

Ademola Abass, head of the Peace and Security Programme at the United Nations University on Comparative Regional Integration Studies (UNU-CRIS) said that such tinkering with burdens of proof is both unnecessary and dangerous because the Convention authorizes intervention based on suspicion of genocide and ensures that there are genuine reasons for the violation of sovereignty. Abass pointed out that "not every killing in a war front automatically qualifies as mass atrocities in international law." There is a risk if the goal posts of the Genocide Convention were widened that actors could respond to public pressure and "simply jump on the bandwagon without doing their homework," he said. While Verdeja added "It shouldn't be only a focus on the immediate factors that trigger genocide, war crimes, crimes against humanity, ethnic cleansing - the mass atrocities - but it should be about deep structural and material conditions," Verdeja added. "Otherwise we would end up basically trying to put out fires once the fire has already started." [542].

[363]

13. 6. The International Role Of Human Rights Activists. Fallujah As Example

1. The Justice For Fallujah campaign - Italy: After a long period of starting there to explain away what happened in Fallujah, we managed to launch the idea of justice for Fallujah international campaign in cooperation with the Italian organization Bridge To ... (Un Ponte Per or UPP). This campaign includes the collection of signatures from various Italian community people in order to put pressure on the Commission on Human Rights in the Council of Representatives and Italian government in order to provide assistance to Fallujah. The city is suffering because of what has happened from the effects of disastrous destruction during the two battles of 2004 and use of prohibited weapons that resulted in daily disaster including deformed children and serious cancerous diseases among different age groups. The Italian organization UPP had a significant role in assisting Iraqi people during the economic embargo against Iraq and brought humanitarian aid. I have been involved with them in the local and international activities inside and out of Italy to promote the facts of the situation in Iraq under Western occupation. In addition to informing Italian people about the need to withdraw their troops from Iraq this activities helped somehow in the advent of a Roman Prodi government, which has made this Just demand, which was one of the slogans during Prodi's election campaign in Italy.

As a result of continuous efforts, it was decided to launch the international campaign first by a meeting which started with members of the Human Rights Commission of the Italian Senate, and then went to one of the major halls in the University of Rome to hold a press conference and a seminar open to college students to explain all the effects of what happened in Fallujah on the health environmental, political, and legal levels. It was planned that we should invite representatives of the international press agencies to join the press conference with me in the seminar as well as the president of the Italian organization (UPP) Ms. Martina as well as one of the Italian judges from the Constitutional Court (Mr. Francesco Gallo), and also Mr. Francesco Martona from *Sinistra Ecologia Liberta* party. a representative of one of the left-wing parties supporting the case of Fallujah

But political interference prevented the implementation of the action plan and changed its goals in the following way: 1. There was an apology by the parliamentary committee about their meeting with organizers of the campaign after they asked to postpone the meeting three times previously!!, 2. The organizers changed the agreement and did not invite the international press as scheduled and limited it to some of the local press, 3. The Italian organizers delayed the start and then they sent a parliamentary group to Baghdad to warn them about this campaign which would cause may problems to the new government there. As a consequence the deputies in former PM Ayad Allawi's group started to request parliament to consider the first battle of Fallujah as a war crime and to provide financial compensation in accordance with the Iraqi constitution for the victims of the mass graves. But without they mentioning that the first battle also was genocide by the occupation forces. The parliamentary group of ex PM Maliki a greed to this request with one condition, that Ayad Allawi should be tried because he gave order to the occupation forces for the crimes of the second battle of Fallujah. Therafter the parlimentary group around Allawi threatened the Maliki group that if they open cases against Allawi then the latter will also open genocide cases against Maliki for crimes such as killing all the Zarqa village civilians in 2006. In the midst of this political wrangling parliament lost its way and could not arrive at a new decision to compensate the victims and the campaign could not be launched. [14A]

The international political intervention to thwart the efforts of organizations and human rights defenders reveal the importance of the Fallujah case at the international level, and the fear to open its files internationally because of the involvement of some international and local sides. This event gives an incentive for activists and defenders of the victims to continue to deliver the case to the international level, which parallels the magnitude of the crimes committed there.

GLI EFFETTI DELLE GUERRE UMANITARIE
IL CASO DI FALLUJA

lunedì 18 aprile - ore 18
Dipartimento di Studi Orientali
Via Principe Amedeo 182/b - Aula 9

Introduce
Laura Guazzone
Università di Roma La Sapienza

Modera
Francesco Martone
Forum Politiche Internazionali, Sinistra Ecologia e Libertà

Per un giusto processo internazionale sui crimini contro l'umanità commessi a Falluja
Muhammed Tareq, Rete di Monitoraggio dei Diritti Umani in Iraq – MHRI

Crimini di guerra e crimini contro l'umanità a Falluja
Domenico Gallo, Giuristi Democratici

Le conseguenze della guerra sulla salute e sull'ambiente
Loretta Mussi, Presidente di Un ponte per...

SAPIENZA
Università di Roma

Sguardo sul Medio Oriente

Informazioni:
info@unponteper.it
tel 0644702906
www.unponteper.it

[366]

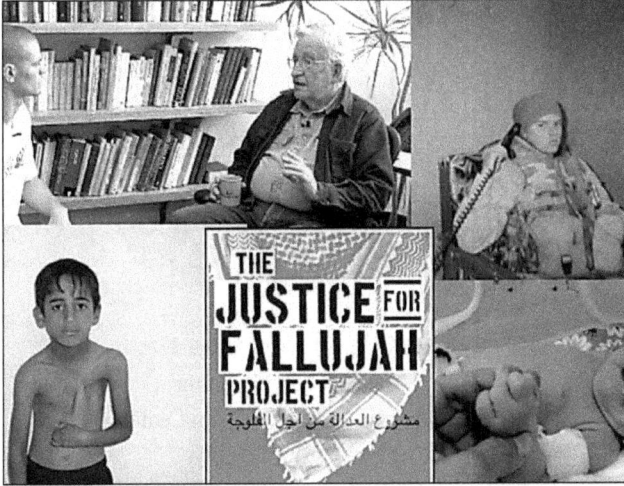

2. Annual Conference of the anniversary of Fallujah' battles - America: One of the repercussions of the Fallujah case is how it affected one of the Marines who fought in the second battle in Fallujah, Ross Caputi. He was suffering from memories of the mass killings, which he saw during the battle. After an internal conflict and remorse, Ross decided eventually to help the victims of Fallujah. In the first contact between us, he showed the potential to help the people of Fallujah through the publishing of his testimony. Actually I inserted his testimony in the comprehensive report submitted to the meetings of the Human Rights Council of UN in Geneva on September 2010, as well as sending him the testimony copy to keep a file of the case we have. Over time, the idea began to grow with Ross to decide during his time as a student at the College of Law in one of an American university to starts a popular campaign to publicize what happened in Fallujah. And here he decided to launch his project about remember Fallujah (The Remember Fallujah Project). He held the first public conference in November 2010 and continued in 2011 and at the same time of November on the anniversary of the second battle of Fallujah in which he participated as a Marine soldier. (http://thefallujahproject.org/home/).

17 NOVEMBER 2011

FALLUJAH: A LOST GENERATION?
FREE SCREENING
PLUS
Q & A WITH DIRECTOR, FEURAT ALANI

6PM Thursday November 17th
1st Fl. Screening Room
King Juan Carlos I of Spain Center
New York University
53 Washington Square South
(betw. Thompson and Sullivan)
Please bring a photo ID

After two brutal sieges in 2004, Fallujah, Iraq is plagued with cancer, birth defects and death.
REMEMBER FALLUJAH WEEK
www.thefallujahproject.org

THE
JUSTICE FOR FALLUJAH
PROJECT

CO-SPONSORED BY NYU ENGLISH
MODERN WORKING GROUP

NYUMODERNWORKINGGROUP.WORDPRESS.COM

Then Ross' project produced a short documentary film about some of the crimes committed by US forces in Fallujah, Iraq entitled "Fear Not the Path of Truth" which won the Changemaker Award at the Traverse City Film Festival.

Predestination dictated that I and Ross should be together at different times. The first time, we were enemies during the second battle in Fallujah (November 2004), and Ross was fighting with US Marines while I was with Iraqi journalist Ali Fadhil, on the outskirts of Fallujah, trying to gather information from eyewitnesses and civilians fleeing the city. While the second time was after Ross decided to champion the cause of Fallujah and help victims who have been affected because of the aggressive policy of his country. Ross is an example of the triumph of the path of goodness in the end our humanity as human beings returns and we turn away from the lies and criminal political agendas.

Photos of Ross

3. Brussels Tribunal - Belgium. Its founder was Dirk Adriaensens from Belgium and supported by European groups opposed to Western occupation of Iraq. This tribunal established many people's courts led by international judges to issue popular and judicial informal decisions criminalizing the crimes of the occupation and lifting these decisions to international organizations as one of the means of putting pressure and exposing these violations. (http://brussellstribunal.org/)

4. Also a number of European and international organizations, set up campaigns and awareness activities and campaigns to create awareness in the media and political parties in their respective countries, in order to mobilise international public opinion about the fact that there are violations in Iraq.

13. 7. Conclusion

All the previous facts listed confirm the crime of a war of aggression against an independent country Iraq by the United States and Britain. Now new documents confirm there was prior intent to commit this crime a year prior to

[369]

the war through what it called by the Western press "a deal in blood". This agreement between PMs of UK Tony Blair and former president of US George W. Bush revealed the shocking fact that they failed to disclose the real aim of the war. Blair was talking about diplomatic solutions one year before war, while the latter documents revealed that he gave the promises to Bush Jr. in a timely manner to support the war. He told voters: 'We're not proposing military action' – in direct contrast to what the secret email now reveals [690].

It is true that there are other governments helping in this crime for their own interests. For this reason, I want to ask the people whose governments supported this invasion (in direct or indirect ways) to consider the following questions:

1. Do you believe now, after destroying Iraq and all its institutions, that there is an imbalance in your political and judicial system, which allowed this crime to be committed and allowed the peace and security in the Middle East to be threatened??
2. Will you try now to repair this flaw that allowed impunity and will encourage future politicians to repeat these tragedies? Or will you close your eyes and accept the myths and lies?
3. Do you think that progress or well-being can be based on damage and harm to others and is it possible to build a good life governed by bad politicians?
4. Will you help us in publishing facts and opening the eyes of your people, in order to bring criminals who give us this suffering till now to justice??
5. Will you re-elect those who marketed lies, and has feared facing the victims and who prevent the delivery of justice to them?? Or will you re-elect those who gloss over the crimes, who do not respect the right of peoples to self-determination, as well as not respecting your right to know the truth?

God created the human and gave him the honor to be his successor on our earth and to make it like paradise for humanity as an application of the principles of good and love that God wants. Are we acting like this for the good or are we with the bad side?

I would like to finish this book by reminding you of some of the most important lessons learned from the crime of occupation or invasion of Iraq, as provided in assessments by some international actors after 13 years of this war of aggression:

[370]

- **Koffi Annan**: The second and much more proximate cause of the instability we are witnessing today was the invasion of Iraq in 2003. I spoke against it at the time, and I am afraid my concerns have proved well-founded. The folly of that fateful decision was compounded by post-invasion decisions. The wholesale disbandment of the security forces, among other measures, poured hundreds of thousands of trained and disgruntled soldiers and policemen onto the streets. Subsequently, the rush to create an instant democracy, as if elections sufficed in the absence of democratic tradition or sound institutions, ushered in corrupt, repressive and sectarian governance [683].

- **Noam Chomsky**: The Iraq war is the first in imperial history that was massively protested even before it was officially launched. That did not prevent the aggression, but there is good reason to believe that it limited the means of destruction employed by the invaders, who never even contemplated what was done to South Vietnam by Kennedy and Johnson in the absence of organized protest. Had protests continued at a high level the effects would have been greater. We should also learn the importance of encouraging public discussion and understanding of the causes of the continued resort to violence and subversion to control much of the world, to nip future exercises in the bud, and to change the structures of power in our own societies that engender such crimes. [407].

- **Hans Blix** (Chief Inspector of weapons of mass destruction in Iraq before the occupation): Iraq War was a terrible mistake and violation of U.N. charter. The war aimed to make Iraq a model democracy based on law, but it replaced tyranny with anarchy and led America to practices that violated the laws of war. The most important lesson of the Iraq War, I think, has been that overconfidence in military power has been replaced by an understanding that there are severe limitations on what can be achieved by military means. Intervening swiftly with arms and crippling strikes might be easy for a great power, but achieving desired political aims is another matter and exiting may be hard -- the phrase "If you break it, you own it" comes to mind. Vietnam, Afghanistan, and Iraq have been long and costly engagements with very mixed results. Since then prudence has held the U.S. back in the case of Libya and so far in Syria. Another important lesson is that today armed international interventions are likely to be condemned by much of the world unless they are clearly in self-defense or have been authorized by the Security Council. Iraq was neither. Unless we remember this going forward, I fear there is nothing stopping this kind of tragedy from being repeated [405].

- **William Blum:** From 1945 to 2003, the United States attempted to overthrow more than 40 foreign government, and tried to crush more than 30 national popular movement against dictatorships and bombed 25 countries approximately, which resulted in the end of several lives of millions of people and exposed more millions to despair and suffering life [426].

- **Sebastian Fischer** (Correspondent for Der Spiegel, Germany): The most important ten lessons can be learned after ten years of the invasion of Iraq are: 1) it was a "dumb war", 2) The war damaged America's image, 3) The war discredited the CIA, 4) The war divided the nation, 5) The war fueled Obama's victory in the presidential election, 6) It was the war of the neocons, 7) The neocons learned little from the war, 8) The Iraq War paved the way to the shadow war, 9) The war shaped America's stance toward the Arab Spring, 10) The effects of the war pervade the country [521].

- **Bruce Riedel**, Formerly a senior CIA official and presidential adviser. There is a national consensus (that) it was a dumb war, (that) the costs were enormous and that it was one of the country's biggest mistakes." The shadow of this war "weighs heavily" on the stances that America is now assuming toward Iran, Syria and Libya. The war's legacy "will haunt America for years." [521].

- **Jeremy Corbyn** (The presidential of the British Labour Party): 'Let us make it clear that Labour will never make the same mistake again, will never flout the United Nations and international law [685].

- **Dr. Rahim al-Kubaisi:** Crimes against humanity, no statute of limitations, all crimes and violations must continue to be documented in an attempt to bring claims in US courts [A7].

Finally, our Holy land is the land of the prophets, and of it came out the first civilized law teaching the human meaning of the rules of civil life. From Baghdad, came out the finest science and inventions that has been credited later in the progress of the industrial revolution in Europe. All the occupying

[372]

powers have passed on and ended with defeat on our land, and our free people will not renounce its rights against criminals.

What we presented in this book of facts is a drop in the ocean to confirm to the world that the stubbornness and patience of freemen in Iraq is greater than what you read in the history books. Our goal is justice and from God we keep our strength and perseverance in the pursuit of it.

REFERENCES

1. National Ground Intelligence Center (NGIC). SECRET//NOFORN//20310306
2. Jernej Letnar (Researcher, Institute for European Constitutional, International Law and Law of Economics). Corporate human rights abuses require stronger international and domestic legal regimes. Tuesday, May12, 2009. JURIST
3. Byron L. Warnken. Blackwater, Garrity, and Immunity: What Does It All Mean? (JURIST Guest Columnist from the University of Baltimore School of Law). November 12, 2007
4. Special Interview with victim' family, as well to vedio interview.
5. Samira Alaani, Muhammed Tafash, Christopher Busby, Malak Hamdan, Eleonore Blaurock-Busch. 2011. Uranium and other contaminants in hair from the parents of children with congenital anomalies in Fallujah, Iraq. Conflict and Health, 5:15. http://www.conflictandhealth.com/content/5/1/15
6. Samira Alaani, Mozhgan Savabieasfahani, Mohammad Tafash, Paola Manduca. 2011. Four Polygamous Families with Congenital Birth Defects from Fallujah, Iraq. Int. J. Environ. Res. Public Health, 8: 89-96. http://www.ncbi.nlm.nih.gov/pmc/articles/PMC3037062/
7. Chris Busby, Malak Hamdan, and Entesar Ariabi. 2010. Cancer, Infant Mortality and Birth Sex-Ratio in Fallujah, Iraq 2005–2009. Int. J. Environ. Res. Public Health, 7, 2828-2837. http://www.mdpi.com/1660-4601/7/7/2828
8. Depleted Uranium Crisis, Muslim Peacemaker Teams: December 2007. www.mpt-iraq.org.
9. International Court of Justice, Reports of Judgments, Advisory Opinions and orders, Legality of the threat or use of nuclear weapons, Advisory Opinion of 8 July 1996.
10. Commission on Health and the Environment, Al-Anbar Provincial Council,Western Iraq Center for Congenital anomalies Registry and Surveillance at Maternity and Children Teaching Hospital in Ramadi, 20/03/2011.
11. Knut Dörmann and Laurent Colassis. 2004. International Humanitarian Law in the Iraq Conflict. In : The German Yearbook of International Law, 47 : 293–342. Duncker & Humblot, Berlin.
12. CPA, Regulation 1 of 16 May 2003, Sect. 1 para 1. The letter from the Permanent Representatives of the UK and the US to the UN, addressed to the President of the Security Council, 8 May 2003, UN Doc. S/2003/538.
13. Donald Rumsfeld, Known and Unknown: A memoir. 2011. Pengui n Group (USA) Inc., 375 Hudson Street, New York, New York 10014, U.S.A.
14. Reynolds, Paul. "White Phosphorus: Weapon on the Edge." BBC News. 16 Nov. 2005. 16 Feb. 2008 .http://news.bbc.co.uk/2/hi/americas/4442988.stm.
15. Popham, Peter. "US Intelligence Classified White Phosphorus as 'Chemical Weapon'" The Independent. 23 .Nov. 2005. 17 Feb. 2008
16. DARRIN MORTENSON. Violence subsides for Marines in Fallujah. Sunday, April 10, 2004. North County Times (Escondido, California).
17. Toshikuni DOI.Fallujah, April 2004. http://www.doi-toshikuni.net/falluja2004/e/index.html
18. Francis A. Boyle. Obliterating Fallujah. A War Crime in Real Time.November, 15,2004

19. Lieutenant Colonel John P. Piedmont. 2010. DET ONE. U.S. MARINE CORPS, U.S. SPECIAL OPERATIONS, COMMAND DETACHMENT, 2003-2006, U.S. Marines in the Global War on Terrorism. History Division, United States Marine Corps, Washington, D.C.

20. From Wikipedia, Force Reconnaissance Company, http://en.wikipedia.org/wiki/1st_Force_Reconnaissance_Company (last visited 22 November 2012)

21. From Wikipedia, Marine Corps Special Operations Command Detachment One http://en.wikipedia.org/wiki/MCSOCOM_Detachment_One .(last visited 22 November 2012)

22. "Marines Suspend Fallujah Offensive," Marine Corps News, 13 April 2004.

23. Military Operations On Urban Terrain, Marine Corps Warfighting Publication (MCWP) 3-35.3 (Quantico, VA: April 1998), pp. 1-16.

24. CNN, "General: It's 'Fun to Shoot Some People,'" CNN.com, February 4, 2005. See: www.cnn.com/2005/US/02/03/general.shoot .(last visited 22 November 2012)

25. Constable, Pamela (2004) 'A Wrong Turn, Chaos and a Rescue', Washington Post, 15 April .

26. Walking Ghosts: Murder and Guerrilla Politics in Colombia .Steven Dudley 2003 .Taylor & Francis, Inc.

27. "Second Day of Fighting at al-Falluja," P. Mitchell Prothero, UPI, April 30, 2003. http://www.upi.com/Business_News/Security-Industry/2003/04/30/Second-day-of-fighting-at-al-Falluja/UPI-97261051713329/ .(last visited 22 November 2012)

28. Rogue State .A Guide to the Worlds Only Superpower. William Blum. 2002. Zed Books – London.

29. From (William Blum. Rogue State, 2002) (New York Times, March 9, 1982, p.l; March 23, 1982, p.l and 14; The Guardian (London) November 3, 1983, March 29, 1984; Washington Post, May 30,1986)

30. Who Won the Battle of Fallujah? Mr. Keiler, a former captain in the Army's Judge-Advocate General Corps The Naval Institute: Proceedings 2004. (MCWP 3-35.3, pp. 1-17 and 2-7)

31. Jackie Spinner, "Artillerymen Clear Path for the Infantry," The Washington Post, 11 November 2004; Associated Press, 8 November 2004.(from 30).

32. E.g., Mackubin Thomas Owens, "Two, Three, Many Fallujahs," The Weekly Standard, 6 December 2004; Jack Kelly, "U.S. Tactic, Training Kept Casualties Down in Fallujah" (citing author and retired Army LCol Ralph Peters), The Pittsburg Post-Gazette, 21 November 2004.(from 30).

33. A Matter of Principle .Humanitarian Arguments for War in Iraq. Thomas Cushman. University of California Press .2005

34. THE FIGHT FOR FALLUJAH - TF 2-2 IN FSE AAR: Indirect Fires in the Battle of Fallujah By Captain James T. Cobb, First Lieutenant Christopher A. LaCour and Sergeant First Class William H. Hight" Field Artillery.March-April 2005.

35. Interview with His Royal Highness Prince Hassan of Jordan. ICRC. Volume 89 Number 868 December 2007

36. WISER IN BATTLE,A Soldier's Story. LT. GEN. RICARDO S. SANCHEZ with Donald T. Phillips HarperCollins Publishers Inc.2008

37. Intelligence Cooperation and the War on Terror. Anglo-American security relations after 9/11 .Adam D.M. Svendsen. Taylor & Francis e-Library.2010

38. Failure to protect. A case for the prohibition of cluster munitions. Dr. Brian Rappert and Richard Moyes. Landmine Action. 2006.

39. Ministry of Defence. Operations in Iraq: First Reflections, July 2003. (From 38)

40. Figures given in Human Rights Watch, Off Target, New York: Human Rights Watch, 2003. (From 38).

41. The European Parliament. European Parliament resolution on cluster bombs. B5-0765, 0775, 0782 and 0789/2001 2001. Further in this resolution, the parliament called for additional examination of the ERW effects of submunitions and for steps to improve their reliability. In 19 January 2006, the European Parliament agreed a resolution on disability and development that stated it: 'Supports fully, given the effects especially on child victims, the global battle to eradicate anti-personnel landmines and other related controversial weapon systems such as cluster submunitions. (From 38).

42. Testimonies of Crimes Against. Humanity in Fallujah. Towards a Fair International Criminal Trial. CCERF and MHRI. 15th Session of the Human Rights Council. United Nations, Geneva, 13 September - 1 October 2010

43. The United Nations Commission on Human Rights: SubCommission on Prevention of Discrimination and Protection of Minorities, Resolution. International Peace and Security as an Essential Condition for the Enjoyment of Human Rights, Above All, the Right to Life. 1996/16, 29 August 1996.

44. Cluster Bombs over Kosovo. Thomas Michael McDonnell. Arizona Law Review 2002 44(1): 34. (From 38).

45. 2008 Convention on Cluster Munitions. International Committee of the Red Cross. Geneva, Switzerland. www.icrc.org

46. Human rights in Iraq's transition: the search for inclusiveness: John P. Pace. International Review of the Red Cross. Volume 90 Number 869 March 2008. http://www.icrc.org/eng/assets/files/other/irrc-869_pace.pdf. (last visited 22 November 2012)

47. Security Council document, UN Doc. S/2003/538

48. Iraq war illegal, says Annan. BBC News, 16 September 2004, available at: http://news.bbc.co.uk/2/hi/middle_east/3661134.stm.(last visited 22 November 2012)

49. Dispatches: Iraq's missing billions, produced by Guardian Films for Channel4.

50. 3rd Armored Cavalr Regiment "Brave Rifles".Global Security org. www.globalsecurit.org/militar/agenc/arm/3acr.htm

51. The Old Ironsides Report. Wednesday, January 14, 2004.

52. The Fallujah Model. Rebecca Grant. Air Force Magazine. February 2005.

53. "Rebuilding Iraq: Preliminary Observations on Challenges in Transferring Security Responsibilities to Iraqi Military and Police," Statement of Joseph A. Christoff, Director of International Affairs and Trade at the Government Accountability Office, submitted to the US House of Representatives Subcommittee on National Security, Emerging Threats, and International Relations on March 14, 2005, pg. 11.

54. Fire Bombs in Iraq: Napalm By Any Other Name. Alison Klevnäs, Per Klevnäs, Rachel Laurence, Mike Lewis and Jonathan Stevenson. Iraq Analysis Group, March 2005. www.iraqanalysis.org , see also: Martin Savidge, "Protecting Iraq's Oil Supply" CNN (March 22, 2003).

55. A New Military Strategic Communications System. A Monograph by MAJ Robert F. Baldwin U.S. Army. School of Advanced Military Studies United States Army Command and General Staff College Fort Leavenworth, Kansas. 2006-2007

56. A war crime or an act of war?? Stephen C. Pelletiere. The New York Times. Januar 31, 2003. http://www.informationclearinghouse.info/article1148.htm

57. Endless Torment: The 1991 Uprising in Iraq And Its Aftermath, Human Rights Watch, June 1992.(From 54).

58. Dead bodies are everywhere", *Sydney Morning Herald*, 22 March 2003. http://www.smh.com.au/articles/2003/03/21/1047749944836.html

59. 'Sailors Offload Ammo For U.S. Marines', Defend America, US Dept. of Defense, 2 February 2003.(From 54).

60. Post - Transition violence in Iraq (2004 - 2005): The military perspective of an insider. Colonel Jabbar Naeemah Karam and Dr. Sherifa Zuhur. U.S. Army War College, Carlisle Barracks, Pennsylvania,2006.

61. Beyond Close Air Support. Forging a new air-ground partnership. Bruce R. Pirnie, Alan Vick, Adam Grissom, Karl P. Mueller, David T. Orletsky. RAND Corportation. 2005.

62. Eyewitness to War, Volume I. The US Army in Operation AL FAJR: An Oral History. 2006. Kendall D. Gott, John McCool, Matt M. Matthews, Colette Kiszka, Jennifer Vedder, Jennifer Lindsey, Christopher K. Ives. Army Combined Arms Center, Combat Studies Institute, Fort Leavenworth, KS, 66027

63. Defensive operations in the media battlespace: Operation Iraqi Freedom. 2006, Master degree of Military Art and Science Strategy. Patrick Proctor. US Army Command and General Staff College,1 Reynolds Ave., Fort Leavenworth,KS,66027-1352

64. 10th Annual Command and Control Research and Technology Symposium: The Future of C2. Multinational Force and Host-Nation Administration in Wartime Iraq, an Inter-ministerial Approach. Topic: C4ISR/C2 Architecture: A Case Study of Iraqi-MNF Interoperability in Iraq, 2005. Colonel John R. Ballard. Washington D.C.

65. Shared Awareness in Urban Operations.2005. Lt Col Carl H. Block, Joint Military Operations Department.Naval War College .Newport, RI 02841-1207.

66. AGM-65 Maverick, GlobalSecurity.org. http://www.globalsecurity.org/military/systems/munitions/agm-65.htm

67. Battle for Fallujah, our warfighters towered in maturity and guts . Brief comments on air power in urban airfare . April 28, 2005. Talking Proud, Service & Sacrifice. http://www.talkingproud.us/Military/FallujahIntro/FallujahAirPower/FallujahAirPower.html

68. What is the role of the joint forces air component commander as airspace control authority during stability operations?? 2007. Major Francisco M. Gallei, Master' Thesis of Military Art and Science. U.S. Army Command and General Staff College. Ft. Leavenworth, KS 66027.

69. All-out assault on Fallujah. Toby Harnden (Fallujah) and Alec Russell (Washington). 9 November 2004. The Telegraph. http://www.telegraph.co.uk/news/worldnews/middleeast/iraq/1476220/All-out-assault-on-Fallujah.html

70. America's mercenaries: war by proxy. 2006. Major Kevin Collins, USMC. Master' Thesis of Military Art and Science. U.S. Army Command and General Staff College. Ft. Leavenworth, KS 66027.

71. Q&A: Private Military Contractors and the Law. Human Rights Watch, October 21, 2004.

72. Haditha and Fallujah cases on the 2008 docket. Monday, December 31, 2007. Mark Walker. North County Times.

73. A look at some of the incidents involving private contractors firing on Iraqi civilians. The Associated Press. September 17, 2007.

74. Investigating Officer's Report. 2 October 2007. From: Lt. Col. Paul J. Ware (WESTPAC, Navy-Marine Corps Trial Judiciary), To: Commander James N. Mattis (US Marine Corps Forces, Central Command). Name of accused: SSGT Frank D. Wuterich (3rd BN, 1st Marines), Date of Charges: 21 Dec. 2006.

75. The Promise of Precision. 2010. Colonel Michael McCarthy. Colonel Phillip Tissue. U.S. Army War College, Carlisle Barracks, PA 17013-5050

76. Report: Blackwater skimped on security before Fallujah ambush. 27 September 2007. Joseph Neff and Jay Price. McClatchy Newspapers. McClatchy Washington Bureau.

77. Military contractors: How earlier integration in the planning process would achieve greater mission success. 3 May, 2010. Lieutenant Commander Kevin B. O'Brien (US Navy). A paper submitted to the Faculty of the Naval War College in partial satisfaction of the requirements of the Department of Joint Military Operations.

78. The future use of corporate warriors with the U.S. Armed Forces: legal, policy, and practical considerations and concerns. 1 July 2009. David A. Wallace. Defense A. R. Journal.

79. International Humanitarian Law and the Regulation of Private Military Companies. February 8-9 2007. Lindsey Cameron, University of Geneva, Switzerland. Conference «Non-State Actors as Standard Setters: The Erosion of the Public-Private Divide», Switzerland. ((*These two examples have been officially recognized by the former Special Rapporteur on the Right of Peoples to SelfDetermination and its application to peoples under colonial or alien domination or foreign occupation:Use of mercenaries as a means of violating human rights and impeding the exercise of the right of peoples to self-determination, Mrs. Shaista Shameem,in her annual report. See UN Doc. E/CN.4/2005/14 at para. 50 (2004). Both the Fay Report and Taguba Report recommended referral to the US Department of Justice for potential criminal prosecution for these events. See Major General George R. Fay, A15-6 Investigation of the Abu Ghraib Detention Facility and 205 6 Military Intelligence Brigade 130-34, August 23 2004, online: http://www4.army.mil/ocpa/reports/ar156/index.html (last visited 20 September 2006). The report enumerates incidents in which private contractors were allegedly involved, including (but not limited to) rape (Incident 22), use of "unauthorized stress positions" (Incident 24) use of dogs to aggress detainees (Incidents 25 and 30), humiliation (Incident 33). See also pp. 131 – 134 for MG Fay's findings regarding the civilians (private military company employees) he investigated. See also http://www.dod.mil/pubs/foi/detainees/taguba/ (last visited 20 September 2006) for the report of Major General Antonio M. Taguba, Article 15-6 Investigation of the 800 Military Police Brigade [hereafter Taguba Report].*))

80. International assistance for victims of use of nuclear, radiological, biological and chemical weapons: time for a reality check? June 2009. Robin Coupland and Dominique Loye. International Review of Red Cross, Volume 91 Number 874.

81. Britain's secret army in Iraq: Thousands of armed security men who answer to nobody. Robert Fisk and Severin Carrell. Independent (UK), 28 March 2004

82. European Security and Private Military Companies: The Prospects for Privatized 'Battlegroups. James K. Wither. The Quarterly Journal 107– 126 (Summer 2005), especially at p. 122.

83. International Convention against the Recruitment, Use, Financing and Training of Mercenaries, 4 December 1989, UNGA Res A/RES/44/34, entered into force 20 October 2001 [http://www.un.org/documents/ga/res/44/a44r034.htm].

84. Convention for the Elimination of Mercenarism in Africa, Organisation of African Unity, Libreville, 3 July 1977, CM/817 (XXXIX), Annex II, Rev. 3 (entered into force 22 April 1985). http://www.africa-union.org/official_documents/Treaties_%20Conventions_%20Protocols/Convention_on_Mercenaries.pdf].

85. Private Security Contractors in Iraq: Background, Legal Status, and Other Issues. August 25, 2008. Jennifer K. Elsea, Moshe Schwartz, Kennon H. Nakamura, Congressional Research Service. The Library of Congress. CRS Report RL32419.

86. U.S. Treatment of Prisoners in Iraq: Selected Legal Issues. May 19, 2005. Jennifer K. Elsea. Congressional Research Service. The Library of Congress. CRS Report RL32395. http://www.au.af.mil/au/awc/awcgate/crs/rl32395.pdf

87. Operation Iraqi Freedom: Strategies, Approaches, Results, and Issues for Congress. April 2, 2009. Catherine Dale. CRS Report for Congress. Congressional Research Service. RL34387.
http://www.fas.org/sgp/crs/mideast/RL34387.pdf

88. No True Glory: A Frontline Account of the Battle for Fallujah. 2005. Bing West, New York: Bantam Books.

89. US used white phosphorus in Iraq. Wednesday, 16 November 2005, 11:25 GMT. BBC NEWS. http://news.bbc.co.uk/2/hi/middle_east/4440664.stm , see also: Pentagon Used White Phosphorous in Iraq. ROBERT BURNS. The Associated Press, Wednesday, November 16, 2005. http://www.washingtonpost.com/wp-dyn/content/article/2005/11/16/AR2005111600374.html

90. Fallujah..The Hidden Massacre. 8 November 2005. documentary film by Sigfrido Ranucci and Maruizio Torrealta, Video documentary shows actual chemical bombing on civilians in Fallujah with testimony of interviewed U.S. soldiers - English, Italian and Arabic, Rai News 24. http://video.google.com/videoplay?docid=8905191678365185391

91. British play lays bare U.S. offensive in Falluja. May 4, 2007. Luke Baker. Reuters

92. U.S. jury acquits ex-Marine in Iraqi killings. Aug 28, 2008. Syantani Chatterjee, Steve Gorman, and Eric Beech. Reuters. http://www.reuters.com/article/2008/08/28/us-usa-iraq-marines-idUSN2836306920080828.

93. US intelligence classified white phosphorus as 'chemical weapon'. Peter Popham and Anne Penketh. Wednesday 23 November, 2005. The Independent.
http://www.gulflink.osd.mil/declassdocs/dia/19950901/950901_22431050_91r.html

94. Mark 77 bomb. From Wikipedia. http://en.wikipedia.org/wiki/Mark_77_bomb (last visited....); and MK77 750lb Napalm, From GlobalSecurity.org.
http://www.globalsecurity.org/military/systems/munitions/mk77.htm

95. Officials confirm dropping firebombs on Iraqi troops, Results are 'remarkably similar' to using napalm, By James W. Crawley, *San Diego Union-Tribune*, August 05, 2003.
http://www.globalsecurity.org/org/news/2003/030805-firebombs01.htm ,
http://legacy.utsandiego.com/news/military/20030805-9999_1n5bomb.html

96. Protocol on Prohibitions or Restrictions on the Use of Incendiary Weapons (Protocol III). Geneva, 10 October 1980. ICRC.
http://www.icrc.org/ihl.nsf/NORM/3AB9E36D37F951ECC1257558003E6A3F?OpenDocument

97. UK Ministry of Defence letter to Alice Mahon (document).
http://www.rainews24.rai.it/ran24/inchiesta/foto/documento_ministero.jpg

98. British Parliament, Written Answers to Questions. *Defense Minister Adam Ingram Denies US Use of Firebombs* (January 11, 2005) Written answers to questions. 11 Jan 2005 : Column 373W. parliament.uk.
http://www.publications.parliament.uk/pa/cm200405/cmhansrd/vo050111/text/50111w01.htm#50111w01.html_sbhd3 , see also: US Lied to Britain Over Use of Napalm in Iraq War. Colin Brown. Friday, June 17, 2005. *Independent/UK*.
http://www.commondreams.org/headlines05/0617-01.htm

99. US hunts Fallujah rebels, blocks aid. November 15, 2004. *AFP/Reuters/ABC News*.

100. IRAQ: US launches mass slaughter in Fallujah. Doug Lorimer. *Green Left weekly.* Wednesday, November 17, 2004. http://www.greenleft.org.au/node/31035
101. US strikes raze Falluja hospital. Saturday, 6 November, 2004. *BBC News.* http://news.bbc.co.uk/2/hi/3988433.stm
102. CNN. http://www.chris-floyd.com/fallujah/warcrime/
103. U.S. Begins Main Assault in Falluja, Setting Off Street Fighting. Dexter Filkins and James Glanz. November 9, 2004. The New York Times.
104. Urban Warfare Deals Harsh Challenge to Troops. Dexter Filkins. November 9, 2004. The New York Times.
105. American Forces Reach Center of Falluja Amid Fierce Fighting. Dexter Filkins and James Glanz. November 9, 2004. The New York Times.
106. Falluja Assault Roils Iraqi Politics. Edward Wong. November 9, 2004. The New York Times.
107. Falluja Offensive Is Seen as a Test of U.S. Pledge to Pacify Iraq in Time for January Elections. Douglas Jehl and Thom Shanker. November 9, 2004. The New York Times. http://www.nytimes.com/2004/11/09/politics/09attack.html?_r=0
108. Blair Defends the Us Onslaught in Fallujah. Evening Standard - London. April 28, 2004
109. Us Bombards Fallujah in Bigley Revenge Raid ; Massive Air Assault On Rebel Stronghold Targets Iraq's Most Wanted Man. Evening Standard - London. October 15, 2004. http://www.chris-floyd.com/fallujah/flv/player.php?url=WARCRIME3.flv
110. Dead-Check in Falluja. Evan Wright. Tuesday, Nov 16 2004. Village Voice.
111. Contractors in the 21st Century "Combat Zone. Richard L. Dunn, (Edgewater, MD: University of Maryland School of Public Policy, Center for Public Policy and Private Enterprise, 2005), 22.
112. U.S.C., Chapter I, Subchapter M, rev. Apr. 1, 1992. From reference 70
113. U.S. Congress, Public Law 108-75, Ronald W. Reagan Defines Authorization Act for 2005, Sect. 1206, 28 October 2004. From reference 70
114. War, Profits, and the Vacuum of Law: Privatized Military Firms and International Law. P. W. Singer. *Columbia Journal of Transnational Law* 42 (2004): 52.
115. Military Operations: Contractors Provide Vital Services to Deployed Forces but Are Not Adequately Addressed in DoD Plans, Government Accountability Office, GAO-03-695, 5 June 2003. http://www.gao.gov/products/GAO-03-695
116. REBUILDING IRAQ. Actions Needed to Improve Use of Private Security Providers. Government Accountability Office, GAO-05-737. July 2005. http://www.gao.gov/assets/250/247252.pdf
117. Gulf war illnesses, DOD's Conclusions about U.S. Troops' Exposure Cannot Be Adequately Supported. Government Accountability Office. GAO-04-159, Jun 1, 2004. http://www.gao.gov/products/GAO-04-159
118. Stabilizing Iraq. An Assessment of the Security Situation. Government Accountability Office. GAO-06-1094T. September 11, 2006. http://www.gao.gov/assets/120/114761.pdf
119. Military operations in urban areas. Alexandre Vautravers. International Review of the Red Cross. Volume 92 Number 878 June 2010. http://www.icrc.org/eng/resources/international-review/review-878-urban-violence/review-878-all.pdf
120. Training and Doctrine Command (TRADOC), Department of the Army, Field Manual FM90-10, Military Operations on Urbanized Terrain (MOUT), Washington, DC, 1979.
121. Private security firms involved in new forms of mercenary activity. UN Working Group. Press Release.UN news center. November 6, 2007. http://www.un.org/apps/news/story.asp?NewsID=24556&Cr=mercenaries#

122.   Mission to Iraq. Report of the Working Group on the use of mercenaries as a means of violating human rights and impeding the exercise of the right of peoples to self-determination. Human Rights Council Eighteenth session, Agenda item 3.12 August 2011. A/HRC/18/32/Add.4.

123.   Use of mercenaries as a means of violating human rights and impeding the exercise of the right of peoples to self-determination. General Assembly. Sixty-first session. 13 September 2006. A/61/341.

124.   Private Contractors and Torture at Abu Ghraib, Iraq. Pratap Chatterjee and A.C. Thompson. May 7th, 2004. CorpWatch. http://www.corpwatch.org/article.php?id=10828&printsafe=1

125.   Shadow Force, Private Security Contractors in Iraq. 2009. David Isenberg. Praeger Security International, 88 Post Road West, Westport, CT 06881, US.

126.   Broader legal definition of 'Mercenary' needed, say Special Rapporteur. As Third committee continues discussion of self-determination, Racism. Press Release. Fifty-eighth General Assembly, Third Committee, 24th Meeting, 27 October, 2003. GA/SHC/3752. http://www.un.org/News/Press/docs/2003/gashc3752.doc.htm

127.   Pentagon reverses position and admits U.S. troops used white phosphours against Iraqis in Fallujah. A daily independent global news hour with Amy Goodman & Juan Gonzalez. November 17, 2005. http://www.democracynow.org/2005/11/17/pentagon_reverses_position_and_admits_u A Debate: Did the U.S. Military Attack Iraqi Civilians With White Phosphorus Bombs in Violation of the Geneva Conventions? NOVEMBER 8, 2005. http://www.democracynow.org/2005/11/8/a_debate_did_the_u_s

128.   White Phosphorus. U.S. Department of Health and Human Services, Public Health Service, *Agency for Toxic Substances and Disease Registry*(ATSDR). CAS≠ 7723-14-0. September 1997. http://www.atsdr.cdc.gov/toxfaqs/tfacts103.pdf

129.   Contractors outnumber troops in Iraq. T. Christian Miller. July 04, 2007. Los Angeles Times. http://articles.latimes.com/print/**2007**/jul/**04**/nation/na-private**4**

130.   By the number, Finding of the detainee abuse and accountability project. Volume 18, No 2(G). April 2006. Human Rights Watch, Human Rights First, and Hhuman Rights and Global Justice.

131.   See e.g. U.S. Const. amend. V, VIII; 18 U.S.C. § 2340 (2006) (defining torture as an offense against U.S. law); Dep't of the Army, Field Manual 34-52 Intelligence Interrogation (1992) (describing the legal standards governing interrogations by U.S. military personnel, and unequivocally stating that binding international treaties and U.S. policy "expressly prohibit acts of violence or intimidation, including physical or mental torture, threats, insults, or exposure to inhumane treatment as a means of or aid to interrogation") ["Army Field Manual"].

132.   Independent Panel to Review DoD Detention Operations, Final Report of the Independent Panel to Review DoD Operations (August, 2004), *available at* http://news.findlaw.com/wp/docs/dod/abughraibrpt.pdf

133.   Major General Antonio Taguba, Preface to Broken Laws, Broken Lives: Medical Evidence of Torture by the U.S. (2008), *available at* http://brokenlives.info/?page_id=23

134.   Report of the International Committee of the Red Cross (ICRC) on the Treatment by the Coalition Forces of Prisoners of War and Other Protected Persons by the Geneva Conventions in Iraq During Arrest, Internment and Interrogation (2004), *available at* http://www.globalsecurity.org/military/library/report/2004/icrc_report_iraq_feb2004.pdf

135. S. Armed Services Comm., 110th Cong., Inquiry into Treatment of Detainees (Comm. Print Nov. 20, 2008) *available at* http://armed-services.senate.gov/Publications/Detainee%20Report%20Final_April%2022%202009.pdf

136. Major General George R. Fay, AR 15-6 Investigation of the Abu Ghraib Detention Facility and 205th Military Intelligence Brigade 10, 70 (2004) ["Fay-Jones Report"], *available at* http://news.findlaw.com/hdocs/docs/dod/fay82504rpt.pdf.

137. Memorandum from Gen. Ricardo Sanchez for Commander of U.S. Central Command on CJTF-7 Interrogation and Counter-Resistance Policy (Sep. 14, 2003), *available at* http://www.gwu.edu/~nsarchiv/torturingdemocracy/documents/20030914.pdf.

138. Lynndie England Convicted in Abu Gharaib Trial, Associated Press, Sept. 26, 2005, *available at* http://www.usatoday.com/news/nation/2005-09-26-england_x.htm.

139. Abu Gharib Officer Cleared of Detainee Abuse. Josh White. Wash. Post, Aug. 29, 2007, *available at* http://www.washingtonpost.com/wp-dyn/content/article/2007/08/28/AR2007082800359.html

140. American Civil Liberties Union, *Lack of United States Accountability and Remedy for Torture and Abuse in the Name of Counter-Terrorism*, Statement submitted to the OSCE Human Dimension Implementation Meeting, HDIM.NGO/0198/11 (Sept. 28, 2011), *available at* http://www.osce.org/odihr/83140

141. President Bush declared: "The United States also remains steadfastly committed to upholding the Geneva Conventions, which have been the bedrock of protection in armed conflict for more than 50 years. These Conventions provide important protections designed to reduce human suffering in armed conflict. We expect other nations to treat our service members and civilians in accordance with the Geneva Conventions. Our Armed Forces are committed to complying with them and to holding accountable those in our military who do not." President George W. Bush, President's Statement on the U.N. International Day in Support of Victims of Torture (June 26, 2004), *available at* http://www.whitehouse.gov/news/releases/2004/06/20040626-19.html.

142. Comm. Against Torture, Conclusions and Recommendations of the Committee Against Torture: United States of America, 36th Sess., May 1-19, 2006, U.N. Doc. CAT/C/USA/CO/2 (July 25, 2006) *available at* http://www.unhchr.ch/tbs/doc.nsf/0/e2d4f5b2dccc0a4cc12571ee00290ce0/$FILE/G064 3225.pdf. The CAT issued the findings in this subsection in response to the U.S. 2006 report. The United States, which is expected to report to CAT every four years, has not yet submitted the report that was due in 2010. *See* Office of the U.N. High Comm'r for Human Rights, http://www2.ohchr.org/english/bodies/cat/reports2011.htm (last visited Nov. 7, 2011). The Committee has expressed concerns similar to the ones noted above in relation to the pending U.S. report. *See* U.N. Comm. against Torture, List of issues prior to the submission of the fifth periodic report of United States of America, 43rd Sess., Nov. 2-20, 2009, U.N. Doc. CAT/C/USA/Q/5 (Jan. 20, 2010), *available at* http://www2.ohchr.org/english/bodies/cat/docs/CAT.C.USA.Q.5.pdf.

143. Contemporary State Terrorism, Theory and Practice. 2010. Richard Jackson ,Eamon Murphy ,Scott Poynting. Routledge, UK, US, Canada.

144. S. Armed Services Comm., Inquiry into the Treatment of Detainees in U.S. Custody 132 (2008) available at http://armed-services.senate.gov/Publications/Detainee%20Report%20Final_April%2022%202009.pdf

145. United Nations, Universal Declaration of Human Rights, Dec. 10, 1948, art. 5, G.A. Res 217A (III), U.N. Doc. A/810 (1948)

146.   Review of DoD-Directed Investigations of Detainee Abuse (U). Office of the inspector general of the department of defense. Deputy Inspector General for Intelligence. Report No. 06-INTEL-10, August 25, 2006.

147.   Statement Submitted to the OSCE Human Dimension Implementation Meeting by the American Civil Liberties Union on: Lack of United States Accountability and Remedy for Torture and Abuse in the Name of Counter-Terrorism. September 28, 2011. Warsaw, Poland.

148.   The private military industry and Iraq: What have we learned and where to text? Peter W. Singer. Geneva, November 2004. Geneva Centre for the Democratic Control of Armed Forces (DCAF). DCAF-hosted 2004 International Security Forum (ISF), held from 4 to 6 October 2004 in Montreux, Switzerland.

149.   'New Role for Mercenaries' (2001), Sebastian Mallaby, Los Angeles Times, *accessed at* http://www.globalpolicy.org/security/peacekpg/reform/2001/mercenaries.htm

150.   'Should We Privatize the Peacekeeping?'(2000), Jonah Schulhofer-Wohl, Washington Post, *accessed at* http://www.globalpolicy.org/security/peacekpg/general/private.htm

151.   US general defends phosphorus use. 30 November, 2005. BBC

152.   "Civilians working for U.S. in Iraq making a bundle: Army Corps is paying Charlotte contractor millions to dispose of munitions,". Kevin Begos and Phoebe Zerwick. Winston-Salem Journal, February 13, 2005.
       http://www.corpwatch.org/article.php?id=11843&printsafe=1

153.   Eyewitness: Ghost city calls for help. Saturday, 13 November, 2004. BBC.

154.   Eyewitness: Smoke and corpses. Thursday, 11 November, 2004. BBC.

155.   In March 2003, President George W. Bush reported to Congress the determination that was required by P.L. 107-243 regarding his exercise of authority for military operations against Iraq. House Document 108-50. March 19, 2003. A report in connection with Presidential Determination under Public Law 107-243. Communication from the President of the United States transmitting a report consistent with Section 3(b) of the Authorization for Use of Military Force Against Iraq Resolution of 2002.

156.   Congressional Oversight and Related Issues Concerning the Prospective Security Agreement Between the United States and Iraq. Michael John Garcia, R. Chuck Mason, and Jennifer K. Elsea. Legislative Attorneys, American Law Division. February 26, 2008. Congressional Research Services. Order Code RL34362.

157.   "The Warrior Class": The Blackwater Videos. April 3, 2012. Harper's Magazine.
       http://harpers.org/archive/2012/04/hbc-90008515

158.   "Privatized Military History, Peter Singer," Chap. 2 in Corporate Warriors:The Rise of the Privatized Military Industry (Ithaca, NY: Cornell University Press, 2003). (From 125)

159.   "What's in a Name? The Importance of Language for the Peace and Stability Operations Industry, J. J. Messner," Journal of International Peace Operations 2, no. 6 (May 1, 2007): 24. (From 125)

160.   "Swift road for U.S. citizen soldiers already fighting in Iraq, Edward Wong," New York Times, August 9, 2005. (From 125)

161.   "Civilian Contractors under Military Law, Marc Lindemann," Parameters (Autumn 2007): 84.http://www.carlisle.army.mil/usawc/parameters/Articles/07autumn/lindeman.pdf

162.   "Census counts 100,000 contractors in Iraq, Renae Merle," Washington Post, December 5, 2006, p. D1. (From 125)

163.   "Contractors outnumber troops in Iraq, T. Christian Miller," Los Angeles Times, July 4, 2007. (From 125)

164.   Contractor crackdown - Civilian contract employees can now be prosecuted under the UCMJ. William Matthews. Armed Forces Journal. Thursday, February 1, 2007.

165.   Farewell To Falluja. Fadhil Badrani. 25 November, 2004. BBC World Service in Arabic.
166.   Falluja's Health Damage. Miles Schuman. December 13, 2004. The Nation Magazine
       http://www.thenation.com/docprint.mhtml?i=20041213&s=schuman
167.   Angeli Distratti.....Falluja: Aprendo le porte dell' inferno. Gianluca Arcopinto,2007.
       http://www.youtube.com/watch?v=mlOvPZs459A
       http://www.youtube.com/watch?v=NjWkbnl6oik&feature=relmfu
       http://www.youtube.com/watch?v=sjJmFwejl4o&feature=related
       http://www.unponteper.it/english/pagina.php?doc=closed
168.   Italy plans Iraq troop pull-out. 15 March, 2005. BBC.
       http://news.bbc.co.uk/2/hi/europe/4352259.stm
169.   Multi - National Force – Iraq. Wikipedia, the free encyclopedia.
       http://en.wikipedia.org/wiki/Multi-National_Force_%E2%80%93_Iraq
170.   Top UN envoy Sergio Vieira de Mello killed in terrorist blast in Baghdad. 19 August 2003.
       UN News Centre.
       http://www.un.org/apps/news/story.asp?NewsID=8023&Cr=iraq&Cr1#
171.   Peter W. Singer. Counterproductive - Private militar contractors harm the
       counterinsurgenc effort in Iraq. Thursday, November 1, 2007, Armed Forces Journal.
172.   Iraq: U.S. Should Investigate al-Falluja, June 16, 2003, Huam Rights Watch.
       www.hrw.org/en/news/2003/06/16/iraq-us-should-investigate-al-falluja
173.   Ali Fadhil, City of ghosts, The Guardian, Tuesday 11 January 2005.
       http://www.guardian.co.uk/world/2005/jan/11/iraq.features11
       http://www.youtube.com/watch?v=11mdMeg8FHc (Channel 4 film)
174.   The Riz Kahn Show. Fallujah's Birth Defects. Al-Jazeera
       http://www.youtube.com/watch?v=pq1MTxXmELg&feature=player_embedded
175.   Iraq in Prospective, An Orientation Guide. Technology Integration Division, Defence
       Language Institute Foreigner Language Center. 2011.
176.   Kenneth Katzman, "Iraq: Post-Saddam Governance and Security," Congressional Research
       Service, 8 June 2009, 3, http://fpc.state.gov/documents/organization/125947.pdf
177.   Jordi Palou-Loverdos, Leticia Armendáriz. The Privatization of Warfare, Violence and
       Private Military & Security Companies: A factual and legal approach to human rights
       abuses by PMSC in Iraq. 2011. The Nova-Institute for Active Non-violance. Creative
       Common, Spain.
178.   Joint Staff (1991). "Possible Use of Phosphorus Chemical Weapons by Iraq in Kurdish
       Areas along the Iraqi-Turkish-Iranian Borders; and Current Situation of Kurdish Resistance
       and Refugees.
       http://www.gulflink.osd.mil/declassdocs/dia/19950901/950901_22431050_91r.html ,
       http://www.gulflink.osd.mil/declassdocs/dia/19950901/
179.   US Army Command and General Staff College. "FM 100-3 US Army Battle Book.
       http://www.fas.org/man/dod-101/army/docs/st100-3/index.htm
180.   The CIA's Intervention in Afghanistan, Interview with Zbigniew Brze zinski, President
       Jimmy Carter's National Security Advise r. Le Nouvel Observateur, Paris, 15-21 January
       1998. www.globalresearch.ca/articles/BRZ110A.html
       http://www.dailypaul.com/283303/hillary-admits-us-funded-beginnings-of-global-
       terrorism&sss=1
181.   Reforming Iraq's Security Sector. Chapter 3, from book 'Developing Iraq's security sector.
       The coalition provisional authority's experience'. Eds. Andrew Rathmell, Olga Oliker,
       Terrence K. Kelly, David Brannan, and Keith Crane. 2005. RAND Corporation. US.

182. Oxford Research Group, 'Learning From Fallujah: Lessons identified'. www.oxfordresearchgroup.org.uk/publications/books/fallujah.pdf (accessed February 5, 2006).

183. SECRET//REL TO USA, MCFI, REO AL HILLAH, IRAQ, 2006 JUNE 8. wlstorage.net/file/us-iraq-intsum-2006-06-08.txt

184. Media is the battlefield, Tactics, Techniques, and Procedures. Center for Army Lessons Learned (CALL). Call Newsletter, No. 07-04 , October 2006. http://call.army.mil

185. Marine Corps Midrange Threat Estimate: 2005-2015. Department of Defense Intelligence Document (Global Threats Branch, Production and Analysis Company, Marine Corps Intelligence Activity). Information Cutoff Date: 1 July 2005.

186. Memorandum for 332 EAMDS/SGPB, Subject: Purn Pit Health Hazards. Department of the air force, 332D AIR EXPEDITIONARY WING, BALAD AIR BASE, IRAQ. 20 Dec. 2006.

187. FM 31-20-3, Foreign internal defense tactics, techniques, and procedures for special forces. Field Manual No. 31-20-3, Department of the Army, Washington, DC, 20 September 1994.

188. Memorandum for record, Subject: TIF SOP 701, Detainee death and reporting procedures. Headquarters, 705th Military Police Battalion (I/R), Camp Bucca, Iraq, APO AE 09375, 19 Feb. 2007

189. Draft Bayji white phosporus incident investigation report, Coalition munitions clearance (CMC), NAD BAYJI, IRAQ. 9 MARCH 2008.

190. Official page of Birth Defects in FGH on facebook. 10th Feb. 2012. http://www.facebook.com/media/set/?set=a.209837189113814.43125.179904905440376&type=1

191. CVW-17 Supports Coalition Ground Forces in Fallujah, Story Number: NNS041122-01, 11/22/2004. By Journalist 1st Class (SW) Christopher E. Tucker, USS John F. Kennedy Public Affairs.NAVY. MIL. www.navy.mil

192. Birth defects in Gaza: Prevalence, type, familiarity and correlation with environmental factors. Awny Naim, Hedaya Al Dalies, Mohammed El Balawi, Eman Salem, Kholud Al Meziny, Raneem Al Shawwa, Roberto Minutolo, and Paola Manduca. 2012. International journal of environmental research and public health. 9

193. Fighting for Fallujah, A New Dawn for Iraq. John R. Ballard. 2006. Praeger Security International. Westport, Connecticut US, London, UK.

194. Operation AL FAJR: A Study in Army and Marine Corps Joint Operations .Matt. M. Matthews. 2006. Combat Studies Institute Press Fort Leavenworth, Kansas. http://usacac.army.mil/cac2/cgsc/carl/download/csipubs/matthews_fajr.pdf http://www.dtic.mil/cgi-bin/GetTRDoc?AD=ADA454930

195. Law of land warfare. Chapter 5, Section III. http://www.fas.org/man/dod-101/army/docs/st100-3/c5/5sect3.htm

196. Eg Mike Marqusee, 10th November 2005. A name that lives in infamy. The Guardian.

197. Rory McCarthy and Peter Beaumont, 14th November 2004. Civilian cost of battle for Falluja emerges. The Observer. United Nations, Emergency Working Group -- Falluja Crisis , "Update Note," (November 11, 2004 and November 13, 2004)

198. F J "Bing" West, July 2005. The Fall of Fallujah. Marine Corps Gazette.

199. John F Sattler, Daniel H Wilson, July 2005. Operation AL FAJR: The Battle of Fallujah-Part II. Marine Corps Gazette.

200. A War Crime Within a War Crime Within a War Crime. George Monbiot. Published in the Guardian 22nd November 2005

201. A 'Crushing' Victory: Fuel-Air Explosives and Grozny 2000 .Lester W. Grau and Timothy Smith, August 2000. The Marine Corps Gazette.

202. There was no doubt that the horrific nature of the attack required a response. CNN noted, "Paul Bremer, the U.S. civilian administrator in Iraq, promised that the deaths of the contractors would 'not go unpunished.'" "Marines, Iraqis Join Forces to Shut Down Fallujah," Cable News Network, April 5, 2004, at www.cnn.com/2004/WORLD/meast/04/05/iraq.main/

203. U.S. Marine Corps Operations in Iraq, 2003–2006. Lieutenant Colonel Kenneth W. Estes , U.S. Marine Corps (Retired).History Division, United States Marine Corps ,Quantico, Virginia. 2009.

204. Shake & Bake: Dual-Use Chemicals, Contexts, and the Illegality of American White Phosphorus Attacks in Iraq.2007. JOSEPH D. TESSIER. PIERCE LAW REVIEW. Vol. 6, No. 2. 323-363

205. http://www.icrc.org/ara/war-and-law/treaties-customary-law/geneva-conventions/overview-geneva-conventions.htm

206. Fallujah children's genetic damage. Simpson J. BBC. http://www.bbc.co.uk/news/world-middle-east-10721562.

207. Reducing the need for surgeons by reducing pollution-derived workload: Is there a role for surgeons?2011. Jamsheer J. Talati, Riaz Agha, Maliha Agha, Richard David Rosin. International Journal of Surgery. 9: 444-450.

208. The United States Military, Chapter 4. From: Risks of Hazardous Wastes. (Eds.) Paul E. Rosenfeld, and Lydia G.H. Feng. 2011. Pp. 49-56. http://www.sciencedirect.com/science/article/pii/B9781437778427000040

209. Pentagon Weighs Cleanups as It Plans Iraq Exit. DINA FINE MARON . The New York Times. Retrieved January 13, 2010. From 208. (http://www.nytimes.com/gwire/2010/01/13/13greenwire-pentagon-weighs-cleanups-as-it-plans-iraq-exit-21915.html?sq=&st=&%2359;1=&%2359;toxic%20waste%20iraq=&equals=&scp=&%2359;cse=&pagewanted=print)

210. Oliver August. America leaves Iraq a toxic legacy of dumped hazardous materials (2010). The Times. Retrieved June 14. From 208.

211. The Iraq war and the International law, Phil Shiner and Andrew Williams. 2008. Hart Publishing, c/o International Specialized Book Services. Portland, Oregon, USA.

212. Operation Phantom Fury – Beginning of the End of al Qaeda in Iraq. Richard S. Lowry. In War College. Armchair General Magazine. 11/4/2009. http://www.armchairgeneral.com/operation-phantom-fury-beginning-of-the-end-of-al-qaeda-in-iraq.htm

213. Anniversary of the Battle for Fallujah. Richard S. Lowry. Armchair General Magazine. November 22, 2010. http://www.armchairgeneral.com/anniversary-of-the-battle-for-fallujah.htm

214. Current US Military Operations and Implications for Military Surgical Training. Joshua A Tyler, Kevin S Clive, Christopher E White, Alec C Beekley, Lorne H Blackbourne, (J. American College of Surgeons ,2010; 211:658–662.

215. U.S. Military Fatalities in Iraq: A Perspective on Year 5. Glenn Kutler. 2008. Foreign Policy Research Institute.

216. Blackwaters for the Blue Waters: The Promise of Private Naval Companies. Claude Berube. 2007. Foreign Policy Research Institute.

217. The Privatization of Security: Lessons from Iraq. Deborah D. Avant. 2006. Foreign Policy Research Institute.

218. Responsibility for protection of medical workers and facilities in armed conflict. Leonard S Rubenstein, Melanie D Bittle. Lancet 2010; 375: 329–40.

[387]

219. Military action in an urban area: the humanitarian consequences of Operation Phantom Fury in Fallujah, Iraq. Cedric Turlan and Kasra Mofarah, NCCI. Humanitarian Exchange. Number 35 • November 2006.http://www.odihpn.org/humanitarian-exchange-magazine/issue-35/military-action-in-an-urban-area-the-humanitarian-consequences-of-operation-phantom-fury-in-fallujah-iraq

220. Promoting aggression and violence at Abu Ghraib: The U.S. military's transformation of ordinary people into torturers. (2009) Adam Lankford. Aggression and Violent Behavior. 14 388–395.

221. CNN, "Blackwater impeded probe into contractors deaths", 27 September 2007. http://articles.cnn.com/2007-09-27/politics/iraq.blackwater_1_erik-princeblackwater-usa-blackwater-team?_s=PM:POLITICS

222. Marines Jail Contractors in Iraq. Tension and Confusion Grow Amid the "Fog of War". David Phinney. Crop Watch. June 7th, 2005. http://www.corpwatch.org/article.php?id=12349&printsafe=1

223. New York Times, "The Other Army", by Daniel Bergner, 14 August 2005. http://www.nytimes.com/2005/08/14/magazine/14PRIVATI.html?sq=zapata%20iraq&st=cse&scp=4&pagewanted=all

224. Military and Paramilitary Activities in and against Nicaragua (Nicaragua v. United States of America). International Court of Justice. Summary of the Summary of the Judgment of 27 June 1986. http://www.icj-cij.org/docket/index.php?sum=367&code=nus&p1=3&p2=3&case=70&k=66&p3=5

225. US Lied to Britain Over Use of Napalm in Iraq War. Colin Brown. Frida, June 17, 2005. Independent/UK.

226. IRAQ: US used chemical weapons in Fallujah assault. Doug Lorimer. Wednesday, March 16, 2005. Green Left Weekly. http://www.greenleft.org.au/node/32947

227. Arms controversy in Iraq. Mark Sappenfield. November 18, 2005. The Christian Science Monitor. http://www.csmonitor.com/2005/1118/p03s01-usmi.html

228. Heavy casualty list ignored as Powell sticks to the same old story. September 15, 2003. Europe Intelligence Wire. Irish Independent. http://www.accessmylibrary.com/coms2/summary_0286-24446445_ITM

229. Iraq, Bureau of Democracy, Human Rights , and Labor. 2005. March 8, 2006. US Department of State. www.state.gov /j/drl/rls/hrrpt/2005/61689.htm

230. The Battle for Fallujah, Al Fajr—the Myth-buster. Dr. William Knarr and Major Robert Castro, US Marine Corps, with Ms. Dianne Fuller. September 2009. Institute For Defense Analysis (IDA). http://www.dtic.mil/dtic/tr/fulltext/u2/a530831.pdf

231. Operation AL FAJR: The Battle of Fallujah-Part II. John F Sattler; Daniel H Wilson. Marine Corps Gazette; Jul 2005; 89, 7; ProQuest Direct Complete pg. 12. http://www.scribd.com/doc/55754179/Operation-AL-FAJR-The-Battle-for-Fallujah-Part-II

232. National Public Radio, —Spread of Iraqi Insurgency Feared in Arab World, Morning Edition, 3 April 2006. From 230.

233. Additionally, comments such as Bring 'em on' by President Bush on 3 July 2003 (Sean Loughlin, 'Bush Warns Militants Who Attack US Troops in Iraq,' CNN.Com/Inside Politics, CNN Washington Bureau, 3 July 2003), and Secretary of Defense Rumsfeld's characterization of the insurgents as deadenders, foreign terrorists and criminal gangs'(Douglas Jehl with David E. Sanger, Iraqis' Bitterness Is Called Bigger Threat Than Terror,' New York Times, 17 September 2003)(*Time Magazine* 11/16/2003) underestimated the power, depth, breadth, and momentum of the building insurgency. From 230.

234. LtCol Dave Bellon, S-2, RCT-1 in 2004, was with TF Scorpion in 2003. He remarked that activities in Fallujah were influencing TF Scorpion's area south of Fallujah in 2003. During one of the raids, TF Scorpion captured a number of insurgents. During tactical questioning he over-heard a flurry of comments about Fallujah. I said to one of the interrogators, Ask them about Fallujah.' And I remember this guy, the look on his face. I'll never forget it. He said, Ah, Fallujah, that's where the real men are.' It just struck me; it's like talking to a guy in Single A baseball and asking him about the big leagues, and him saying 'That's where I am going to go.' And I remember thinking, We are going to fight it out in Fallujah.' LtCol Dave Bellon, telephone interview with Bill Knarr , 4 November 2005. *Morning Edition*, Spread of Iraqi Insurgency'; the broadcast attributed the birth of the insurgency to that event based on interviews with Iraqis. From 230

235. THE STRATEGIC CORPORAL AND THE EMERGING BATTLEFIELD ,THE NEXUS BETWEEN THE USMC'S THREE BLOCK WAR CONCEPT AND NETWORK CENTRIC WARFARE. Master of Arts in Law and Diplomacy Thesis Submitted by James E. Szepesy. March 2005. http://fletcher.tufts.edu

236. Occupying iraq , a history of the coalition provisional authority. James Dobbins , Seth G. Jones , BenJamin Runkle , Siddharth Mohandas. Sponsored by the Carnegie Corporation of New York. International Security and Defense Policy Center of the RAND, National Security Research Division (NSRD). 2009.

237. 'Lessons So Far: Hard Truths to Learn from Israel's War on Hezbollah, Ralph Peters,' *New York Post Online Edition*, 13 August 2006. From 230

238. Greg Lewis, Welsh Troops Face Fallujah Backlash, *Wales on Sunday*, 17 October 2004. http://www.thefreelibrary.com/WELSH+TROOPS+FACE+FALLUJAH+BACKLASH.-a0123320062

239. Incident Reports Fault Blackwater in Fallujah Ambush. Committee on Oversight and Government Reform. http://democrats.oversight.house.gov/index.php?option=com_content&view=article&id=2574%3Aincident-reports-fault-blackwater-in-fallujah-ambush&catid=43%3Ainvestigations&Itemid=1

240. Fourth of July speech – Written by LT Ellen Engleman Conners. http://www.navy.mil/navco/speeches/2004/4july04.txt

241. Historic Wartime Turnover By Navy Reserve Seabee Battalions In Iraq. 11/16/2004. Suzanne Speight and Michael D. Heckman, 1st Marine Engineer Force Public Affairs. Navy News Services. http://www.navy.mil/submit/display.asp?story_id=15940

242. NMCB 14 Sailors Killed in Iraq. 5/3/2004. Special release from the U.S. Department of Defense. Navy News Services. http://www.navy.mil/submit/display.asp?story_id=13122

243. Seabees Gather to Honor Fallen Comrades. 5/21/2004. Siegfried Bruner, Commander, 1st Naval Construction Division Public Affairs. Navy News Services. http://www.navy.mil/submit/display.asp?story_id=13437

244. Private Security Contractors at War, Ending the Culture of Impunity. 2008. Human Rights First. www.humanrightsfirst.org

245. US 'uses incendiary arms' in Iraq. Tuesday, 8 November 2005. BBC News. http://news.bbc.co.uk/2/hi/middle_east/4417024.stm

246. War Crimes Committed by the United States in Iraq and Mechanisms for Accountability. Consumers for Peace and Karen Parker. October 10, 2006.

247. Out of bounds? The approach of the Inter-American System for the promotion and protection of human rights to the extraterritorial application of human rights law. Christina M. Cerna. Center for Human Rights and Global Justice Working Paper, No. 6 2006. NYU School of Law ☒ New York, NY 10012

248. Shake & Bake: Dual-Use Chemicals, Contexts, and the Illegality of American White Phosphorus Attacks in Iraq. Joseph D. Tessier. *PIERCE LAW REVIEW,* Vol. 6, No. 2 . http://law.unh.edu/assets/images/uploads/publications/pierce-law-review-vol06-no2-tessier.pdf

249. Declaration Concerning Asphyxiating Gases, July 29, 1899, 32 Stat. 1779, 187 CONSOL. T.S. 453, available at http://hei.unige.ch/humanrts/instree/1899e.htm. From 248.

250. Protocol for the Prohibition of the Use in War of Asphyxiating, Poisonous, or Other Gases, and of Bacteriological Methods of Warfare, June 17, 1925, 26 U.S.T. 571, 14 I.L.M. 49. From 248.

251. Official Waffling on White Phosphorus Fuels Debate Abroad, Darrin Mortenson, N. COUNTY TIMES (Escondido, Cal.), Nov. 22, 2005, available at http://www.globalsecurity.org/org/news/2005/051122-phosphorus-debate.htm. From 248.

252. U.S. Is Slow to Respond to Phosphorus Charges . SCOTT SHANE. November 21, 2005. The New York Times. http://www.nytimes.com/2005/11/21/international/21phosphorus.html

253. The Use of White Phosphorus Munitions by U.S. Military Forces in Iraq. David P. Fidler. December 6, 2005. American Society of International Law. http://www.asil.org/insights051206.cfm

254. U.S. Department of State, Did the U.S. Use Illegal Weapons in Fallujah?, at http://www.globalsecurity.org/military/library/report/2005/050127-fallujah.htm.

255. Health Action in Crises (WHO/HAC). Highlight – No. 4: Monday, 12 April 2004. http://www.who.int/hac/about/donorinfo/12April2004_MondayHighlights.pdf

256. Health Action in Crises (WHO/HAC). Highlight – No. 37: Monday, 29 November 2004. http://www.who.int/hac/about/donorinfo/29November04_MondayHighlights.pdf

257. Health Action in Crises (WHO/HAC). Highlight – No. 41: Monday, 10 January 2005. http://www.who.int/hac/donorinfo/10January05_MondayHighlights.pdf

258. Phil Stewart, Burning Agent Used in Iraq, Says TV Report, I RISH TIMES (Dublin), Nov. 9, 2005, at 12.

259. U.S. Forces Used "Chemical Weapon" in Iraq, I NDEPENDENT (London), Nov. 16, 2005. In a press conference Brig. Gen. Rick Lynch, spokesman for U.S. forces in Baghdad, told reporters, "[w]e don't use munitions of any kind against innocent civilians. . . . In accordance with all established conventions, [white phosphorus] can be used against enemy combatants." John Daniszewski & Mark Mazzetti, White Phosphorus Use Ignites Debate: Critics Say the U.S. Killed Iraqi Civilians with the Incendiary Weapon. The Pentagon Denies It, L.A. TIMES, Nov. 28, 2005. From 248

260. Erin Emery, Coloradan: Incendiary Killed Civilians, DENVER POST, Nov. 18, 2005, at A1. The article further quotes Maj. Todd Vician, a Pentagon spokesman, as saying: "In Fallujah, the insurgents were in entrenched lines and small holes, and we could not get at them effectively with our munitions. So [white phosphorus shells] were used then to bring the insurgents out of those areas to . . . engage them better with the high-explosive munitions." From 248

261. Al Kamen, Chemical Reactions, W ASH. POST, Nov. 18, 2005, at A21. After the Pentagon's first retraction, the American Embassy in London directed "all questions on [white phosphorus]" to the Pentagon. Andrew Buncombe et al., Incendiary Weapons: The Big White Lie: U.S. Finally Admits Using White Phosphorus in Fallujah—and Beyond, B ELFAST TELEGRAPH, Nov. 17, 2005. On November 22, 2005, William Burns, U.S. Ambassador to Russia, commented: "On the question of [white] phosphorus, we have made clear publicly that we have not undertaken any actions that would violate international law,

and we have not undertaken any actions against civilians." Ambassador Burns' Interview with Gazeta.ru: William Burns, U.S. Ambassador to Russia, Nov. 22, 2005, http://moscow.usembassy.gov/bilateral/statement.php?record_id=23. From 248

262. U.S. Defends Use of White Phosphorus Against Iraq Insurgents, *AFX FIN. NEWS* (London), Nov. 16, 2005, http://www.globalsecurity.org/org/news/2005/051116-phosphorus-defense.htm From 248, see also: The fog of war: white phosphorus, Fallujah and some burning questions. Andrew Buncombe and Solomon Hughes. *Independent*.15 November 2005. http://www.nogw.com/download/2005_fog_of_war_wp.pdf

263. News Briefing with Secretary of Defense Donald H. Rumsfeld and Gen. Peter Pace (U.S. Dep't of Def. news transcript Nov. 29, 2005), available at http://www.defenselink.mil/transcripts/2005/tr20051129-secdef4361.html. From 248

264. Vince Crawly, Top Military Official Calls White Phosphorus "Legitimate Tool," INT'L INFO. PROGRAMS, Dec. 1, 2005, http://usinfo.state.gov/xarchives/display.html?p=washfile-english&y=2005&m=December&x=20051201140216mvyelwarc0.787594. From 248

265. Christopher L. Budihas, So, You're Going to Iraq? Company Commander Shares Successful Tactics, Techniques, I NFANTRY MAG., Sept. 1, 2004, at 23 ("When needed, they [white phosphorus illumination mortars] suppressed enemy personnel in the objective area, suppressed personnel attempting to escape, illuminated the battlefield, and marked targets for rotary-wing air-support. Due to the FOB [forward operating base] being located on the edge of a town, I would periodically (on average four times a week) use mortar illumination rounds as pseudo H&I [harassment and interdiction] fires. My intent was to not cause any unnecessary local national casualties, but I wanted them to know that we were still there and alert."). From 248

266. Paul Reynolds, White Phosphorus: Weapon on the Edge, BBC NEWS, Nov. 16, 2005, http://news.bbc.co.uk/2/hi/americas/4442988.stm. The American ambassador to Italy, Ronald P. Spogli, also denied that white phosphorus had been used as a weapon by the United States.

267. Kyle Rex Jacobson, Doing Business with the Devil: The Challenges of Prosecuting Corporate Officials Whose Business ransactions Facilitate War Crimes and Crimes Against Humanity, 56 A.F. L. REV. 167, 194 (2005). From 248.

268. U.S. ARMY, COMBINED ARMS OPERATIONS IN URBAN TERRAIN, FIELD MANUAL 3-06.11(2002), available at https://atiam.train.army.mil/soldierPortal/atia/adlsc/view/public/9629-1/fm/3-06.11/fm3_06x11.pdf. See also Jonathan P. Edwards, The Iraqi Oil "Weapon" in the 1991 Gulf War: A Law of Armed Conflict Analysis, 40 N AVAL L. REV. 105, 130 (1992) (concluding that the igniting of Kuwaiti oil fields constituted a violation of the law of war). From 248.

269. Convention on the Prohibition of the Development, Production, Stockpiling and Use of Chemical Weapons and on their Destruction, opened for signature Jan. 13, 1993, S. TREATY DOC. NO. 10321, 32 I.L.M. 800, available at http://www.opcw.org/docs/cwc_eng.pdf [hereinafter Chemical Weapons Convention]. The treaty entered into force for the United States and other original signers on April 25, 1997. Organization for the Prohibition of Chemical Weapons, Membership of the OPCW (2007), http://www.opcw.org/html/db/members_ratifyer.html [hereinafter OPCW Membership]. From 248.

270. Chemical Weapons Convention Implementation Act § 229 F(7)(C), 22 U.S.C. § 6701(8)(C). http://www.law.cornell.edu/uscode/text/18/229F From 248. http://www.law.cornell.edu/uscode/pdf/uscode18/lii_usc_TI_18_PA_I_CH_11B_SE_229F.pdf

271.   Colin Powell, U.S. Sec'y of State, Iraq Denial and Deception: Address Before the U.N. Sec. Council (Feb. 5, 2003), available at http://www.whitehouse.gov/news/releases/2003/02/200302051.html. From 248.

272.   Kerry Boyd, Rumsfeld Wants to Use Riot Control Agents in Combat, A RMS CONTROL TODAY, Mar. 2003, available at http://www.armscontrol.org/act/2003_03/nonlethal_mar03.asp. From 248.

273.   Nicholas Wade & Eric Schmitt, Bush's Authorization for Troops to Use Tear Gas is Criticized, I NT'L HERALD TRIBUNE, Apr. 3, 2003, at 3. From 248.

274.   Paul Richter, After the War: Treaty Complicates Crowd Control, L.A. TIMES, Apr. 30, 2003, at A8. From 248.

275.   NATO Training Mission – Iraq. NATO: Wikipedia, the free encyclopedia (withdrawn 12/11). http://en.wikipedia.org/wiki/NATO_Training_Mission_-_Iraq

276.   The Multi-National Force – Iraq (MNF–I) Wikipedia, the free encyclopedia .http://en.wikipedia.org/wiki/Multi-National_Force_%E2%80%93_Iraq.

277.   UN Security Council Resolution 1546. http://en.wikipedia.org/wiki/UN_Security_Council_Resolution_1546

278.   Victims of gross violations of human rights and fundamental freedoms arising from the illegal invasion and occupation of Kuwait by Iraq. **Larisa Gabriel**. SIM special 12. Seminar on the right to restitution, compensation and rehabilitation for victims of gross violations of human rights and fundamental freedoms. http://www.uu.nl/faculty/leg/nl/organisatie/departementen/departementrechtsgeleer dheid/organisatie/onderdelen/studieeninformatiecentrummensenrechten/publicaties/s imspecials/12/Pages/default.aspx

279.   United States Military Compensation to Civilians in Armed Conflict. May 2010. Center for Civilians in Conflict. http://civiliansinconflict.org/uploads/files/publications/CENTER_Condolence_White_Pap er_2010.pdf

280.   Geneva Protocol for the Prohibition of the Use in War of As phyxiating, Poisonous or Other Gases, and of Bacteriological Methods of Warfare, June 17, 1925, 44 LNTS 65; Convention for the Prohibition of the Development, Production, Stockpiling and Use of Chemical Weapons and on Their Destruction, Jan. 13, 1993, 32 ILM 800 (1993).

281.   Ex-officer alleges Iraq cover-ups. Richard Norton-Taylor. The Guardian, Sunday 11 October 2009. http://www.guardian.co.uk/uk/2009/oct/11/exofficer-alleges-iraq-coverups?INTCMP=ILCNETTXT3487

282.   Court: Britain obligated to probe civilian deaths in Iraq. CNN Wire Staff. July 7, 2011. http://edition.cnn.com/2011/WORLD/europe/07/07/uk.iraq.deaths/index.html

283.   David Feldman. UK Human Rights Litigation After the Iraq War. JURIST - Forum, Jan. 17, 2012, http://jurist.org/forum/2012/01/david-feldman-uk-iraq.php

284.   Curtis Doebbler, The use of Force Against Iraq and Other Violations of International Law and Impunity, JURIST - Forum, Dec. 19, 2011, http://jurist.org/forum/2011/12/curtis-doebbler-iraq-retrospective.php , see also: "Dutch inquiry says Iraq war had no mandate". news.bbc.co.uk. 2010-01-12. http://news.bbc.co.uk/2/hi/europe/8453305.stm , Al Jazeera, 12 Jan 2010, "Dutch Inquiry: Iraq Invasion was Illegal, http://english.aljazeera.net/news/europe/2010/01/2010112144254948980.html

285. Military and Paramilitary Activities in and against Nicaragua (Nicaragua v. United States of America). International Court of Justice. 27 June 1986. http://www.icj-cij.org/docket/index.php?sum=367&code=nus&p1=3&p2=3&case=70&k=66&p3=5

286. Onward Muslim Soldiers, How jihad still threatens America and the west. 2003. Robert Spencer. Regnery Publishing, Inc. An Eagle. U.S.

287. Contractors' support of U.S. operations in Iraq. Congress of the United States , Congressional Budget Office. August 2008.

288. COMPLAINT IN THE UNITED STATES DISTRICT COURT FOR THE DISTRICT OF COLUMBIA. CCRjustice.org.Case 1:07-cv-02273-RBW,Document 1, Filed 19/12/2007. Page 1-16. http://ccrjustice.org/files/Albazzaz_Complaint_12_07.pdf

289. Alien Tort Statute - Wikipedia, the free encyclopedia. http://en.wikipedia.org/wiki/Alien_Tort_Statute

290. Convicted ex-Blackwater contractor sentenced to 2.5 years in prison for manslaughter. JURIST. Tuesday, June 28, 2011. http://jurist.org/paperchase/2011/06/Convicted-ex-blackwater-contractor-sentenced-to-2.5-years-for-manslaughter.php

291. U.S. Examines Whether Blackwater Tried Bribery. MARK MAZZETTI and JAMES RISEN. January 31, 2010. The New York Times. http://www.nytimes.com/2010/02/01/world/middleeast/01blackwater.html?_r=0

292. Blackwater under investigation for bribing Iraq officials following 2007 deaths: NYT. JURIST. Monday, February 01, 2010. http://jurist.org/paperchase/2010/02/blackwater-under-investigation-for.php

293. 2nd ex-Blackwater contractor gets 30 months for manslaughter. Bill Sizemore.The Virginian-Pilot. June 28, 2011. http://hamptonroads.com/2011/06/2nd-exblackwater-worker-gets-30-months-manslaughter

294. Trial begins for last US Marine charged in Haditha killings. JURIST. Tuesday, January 10, 2012. http://jurist.org/paperchase/2012/01/trial-begins-for-last-us-marine-charged-in-haditha-killings.php

295. Jurist Newsletter supported by University of Pittsburgh School of Law. www.jurist.org

296. Final marine tried in Haditha killings pleads guilty. JURIST. Tuesday, January 24, 2012. http://jurist.org/paperchase/2012/01/final-marine-tried-in-haditha-killings-pleads-guilty.php

297. British troops face backlash from US Fallujah assault. 16 October 2004. The Telegraph. http://www.telegraph.co.uk/news/1474282/British-troops-face-backlash-from-US-Fallujah-assault.html

298. The Road from Los Alamos 17. Hans A. Bethe. 1991

299. Marines return to Fallujah, no shots fired. Sgt. Jose E. Guillen, 1st Marine Division. May 12, 2004.Marines.http://www.1stmardiv.marines.mil/News/NewsArticleDisplay/tabid/8585/Article/87320/marines-return-to-fallujah-no-shots-fired.aspx

300. Intelligence discoveries paint picture of enemy in Fallujah. Sgt. Jose E. Guillen,1st Marine Division,April,14,2004.Marines. http://www.1stmardiv.marines.mil/News/NewsArticleDisplay/tabid/8585/Article/87274/intelligence-discoveries-paint-picture-of-enemy-in-fallujah.aspx

301. Small platoon takes on big challenge for RCT-1. Sgt. Jose E. Guillen,1st Marine Division,April,15,2004.Marines.http://www.1stmardiv.marines.mil/News/NewsArticleDisplay/tabid/8585/Article/87277/small-platoon-takes-on-big-challenge-for-rct-1.aspx

302. US seeks end to Falluja bloodshed. Monday, 12 April, 2004, BBC. http://news.bbc.co.uk/2/hi/middle_east/3618559.stm

303. The legality of the use of white phosphorus by the United States military during the 2004 Fallujah assaults. Roman Reyhani. Journal of Law and Social Change, Vol. 10, 2007.pp. 1-45.
https://www.law.upenn.edu/journals/jlasc/articles/volume10/issue1/Reyhan10U.Pa.J.L.&Soc.Change1(2007).pdf

304. GlobalSecurity.org, operation al-Fajr r (Dawn)/Operation Phantom Fury [Fallujah], http://www.globalsecurity.org/military/ops/oif-phantom-fury-fallujah.htm.

305. US Death Toll in Fallujah Reaches 71, ABC NEWS ONLINE (Austl.), Dec. 2, 2004, available at http://www.abc.net.au/news/newsitems/200412/s1256321.htm.

306. Andrew Buncombe & Solomon Hughes, The Fog of War: White Phosphorus, Fallujah and Some Burning Questions, THE INDEP. (U.K. Online Edition), Nov. 15, 2005, available at http://news.independent.co.uk/world/americas/article327094.ece.

307. US Forces Used 'Chemical Weapon' in Iraq, THE INDEP. (U.K. Online Edition), Nov. 16, 2005. http://news.independent.co.uk/world/americas/article327379.ece.

308. Jackie Spinner, Karl Vick & Omar Fekeiki, US Forces Battle into Heart of Fallujah, WASH. POST, Nov. 10, 2004.

309. U.S. Environmental Protection Agency, Phosphorus, Jan. 2000, http://www.epa.gov/ttn/atw/hlthefwhitepho.html

310. Fallujah residents prepare to return. Dec 23, 2004. ABC News. http://www.abc.net.au/news/2004-12-23/fallujah-residents-prepare-to-return/607508

311. Clashes mar return of Fallujah residents. Dec 24, 2004 . ABC News. http://www.abc.net.au/news/2004-12-24/clashes-mar-return-of-fallujah-residents/607710

312. Fallujah refugees in desperate need of aid: UN. Dec 3, 2004. ABC News. http://www.abc.net.au/news/2004-12-03/fallujah-refugees-in-desperate-need-of-aid-un/596296

313. US retaliates after 8 Marines killed in Fallujah. Dec 14, 2004. ABC News. http://www.abc.net.au/news/2004-12-14/us-retaliates-after-8-marines-killed-in-fallujah/602150

314. US plans December offensive on Iraqi insurgents. Sep 19, 2004. ABC News. http://www.abc.net.au/news/2004-09-19/us-plans-december-offensive-on-iraqi-insurgents/554190

315. Law and corruption a haze in Blackwater. Jun 10, 2010. ABC News. http://www.abc.net.au/news/2010-06-10/law-and-corruption-a-haze-in-blackwater/862448

316. Corruption in Iraq: 'Your son is being tortured. He will die if you don't pay'. Ghaith Abdul-Ahad. The Guardian, Monday 16 January 2012. http://www.guardian.co.uk/world/2012/jan/16/corruption-iraq-son-tortured-pay

317. US general under scrutiny in Iraqi prisoner case. **April 30, 2004.** ABC News. http://www.abc.net.au/news/2004-04-30/us-general-under-scrutiny-in-iraqi-prisoner-case/178440

318. GlobalSecurity.org, White Phosphorus . http://www.globalsecurity.org/military/systems/munitions/wp.htm

319. Toxicity of Military Smokes and Obscurants, in National Academy of Sciences, Vol. 2, 24 (1999). http://www.nap.edu/openbook.php?record_id=9621&page=18

320. 1993 Convention on the Development, Production, Stockpiling and Use of Chemical Weapons and on their Destruction (hereinafter "The Chemical Weapons Convention" or "CWC") art. I(I)(b). The Convention has 178 state parties as of March 19, 2007. From 303.

321. WALTER KRUTZSCH & RALF TRAPP, A COMMENTARY ON THE CHEMICAL WEAPONS CONVENTION 12,(1994). Oxford Commentaries on International Law. From 303

322. David P. Fidler, International Law and Weapons of Mass Destruction: End of the Arms Control Approach?, 14 DUKE J. COMP. & INT'L L. 39, 48-49 (2004).

323. Report to Congress on the Situation in Iraq. General David H. Petraeus, Commander, Multi-National Force–Iraq. 8-9 April 2008. http://www.armed-services.senate.gov/statemnt/2008/April/Petraeus%2004-08-08.pdf

324. The minister of civil war,Bayan Jabr, Paul Bremer, and the rise of the Iraqi death squads.Ken Silverstein. Harper's Magazine.August,2006.http://harpers.org/archive/2006/08/the-minister-of-civil-war/

325. Falluja doctors report rise in birth defects. Thursday, 4 March 2010. BBC News. http://news.bbc.co.uk/2/hi/middle_east/8548707.stm.

326. "The Salvador Option For Syria": US-NATO Sponsored Death Squads Integrate "Opposition Forces". Michel Chossudovsky. 28 May 2012. Global Research. Center for research on Globalization. http://www.globalresearch.ca/the-salvador-option-for-syria-us-nato-sponsored-death-squads-integrate-opposition-forces/31096

327. Tina Susman, "Iraq won't give casualty figures to U.N.," Chicago Tribune, April 26, 2007,p.12. From 331

328. United Nations Assistance Mission to Iraq, Human Rights Report, 1 April - 20 June 2007, at [http://www.uniraq.org/FileLib/misc/HR%20Report%20Apr%20Jun%202007%20EN.pdf]
.

329. Farah Stockman and Bryan Bender, "Iraq violence up as troop levels drop; Value of the surge debated," The Boston Globe, April 7, 2008, p. A1. From 331

330. Sabrina Tavernise, "Wartime low for U.S. soldier deaths in July," New York Times, August 1,2008. From 331

331. Iraqi Civilian Deaths Estimates, Hannah Fischer, Information Research Specialist, Knowledge Services Group. CRS Report for Congress. August 27, 2008. Order Code RS22537. http://www.fas.org/sgp/crs/mideast/RS22537.pdf

332. John Negroponte. From Wikipedia, the free encyclopedia. http://en.wikipedia.org/wiki/John_Negroponte

333. "Nomination of John Negroponte". Congressional Record: (Senate). 2001-09-14. pp. S9431–S9433. Retrieved 2006-07-21. http://www.fas.org/irp/congress/2001_cr/s091401.html from 332

334. Our man in Honduras (Stephen Kinzer for The New York Review of Books, September 20, 2001) http://www.nybooks.com/articles/archives/2001/sep/20/our-man-in-honduras/ from 332

335. R. Earle, "Nights in the Pink Motel:An American Strategist's Pursuit of Peace in Iraq (Annapolis: U.S. Naval Institute, 2008) from 332

336. "Bush Taps Negroponte For Iraq Post". CBS News. 2004-04-09. Retrieved 2006-08-17.

337. El Salvador-style 'death squads' to be deployed by US against Iraq militants – Times Online, January 10, 2005. From The Pentagon's "Salvador Option": The Deployment of Death Squads in Iraq and Syria.Part II. Prof Michel Chossudovsky. Global Research, August 16, 2011.http://www.globalresearch.ca/the-pentagon-s-salvador-option-the-deployment-of-death-squads-in-iraq-and-syria/26043

338. Dahr Jamail, Managing Escalation: Negroponte and Bush's New Iraq Team,. Antiwar.com, January 7, 2007. http://antiwar.com/jamail/?articleid=10289

339. Director of National Intelligence: Statutory Authorities. Richard A Best, Jr.; Alfred Cumming; and Todd Masse Foreign Affairs, Defense, and Trade and Domestic Social

Policy. CRS Report for Congress. Order Code RS22112. April 11, 2005.
http://www.fas.org/sgp/crs/intel/RS22112.pdf

340. The Iraq Federal Police. U.S. Police Building under Fire. Robert M. Perito. October 2011.
United States Institute of Peace. Special Report.
http://www.usip.org/files/resources/SR291_The_Iraq_Federal_Police.pdf

341. Measuring stability and security in Iraq. August 2006. Report to Congress In accordance
with the Department of Defense Appropriations Act 2006. (Section 9010).
http://www.defense.gov/pubs/pdfs/Security-Stabilty-ReportAug29r1.pdf

342. 'What were the causes and consequences of Iraq's descent into violence after the initial
invasion?' 10 November, 2009. Dr Toby Dodge.
http://www.iraqinquiry.org.uk/media/37045/dodge-submission.pdf

343. Foreign Fighters Captured in Iraq come from 27, mostly Arab, Lands", Dexter Filkins. New
York Times, 21 October, 2005. From 342

344. Hannah Allam, „Wolf Brigade the Most Loved and Feared of Iraqi Security Forces", Knight
Ridder Newspapers, 21 May, 2005. From 342

345. Amnesty International, Beyond Abu Ghraib: Detention and Torture in Iraq, (March, 2006),
p. 4. From 342

346. Ghaith Abdul-Ahad, „Tea and Kidnapping – Behind the Lines of a Civil War", The
Guardian, 28 October, 2006. From 342

347. Solomon Moore, „Militias Seen as Spinning Out of Control", Los Angels Times, 12
September, 2006. Abdul-Ahad, „Tea and Kidnapping" and Peter Beaumont, „Inside
Baghdad: Last Battle of a Stricken City", Observer, 17 September, 2006. From 342

348. Patrick Cockburn, Muqtada al Sadr and the Fall of Iraq, (London: Faber and Faber, 2008),
p. 249. From 342

349. Biennial technical report 2009–2010 / Department of Reproductive Health and Research,
including UNDP/UNFPA/WHO/World Bank Special Programme of Research, Development
and Research Training in Human Reproduction. World Health Organization 2011

350. Metal Contamination and the Epidemic of Congenital Birth Defects in Iraqi Cities .M. Al-
Sabbak ,G. Savabi, S. Sadik Ali, Bull Environ Contam Toxicol (2012) 89:937–944.

351. Making the UK safer: detecting and decontaminating chemical and biological agents. The
Royal Society, UK, Policy document 06/04, April 2004.

352. The health effects of depleted uranium munitions. The Royal Society, UK, Document
6/02. March 2002.

353. Fallujah- Looking Back at the Fury. June 29th, 2010. Lance Cpl. Benjamin Harris. MARINES
Magazine.

354. Depleted uranium casts a shadow over peace in Iraq ,New Scientist. 15 April 2003.
Duncan Graham-Rowe, Rob Edwards.

355. The risks of depleted uranium contamination post-conflict: UNEP assessments. Mario
Burger. 2008. http://unidir.org/pdf/articles/pdf-art2760.pdf

356. UNEP, 20 October 2003, Environment in Iraq: UNEP Progress Report, Geneva, at
<postconflict.unep.ch/publications/Iraq_PR.pdf>

357. Interview Brig. Gen. Karl Horst. Frontline, 9 Feb. 2007.
http://www.pbs.org/wgbh/pages/frontline/gangsofiraq/interviews/horst.html

358. CNN: Special Investigations Unit, Death Squads, March 25, 2007. John Roberts.
http://transcripts.cnn.com/TRANSCRIPTS/0703/25/siu.01.html

359. DISPATCHES: THE DEATH SQUADS. FRIDAY 19 JANUARY 2007. Deborah davies. The
channel 4. http://www.channel4.com/programmes/dispatches/articles/iraqs-death-
squads , http://documentaryheaven.com/dispatches-the-death-squads/

360. Interview Gen. David Petraeus. Frontline, 9 Feb. 2007.
http://www.pbs.org/wgbh/pages/frontline/gangsofiraq/interviews/petraeus.html

361. CBS: Death Squads In Iraqi Hospitals. Melissa McNamara. February 11, 2009.
http://www.cbsnews.com/stories/2006/10/04/eveningnews/main2064668.shtml

362. Henry Kissinger: "If You Can't Hear the Drums of War You Must Be Deaf" Alfred
Heinz. 27/11/2011. dailysquib.co.uk.
http://www.dailysquib.co.uk/index.php?news=3089

363. Desk Study on the Environment in Iraq. United Nations Environment Programme (UNEP).
2003. http://www.unep.org

364. Question of the violation of human rights and fundamental freedoms in any part of the
world. Situation of human rights in Iraq, Report submitted by the Special Rapporteur,
Andreas Mavrommatis. E/CN.4/2004/36, 19 March 2004.
http://www.unhchr.ch/Huridocda/Huridoca.nsf/0/f31af14ed598d828c1256e63003c0e5d
/$FILE/G0412182.pdf

365. W. Kalin, Special Rapporteur, Report on the situation of human rights in Kuwait under
Iraqi occupation, UN Doc. E/CN.4/1992/26, 16 January 1992

366. Coalition Provisional Authority, Order No. 7, Penal Code, 9 June 2003, Sections 3 and 4

367. The interrelation of the law of occupation and economic, social and cultural rights: the
examples of food, health and property. Sylvain Vite´. International Review of the Red
Cross. Volume 90 Number 871 September 2008.
http://www.icrc.org/eng/assets/files/other/irrc-871-vite.pdf

368. Convention (IV) Respecting the Laws and Customs of War on Land and Its Annex:
Regulations Concerning the Laws and Customs of War on Land, 18 October 1907 ', in
Dietrich Schindler and Jiri Toman (eds.), The Laws of Armed Conflict, Nijhoff, Dordrecht,
1988, pp. 69–93 (hereinafter Hague Regulations). From 367.

369. Geneva Convention Relative to the Protection of Civilian Persons in Time of War, 12
August 1949 (hereinafter Fourth Geneva Convention), ICRC, Geneva, 1949 : Article 2(2).
From 367.

370. Hague Regulations, above note 6 ; Fourth Geneva Convention, above note 7 ; Protocol
Additional to the Geneva Conventions of 12 August 1949, and Relating to the Protection
of International Armed Conflicts, 8 June 1977, Protocols additional to the Geneva
Conventions of 12 August 1949, ICRC, Geneva, 1977, pp. 3–89. From 367.

371. Blackwater: The Rise of the World's Most Powerful Mercenary Army. Jeremy Scahill.
2008. Nation Books, NY

372. The Forever War. (ed.) Dexter Filkins. Alfred A. Knopf, New York. Borzoi Books. 2008.

373. American Sniper. (eds.)Chris Kyle with Scott McEwen and Jim DeFelice. Harper Collins
Publishers. 2012.
http://www.harpercollins.com/browseinside/index.aspx?isbn13=9780062082350

374. In a state of uncertainty, impact and implications of the use of depleted uranium in Iraq.
ikv pax Christi. This report was financed by the Norwegian Ministry of Foreign Affairs.
http://www.ikvpaxchristi.nl/media/files/in-a-state-of-uncertainty.pdf

375. Huge rise in birth defects in Falluja, Iraqi former battle zone sees abnormal clusters of
infant tumours and deformities. The Guardian. Martin Chulov. Friday 13 November
2009. http://www.guardian.co.uk/world/2009/nov/13/falluja-cancer-children-birth-
defects

376. The Truth Of Iraq's City Of Deformed Babies. Lisa Holland . Tuesday 01 September 2009.
http://news.sky.com/story/720205/the-truth-of-iraqs-city-of-deformed-babies

377. Disturbing story of Falluja's birth defects. John Simpson. Thursday, 4 March 2010.
http://news.bbc.co.uk/2/hi/8548961.stm

378. US claims no depleted uranium used in second Fallujah siege. International Coalition to Ban Uranium Weapons ICBUW.18 April 2011. http://www.bandepleteduranium.org/en/us-claims-no-depleted-uranium-used-in-second-fallu http://www.bandepleteduranium.org/en/docs/160.pdf

379. Growing concern over humanitarian situation in Fallujah. International Coalition to Ban Uranium Weapons ICBUW. 19 November 2009. http://www.bandepleteduranium.org/en/growing-concern-over-humanitarian-situation-in-fal

380. Interview with Dr. Mario Burger, UNEP, Spiez, September 23, 2012. From 374

381. Abdulghani et al, Perinatal and neonatal mortality in Fallujah General Hospital, Fallujah City, Anbar Province, west of Iraq. http://www.scirp.org/journal/health Vol.4, No.9, 597-600 (2012)

382. UNDP (2012) Pilot Assessment of Congenital Birth Defects in Iraq in Six Governorates, project description. Accessed on http://mdtf.undp.org/document/download/6499

383. Si vous le répétez, je démentirai... : Chirac, Sarkozy, Villepin. Jean-Claude Maurice, 2009. PLON. http://www.amazon.fr/Si-vous-r%C3%A9p%C3%A9tez-d%C3%A9mentirai-Villepin/dp/225921021X/ref=sr_1_1?ie=UTF8&qid=1249801129&sr=8-1

384. Iraq: War's legacy of cancer. Dahr Jamail. 15 March, 2013. Al-Jazeera English.http://www.aljazeera.com/indepth/features/2013/03/2013315171951838638.html#.UUP9a7E9M3A.facebook

385. AGM-114 Hellfire. Military Analysis Network. http://www.fas.org/man/dod-101/sys/missile/agm-114.htm

386. Journalists accused of wrecking doctors' lives. An ode to herpetology. Bill Henderson. 6 March 2005. BMJ Publishing Group Ltd.

387. Crimes Against Humanity,A Normative Account. 2005. (ed.) Larry May (Washington University), Cambridge University Press.

388. DEPLETED URANIUM AND CANADIAN VETERANS, A Review of Potential Exposure and Health Effects, A Report Prepared for the Minister of Veterans Affairs by the Scientific Advisory Committee on Veterans' Health. January 2013.

389. Epidemic of birth defects in Iraq and our duty as public health researchers. 15 Mar 2013. Mozhgan Savabieasfahani. Al Jazeera English. http://www.aljazeera.com/indepth/opinion/2013/03/2013312175857532741.html

390. Scientists urge shell clear-up to protect civilians. Royal Society spells out dangers of depleted uranium. Paul Brown. The Guardian. Thursday 17 April 2003. http://www.guardian.co.uk/world/2003/apr/17/highereducation.science

391. Research Working Group of the Persian Gulf Veterans Coordinating Board. Annual report to Congress. Washington, DC: Department of Veterans Affairs, 1999.

392. UN General Assembly supports precautionary approach to depleted uranium weapons. 3 December 2012 - ICBUW.http://www.bandepleteduranium.org/en/unga-2012-vote

393. The Gulf War Depleted Uranium Cohort at 20 years: Bioassay Results and Novel Approaches to Fragment Surveillance. McDiarmid MA, Gaitens JM, Hines S, Breyer R, Wong-You-Cheong JJ, Engelhardt SM, Oliver M, Gucer P, Kane R, Cernich A, Kaup B, Hoover D, Gaspari AA, Liu J, Harberts E, Brown L, Centeno JA, Gray PJ, Xu H, Squibb KS. Health Phys. 2013 Apr;104(4):347-361. http://www.ncbi.nlm.nih.gov/pubmed/23439138

394. Lebanon Post-Conflict Environmental Assessment. United Nations Environment Programme (UNEP). January 2007. http://postconflict.unep.ch/publications/UNEP_Lebanon.pdf

395. The emergence and decline of the debate over depleted uranium munitions (1991-2004). Dan Fahey, 20 June 2004. http://www.wise-uranium.org/pdf/duemdec.pdf

396. Gulf War Veterans: Evidence for Chromosome Alterations and their Significance. Jo Nijs, and Garth L. Nicolson. Journal of Chronic Fatigue Syndrome 2004; 12(1):79-83. http://www.immed.org/GWI%20Research%20docs/06.26.12.updates.pdfs.gwi/Nigs-NicolsonJCFS-GWI.pdf

397. Technical Report on Capacity-building for the Assessment of Depleted Uranium in Iraq. United Nations Environment Programme, Geneva, August 2007. http://postconflict.unep.ch/publications/Iraq_DU.pdf

398. Depleted Uranium Munitions, Comments of the International Committee of the Red Cross. NATO Information. 2 April, 2001.Geneva.http://www.nato.int/du/docu/d010402a.htm

399. Council of Europe calls for ban on DU weapons. Press release 24,Jan.2001. http://press.coe.int/cp/2001/51a(2001).htm

400. European Parliament Makes Fourth Call for DU Ban. 22 November 2006 - ICBUW. http://www.bandepleteduranium.org/en/a/89.html

401. Book I: weapon contamination environment. Ben Lark and Lena Eskeland. ICRC. 2005. http://www.icrc.org/eng/assets/files/other/mine_action_i_web.pdf

402. UN Subcommission condemns DU weapons. UN Press Release, 04 Sep 1996, HR/CN/755: Subcommission on prevention of discrimination and protection of minorities concludes forty/eighty session.

403. Congenital birth defect study in Iraq: frequently asked questions. http://www.emro.who.int/irq/iraq-infocus/faq-congenital-birth-defect-study.html

404. Why Bush, Blair should be charged with war crimes over Iraq invasion. Michael Mansfield, 2013. CNN. http://edition.cnn.com/2013/03/19/opinion/iraq-war-bush-blair/index.html?sr=fbmainintl

405. Hans Blix: Iraq war was a terrible mistake and violation of UN charter. Hans Blix. March 19, 2013. CNN. http://edition.cnn.com/2013/03/18/opinion/iraq-war-hans-blix/index.html

406. Revealed: hand of Iran behind Britons' Baghdad kidnapping. Mona Mahmood, Maggie O'Kane, Guy Grandjean. The Guardian, Wednesday 30 December 2009. http://www.guardian.co.uk/world/2009/dec/30/iran-britons-baghdad-kidnapping

407. CHOMSKY ABOUT THE WAR IN IRAQ. Mike Powers. 26-03-2013. http://www.brussellstribunal.org/article_view.asp?id=856#.UVM7RBdPOVi

408. Revealed: Pentagon's link to Iraqi torture centres. Mona Mahmood, Maggie O'Kane, Chavala Madlena and Teresa Smith .The Guardian, Wednesday 6 March 2013. http://www.guardian.co.uk/world/2013/mar/06/pentagon-iraqi-torture-centres-link?INTCMP=SRCH

409. Pentagon investigating link between US military and torture centres in Iraq. Ewen MacAskill and Mona Mahmood. The Guardian, Thursday 7 March 2013. http://www.guardian.co.uk/world/2013/mar/07/pentagon-investigating-link-military-torture

410. From El Salvador to Iraq: Washington's man behind brutal police squads. Mona Mahmood, Maggie O'Kane, Chavala Madlena, Teresa Smith, Ben Ferguson,Patrick Farrelly, Guy Grandjean, Josh Strauss, Roisin Glynn, Irene Baqué, Marcus Morgan, Jake Zervudachi and Joshua Boswell. The Guardian, Wednesday 6 March 2013. http://www.guardian.co.uk/world/2013/mar/06/el-salvador-iraq-police-squads-washington

411.   Iraq 'failing to tackle death squads'. Peter Beaumont. The Guardian, Friday 29 September,2006.http://www.guardian.co.uk/world/2006/sep/29/iraq.topstories3?INTC MP=SRCH

412.   Fanning sectarian flames. Leader, The Guardian, Thursday 23 February 2006. http://www.guardian.co.uk/world/2006/feb/23/iraq.mainsection?INTCMP=SRCH

413.   US allies are behind the death squads and ethnic cleansing. Jonathan Steele.The Guardian, Friday,14 April 2006. http://www.guardian.co.uk/commentisfree/2006/apr/14/comment.iraq?INTCMP=SRCH

414.   Colonel Gregg P. Olson. http://www.johnfry.com/pages/IconBioOlson.html

415.   Crime of aggression. Wikipedia. http://en.wikipedia.org/wiki/Crime_of_aggression http://treaties.un.org/doc/publication/CN/2010/CN.651.2010-Eng.pdf

416.   ICC nations define crime of aggression". Retrieved 26 December 2011. http://jurist.org/paperchase/2010/06/icc-nations-adopt-crime-of-aggression.php

417.   "Special Briefing: U.S. Engagement With the ICC and the Outcome of the Recently Concluded Review Conference". United States Department of State. 2010-06-15. Retrieved 2012-05-16. http://www.state.gov/j/gcj/us_releases/remarks/143178.htm

418.   Frequently Asked Questions. The Office of The Prosecutor (OTP), International Criminal Court site. http://www.icc-cpi.int/en_menus/icc/structure%20of%20the%20court/office%20of%20the%20prosecut or/faq/Pages/faq.aspx#id_2

419.   The States Parties to the Rome Statute. International Criminal Court site. http://www.icc-cpi.int/EN_Menus/ASP/States%20Parties/Pages/the%20states%20parties%20to%20the %20rome%20statute.aspx

420.   Letter of The Office of the Prosecutor to senders on Iraqi situation. ICC. 9 February 2006. http://www.icc-cpi.int/NR/rdonlyres/FD042F2E-678E-4EC6-8121-690BE61D0B5A/143682/OTP_letter_to_senders_re_Iraq_9_February_2006.pdf

421.   "Off Target" The Conduct of the War and Civilian Casualties in Iraq. HRW. December 12, 2003. http://www.hrw.org/reports/2003/usa1203/

422.   Preliminary Examinations. ICC. http://www.icc-cpi.int/en_menus/icc/structure%20of%20the%20court/office%20of%20the%20prosecuto r/comm%20and%20ref/Pages/communications%20and%20referrals.aspx#1

423.   Iraq Pulls Out Of International Criminal Court, Radio Free Europe, 2005-03-02. http://www.rferl.org/content/article/1057782.html

424.   Groups Urge Iraq to Join International Criminal Court, Common Dreams, 2005-08-08. http://www.commondreams.org/cgi-bin/print.cgi?file=/headlines05/0808-06.htm

425.   War and Occupation in Iraq. Report prepared by Global Policy Forum, June 2007. James Paul Céline Nahory, Rachel Laurence, Mike Lewis, Philippa Curran, Anna Dupont, Peter Jenkins, and Alice Skipper. http://www.humanitarianibh.net/english/reportes/War%20Occupation%20in%20Iraq.pd f

426.   Killing the hope, U.S. Military and CIA Interventionss Since World War II. William Blum. Zed Books Ltd, 2004.

427.   Los Angeles Times, 12 June 1991, p. I; 26 September, p. 16; occurred on 18 January 1991. From 426.

428.   The Guardian (London), 20 February 1991, p. 1, entitled: "Bombs rock capital as allies deliver terrible warning". From 426.

429.   Washington Post, 23 June 1991, p. 16. From 426.

430.   Los Angeles Times, 7 September 1994, p. 6. From 426.

431. Washington Post, 13 January 1985, p. A30. The unnamed official may have been CIA Director Stansfield Turner who is quoted as saying something very similar in Wciner pp. 146-7. From 426.

432. New York Times, 17 January 2003, p. 10. From 426.

433. UN Security Council Meeting 4701 on Iraq, Verbatim Transcript S/PV.4701 (February 5, 2003) p.5 .From 425.

434. See US Central Intelligence Agency, Comprehensive Report of the Special Advisor to the DCI on Iraq's WMD (September 30, 2004) . From 425.

435. Richard Clarke, Against all Enemies (New York, 2004) Clarke was the chief counter-terrorism expert on the National Security Council in the Bush administration's early years. From 425.

436. Sir Christopher Meyer, DC Confidential (London, 2005). Meyer was the UK ambassador in Washington at the time. From 425.

437. "Iraq: Prime Minister's Meeting, 23 July [2002]" Secret memorandum of a meeting of senior UK civil servants and ministers at 10 Downing Street, leaked to the Sunday Times and published May 1, 2005. Its authenticity has never been disputed. See Walter Pincus, "British Intelligence 'Warned of Iraq War'" Washington Post (May 3, 2005) From 425.

438. "Powell Calls Pre-Iraq U.N. Speech a 'Blot' on his Record" Associated Press (September 8, 2005). From 425.

439. Assessment of the British Government, Iraq's Weapons of Mass Destruction (September 24, 2002) and UK 10 Downing Street, Iraq: Its Infrastructure of Concealment, Deception and Intimidation (February 3,2003). From 425.

440. Ross worked at the UK's UN Mission for four and a half years, from December 1997 until June 2002.His testimony was kept secret and only made public 30 months later after pressure from members of Parliament. See "Full Transcript of Evidence given to the Butler Inquiry, Supplementary Evidence Submitted by Mr. Carne Ross, Director, Independent Diplomat," dated June 9, 2004, published by the Independent (December 15, 2006). See Colin Brown and Andy McSmith, "Diplomat's Suppressed Document Lays Bare the Lies Behind Iraq War" Independent (December 15, 2006). From 425.

441. US Senate, 109th Congress, 2nd Session, Report of the Select Intelligence Committee on Postwar Findings on Iraq's WMD Programs and Links to Terrorism and How They Compare with Prewar Assessments (September 8, 2006). A report by the Inspector General of the Department of Defense, released to the Congress on April 5, 2007, Came to the same conclusion. See "Hussein-Qaeda Lind 'Inappropriate,' Report Says" Bloomberg News (April 6, 2007) From 425. http://www.gpo.gov/fdsys/pkg/CREC-2006-09-08/pdf/CREC-2006-09-08.pdf

442. White House Press Release, Remarks by the President to the Military Personnel and Their Families Marine Corps Base Camp Lejeune, North Carolina (April 3, 3003). From 425.

443. White House Press Release, Iraq Coalition (March 27, 2003) From 425.

444. See for example US Department of State, Office of the Coordinator for Counterterrorism, "Patterns of Global Terrorism" (April 29, 2004); US CENTCOM, "International Contributions to the War on Terror" (January 10, 2005); Sewell Chan, "Rumsfeld Thanks Kazakhstan" Washington Post (February 26, 2004); Globalsecurity.org, Iraq Coalition Troops (February 2007) From 425.

445. Jim Garamone, "More than 100,000 Coalition Troops in Iraq" American Forces Press Service (March 31, 2003) From 425. http://osd.dtic.mil/news/Mar2003/n03312003_200303316.html

446. The White House website notes that the Ministry of Health was "completely looted". For details on the Oil Ministry see Andras Riedlmayer, "Yes the Oil Ministry Was Guarded" Iraq War and Archeology (May 7, 2003) From 425.

447. Department of Defense, *News Briefing by Secretary of Defense Donald Rumsfeld and General Richard Meyers* (April 11, 2003). See Sean Loughlin, "Rumsfeld on Looting in Iraq"

448. UN Security Council Resolutions S/RES/1637(2005) and S/RES/1723 (2006). From 425.

449. Maggie Farley and Richard Boudreaux, "Mexico's Envoy to UN Leaves, With Defiance" *Los Angeles Times* (November 22, 2003) From 425.

450. Bremer had served in the State Department for many years and from 1989-2000 had been a Managing Director of Kissenger Associates. His biographies describe him as a counter-terrorism expert. See the bio presented by the CPA website http://www.iraqcoalition.org/bremerbio.html

451. Human Rights Watch, Violent Response: the U.S. Army in al-Falluja (June 17, 2003) From 425.

452. Seymour Hersh, "Moving Targets" *New Yorker* (December 15, 2003). Also see Matthew B. Stannard, "Special Forces Have Scoped Iraq for Weeks" *San Francisco Chronicle* (March 21, 2003) From 425.

453. Thom Shanker, "Special Operations in Iraq: High Profile But in the Shadow," *New York Times* (May 29, 2007) and Human Rights First, "Command's Responsibility," (February, 2006) From 425.

454. Amnesty International USA, *Human Rights Responsibilities of Private Companies Operating in Iraq*. From 425. http://www.amnestyusa.org/pdfs/corpwatchl3rpt.pdf

455. Dana Priest and Josh White, "Before the War, CIA Reportedly Trained a Team of Iraqis to Aid US" *Washington Post* (August 3, 2005) From 425. http://en.citizendium.org/wiki/Scorpions_(Iraq_War) , http://www.washingtonpost.com/wp-dyn/content/article/2005/08/02/AR2005080201579_pf.html

456. Human Rights First, *Command's Responsibility* (February 2006) p. 8. The detainee was Major General Abed Hamed Mowhoush .From 425.

457. Robert Dreyfuss, "Phoenix Rising" *The American Prospect* Volume 15, Issue 1 (January 1, 2004) . From 425.

458. Michael Hirsh and John Barry, "The Salvador Option" *Newsweek* (January 14, 2005) From 425.

459. Peter Maass, "The Way of the Commandos" *New York Times Magazine* (May 1, 2005). Another important advisor who had been involved in US Latin American counter-insurgency operations was Steven Casteel. From 425.

460. The *Wall Street Journal* identified six of these units. See Greg Jaffe, "New Factor in Iraq: Irregular Brigades Fill Security Void" *Wall Street Journal* (February 16, 2005) and "Bands of Brothers New Factor in Iraq: Irregular Brigades Fill Security Void" *Wall Street Journal* (February 23, 2005). See esp. A.K. Gupta, "Let a housand Militias Bloom" NYC Indymedia Center (April 22, 2005) and A.K. Gupta, "Iraq: Militias and Civil War" *Z Magazine* (December 2006) .From 425.

461. Lionel Beehner, "Iraq: Militia Groups" *Council on Foreign Relations* (June 9, 2005)

462. Michale Hirsch and John Barry, "Special Forces May Train Assassins, Kidnappers in Iraq" *Newsweek* (January 14, 2005) and Peter Maas, "The Way of the Commandoes" *New York Times Magazine* (May 1, 2005) From 425.

463. Ned Parker, "Divided Iraq Has Two Spy Agencies" *Los Angeles Times* (April 15, 2007) From 425.

464. Yochi J. Dreazen and Christopher Cooper, "Behind the Scenes, US Tightens Grip on Iraq's Future" *Wall Street Journal* (May 13, 2004). Also see Bradley Graham and Robin Wright, "Aid to Iraq Ministries To Shift to Pentagon" *Washington Post* (September 26, 2005) From 425.

465. James W. Crawley, "Officials Confirm Dropping Firebombs on Iraqi Troops" *San Diego Union-Tribune* (August 5, 2003) From 425.

466. Iraq Analysis Group, *Fire Bombs in Iraq: Napalm by Any Other Name* (March/April 2005) From 425.

467. Jason E. Levy, "TTPs for the 60mm Mortar Section" *Infantry Magazine* (May/June 2004) and Captain James T. Cobb, First Lieutenant Christopher A. LaCour and Sergeant First Class William H. Hight, "The Fight for Fallujah" *Field Artillery* (March/April 2005) From 425.

468. Scott Peterson, "Remains of Toxic Bullets Litter Iraq" *Christian Science Monitor* (May 15, 2003) From 425.

469. Human Rights Watch, Off Target: *The Conduct of the War and Civilians Casualties in Iraq* (December 2003) From 425.

470. 26 Countries' WMD Programs; A Global History of WMD Use. *Pro. Con. Org*. http://usiraq.procon.org/view.resource.php?resourceID=000678

471. Chemical weapons and the United Kingdom. From *Wikipedia*. http://en.wikipedia.org/wiki/Chemical_weapons_and_the_United_Kingdom

472. Chemical warfare, From Wikipedia. http://en.wikipedia.org/wiki/Chemical_warfare

473. MK-77750lb Napalm. *GlobalSecurity.org*, http://www.globalsecurity.org/military/systems/munitions/mk77.htm

474. You asked for my evidence, Mr Ambassador. Here it is. Naomi Klein. *The Guardian*. Saturday 4 December 2004. http://www.guardian.co.uk/world/2004/dec/04/iraq.usa, see also: Journalists Tell of US Falluja Killings. Adam Porter. Thursday, March **17, 2005**. *Aljazeera*. http://www.commondreams.org/headlines05/0317-02.htm

475. Smoking while Iraq burns. Naomi Klein. *The Guardian*. Friday 26 November 2004 . http://www.guardian.co.uk/world/2004/nov/26/usa.iraq

476. Who seized Simona Torretta? Naomi Klein and Jeremy Scahill. *The Guardian*. Thursday 16 September 2004. http://www.guardian.co.uk/world/2004/sep/16/usa.iraq

477. Die, then vote. This is Falluja. Naomi Klein. *The Guardian*. Saturday 13 November 2004. http://www.guardian.co.uk/politics/2004/nov/13/iraq.iraq

478. Fallujah assault underway; Baghdad church burning. *USA TODAY* . 11/7/2004. http://usatoday30.usatoday.com/news/world/iraq/2004-11-07-emergency-iraq_x.htm

479. Iraq report focuses blame on CIA. John Diamond, *USA TODAY*. 7/11/2004. http://usatoday30.usatoday.com/news/world/iraq/2004-07-11-iraq-intelligence_x.htm

480. U.S. drives into heart of Fallujah / Army, Marines face rockets and bombs in battle to take insurgents' stronghold / ADVANCING: 70% of city reported under American control. *San Francisco Chronicle*. Wednesday, November 10, 2004. http://www.sfgate.com/news/article/U-S-drives-into-heart-of-Fallujah-Army-2637064.php

481. IRAQ: 'Unusual Weapons' Used in Fallujah. Dahr Jamail. *Inter Press Service*. Nov. 25, 2004. http://www.ipsnews.net/2004/11/iraq-unusual-weapons-used-in-fallujah/

482. Falluja Was Wiped Out. Rüdiger Göbel. *Junge Welt*. Feb. 26, 2005. http://www.countercurrents.org/iraq-awad100305.htm , see also: Diving Into Falluja. Maker Mark Manning. *Santa Barbara Independent*. 03/24/2005. http://www.informationclearinghouse.info/article8353.htm, In Fallujah, U.S. Declares

War on Hospitals, Ambulances. Brian Dominick. The New Standard. Nov 9, 2004. http://www.nogw.com/download/2004war_hosp.pdf

483. IRAQ: Red Crescent Society makes plans for Fallujah camp. *IRIN*. 15 April 2004. http://www.irinnews.org/Report/23682/IRAQ-Red-Crescent-Society-makes-plans-for-Fallujah-camp , see also: IRAQ: Baghdad hospital treating injured from Fallujah. *IRIN*. 14 April 2004. http://www.irinnews.org/Report/23679/IRAQ-Baghdad-hospital-treating-injured-from-Fallujah

484. Falluja Atrocities Expose True Face of U.S. War. Joseph Nevins. Friday, December 10, 2004. *CommonDreams.org*. http://www.commondreams.org/views04/1210-23.htm

485. Iraqi Inquiry, www.iraqinquiry.org.uk/about.aspx

486. Clinton Admits We Created al Qaeda But Lies About Why and When. Scott Creighton. Willyloman. May 9, 2012. http://willyloman.wordpress.com/2012/05/09/clinton-admits-we-created-al-qaeda-but-lies-about-why-and-when/ https://www.youtube.com/watch?feature=player_embedded&v=gssjVvE0_QU#at=22

487. Gen. Georg Casey' speech in annual conference of Mojahedin organization. Paris, France. 23 June 2013. http://www.mojahedin.org/Pagesar/linksdetails.aspx?downloadfile=../links/other/2013 0623_Ceisi.flv*2164 , http://www.youtube.com/watch?feature=player_embedded&v=BGMQKrPOxek

488. Susan Lindauer's Mission To Baghdad. The New York Times. David Samuels, August 29, 2004. http://www.nytimes.com/2004/08/29/magazine/susan-lindauer-s-mission-to-baghdad.html?pagewanted=all&src=pm ,

489. The Iran-Contra Affair 20 Years On. The National Security Archive (George Washington University), 2006-11-24. http://www.gwu.edu/~nsarchiv/NSAEBB/NSAEBB210/, read also: Iran–Contra affair - Wikipedia, the free encyclopedia. http://en.wikipedia.org/wiki/Iran%E2%80%93Contra_affair,Walsh Iran / Contra Report - Chapter 28 George Bush http://www.fas.org/irp/offdocs/walsh/chap_28.htm, The Regan-Bush Era Iran Hostage Crisis Subterfuge, October Surprise' and Iran-Contra. http://www.nlpwessex.org/docs/irancontra.htm

490. Fair Game: My Life as a Spy, My Betrayal by the White House. Valerie Plame Wilson. 2007. Simon & Schuster. US. http://en.wikipedia.org/wiki/Fair_Game:_My_Life_as_a_Spy,_My_Betrayal_by_the_White_House , http://en.wikipedia.org/wiki/Fair_Game_(2010_film)

491. The Politics of Truth: Inside the Lies that Led to War and Betrayed My Wife's CIA Identity: A Diplomat's Memoir. http://en.wikipedia.org/wiki/The_Politics_of_Truth

492. The Long-Term Psychosocial Impact of a Surprise Chemical Weapons Attack on Civilians in Halabja, Iraqi Kurdistan. Jonathan Dworkin, Marta Prescott, Rawan Jamal, Soran Ali Hardawan, Aras Abdullah, and Sandro Galea. *The Journal of Nervous and Mental Disease*. Volume 196, Number 10, October 2008. http://deepblue.lib.umich.edu/bitstream/handle/2027.42/61176/dworkin_long?sequence=1

493. Enforcing the Ban on Chemical Weapons. Mea Sucato. *Sustainable Development Law & Policy*. Volume 6. Issue 3 Spring 2006. http://digitalcommons.wcl.american.edu/cgi/viewcontent.cgi?article=1350&context=sdlp

494. Speech of retired war college Professor and CIA-analyst Stephen C. Pelletiere. 29 Jan. 2003. St. Bonaventure University, Olean, NY. USA. http://www.youtube.com/watch?v=H-rxlWnZslY

495. United States Defense Intelligence Agency, Special Security Offices, 'Iran-Iraq: war update', 23 March 1988, Envelope PTTSZYUW RUEKJCS2867 0850428-SSS–RUEALGX, as

cited in Jean Pascal Zanders, 'Allegations of Iranian Chemical Weapons use in the 1980-88 Gulf War', SIPRI research note, 21 March 2001. From ((Iraq and Chemical & Biological Warfare: A Chronology of Events Volume I — 1960s to 1990. Richard Guthrie and Julian Perry Robinson. 2007. http://www.cbw-events.org.uk/EXIQ88Q1.PDF))

496. Did President Bush Mislead the Country in His Arguments for War with Iraq? JAMES P. PFIFFNER. George Mason University. *Presidential Studies Quarterly* 34, no. 1 (March) 2004. https://dk-media.s3.amazonaws.com/AA/AT/gambillingonjustice-com/downloads/275071/Did_President_Bush_Mislead_the_Country_in_His_Arguments_for_War_with_Iraq.pdf

497. Report on the U.S. intelligence community's prewar intelligence assessments on Iraq. Ordered Reported on July 7, 2004. SELECT COMMITTEE ON INTELLIGENCE UNITED STATES SENATE. http://web.mit.edu/simsong/www/iraqreport2-textunder.pdf

498. The Accidental Guerrilla, Fighting small wars in the midst of a big one. David Kilcullen, 2009. Oxford University Press, Inc. Oxford New York, U.S.

499. Robert Fisk: Seen through a Syrian lens, 'unknown Americans' are provoking civil war in Iraq. Friday 28 April 2006. *The Independent.* http://www.independent.co.uk/voices/commentators/fisk/robert-fisk-seen-through-a-syrian-lens-unknown-americans-are-provoking-civil-war-in-iraq-475889.html

500. UK soldiers 'freed from militia'. *BBC.* Tuesday, 20 September 2005. http://news.bbc.co.uk/2/hi/middle_east/4262336.stm, http://www.csmonitor.com/2005/0920/dailyUpdate.html

501. British Chief Police Investigator in Basra dies under mysterious circumstances. Michel Chossudovsky. October 17, 2005. GlobalResearch.ca. http://www.scoop.co.nz/stories/HL0510/S00242.htm

502. Were British Special Forces Soldiers Planting Bombs in Basra? Michael Keefer, September25, 2005. *Global Research.* http://www.globalresearch.ca/were-british-special-forces-soldiers-planting-bombs-in-basra/994

503. Robert Fisk shares his Middle East knowledge. Tony Jones. *Australian Broadcasting Corporation.* TV PROGRAM TRANSCRIPT. 02/03/2006. http://www.abc.net.au/lateline/content/2006/s1582067.htm

504. Who Killed Margaret Hassan? Robert Fisk. November 17, 2004. *The Independent.* http://www.countercurrents.org/fisk181104.htm

505. Anyone Remember Abu Ghraib? Robert Fisk. 29 September, 2004.*The Independent.* http://www.countercurrents.org/iraq-fisk290904.htm

506. Atrocity In Fallujah. Robert Fisk. April 2, 2004 .*The Independent.* http://www.countercurrents.org/iraq-fisk020404.htm

507. Britain "apologizes" for terrorist act in Basra. *Global Research.* October 15, 2005. http://www.globalresearch.ca/britain-apologizes-for-terrorist-act-in-basra/1094 , http://news.bbc.co.uk/2/hi/middle_east/4264614.stm

508. Iraqi MP accuses British Forces in Basra of "Terrorism". *Global Research.* September 20, 2005. http://www.globalresearch.ca/iraqi-mp-accuses-british-forces-in-basra-of-terrorism/983 ,http://www.guardian.co.uk/world/2005/sep/24/uk.military

509. Occupiers Spend Millions On Private Army Of Security Men. Robert Fisk and Severin Carrell. 02 April, 2004. *The Independent.* http://www.countercurrents.org/iraq-carrell020404.htm

510. VIDEO: Controversial Cockpit Video on the Strafing of Civilians in Fallujah: Pentagon Investigating its own War Crimes. *Global Research.* 10 October 2005.

http://www.globalresearch.ca/video-controversial-cockpit-video-on-the-strafing-of-civilians-in-fallujah-pentagon-investigating-its-own-war-crimes/576

511. Canada train plot: Iran's al-Qaeda problem. Kasra Naji. 23 April 2013. *BBC Persian*. http://www.bbc.co.uk/news/world-asia-22269352

512. Iran denies link to Canada train 'al-Qaeda plot. 23 April 2013. *BBC*. http://www.bbc.co.uk/news/world-us-canada-22263325

513. Mystery in Iraq: Are US Munitions to Blame for Basra Birth Defects? Alexander Smoltczyk. December 18, 2012. *SPIEGEL*. http://www.spiegel.de/international/world/researchers-studying-high-rates-of-cancer-and-birth-defects-in-iraq-a-873225.html

514. Metal Contamination and the Epidemic of Congenital Birth Defects in Iraqi Cities. 2012. M. Al-Sabbak, S. Sadik Ali, O. Savabi, G. Savabi, S. Dastgiri, M. Savabieasfahani. *Bull Environ Contam Toxicol*. 89: 937–944. http://link.springer.com/content/pdf/10.1007%2Fs00128-012-0817-2.pdf

515. British Soldiers 'Kicked Iraqi Prisoner To Death'. Robert Fisk. *The Independent*. 05 January, 2004. http://www.countercurrents.org/fisk050104.htm

516. A/HRC/13/42 - Office of the High Commissioner for Human Rights. 19 February 2010. http://www2.ohchr.org/english/bodies/hrcouncil/docs/13session/A-HRC-13-42.pdf

517. Depleted uranium used by US forces blamed for birth defects and cancer in Iraq. July 23, 2013. *Russia Today Channel*. http://rt.com/news/iraq-depleted-uranium-health-394/

518. Wesley Clark (US 4 Star General), US will attack 7 countries in 5 years. http://www.youtube.com/watch?v=Ha1rEhovONU, http://en.wikipedia.org/wiki/Wesley_Clark http://www.youtube.com/watch?v=zv71cJdRHUI , The Truth about Osama bin Laden and Iraq, General Clark was the special guest at the Warren County Democrats Fall Dinner on Saturday, September 30th, 2006 in Indianola, Iowa: http://www.youtube.com/watch?v=_8aOiMmekGk

519. Canada cuts diplomatic ties with Iran. Saeed Kamali Dehghhan. *The Guardian*. Friday 7 September 2012. http://www.guardian.co.uk/world/2012/sep/07/canada-cuts-diplomatic-ties-iran

520. Scandal-hit US firm wins key contracts. Antony Barnett, Sunday April 13, 2003. *The Observer*. http://www.freerepublic.com/focus/f-news/893279/posts

521. 10 Lessons from America's 'Dumb War'. Sebastian Fischer. 03/20/2013. *SPIEGEL*. http://www.spiegel.de/international/world/ten-lessons-america-learned-from-the-2003-iraq-war-a-890066.html

522. Iran confirms al-Qaeda suspect handover. Monday, 12 August, 2002. *BBC*. http://news.bbc.co.uk/2/hi/middle_east/2189223.stm

523. US warns Iran over al-Qaeda help. Pam O'Toole. Tuesday, 12 February, 2002. *BBC*. http://news.bbc.co.uk/2/hi/middle_east/1817141.stm

524. Bush warns Iran on terror. Thursday, 10 January, 2002. *BBC*. http://news.bbc.co.uk/2/hi/americas/1753521.stm

525. Thousands of Iraqi detainees at risk of torture after US handover. 13 September 2010. *Amnesty*. http://www.amnesty.org/en/news-and-updates/report/thousands-iraqi-detainees-risk-torture-after-us-handover-2010-09-13

526. Iraq war logs: secret files show how US ignored torture. Nick Davies, Jonathan Steele, and David Leigh. Friday 22 October 2010. *The Guardian*. http://www.guardian.co.uk/world/2010/oct/22/iraq-war-logs-military-leaks

527. Supreme Court declines to take up Abu Ghraib detainee lawsuit. Warren Richey, June 27, 2011. *The Christian Science Monitor*.

http://www.csmonitor.com/USA/Justice/2011/0627/Supreme-Court-declines-to-take-up-Abu-Ghraib-detainee-lawsuit

528. CIA 'tortured and sodomised' terror suspect, human rights court rules. Richard Norton-Taylor. Thursday. 13 December 2012. *The Guardian*.
http://www.guardian.co.uk/law/2012/dec/13/cia-tortured-sodomised-terror-suspect

529. Globalizing torture CIA secret detention and extraordinary rendition. 2013. Amrit singh. *Open Society Justice Initiative*.
http://www.opensocietyfoundations.org/sites/default/files/globalizing-torture-20120205.pdf , http://www.opensocietyfoundations.org/reports/globalizing-torture-cia-secret-detention-and-extraordinary-rendition

530. CIA rendition report author believes UK could face human rights court. Ian Cobain. Tuesday 5 February 2013. *The Guardian*.
http://www.guardian.co.uk/world/2013/feb/05/cia-rendition-report-uk-court

531. Poland admits role in CIA rendition programme. Ian Traynor. Monday 22 February 2010. *The Guardian*. http://www.guardian.co.uk/world/2010/feb/22/poland-cia-rendition-flights?INTCMP=SRCH

532. Q&A: rendition flights. Ian Cobin, Thursday 7 June 2007. *The Guardian.*
http://www.guardian.co.uk/world/2007/jun/07/usa.ciarendition?INTCMP=SRCH

533. Torture by the book. Vikram Dodd, Thursday 6 May 2004. *The Guardian*.
http://www.guardian.co.uk/world/2004/may/06/usa.iraq3?INTCMP=SRCH

534. U.S. Army and CIA interrogation manuals. From Wikipedia, the free encyclopedia.
http://en.wikipedia.org/wiki/KUBARK_Counterintelligence_Interrogation#CIA_manuals

535. Bombing of Hamburg, Dresden, and Other Cities. 28 Mar 1942 - 3 Apr 1945. C. Peter Chen. *World War II Database*. http://ww2db.com/battle_spec.php?battle_id=55

536. US troops killed in Falluja sweep. Friday, 26 November, 2004. *BBC News*.
http://news.bbc.co.uk/2/hi/middle_east/4044235.stm

537. Historic Royal Speeches and Writing. The British Monarchy web site.
[http://www.royal.gov.uk] GEORGE VI (r. 1936-1952). Broadcast, outbreak of war with Germany, 3 September 1939. http://www.royal.gov.uk/pdf/georgevi.pdf

538. Joint written statement submitted by the International Youth and Student Movement for the United Nations, a non-governmental organization in general consultative status - The impact of ten years of occupation on Iraqi children. Session 24th. A/HRC/24/NGO/133. 09/09/2013. http://daccess-dds-ny.un.org/doc/UNDOC/GEN/G13/168/98/PDF/G1316898.pdf?OpenElement

539. The International Response to Conflict and Genocide: Lessons from the Rwanda Experience. 1996. John Eriksson. Joint Evaluation of Emergency Assistance to Rwanda.
http://www.oecd.org/derec/50189495.pdf

540. Responding to Genocide: The Politics of International Action. 2013. Adam Lupel Ernesto Verdeja. Lynne Rienner Publishers.

541. The Responsibility to Protect. 2001. Report of the International Commission on Intervention and State Sovereignty. The International Development Research Centre - ICISS. Ottawa, Canada. http://responsibilitytoprotect.org/ICISS%20Report.pdf

542. The politics of preventing genocide. Anjli Parrin. 3 December 2013. IRIN.
http://www.irinnews.org/printreport.aspx?reportid=99253

543. Online News Hour: Scott Ritter — August 31, 1998.
http://www.pbs.org/newshour/bb/middle_east/july-dec98/ritter_8-31.html

544. "U.N. Panel Finds No Evidence to Link Iraq, Al-Qaeda," online version, Associated Press, retrieved June 26, 2003, from http://www.truthout.org. From 496.

545.   "Invasion right but 'illegal', says US hawk". Burkeman, Oliver (November 21, 2003). Melbourne: The Age.
       http://www.theage.com.au/articles/2003/11/20/1069027255087.html

546.   "War critics astonished as US hawk admits invasion was illegal". London: The Guardian. Oliver Burkeman and Julian Borger (November 20, 2003). http://www.theguardian.com/uk/2003/nov/20/usa.iraq1

547.   Legality of the Iraq War. From Wikipedia.
       http://en.wikipedia.org/wiki/Legality_of_the_Iraq_War#cite_note-aljazeera1-24

548.   U.S. Department of State, Daily Press Briefing, INDEX, MONDAY, DECEMBER 1, 1997. Briefer: JAMES P. RUBIN.
       http://secretary.state.gov/www/briefings/9712/971201db.html

549.   Select Committee on International Development Second Report. The impact of sanctions.
       http://www.publications.parliament.uk/pa/cm199900/cmselect/cmintdev/67/6707.htm

550.   Report of the second panel established pursuant to the note by the president of the Security Council of 30 January 1999 (S/1999/100), concerning the current humanitarian situation in Iraq. Annex II of S/1999/356. 30 March, 1999.
       http://www.casi.org.uk/info/panelrep.html

551.   Iraq surveys show 'humanitarian emergency'. Wednesday, 12 August 1999: The first surveys since 1991 of child and maternal mortality in Iraq. UNICEF.
       http://www.unicef.org/newsline/99pr29.htm

552.   Open letter and report about torture in Iraq: Conservation Center of Environmental & Reserves in Fallujah-CCERF.19
       Oct.2006.http://3.iraksolidaritet.se/customers/iraksolidaritet/uploadfiles/Fallujah_torture_2003-
       2004_finally.pdf,http://www.yumpu.com/en/document/view/20012094/conservation-center-of-environmental-reserves-iraksolidaritet

553.   UN warns on Iraq environment fate. Thursday, 10 November 2005. BBC.
       http://news.bbc.co.uk/2/hi/4425562.stm

554.   Fallujah: the April 2004 Siege. Jo Wilding. 14 April 2004. Brussells Tribunal.
       http://www.brusselstribunal.org/pdf/Fallujah.pdf Also: "Getting Aid Past US Snipers Is Impossible". Jo Wilding, Guardian. (April 17, 2004), from 555.

555.   War and Occupation in Iraq - Chapter 6, Attacks on Cities. Global Policy Forum.
       https://www.globalpolicy.org/component/content/article/168/37150.html#_edn43

556.   Major General Charles H. Swannack, Jr., Commander, 82nd Airborne Division, *Special Operational Briefing from Baghdad* (November 18, 2003). From 555.

557.   Dahr Jamail, "Fallujah Delux" *ZNet* (June 15, 2006). From.555

558.   As cited in "Urgent Aid Required as Displacement Increases in Talafar" United Nations Integrated Regional Information Networks (September 14, 2004). From 555.

559.   United Nations, Report of the Special Rapporteur on the Right to Food, Jean Ziegler, to the Human Rights Commission (January 24, 2005) Document E/CN.4/2005/47

560.   "UN Food Envoy Says Coalition Breaking Law in Iraq " Reuters (October 14, 2005)

561.   Adrian Blomfield, " Police Fire at Reporters as US Tanks Roll Up To Shrine" Telegraph (August 16, 2004)

562.   " Iraq Evicts Reporters from Najaf" Associated Press (August 16, 2004)

563.   Reporters Without Borders, Annual Report 2004

564.   Amnesty International, Iraq : Civilians under Fire (April 2003)

565.   Karl Vick, "Fallujah Strikes Herald Possible Attack" Washington Post (October 16, 2004)

566.   Brian Conley, " Ramadi Becomes Another Fallujah " Inter Press Service (June 5, 2006)

567. Sengupta, op.cit. From 555.
568. Iraq Body Count, A Dossier on Civilian Casualties in Iraq (2003-2005)
569. Indiscriminate and Especially Injurious Weapons. Chapter 3. From 555.
570. World Health Organization, Detailed Situation Report in Talafar (August 19, 2005)
571. Jo Wilding, "Getting Aid Past US Snipers Is Impossible" Guardian. (April 17, 2004)
572. UN Assistance Mission for Iraq (UNAMI), Human Rights Report (July 1- August 31, 2006) p. 13. The district was al-Eakan al-Jadida.
573. Brian Dominick, "In Fallujah , US Declares War on Hospitals, Ambulances" New Standard (November 12, 2004)
574. UN Assistance Mission for Iraq (UNAMI), Human Rights Report (November 1- December 31, 2005) p.5
575. Scott Baldauf , "The Battle of Najaf" Christian Science Monitor (August 9, 2004)
576. UN Assistance Mission for Iraq (UNAMI), *Human Rights Report* (November 1- December 31, 2005) p.5
577. UN Assistance Mission for Iraq (UNAMI), *Human Rights Report* (July 1- August 31, 2006) p. 12
578. UN Assistance Mission for Iraq (UNAMI), *Human Rights Report* (November 1- December 31, 2006) p. 27
579. UN Assistance Mission for Iraq (UNAMI), *Human Rights Report* (July 1- August 31, 2006) p. 5
580. For example, see "Medical Need Massive in Fallujah – Red Crescent" United Nations Integrated Regional Information Networks (November 10, 2004). Spokesman for the Iraq Red Crescent Society (IRCS), Firdoos al-Abadi added: (We have supplies and people who want to help. People are dying due to the shortage of medical materials and other needing food and water, but you have to watch them die because US troops do not let you go in).
581. "Aid Agencies Unable to Enter Samarra" United Nations Integrated Regional Information Networks (March 22, 2006)
582. Cited in Chris Shumway , "More Reports of US War Crimes in Najaf as Major Assault Looms" *New Standard* (August 11, 2004)
583. UN Assistance Mission for Iraq (UNAMI), *Human Rights Report* (September 1 – October 31, 2005)
584. Abdul-Qader Saadi, "Fallujah Death Toll for Week More than 600" *Associated Press* (April 12, 2004)
585. "Cost of Iraq Reconstruction Calculated" United Nations Integrated Regional Information Networks (September 8, 2004)
586. Ellen Knickmeyer, "US Airstrikes Take Toll on Civilians" *Washington Post* (December 24, 2005)
587. Amnesty International, *Iraq: End Bloodshed and Killing of Children* (October 1, 2004)
588. Knickmeyer, *op.cit.*
589. Patrick Cockburn, "US Soldiers Bulldoze Farmers' Crops" *Independent* (October 12, 2003)
590. Dahr Jamail and Ali Fadhil, "Rebuilding? Not for Fallujah" *Inter Press Service* (June 25, 2006)
591. "Clean-up Process Starts in Najaf Following Fighting" United Nations Integrated Regional Information Networks (August 31, 2004)
592. "Cost of Iraq Reconstruction Calculated" United Nations Integrated Regional Information Networks (September 8, 2004)
593. *Ibid.*

594. Dexter Filkins, "In Ramadi, Fetid Quarters and Unrelenting Battles" *New York Times* (July 5, 2006)

595. Monte Morin, "US Troops Razing Ramadi Buildings to Renew Security" *Stars and Stripes* (September 2, 2006)

596. Maher Mohammad , "Iraq Urges US Troops to Leave Najaf" *Reuters* (August 11, 2004)

597. "Najaf Officials Quit in Protest". *al-Jazeera* (August 13, 2004)

598. "Iraqi Governing Council Members Denounce US Action" *Radio Free Europe* (April 9, 2004).

599. "Governing Council Blasts Fallujah Genocide'" Financial Times (April 10, 2004)

600. Qassim Abdul-Zahra, "Iraq PM Criticizes US-Led Attack". *Associated Press* (August 7, 2006)

601. "Kofi Annan's Letter: Fallujah Warning" *BBC* (November 6, 2004)

602. Office of the High Commissioner for Human Rights, *Statement read by José Luis Dias, Spokesperson* , at the regular press briefing held at the UN Office in Geneva (November 16, 2004)

603. Tim Whitmire "Ex-Soldier Charged with Rape, Murder" *Associated Press* (July 3, 2006)

604. Rick Jervis & Andrea Stone, "Four More Soldiers Accused of Rape, Murder in Iraq " *USA Today* (July 9, 2007)

605. As quoted in "Iraq Rape Soldiers given Life Sentence" *Guardian* (November 17, 2006)

606. Mathew Schofield, "Iraqi Policy Report Details Civilians' Deaths and Hands of US Troops" *Knight Ridder (McClatchy)* (March 19, 2006)

607. Josh White and Sonya Geis, "8 Troops Charged In Death Of Iraqi" *Washington Post* (June 22, 2006)

608. Carolyn Marshall, "Corpsman Who Failed to Halt Killing of Iraqi Receives Prison Sentence" *New York Times* (October 7, 2006)

609. *Ibid*.

610. Richard Engel, "What Happened in Haditha" *NBC News* (May 30, 2006)

611. [44] David S. Cloud, "Marines Have Excised Evidence on 24 Iraqi Deaths" *New York Times* (August 18, 2006)

612. David S. Cloud, "Inquiry Suggests Marines Excised Files on Killings" *New York Times* (August 18, 2006)

613. Thomas E. Ricks, " Probe Into Iraq Deaths Finds False Reports" *Washington Post* (June 1, 2006)

614. "'Simple Failures' and â€˜Disastrous Results': Excerpts from Army Maj. Gen. Eldon A. Bargewell's report" *Washington Post* (April 21, 2007)

615. "US Military Trial Ordered in Iraq Murder Cases" *Reuters* (October 19, 2006)

616. Sonya Geis, "Hearings Begin for Marines Accused of Killing Iraqi" *Washington Post* (August 31, 2006)

617. Mathew Schofield, Iraqi Policy Report Details Civilians' Deaths and Hands of US Troops, *Knight Ridder Newspapers (McClatchy)* (March 19, 2006)

618. Will Dunham, "Troops Cleared in Iraqi Deaths in Ishaqi" *Reuters* (June 2, 2006)

619. Mathew Schofield, *op.cit* .

620. Ziad Khalaf, "Raid Kills 11, Mostly Women and Children" *Associated Press/Army Times* (March 15, 2006)

621. Mathew Schofield, *op.cit* .

622. "New an Iraq Massacre' Tape Emerges" *BBC* (June 2, 2006)

623. Fitzroy Sterling, "Still Seeking Answers in US Checkpoint Killing" *Inter Press Service* (June 24, 2006)

624. Multinational Force in Iraq and US Army Medical Command, *Final Report : Mental Health Advisory Team IV Operation Iraqi Freedom 05-07* (November 17, 2006) p.42

625. Josh White, Charles Lane and Julie Tate, "Homicide Charges Rare In Iraq War" *Washington Post* (August 28, 2006)

626. "Convictions in US Cases Rare in Iraq" *United Press International* (August 28, 2006)

627. Cited in White, Lane and Tate, *op.cit.*

628. Richard A. Oppel "Iraqi Assails US for Strikes on Civilians" *New York Times* (June 2, 2006)

629. Brian Brady "Furious Iraq Demands Apology as US Troops Are Cleared of Massacre" *Scotland on Sunday* (June 4, 2006)

630. UNHCR, Press Briefing by UNHCR Spokesperson Ron Redmond (March 20, 2007)

631. Int. Herald Tribune. Article on game over book about Iranian role in Iraqi violence. https://www.youtube.com/watch?feature=player_embedded&v=BYH5zUtpGCc

632. Qassem Suleimani: the Iranian general 'secretly running' Iraq. Martin Chulov. The Guardian, Thursday 28 July 2011. http://www.theguardian.com/world/2011/jul/28/qassem-suleimani-iran-iraq-influence

633. The shadow commander. Dexter Filkins, 30 September, 2013. The New Yorker. http://www.newyorker.com/reporting/2013/09/30/130930fa_fact_filkins

634. "Iranian who brokered Iraqi peace is on U.S. terrorist watch list". McClatchy Newspapers. 31 March 2008. http://www.mcclatchydc.com/2008/03/31/32141/iranian-who-brokered-iraqi-peace.html.

635. Abbas, Mushreq (12 March 2013). "Iran's Man in Iraq and Syria". http://www.al-monitor.com/pulse/originals/2013/03/soleimani-iraq-syria-difference.html?utm_source=&utm_medium=email&utm_campaign=6518

636. COUNCIL IMPLEMENTING REGULATION (EU) No 611/2011 of 23 June 2011. http://eur-lex.europa.eu/LexUriServ/LexUriServ.do?uri=OJ:L:2011:164:0001:0003:EN:PDF

637. "Ordinance instituting measures against Syria". Federal Department of Economy. http://www.baselgovernance.org/fileadmin/docs/news/09.09.2011.Ordinance__amedment__Syria_ENG.draft.pdf

638. Ali Mamouri, The Enigma of Qasem Soleimani And His Role in Iraq, Al-Monitor, 13 October 2013. http://www.al-monitor.com/pulse/originals/2013/10/the-enigma-behind-qassem-suleimani.html

639. "Designation of Iranian Entities and Individuals for Proliferation Activities and Support for Terrorism". United States Department of State. 25 October 2007. Archived from the original on 12 March 2008. http://web.archive.org/web/20080312042926/http://www.state.gov/r/pa/prs/ps/2007/oct/94193.htm

640. Chapter 3, Ellen Knickmeyer and K. I. Ibrahim. Bombing Shatters Mosques in Iraq: Attack on Shiite Shrine Sets Off Protests, Violence. Washington Post, February 23, 2006, A1. From 498.

641. Chapter 3, discussion with translator, May 2007, Baghdad, in Fieldnotes: Iraq 2007, un published field notebook entry in the author's possession. From 498.

642. Chapter 3, Conversation with locally employed staff, Baghdad embassy, March 2006, Fieldnotes 01/2006. From 498.

643. Chapter 3, Field note, Monday, March 6, 2006, Baghdad, Fieldnotes 01/2006. From 498.

644. Chapter 3, Author's personal review of BUA slides from January – June 2006, on the shared MNF-I hard drive, over several weeks in June 2007. From 498.

645. Chapter 3, Interview with Colonel A. K. M., counterinsurgency schoolm Taji, June 18, 2007, Fieldnotes Iraq2007 no. 3, unpublished field notebook entry in the author's possession. From 498.

646. The White House, President's Address to the Nation, January 10, 2007; http://www.white_house.gov/news/released/2007/01/20070110-7.html.

647. Chapter 3, Colin Khal, Michele Flournoy, and Shawn Brimley, Shaping the Iraq Inheritance (Washington, D.C.: Center for a New American Security, 2008), 21. From 498.

648. Chapter 3, I am indebted to Dr. Steve Biddle of the Council on Foreign Relations for this insight. From 498.

649. UNAMI - Human Rights Report, 1 January– 28 February 2006. www.unami.unmission.org

650. UNAMI - Human Rights Report, November – December 2005. www.unami.unmission.org

651. Report Shows Torture Is Widespread in Iraq. Mark Kukis. TIME. Friday, 17 April 2009.http://content.time.com/time/world/article/0,8599,1892038,00.html

652. Pentagon Reverses Position and Admits U.S. Troops Used White Phosphorus Against Iraqis in Fallujah. Thursday, November 17, 2005. Democracy Now! http://www.democracynow.org/2005/11/17/pentagon_reverses_position_and_admits_u

653. Bush Torture Memo Approved Use of Insects. Michael Scherer. TIME. April 16, 2009. http://content.time.com/time/nation/article/0,8599,1891812,00.html

654. Iraq frees Hezbollah commander who helped mold Shia terror groups Thomas Joscelyn & Bill Roggio. The Long war Journal. November 16, 2012. http://www.longwarjournal.org/archives/2012/11/iraq_frees_hezbollah.php.

655. US releases 'dangerous' Iranian proxy behind the murder of US troops. Bill Roggio. The Long war Journal. December 31, 2009. http://www.longwarjournal.org/archives/2009/12/us_releases_dangerou.php

656. US released senior Iranian Qods Force commander. Bill Roggio. The Long war Journal. July 27, 2009. http://www.longwarjournal.org/archives/2009/07/us_released_senior_iranian_qods_force_commander.php

657. Iran and al Qaeda in Iraq. Bill Roggio. The Long war Journal. January 6, 2007. http://www.longwarjournal.org/archives/2007/01/iran_and_alqaeda_in.php

658. Iraq Expels 2 Iranians Detained by U.S. Sudarsan Raghavan and Robin Wright, Washington Post. Saturday, December 30, 2006. http://www.washingtonpost.com/wp-dyn/content/article/2006/12/29/AR2006122901510.html

659. Iran's Secret Plan For Mayhem. ELI LAKE, January 3, 2007. http://www.nysun.com/foreign/irans-secret-plan-for-mayhem/46032/

660. Iran, Hezbollah train Iraqi Shia "Secret Cells". Bill Roggio. The Long war Journal. July 2, 2007. http://www.longwarjournal.org/archives/2007/07/iran_hezbollah_train.php

661. Iranian-backed Shia terror group kidnaps US civilian in Baghdad. Bill Roggio. The Long war Journal. February 6, 2010. http://www.longwarjournal.org/archives/2010/02/iranianbacked_shia_t.php

662. Civilization versus Barbarism? Noam Chomsky interviewed by M. Junaid Alam. Left Hook, December 17, 2004. http://www.chomsky.info/interviews/20041217.htm

663. US arms trader to run Iraq. Oliver Morgan, The Observer, Sunday 30 March 2003.

664. "Unreported: The Zarqawi Invitation", Greg Palast, ZNet, June 10, 2006. Also see: No End in Sight is a 2007 documentary film produced by Charles H. Ferguson. http://en.wikipedia.org/wiki/No_End_in_Sight

665. Memo to Bremer from Office of General Counsel, CPA dated 22 May 2003. http://www.dod.mil/pubs/foi/operation_and_plans/CPA_ORHA/Doc_128_CPA_Leg

666. Countering The Changing Threat of International Terrorism. Washington, D.C.:U.S. Government Printing Office. ISBN 978-0756710576.

667. Making the Nation Safer: The Role of Science and Technology in Countering Terrorism. Washington, D.C.: The National Academies Press. 2002. ISBN 978-0-309-08481-9.

668. "What Bremer Got Wrong" Rosen Nir. May 16, 2007. *The Washington Post.* http://www.washingtonpost.com/wp-dyn/content/article/2007/05/15/AR2007051501322.html

669. "Coalition Provisional Authority Order Number 2: Dissoulution of Entities". The Coalition Provisional Authority. August 23, 2003. http://www.iraqcoalition.org/regulations/20030823_CPAORD_2_Dissolution_of_Entities _with_Annex_A.pdf

670. "Blackwater Case Will Go to Iraqi Criminal Courts". Glanz, James; Sabrine Travernise. September 22, 2007. *New York Times.* http://www.nytimes.com/2007/09/22/world/middleeast/22cnd-blackwater.html?_r=0

671. "Iraq to end contractor 'immunity'". September 25, 2007. *BBC News.* http://news.bbc.co.uk/2/hi/middle_east/7012853.stm , see also: "Blackwater staff face charges". September 23, 2007. *CNN.* http://edition.cnn.com/2007/WORLD/meast/09/23/blackwater.probe/index.html

672. Oversight of funds provided to Iraqi Ministries through the National Budget Process - Special Inspector General: Iraq reconstruction at the Wayback Machine (archived September 30, 2005). https://web.archive.org/web/20050930130859/http://www.sigir.mil/pdf/dfi_ministry_re port.pdf , See also: "Audit: U.S. lost track of $9 billion in Iraq funds". January 31, 2005. *CNN.* http://edition.cnn.com/2005/WORLD/meast/01/30/iraq.audit/

673. Toll in Iraq's Deadly Surge: 1,300. Ellen Knickmeyer and Bassam Sebti. Washington Post. Tuesday, 28 February 2006. http://www.washingtonpost.com/wp-dyn/content/article/2006/02/27/AR2006022701128.html

674. Is it a civil war, or isn't it? July 28, 2006. Monica Duffy Toft. monica_toft@harvard.edu. http://www.niemanwatchdog.org/index.cfm?askthisid=220&fuseaction=Ask_this.view

675. Sectarian Strife in Iraq Imperils Entire Region, Analysts Warn. Ellen Knickmeyer. Washington Post. Thursday, 16 November, 2006. http://www.washingtonpost.com/wp-dyn/content/article/2006/11/15/AR2006111501490_pf.html

676. NBC deems Iraq to be in 'civil war'. CHRISTINE LAGORIOCBS/APNovember 27, 2006. http://www.cbsnews.com/news/nbc-deems-iraq-to-be-in-civil-war/

677. Global Overview 2015. Internal Displacement monitoring Center. http://www.internal-displacement.org/global-overview/

678. Criminals, Militias, and Insurgents: Organized Crime in Iraq. Phil Williams. SSI Book Launch CLAI, George Washington University August 26, 2009. https://books.google.at/books?id=ZEEFjZRPucgC&pg=PT41&lpg=PT41&dq=EFFECT+OF+C RIMINAL+MILITIA+ON+society&source=bl&ots=XKc8Tr1UFc&sig=amuNKEOzoz-GIS5ZjGPzUaB_-ok&hl=en&sa=X&redir_esc=y#v=onepage&q=EFFECT%20OF%20CRIMINAL%20MILITIA%2 0ON%20society&f=false http://www2.gwu.edu/~clai/recent_events/2009/Aug%202009%20-%20Crime%20in%20Iraq/Criminals_Militias_Insurgents_PowerPoint.pdf

679. Judge Radhi Testifies on Iraq Corruption; GOPers Attack-UPDATE. David Corn, The Nation. 5th October 2007. http://www.thenation.com/article/judge-radhi-testifies-iraqi-corruption-gopers-attack-update/

680. The interviews and confessions of minister of justice in Iraq Mr. Hassan Shamary. https://www.youtube.com/watch?v=HT4k9lLx5vI https://www.youtube.com/watch?v=9Jdw4GWcqA4

681. Former Blackwater guards sentenced for killing Iraqi civilians. Tuesday 14 April 2015 Dominic Yobbi. JURIST.
http://jurist.org/paperchase/2015/04/former-blackwater-guards-sentenced-for-killing-iraqi-civilians.php,
http://www.alhurra.com/content/life-term-for-one-blackwater-ex-guard-30-years-for-other/269042.html#ixzz3jvQVrxvm

682. Baghdad official who exposed executions flees. Jonathan Steele, 2 March 2006. The Guardian. http://www.theguardian.com/world/2006/mar/02/iraq.jonathansteele

683. The end of the Middle East as we know it? Munich Security Conference 2015, Opening Remarks by Kofi Annan. February 2015.
http://kofiannanfoundation.org/newsroom/speeches/2015/02/end-middle-east-we-know-it

684. Powell Was More Skeptical Than Thought About Threat From Iraq, Annan Says. Rick Gladstone. August 30, 2012. The New York.
http://kofiannanfoundation.org/newsroom/news/2012/08/powell-was-more-skeptical-about-iraq-previously-thought-annan-says

685. Jeremy Corbyn to apologise for Iraq war on behalf of Labour if he becomes leader. Ewen MacAskill. The Guardian. 21 February 2015.
http://www.theguardian.com/politics/2015/aug/20/jeremy-corbyn-apologise-iraq-war-behalf-labour-leader

686. Iran's Support for Terrorism in the Middle East. Matthew Levitt. U.S. Senate, Committee on Foreign Relations, Subcommittee on Near Eastern and Central Asian Affairs, July 25, 2012. http://www.washingtoninstitute.org/policy-analysis/view/irans-support-for-terrorism-in-the-middle-east,
http://www.washingtoninstitute.org/uploads/Documents/testimony/LevittTestimony201 20725.pdf

687. Human Rights Report. UNAMI. 1 November - 31 December 2006.

688. Human Rights Report. UNAMI. 1 July - 31 December 2007.

689. A grim log from the Iraq war goes to a future wing of the Marine museum. Michael E. Ruane. 10 October 2015. The Washington Post.
https://www.washingtonpost.com/local/a-grim-log-from-the-iraq-war-goes-to-a-future-wing-of-the-marine-museum/2015/10/10/a32e20b8-6946-11e5-8325-a42b5a459b1e_story.html

690. Smoking gun emails reveal Blair's 'deal in blood' with George Bush over Iraq war was forged a YEAR before the invasion had even started. Glen Owen and William Lowther. Daily Mail. 18 October 2015. http://www.dailymail.co.uk/news/article-3277402/Smoking-gun-emails-reveal-Blair-s-deal-blood-George-Bush-Iraq-war-forged-YEAR-invasion-started.html#ixzz3ovCxdXLD

691. Top US military official repeatedly warned Iraq about troop's conduct. James Gordon Meek, Brian Ross & Rym Momtaz. 12 March 2015.
http://abcnews.go.com/International/head-us-military-repeatedly-warned-iraq-troops-conduct/story?id=29599056

692.   Isis vs Shia militia in Iraq: Atrocity rivalry sees brutal videos of torture spread online. Tom Porter. June 3, 2015. http://www.ibtimes.co.uk/isis-vs-shia-militia-iraq-atrocity-rivalry-sees-brutal-videos-torture-spread-online-1504255

693.   The U.S. is providing air cover for ethnic cleansing in Iraq. Foreign Policy. Michael Weiss & Michael Pregent. 28 March 2015. http://foreignpolicy.com/2015/03/28/the-united-states-is-providing-air-cover-for-ethnic-cleansing-in-iraq-shiite-militias-isis/

694.   Iraq: Militia Abuses Mar Fight Against ISIS. Human Rights Watch. September 20, 2015. https://www.hrw.org/news/2015/09/20/iraq-militia-abuses-mar-fight-against-isis

695.   Iraq: Pro-Government Militias' Trail of Death. Human Rights Watch. 31 July 2014. https://www.hrw.org/news/2014/07/31/iraq-pro-government-militias-trail-death

696.   Iraq: Evidence of war crimes by government-backed Shi'a militias. Amnesty. 14 October 2014. https://www.amnesty.org/en/latest/news/2014/10/iraq-evidence-war-crimes-government-backed-shi-militias/

697. A deadly spiral of sectarian violence - a year on from IS onslaught on Iraq. Amnesty. 10 June 2015. https://www.amnesty.org/en/latest/news/2015/06/a-deadly-spiral-of-sectarian-violence-a-year-on-from-is-onslaught-on-iraq/

698. Elevated titanium levels in Iraqi children with neurodevelopmental disorders echo findings in occupation soldiers. M. Savabieasfahani , S. Alaani, M. Tafash, S. Dastgiri, M. Al-Sabbak. January 2015, 187:4127. Environmental Monitoring and Assessment. http://link.springer.com/article/10.1007/s10661-014-4127-5/fulltext.html

699. Incidence of cancer in Fallujah above 10 years age with over view of common cancers in 2011. Abdulwahab A. R. Al-Faluji1*, Salih Hussein Ali1*, Arkan A. Jasem Al-Esawi. Vol.4, No.9, 591-596 (2012). Health. https://drive.google.com/file/d/0BzqPDqS2-cm6VXdHbXpLSC1kcFk/view

700. Chaplains re-visit Phantom Fury. Cpl. Seth Star, I Marine, Expeditionary Force, September / 22 / 2015. MARINE CORPS BASE CAMP PENDLETON, Calif. http://www.marines.mil/mobile/News/View/tabid/16335/Article/618199/chaplains-re-visit-phantom-fury.aspx

701. Approximately 300 academics have been killed. Charles Crain. USA TODAY. 1/17/2005. http://usatoday30.usatoday.com/news/world/iraq/2005-01-16-academics-assassinations_x.htm

702. Special Report Scientists become targets in Iraq. Declan Butler. Nature 441, 1036-1037 (29 June 2006) . http://www.nature.com/nature/journal/v441/n7097/full/4411036a.html

703. Iraq's academics targeted by militias. BBC.5 January 2007. http://news.bbc.co.uk/2/hi/talking_point/6224427.stm

704. . Iraq ten years on: ivory tower under siege. Matthew Schweitzer. MARCH 2013.Le Monde Diplomatique. http://mondediplo.com/blogs/iraq-ten-years-on-ivory-tower-under-siege

705. Christopher Bollyen, Controlled Press Ignores Criminal Obliteration of Fallujah, Centre for Research on Globalization, American Free Press, 2 December 2004. http://globalresearch.ca/articles/BOL412A.html. From book "URANIUM IN IRAQ, The Poisonous Legacy of the Iraq Wars" edietied by Abdul-Haq Al-Ani & Joanne Baker, June 2009, Vandeplas Publishing.

Arabic Reference (A*)

1. Could you sue the US Army? Al Jazeera Net-Baghdad, 14 Aprile 2010.
    http://www.aljazeera.net/humanrights/pages/b13984b0-9571-4be4-bfe5-
    f4bcbc6b3aba#.ULDlw-7haLk.facebook
2. In a personal meeting with representatives of the Office of Human Rights at the United
    Nations Assistance Mission for Iraq UNAMI in 2005.
3. Have been affected psychologically from the second Gulf War. To criticize the decision of
    Iraq to compensate Americans. Al Jazeera Net-Baghdad 11/10/2010
4. The price of the Iraqi $ 2,500 by decision of US. Al Jazeera Net-Baghdad. 04/05/2004
5. The Iraqi opposition conference agreed on a plan of action for the future. BBC, London, 17-
    12-2002.
    http://news.bbc.co.uk/hi/arabic/middle_east_news/newsid_2583000/2583409.stm
6. Fallujah. Wikipedia, the free encyclopedia,
    https://ar.wikipedia.org/wiki/%D8%A7%D9%84%D9%81%D9%84%D9%88%D8%AC%D8%A9
7. Professor in Public Law: America imposed itself on the Security Council to adopt a resolution
    that legitimizes the occupation. Russia Today. 03/22/2013.
    http://arabic.rt.com/prg/telecast/658090/
8. Chapter VII: Action with respect in cases of threats and breach of peace and acts of
    aggression. http://www.un.org/ar/documents/charter/chapter7.shtml
9. The organizer a sit-in Fallujah: The military involved in killing of 480 people after the 2nd
    battle of Fallujah. Voices of Iraq Agency. 31/01/2013.
    http://ar.aswataliraq.info/(S(pwfw5obsdkzfjj55ywecbc55))/Default1.aspx?page=article_pag
    e&id=311196
10. US intelligence employee Valerie made her story in front of Congress that triggered a
    political uproar. Richard Libby & Walter Pinkas. Middle East newspaper - London. March 17,
    2007. http://www.aawsat.com/details.asp?issueno=10261&article=410994#.UffRJTssVil
11. Figures and documents. Slaughter of the US military in Iraq and Afghanistan. Aamer Abdul-
    Moneim.https://bahrainforums.com/vb/%C7%E1%DA%D1%C8-
    %E6%C7%E1%DA%C7%E1%E3/1071911.htm
12. Cancer. A new war on the sons of Iraq: Russia Today channel.
    http://arabic.rt.com/news/47418/
13. Documents of Iranian roles in the US war on Iraq. Sunday, 3rd June, 2012 Dr. Abdasattar
    Rawi - Iraq's ambassador to Iran before the occupation. Al-Watan newspaper / Bahrain.
    http://www.alwatannews.net/NewsViewer.aspx?ID=HOMbw7js11GMaQUGTXzZ7w933339
    933339&SearchID=xMmGAfx8QDwc9UGIsrvSCg933339933339
14. Iraqia block exclude its leader from the consequences of their request to be considered an
    attack Fallujah as genocide. Hamza Mustafa. Middle East's newspaper of London. April 6,
    2011.
    http://www.aawsat.com/details.asp?section=4&issueno=11817&article=615990&search=%
    C7%E1%DD%E1%E6%CC%C9%202004&state=true#.UfXN_NI5lrU
15. Meetings of Russia Today, Sumerian and Abbasid channels with Mr. Salem al-Jumaili. In
    addition to personal contacts with him directly.
    http://www.youtube.com/watch?v=qmA2lvyeiT8 ,
    http://www.youtube.com/watch?v=jKNfVsOVjrQ ,
    http://www.youtube.com/watch?v=XEm4dBnMw-Y ,

http://www.youtube.com/watch?v=gqOyUBtOIhs,
http://www.youtube.com/watch?v=gq_VIWUsOR0

16. Interviews of former Iraqi intelligence chief Mohammed al-Shahwani with Al-Arabiya and Al-Sharqyia Channels. http://www.youtube.com/watch?v=pEdOPo6c4cc ,
http://www.youtube.com/watch?v=_Hwfl95ZxNQ ,
http://www.youtube.com/watch?v=KPc_G6tAhzU ,
http://www.youtube.com/watch?v=xpkCnPeWED0 ,
http://www.youtube.com/watch?v=b8x4jLaZsi0

17. Iraq and the US toxic waste. Abdul Hussein Shaaban. Al-Mustaqbal Lebanese newspaper. Saturday 20 July, 2013 - No. 4752 - Opinion and thought - Page 19.
http://www.almustaqbal.com/storiesv4.aspx?storyid=579924

18. Announcement of Mr. Abtahi, former Iranian vice President of Khatami, Posted on Shiite News Agency. http://ebaa.net/khaber/2004/01/15/khaber001.htm

19. Al-Rubaie told «Middle East»: Soleimani, a senior officer in the Quds Corps and has the final sdecision in the Iraqi file. Maad Faiad. 30 June 2010. Middle East. London.
http://www.aawsat.com/details.asp?section=4&issueno=11537&article=576139

20. Muqtada al-Sadr's: I am trying to visit Arab countries ... and on Maliki visiting the yards of Sunni sit. Al-Hayat newspaper. Moushreq Abbas and Sarmad al-Tai, Sunday, 22 December 2013.

21. Parliamentary security committee: We opened an investigation file of armor ... and its disappearance raises doubts. Baghdadi News. October 11 (2015).
http://www.albaghdadia.com/iraqnews/item/45142-2015-10-11-12-28-52

22. Interview with Major General Ghazi Aziza. The Political Memory program. Al Arabiya Channel. 16 October 2015. https://www.alarabiya.net/programs/politic-memory.html

23. Black Box program. Al-Jazeera Channel. 22-10-2015.
http://www.aljazeera.net/programs/black-box/2015/10/18/%D9%86%D9%88%D8%B1%D9%8A-%D8%A7%D9%84%D9%85%D8%A7%D9%84%D9%83%D9%8A-%D8%A7%D9%84%D8%B5%D9%88%D8%B1%D8%A9-%D8%A7%D9%84%D9%83%D8%A7%D9%85%D9%84%D8%A9